Storms
and Dreams

Storms
and Dreams

LOUIS DE BOUGAINVILLE:
SOLDIER, EXPLORER, STATESMAN

JOHN DUNMORE

NONSUCH

First published 2005

Nonsuch Publishing Limited
The Mill
Brimscombe Port
Stroud
Gloucestershire
GL5 2QG

For more information on books relating to exploration and travel
visit our web site www.nonsuch-publishing.com

ISBN 1-84588-076-5

Text design and production by BookNZ
Cover design by Dexter Fry
Printed in China through Colorcraft Ltd., Hong Kong

CONTENTS

PART 4: SAILING AROUND THE WORLD

PART 5: WAR AND REVOLUTION

MAPS

Part 1

EARLY YEARS

PROLOGUE: CHRISTENING

13 November, 1729. Church of Saint-Merri, Rue Saint-Martin, Paris

'EGO TE BAPTIZMO Ludovicus Antonius.'

The day-old baby shook his head weakly as the elderly priest poured a few drops of water on his brow. But he did not utter a cry, his eyes shut against the encroaching world. The nursemaid who proudly held him in her arms smiled at the father standing opposite her at the baptismal font, dressed as usual in sober black, with only a touch of white lace at his throat and his wrists to mark the occasion.

'In nomine Patris and Filii et Spiritus Sancti.' The priest wiped his hands and handed the linen handkerchief back to his waiting acolyte. He made a final sign of the cross over the child and, dignified yet respectful, turned to shake hands with Pierre-Yves Bougainville. 'You have a handsome child, Messire. I have no doubt that he will bring honour to his family. And now he is a good Christian, ready to face the world.' The priest then shook hands with the baby's godfather and uncle, Antoine d'Arboulin, exchanging a few words with him. Now he was almost obsequious, for this was a man of a higher social standing than Bougainville.

The small party made its way slowly through the semi-gloom of the church, preceded by a fat, uniformed beadle bearing his long staff, which he tapped on the flagstones. The acolyte behind him swung a brass censer from which rose the sickly smell of incense. As the priest had said, 'Incense keeps the smells of humanity out of the house of the Lord.' As was the custom, especially when members of a well-to-do family took part in a church ceremony, a mendicant friar slid silently out of the shadows and asked prayerfully for a donation towards the poor. Pierre-Yves signalled to his major-domo to give the man a few coins.

When they reached the door, the noises and smells of the street came up to meet them. The beggars were more clamorous than the friar: they thrust out their gnarled hands at the guests, jostling them as they made their way down the stone steps. Children, ragged, unkempt and shrill, called out for gifts, waving thin arms in a mixture of greeting and appeal. From their doorsteps, women watched, interrupting their gossip for a moment to see how the group of city bourgeois would cope with the situation.

The major-domo knew what to do. He thrust the more insistent beggars out of his way, then threw a handful of small coins and sweetmeats over their heads and beyond the children onto the wet cobblestones. In the resulting mêlée the stronger or more nimble gave little quarter. The major-domo then led Bougainville, with his new-born son and his maid, into the waiting carriage. The horse gave a weary tug and ambled slowly down the street, followed by the christening party. From time to time, a handful of sweets scattered behind them kept the following rabble at bay.

They soon reached the Bougainville home, in the Rue Barre du Bec, an old, not to say ancient street, but dignified still. A handful of small shops and an occasional stall broke the line of discreet houses, their doorways slightly recessed in the grey stone walls. Behind, at intervals, stood larger homes, set apart, where noble families lived.

The street formed part of what had been the Marais, the 'Marsh'. Now it was a little old-fashioned, tired perhaps after a turbulent but proud history, 'sad', someone has written, as though regretting a past that was fading away. It contained impressive homes dating back to the seventeenth century and a few more would be completed in years to come, but they were often cheek by jowl with those of artisans and shopkeepers. Some of the younger nobles were beginning to move out to the newer districts, with their wider streets and larger gardens.

Pierre-Yves Bougainville's home was comfortable by contemporary standards, although in no way ostentatious. It would not have done for a respected lawyer, with a growing reputation among the city administrators, to splash his wealth about and seek to ape the nobility. The house was sheltered from the hurly-burly of the street by a high wall. A double carriage entrance opened out into a courtyard, with a well in one corner, a modest garden, a door to the main house and a smaller one for the servants' quarters. A smaller courtyard led to sheds and storerooms, and a place for the carriage. It was quiet, welcoming, discreet, almost smug.

Pierre left the nurse to take the baby into her quarters and walked upstairs to report to his wife. If the outside of the house was discreet, the private quarters reflected a growing opulence. Marie-Françoise Bougainville's bedroom was hung with rich damask and tapestries; the November gloom was relieved by candles burning in ornate silver candlesticks; a table inlaid in the new Louis XV style stood in one corner, a large bowl of flowers at its centre.

He had made what everyone agreed was a good marriage. His wife was one of the D'Arboulins, a well-connected, respected and influential family, with a wide network of useful contacts. These links with acquaintances and relatives were as valuable as the substantial dowry she had brought with her.

Marie-Françoise was propped up against white linen pillows in the middle of the large bed. 'It went well,' Pierre said. 'Brief, but well organised. We will have another ceremony at home to celebrate our son's birth once you have recovered.'

She was a good wife, he reflected as he went downstairs to the salon where his guests were gathering. He was indeed a fortunate man.

Neither could have guessed that she had fewer than five years to live.

1. Two Brothers

1741–52

PIERRE-YVES BOUGAINVILLE was formally ennobled in 1741 when he was elected to the prestigious Paris *échevinat*, the increasingly powerful municipal council that was gradually taking over the administration of the city. To be an *échevin* meant automatic entry to the ranks of the nobility – not, admittedly, the true aristocracy, but the upper levels of the middle class, the *noblesse de robe*. Made up of administrators and lawyers, the *échevinat* was untainted by any connections with trade and commerce. More significantly, as the eighteenth century progressed, it was beginning to encroach on the power and privileges of the traditional nobility, the *noblesse d'épée*, the descendants of noble families and the courtiers who surrounded the king almost as of right. The aristocrats, claiming power as their birthright, might look down on the *noblesse de robe*, but its members' role in the administration of the kingdom and the larger cities increasingly earned them respect and influence.

For years now, the Paris municipal authorities had been nibbling away at the traditional powers of the aristocracy. The Châtelet, a grim structure serving as police headquarters, law courts and temporary prison, was the city's administrative centre, where the most powerful lawyers and officials congregated and ruled over the capital. Supplicants from far and wide crowded its corridors, seeking favours and exemptions, so that its influence was spreading across to the court at Versailles and to the provincial cities. The Châtelet saw to such matters as street cleaning and fire and flood protection; it ran the police, supervised the trades corporations and had a hand in a host of other functions. It was also responsible for the city's lighting which, as one visitor commented, turned every night, whether wet or fine, into a bright moonlit evening. The city, it was predicted, would one day rise to such prominence that it could challenge even the king.

Pierre-Yves was now Monsieur *de* Bougainville. That little word made a great difference to one's status and the respect one inspired in others. His position at the Châtelet brought him an increasing number of influential acquaintances. He had friends among the traditional nobility and among the rising new thinkers and scientists who would be known as the *philosophes*, the backbone of the European Age of Enlightenment.

His wife had died in 1734, when Louis was not quite five years old. Pierre-Yves coped with his loss in silence, devoting himself to legal matters and steadily building up his growing influence in city administration. On the personal level, he turned for support to a close family friend and near neighbour, Madame Catherine Hérault de Séchelles, the wife of René Hérault, a former *lieutenant général de police*. Hérault, a powerful man at the Châtelet, had gained fame as the instigator of street nameplates – 'On 16 January 1728 they began to place in every street in Paris two tin plates on which the name of the street was written in large black letters'[1] – an innovation for which Parisians and visitors trying to find their way through the twisting labyrinths of streets were endlessly grateful. Louis regarded Madame Hérault as a substitute mother, calling her '*Maman*' and spending much of his time with her lively, active son Jean-Baptiste. As young teenagers they spent time in aristocratic salons and Jean-Baptiste urged Louis to look forward to a career in society and the wider world – in fact to a military life.

Louis also grew up under the influence of his protective older brother, Jean-Pierre, his senior by eight years, an asthmatic who would later develop tuberculosis. A gifted, studious boy, with a flair for the classics as well as for mathematics and the new sciences, he looked to Louis to fulfil the dreams that his own health would not allow him to transform into reality.

For a time the two brothers went to a college. It was usual for sons of the well-to-do to be sent to a boarding establishment run by some religious order, but this was not really suitable for the frail Jean-Pierre. His father seesawed between sending him back to school and keeping him at home with his books, taught by a succession of visiting tutors. He soon adopted much the same policy for young Louis, and their friend Hérault, with his own tutors, completed a talented and almost inseparable trio.

They became well versed in the classics, studying both Latin and Greek, and tackled mathematics, astronomy and various branches of the sciences. And both Madame Hérault and Pierre-Yves were quite happy to see their boys studying history, politics and the rudiments of military science. To all this was added the art of fencing, still indispensable for the well-born in that age, though the lethal duels that had threatened to decimate the ranks of the nobility under Louis XIII and Louis XIV were now mercifully infrequent.

An early love of fencing brought Louis in touch with a number of minor noblemen, young and old. Nearby lived the Marquis de Chailly, a retired musketeer equally renowned for his wit. He gave dinner parties to which he invited a wide range of friends – the Marquis de Saint-Marc, the Comte de Lameth, the Président de Rosambo, the Chevalier de Chastellux, the Count de Caulaincourt, the Marquis de la Grange. After dinner, the salon became a fencing hall, Louis facing the Comte de Lameth in particular, but also some of the younger guests.

He learned other valuable skills, such as card-playing and dancing, and developed a talent for composing short poems or epigrams, and engaging in flirtatious conversation with ladies, young and not-so-young. All this would prove valuable in later life, transforming him into a witty and charming courtier.

As was normal, Pierre-Yves de Bougainville had expected at least one of the boys to follow the family tradition and enter the legal profession. There were two kinds of barristers at the time: an *avocat en parlement*, a highly regarded but essentially honorific title, and an *avocat au parlement*, a lawyer who actually practised. Jean-Pierre qualified as an *avocat en parlement*, but his health kept him mostly in his study. Pierre-Yves pinned his hopes on his second son, but there is no real evidence that Louis ever studied law – even though most of his biographers take this for granted. René de Kerallain, for instance, writes: 'Louis-Antoine also began work among the legal fraternity, which later enabled him, when in Canada, to argue like a jurist and talk of Roman law.'[2] But there is no record of him in the lists of *avocats* and it seems far more likely that he gained his knowledge of the law from his father, his brother and their colleagues, though he may have done some perfunctory studies to please Pierre-Yves.

Instead, Louis, a pleasant, lively young man about town, followed his friend Jean-Baptiste Hérault into the army. He was not really a born soldier and, to some extent, drifted into the army because young Hérault was so enthusiastic about it. His father raised no objection. Although Hérault might be leading Louis into wild adventures, Jean-Pierre was a great influence on his brother and would remain a steadying one. Pierre-Yves also realised that a military career for Louis would allow the Bougainvilles to move from the *nobles de robe* to the *nobles d'épée*. So, in 1750, Louis de Bougainville and Jean-Baptiste Hérault joined the Black Musketeers.

It was a period of relative peace. Two major European conflicts had come to an end, both linked to political manoeuvrings as the major powers shifted from their traditional alliances.

The War of the Polish Succession had broken out in 1733, but ended in 1735. It was a complex dispute over whether Stanislas Leszczynski, supported by the Polish nobility, or Augustus of Saxony, supported by Russia and Austria, should get the throne. Augustus won and Stanislas was given the Duchy of Lorraine as a consolation, under the protection of France. When Stanislas died, Lorraine would formally become part of France.

Another war then broke out over who would succeed to the Austrian throne. Charles VI, Archduke of Austria and Holy Roman Emperor, died in 1740. His

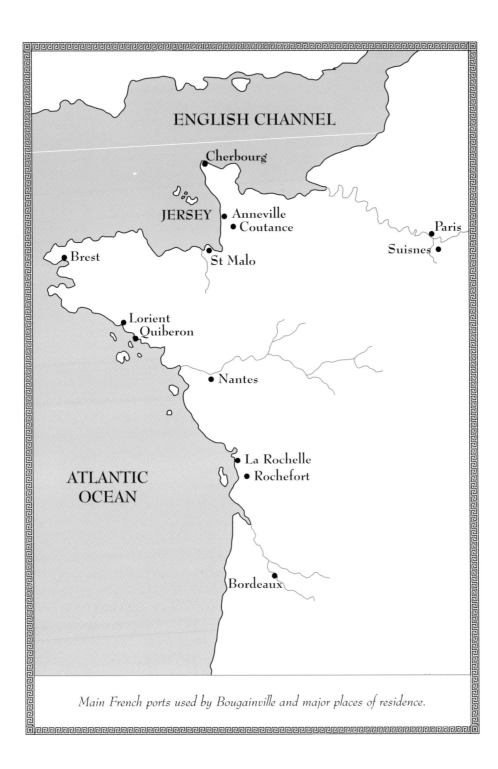

Main French ports used by Bougainville and major places of residence.

daughter Maria Theresa was all set to succeed him, but others challenged her claim. Prussia began by invading Silesia, others joined in and soon an alliance of European powers faced Holland and Britain for a war marked by a long series of victories and defeats. It ended in 1748, with Maria Theresa securely on the throne, and the various rulers retaining their lands, apart from Silesia which went to Prussia and several Italian dukedoms which passed to Spain.

Louis XV had been reluctant to join a conflict that had initially seemed little more than a local quarrel between various German-speaking princes. Backed by his elderly minister, the Cardinal de Fleury, he had at first tried to adopt the stance of 'Europe's arbitrator', but had soon been forced to give in to the more warlike parties and face up to the Prussians and the British in an all-out struggle from 1743–4. The French campaigns were relatively successful but Louis XV agreed to return the lands his armies had conquered, wanting to show that France had merely been defending herself and was not after territorial aggrandisement. Europe was surprised by this attitude, but in no way grateful. And the French people, although glad that the costly conflict had come to an end, were similarly unimpressed. 'You're as stupid as the peace,' was an insult commonly used by fishwives.

The peace did not extend to North America and India, where the rivalry between Britain and France gave rise to constant local clashes and incidents. But the French in general, and the *philosophes* in particular, were not interested in colonial possessions: they were more attracted by political reform, admiring the British trend towards parliamentary democracy – or at least Britain's working partnership between the Crown and Parliament. It was not quite the kind of democracy many of the philosophers dreamt of, but it seemed to work. The power of England's king was still very considerable, but it was tempered by the role of the House of Lords and the House of Commons.

In France, the king ruled as an absolute monarch, needing only to manoeuvre between various squabbling factions: a clique of bigots supporting the dauphin; the *grands nobles*, influential members of the higher nobility, each with their own self-serving agendas; the ministers and others who belonged to the circle of the Marquise de Pompadour, who was the king's mistress; and the upper clergy and senior magistrates. Dealing with all these groups, while coping with the financial problems resulting from the various wars, required more skill and energy than Louis XV, weary and sometimes bored after thirty years on the throne, was able to marshal.

It was not, however, a bad time to join the army. Peace seemed reasonably assured. The king displayed no desire for any further conquests or military campaigns. Promotion could be earned, not on the field of battle, but in regimental gatherings and in salons. The name 'musketeers' evokes the figure of D'Artagnan and his swashbuckling, duelling friends, immortalised by Alexandre Dumas. But the Black Musketeers, so called from their black horses, were dragoons, young men belonging to good families. They were in no way an élite military unit, rather part of an induction and training group: both Louis and Jean-Baptiste were soon posted to larger, more structured regiments, notably the Picardy militia, where Louis became *aide-major*.

Military life made few demands on their time. Most of the young officers spent their leisure time hunting, visiting noble families in the neighbourhood, playing cards or roistering about. Louis kept in touch with his brother and continued to be advised by him in his study, especially in the fields of astronomy and classical history. And he found a number of like minds in the army. In the Age of Enlightenment, there was nothing unusual in young officers discussing philosophy, social problems and the development of scientific knowledge.

Jean-Pierre Bougainville was rapidly acquiring a reputation among French scholars. In 1754 he was accepted as one of the forty members of the *Académie des Inscriptions et Belles-Lettres* of which the secretary was the historian and archaeologist Nicolas Fréret, who became his personal mentor, guiding him, and Louis, towards classical studies and early travel literature. Jean-Pierre wrote a study on the relationship between ancient Greece and its colonial outposts around the Mediterranean, and began a major work, *Parallèle de l'expédition d'Alexandre dans les Indes avec la conquête des mêmes contrées par Koulikhan*, which was published in 1752. (Kuli Khan, also known as Nadir Shah, had died in 1747.) In the following year, he published *Éclaircissements sur l'origine et les voyages de Pythéas de Marseille*, before turning to the discoveries made along the coast of Africa by the Carthaginians.

Fréret also introduced both brothers to a number of other erudite researchers. Realising that young Louis was more interested in mathematics than in history, he sought a suitable tutor for him and found one with an outstanding reputation. Alexis-Claude Clairault, himself the son of a mathematician, had been a member of the *Académie des Sciences* since the age of eighteen and a specialist in the movements of the moon and planets. In 1736 he had travelled to Lapland with Pierre de Maupertuis on an expedition aimed at determining the true shape of the globe. In 1743, Clairault published his major work, *Théorie de la figure de la terre*; this would be followed in 1750 by his *Théorie de la lune*, for which he was awarded the prize of the St Petersburg Academy.

The Bougainville brothers were given access to the libraries of Fréret, Clairault and others. This enabled them to consult the works of Pierre de Maupertuis: his *Eléments de géographie*, published in 1742, his *Astronomie nautique* (1745) and his *Essai de cosmologie* (1750). They avidly read the first volumes of Leclerc de Buffon's monumental *Histoire naturelle*, which appeared in 1749 and would eventually total forty-four volumes.

Jean-Pierre came across reports sent to Fréret by Jean-Baptiste Charles Bouvet de Lozier (or Lozier Bouvet) who had sailed into the southern Indian Ocean in 1738–9 on his search for the mythical southern continent – which he believed he had discovered – and new trading outposts for the French India Company. This helped to move Jean-Pierre's earlier interest in the voyages of antiquity to lands that remained undiscovered. He would maintain this interest as discussions grew about possible exploration of the South Seas. As Buffon had just written in his chapter on geography:

> Today, in spite of all the knowledge that has been acquired through the mathematical sciences and the discoveries of navigators, a great many things still need to be found and vast countries to be discovered. Almost all the land that lies near the Antarctic pole is unknown to us: all we know is that it exists and that it is separated from all the other continents by the Ocean; there are also a number of places to discover near the Arctic pole, and we must admit, with a touch of regret, that the earlier ardour motivating the search for new lands has cooled quite considerably for more than a century.[3]

New discoveries were waiting for someone with enthusiasm and energy. Unable to travel himself, Jean-Pierre would realise his dreams vicariously through his younger brother.

Clairault provided the knowledge and training that Louis would find so useful, indeed essential, during his great circumnavigation. It explains what has struck so many commentators as strange: that a man with an army background and no naval experience could have led an expedition of two ships through little known and largely uncharted waters, navigating skilfully through island groups and chains of atolls and plotting with accuracy the route he was following.

More immediately, however, his army duties had to be attended to. International relations were again showing signs of strain and war in Europe seemed imminent. Louis was appointed aide-de-camp to a famous military commander, Lieutenant-General François Chevert. At the end of 1753, he left to join him at Sarrelouis on the eastern frontier.

2. POLITICS AND DIPLOMACY

1753–5

CHEVERT HAD GAINED his reputation during the recent War of the Austrian Succession. Following one of that conflict's complex manoeuvres, France had, jointly with Prussia, taken over the city of Prague. In 1742, however, Prussia temporarily withdrew from the war and, left on their own, French troops found themselves trapped in the city. In December, Charles Louis August Fouquet, Comte Belle-Isle and Marshal of France, began a skilful, if costly, strategic withdrawal, succeeding in bringing some 14,000 men, with their horses, guns and other supplies, back to the French lines along the Rhine. This meant a heroic struggle, marching through forests and snow, with little rest and food. Wounded and sick soldiers were left to die in the bitter cold; many were robbed and killed by groups of pursuing soldiers or by local peasants.

Chevert had stayed behind in Prague with 4000 soldiers, mostly ill men or second-liners. His task was to hold out in Prague for as long as he could while Belle-Isle got away with his regiments. Chevert managed to hold out for a few weeks, and gained more time and eventual fame by arguing over the terms of surrender. The Austrian commander insisted on an unconditional surrender, but Chevert refused, saying that he would leave only with full military honours. The Austrian general wanted victory rather than the mere departure of the enemy with flags flying, whereupon Chevert threatened to fight to the last man, a threat that finally got him his wish, and the garrison was allowed to return to France under somewhat better conditions than Belle-Isle's troops.

For Louis de Bougainville to obtain a posting as Chevert's aide-de-camp a mere three years after joining up meant that strings had been pulled. Both Madame Hérault and Louis's father had obviously contacted relatives, friends and acquaintances. But Louis had even better backers, notably his uncle, Jean-Potentien d'Arboulin. The younger brother of Louis's deceased mother, Marie-Françoise, he was the perfect example of the French courtier, charming, amusing, tactful, discreet, with a marked gift for intrigue. He had collected several lucrative positions, largely sinecures, including that of *Directeur des Postes de l'Orléanais*. These ensured him a comfortable income, but above all valuable connections. One of these was Le Normant de Tournehem, a former French ambassador to Sweden, a director of the French India Company and a *fermier-général* or tax collector – a valuable post, since tax collectors made a profit on the revenue they managed to collect on behalf of the Crown. More significantly, though, Tournehem had once been the protector of the most powerful woman in France, the Marquise de Pompadour.

Born with the distinctly plebeian name of Jeanne-Antoinette Poisson (Joan Fish), she had raised herself successfully from the merchant class. Her father, François, had worked for the Pâris brothers, contractors to the government. He had supplied Provence with food during the plague of 1720 and helped his employers to bring corn to the capital in 1725 when a bad harvest caused serious shortages. It was a popular service, and highly profitable, but it also involved Poisson and his associates in some shady deals, for which he manfully shouldered all the responsibility. He fled the country while the Pâris brothers skilfully mended fences.

He left behind his wife Louise-Madeleine and their two children. Madame Poisson became the *protégée* and mistress of Le Normant de Tournehem. He helped Jeanne-Antoinette by financing her board in a college and eventually finding her a suitable husband, his own nephew Charles Guillaume Le Normant d'Étioles. She was nineteen, beautiful, well educated, witty and financially secure. Her father had by then been able to return home and renew his contacts. Everything was propitious for her to appear at court and in time attract Louis XV's attention. She succeeded in early 1745 and became his official mistress. She was twenty-three.

The numerous enemies she accumulated over the years, overwhelmingly as a result of jealousy, never forgot her humble origins. It is said that, after her death, one whispered that, if anyone ever dug where she was buried, they would find fish bones (*arêtes de poisson*).

Louis XV soon gave her a more suitable title – Madame d'Étioles still belonged to the lower levels of the nobility – and she became the Marquise de Pompadour. The king needed a young, pretty and active companion. His wife, Maria Leszczynska, the daughter of Stanislas, the deposed King of Poland, was forty-three, seven years older than Louis, and fairly plain. Tired after giving birth to ten children, all but one a boy, she had long sought refuge in religion. It is said that she kept the king out of her bedroom on Sundays, holy days of obligation and special saints' days. Court gossip, always inventive and seldom kind, reported that the king had finally sought consolation elsewhere after stalking out of her room one night, shouting that he had never heard of the particular saint she was using as an excuse on this occasion.

The queen bore no grudge against the marquise, who was always courteous and deferential towards her. Maria believed that Pompadour was preferable to some of the more flighty court ladies Louis XV had earlier courted. The affair suited her, and she even feared that, unlike her marriage, it might not last. This was a concern shared by Jeanne herself, who set about ensuring that her influence would not wane when the king tired of her. She created a complex network of friends and acquaintances, writing regularly to ministers, ambassadors and military leaders, and revealing a sound grasp of French and international politics. One of her correspondents was Chevert; another was the Duc de Mirepoix.

She also gathered around her a small group of supporters and agents, whom she entrusted with confidential tasks. This included D'Arboulin, who became one of her intimates and whom she called Boubou. Among the services he rendered to her was attempting to persuade her husband to accept the position of French ambassador to Turkey. Étioles, however, liked life in Paris and he had struck up a lasting relationship with a young dancer at the Opéra. D'Arboulin arranged a compromise: he obtained Étioles' assurance that he would not interfere with his wife's affair and his agreement to a form of legal separation.

Later, he rendered Madame de Pompadour another service, somewhat more shady, but critical to the maintenance of her position at court. He arranged the interception of a letter written by the Minister of War, the Comte d'Argenson, to his mistress. In it he told her that she would soon be welcome at Versailles and would replace the marquise in the king's affections. Then, he wrote, 'we shall be masters of the den' (*tripot*, a word that means both gambling house and brothel). D'Argenson, whom the king had grown to dislike anyhow, was dismissed and the marquise's position at court reinforced.

The influence of Madame de Pompadour undoubtedly played a part in Louis de Bougainville's next appointment. On 12 October 1754 he was sent to London as part of the Duc de Mirepoix's staff, with the title of third secretary. He was now a junior diplomat, about to enter a wide circle of learned and influential people.

Mirepoix, a man with diplomatic experience and many contacts in England, was facing a difficult task. On the Indian continent, warlike operations had never really come to an end. Robert Clive had defeated the French at Arcot in 1751 and captured Trichonopoly in the following year. The French commander Joseph François Dupleix, while skilfully manipulating the anti-British Indian princes, had gradually lost support in France and was recalled in 1754. The French Indian empire was now no more than a dream.

A similar situation was developing in North America, where French–British relations had been deteriorating since the end of the war. France held most of the area north of the St Lawrence River as far as the Great Lakes. The only exception was the northernmost region, which lay under the control of the Hudson's Bay Company. To the east, Nova Scotia, known as Acadia, was under French control. To the south and west, France controlled Louisiana – named after Louis XIV – an area even more extensive than the present American state of that name, reaching up along the Mississippi River to the Great Lakes. In effect, therefore, French possessions were blocking the British from further growth in Canada and technically boxed in their thirteen colonies between the Allegheny Mountains and the Atlantic Coast. This threatened their progress inland across the Ohio and Mississippi Rivers. Both the British colonists and the politicians in London saw an advance towards the west as not merely desirable, but essential. Success for either side depended on controlling key points along the rivers and the western hills, and gaining influence with the Indian tribes.

The French were greatly outnumbered by the British. France had always put colonial settlements on the back burner. Faraway places might be good enough for adventurers, no-hopers and minor criminals, but civilised life could be lived only in Europe. By the mid-1750s there were fewer than 80,000 settlers of French origin in the whole of Canada, Acadia and Louisiana, compared with close to a million British and other non-French colonists and settlers spread out along the Atlantic seaboard.

The peace treaty of 1748 had included a provision for a British–French commission to settle the vague and disputed western and northern frontiers of North America. This might prevent local disputes breaking out into a regional war. Within a couple of years, the commissioners had to concede that they had made no progress and the French administrators in Canada decided it was time to strengthen their position by consolidating their hold on the land west of the Alleghenies. The Marquis de La Galissonière, the Governor of French Canada, or 'New France', placed a number of lead plaques along the Ohio River: the fleur-de-lys and the message engraved on them indicated that this was French territory.

The British colonists took steps to establish their own claims simply by settling in the disputed lands. To be fair, they did not come across some of La Galissonière's plaques until well after the event. The French authorities realised that plaques, however attractive, were ineffective, and that the only way to stop further encroachments was to build a line of forts to hold the Ohio Basin. A clash was now inevitable.

The figure of George Washington, then a major in the Virginian forces, dominates the story at this point. In 1754 he was sent to capture a stockade named Fort Duquesne (on the site of present-day Pittsburgh). He first built up his own small blockhouse, Fort Necessity, to prepare the way. He then heard that a French military detachment of some thirty men were encamped nearby. On the night of 27 May he and his soldiers crept up, surrounded the French and promptly forced their surrender. Ten Frenchmen were killed, including the officer in charge, Coulon de Jumonville. What might have been a minor and relatively bloodless skirmish became a major incident, because Jumonville's mission had not been an aggressive one aimed at capturing Fort Necessity: he had come only to remind the Virginian force that they were on French territory and require them to withdraw. Jumonville was killed as he waved his credentials and shouted that his mission was a peaceful one. The facts of the Jumonville affair are not easy to establish. The Virginians would not have understood what the French officer was saying and assumed that he was urging his men to fight, but the incident shocked French Canada, and public opinion back in France labelled it the treacherous murder of an envoy on a peaceful mission.

Retribution was prompt. Jumonville's own brother, Villier, led a force of some 900 men to retake Fort Necessity. After a nine-hour battle, Washington was forced to negotiate. Villier maintained that, since France and Britain were not at war and his brother had been sent merely to warn off the Virginians, his death should be regarded as a murder. Indeed, this had become the official French position. Villier did not press his point, however, but agreed to an honourable capitulation that would allow the Virginians to retire to their base at Albany, taking their wounded with them.

Washington was first required to sign an admission of guilt for the *assassinat* of Coulon de Jumonville. This word, assassination, was apparently interpreted by the Virginian negotiators as simply meaning his death in battle.

The incident would haunt George Washington for years. The British took the view that he had been misled by his negotiators and had not quite understood the document, but the French continued to maintain that 'he had indeed signed, possibly in a moment of panic, but with sufficient understanding, an admission of his guilt'.[1] Ironically, Washington and his men marched out of Fort Necessity on 4 July, a date that Washington was to make forever glorious in the history of the independent country he would one day create – with French support.

The worsening situation in Canada led Britain to dispatch two regiments to Virginia. A total of 1000 men were sent. To these would be added a further 1400 men to be enlisted in America. To counter this threat, the French government sent reinforcements from France. During April 1755 eighteen warships, with 3000 men aboard, were readied in Brest and Rochefort. The expedition was placed under the command of Baron Ludwig August Dieskau, an experienced soldier who had served with distinction in the War of the Austrian Succession. A new Governor of Canada was appointed, Philippe de Rigaud de Vaudreuil, a Canadian by birth and a man with naval experience.

The Duc de Mirepoix's task, meanwhile, was to reassure the British authorities in London that France was not sending troops in anticipation of a war, but strengthening its Canadian colony. The British government contended that it was trying to maintain law and order in its own territories. Neither side believed the other. The bad faith behind these manoeuvres became evident once the French ships approached the American continent. Three vessels became separated from the convoy, losing their way in the fog. When the sky cleared, they found themselves close to the Newfoundland Bank, face to face with British warships. It was widely reported in France that a British captain then assured the French that the two countries were still at peace … before firing at them. Two of the French ships were disabled and captured, and eight companies of infantry taken prisoner. The third vessel managed to escape under cover of fog. This incident, still in peacetime, led to the end of the negotiations and the recall, in July 1755, of Mirepoix and his embassy. Bougainville's brief stay in England had come to an end.

It is difficult to determine what functions young Louis-Antoine de Bougainville had carried out in London. He had little experience of the ramifications of France's foreign policy and even less of the workings of the Ministry of Foreign Affairs, although he was a fast learner, intelligent and observant. To some extent, his role was akin to a modern junior cultural attaché. What he did have was a set of introductions to the world of science, provided through his brother. This gave him a number of contacts inside London society, ensured by his uncle D'Arboulin and by the Marquise de Pompadour, to whom the English were well disposed, keen to make use of her influence on Louis XV. Bougainville also made a number of additional contacts at the numerous receptions he had to attend as part of his work.

More significantly, he had an important scientific publication to his credit. It was a study of the calculus, an impressive work for a young man of twenty-five. The *Traité de calcul intégral* or, to give it its full title, *Traité de calcul intégral pour servir à l'Analyse des infiniments petits de M. le Marquis de L'Hôpital* (Treaty on the calculus to be used for the study of Mr de L'Hôpital's work on infinitesimals), was published in two volumes in 1754 and 1755. The subject was of interest to English scientists and philosophers: Isaac Newton had worked on the calculus, developing what he called the calculus of fluxions, while more recently the philosopher Bishop George Berkeley had ridiculed the notion of infinitely small quantities and even the calculus itself. Louis had been guided towards this discipline by Clairault and Jean-Pierre; it became a most useful contribution to his eventual career. Skilfully, he dedicated the first volume to the War Secretary, the Comte d'Argenson: 'It was under your eyes that I entered the field of science. It is my duty to offer you the first fruits of my labours.'[2] To avoid being confused with his better-known older brother, he signed himself 'Bougainville the Younger'.

Louis's many contacts in London scientific and literary circles proved useful to Mirepoix in promoting the French cause among the educated and frequently non-political élite. There was an understanding between European scientists that transcended national rivalries, and continued throughout the century and into the next. Modern readers accustomed to the concept of 'total war' find it difficult to understand how savants could correspond, and even visit each other, while their countries were locked in bitter conflict. The situation is well expressed in the title of G.R. De Beer's book, *The Sciences Were Never at War*. This relationship, however, did little to lessen the enmity that divided the nations or to tone down the propaganda of government pamphleteers. Mirepoix did his best in the unsympathetic atmosphere of Britain's capital, but with little success. His young aide was much more effective.

Bougainville's acceptance by and popularity in London are reflected in his unchallenged election as a Fellow of the Royal Society on 8 January 1756, when the French and British were at war.

He had been nominated on 9 April 1755 by a small group of French and English members. The nomination certificate reads as follows:

> We the undersigned, foreign associates of the Royal Society of London, hereby declare that Mr de Bougainville the younger, author of a Treatise on the calculus of which he has already published the first part, with the second part currently being at the printers, seems to us to be worthy on account of his knowledge of transcendental geometry to be admitted into the Royal Society of London. Signed in Paris on this ninth day of April 1755.
>
> The above-mentioned M de Bougainville being desirous of the Honour of becoming a Member of this Society, we, from our personal knowledge of him or of his works recommend him as fully qualified, and worthy of that Honour
>
> Proposers (those Fellows supporting candidature): D'alembert; Clairaut; Le Monnier; De Gua de Malves
> Ja Short; J Robertson; Geo L Scott; Tho Simpson[3]

Jean le Rond D'Alembert was a *philosophe* with a Europe-wide reputation. He had written a *Mémoire sur le calcul intégral* at the age of twenty-two and a *Traité de la dynamique* at the age of twenty-six, and had recently been elected to the French Academy. Clairault was Bougainville's friend and tutor. Pierre Charles Le Monnier was a friend of both Maupertuis and Clairault, with whom he had travelled to Lapland while only in his early twenties, and of the English astronomer James Bradley and the Scottish astronomer and optical instrument maker James Short. Jean-Paul de Gua de Malvès was a professor of philosophy who was involved in early work on the great *Encyclopédie ou Dictionnaire Raisonné des Sciences, des Arts et des Métiers* edited by Denis Diderot and D'Alembert. The others were probably John Monteith Robertson, George Lewis Scott (from Hanover) and Thomas James Simpson. All were influential scientists, highly regarded in their various fields.

Louis was clearly a young man of promise, with sound achievements to his credit, and he would always be fondly remembered by the many friends he made during his stay in London. His association with savants in England had, too, opened his eyes to the growing interest in Pacific exploration. His time at the French embassy had confirmed that the British had great ambitions in North America and elsewhere; it became clear to him that they also had their eyes on the great Pacific. Jean-Pierre de Bougainville's friend Nicolas Fréret had been a collaborator of Guillaume Delisle, the Royal Geographer, and of his successor Philippe Buache, whose charts of Pacific and eastern waters were widely known. However, they contained many blanks and potential errors. Louis and Jean-Pierre had also discussed the voyage of Bouvet de Lozier to the southern Atlantic and what might be done to continue his investigations. All these could be jeopardised by the British if they started a drive for exploration, which inevitably would be followed by conquest. And then the French would be shut out.

But for the moment these matters had to be put aside. After a brief visit to Paris to see his family and his friends, Louis set out to rejoin his regiment, which was currently stationed at Richemont, in Lorraine.

3. A Soldier of France

1755

FRANCE AND BRITAIN may well have been officially at peace in 1755, but this did not prevent a considerable number of warlike incidents. The year had begun with lengthy discussions about the Jumonville affair. The French had to some extent avenged the young man's death by taking George Washington prisoner; and the British Prime Minister, Lord Newcastle, seemed ready to negotiate a settlement. But they could not agree on the boundary dividing the French and the British American colonies. The negotiators brought out their maps, but these revealed wide differences: Mirepoix's showed two rivers where Newcastle's had only one, a stretch of flat land where the English had a mountain, and an outpost labelled as French which Newcastle claimed was British. Little good faith was shown during the negotiations, and there was minimal hope of reaching an agreement.

Meanwhile, the British were strengthening their forces. By February, British reinforcements had begun to land in Canada and in Virginia. The French countered this by sending their own troops to Canada in May, and this led to the seafight off Newfoundland in which two French ships and their complements were captured. Admiral Edward Boscawen had not attacked without clear instructions. Both he and Admiral Francis Holbourne had received orders from the Admiralty, Boscawen on 16 April and Holbourne on 9 May. Boscawen's assault on French naval units and other vessels, carried out in peacetime, may well have been considered as mere piracy by the French, but they were not unauthorised random raids by hot-headed commanders.

Similarly, General Edward Braddock, commander of the British land forces based in Virginia, had instructions to attack Fort Duquesne and drive the French away from the Ohio valley. In spite of their indignant protests, however, the French were not unaware of the situation. They had not been taken in by the assurances from the Colonial Secretary, Sir Thomas Robinson, that Britain had no intention of disturbing the peace or of upsetting the balance in North America. And the French had sent their own secret instructions to Ange Duquesne, the Governor of New

France, to attack Fort Halifax, a British outpost recently built on the Kennebec River, which presented a danger to Quebec further north.

Braddock wasted no time in preparing his campaign. Two regiments would advance on Fort Duquesne, another led by William Shirley, the Governor of Massachusetts, would attack a fort at Niagara, and a third would attack another French position at Crown Point. The British might claim that they were merely clearing the French from British soil, but Crown Point had been French for a quarter of a century and Niagara for three times as long.

The British plans all went wrong. When Braddock set out for Fort Duquesne, he had little support from the colonial governors. A general in the old mould, he had originally joined the Coldstream Guards and served in a number of campaigns in Europe. He was accustomed to the traditional form of eighteenth-century warfare, in which officers marched their troops in full uniform to form a line facing the enemy, who prepared for battle in the same way. The most famous – and possibly the most absurd – example of such manoeuvres was the Battle of Fontenoy in 1745, when a French officer stepped forward, saluted and invited the British to fire the first volley. His 'Tirez les premiers, Messieurs les Anglais' is an oft-quoted instance of this gentlemanly form of combat, less appreciated no doubt by the victims of the resulting murderous burst of firing than by the patriotic commentators in the drawing rooms back home.

Braddock intended to fight his war the old style. He crossed the Monongahela River, advancing towards Fort Duquesne with 'music, banners, mounted officers, red-coated regulars and blue-coated Virginians'.[1] The terrain was quite unsuitable for such marches: these were primeval forests and uncultivated hillsides, not well-tilled European farmlands. Furthermore, his opponents were not professional soldiers led by young noblemen, but French Canadian rangers and their Indian allies. Hidden behind the trees, they attacked and threw the whole force into confusion. As one of the soldiers is reported to have told his officer, 'We would fight, if we could see anyone to fight against.' Two-thirds of Braddock's men and officers were killed, and he himself was mortally wounded. It was 8 July.

Meanwhile, Major-General Shirley was preparing his advance towards Fort Niagara. Making their way through swamp and forests, struggling to ford streams and rivers, his men were soon affected by fever. They dragged supplies along with them, but these soon proved inadequate. Reaching the shore of Lake Ontario, they stared in dismay at Fort Oswego, a 'miserable little fort' quite inadequate as a base for an attack against well-defended Fort Frontenac or Niagara. Faced by superior French forces, and with many of his men too sick to fight, Shirley decided to turn back and go home the way he had come. It was September.

A third force under Sir William Johnson, though, could claim some successes against the French during an attempt to capture Crown Point. The French had advanced down Lake Champlain and met the British on the shores of Lake George. The inevitable series of ambushes cost Johnson a number of officers and men, but he succeeded in defeating the French after a relatively long battle. He was wounded, however, and could not make up his mind whether to advance further or to rest his men. This gave the French the opportunity to regroup and fortify their positions. After some weeks, with an early cold autumn causing great distress among the wounded and further dispiriting his men, Johnson gave up his plan to attack Crown Point.

The French may have felt satisfied at the outcome of these summer combats, but they became indignant when they learned of the campaign that had been carried out at the same time against the French Acadians in Nova Scotia. This group had been under British control since 1713 when the Peace of Utrecht transferred the territory to the British Crown. They had accepted their new citizenship, but had insisted that, in view of their French origins and their continuing links with distant relatives in France, they should be allowed to remain neutral during the disputes between Britain and France. This caused lasting suspicion among the British authorities, and in 1749 they had set up the naval base of Halifax which became the new capital of the territory.

As the situation deteriorated, the Acadians found themselves torn between the need to placate their British rulers and their continuing loyalty towards the King of France and the Catholic religion. Pressure from the Vicar-General for Nova Scotia, Father Louis-Joseph Le Loutre, caused a number of them – probably between 2000 and 3000 – to move to Quebec, crossing the boundary line of the Missaguash River, but settling not very far from it.

This emigration was interpreted by the British, especially by Governor Shirley and by Charles Lawrence, the Governor of Nova Scotia, as evidence of the Acadians' disaffection. Given a free hand by London to take whatever measures they felt necessary to prevent the Acadians from aiding the French in the forthcoming struggle, Shirley and Lawrence sent Robert Moncton to capture any French outpost that lay in his way and remove all the remaining French from Acadia.

Moncton sent Colonel John Winslow to promulgate the order that all the French inhabitants of these districts be removed, carrying with them their money and as much of their household goods as they could carry. The farm buildings and houses were burned, and the villagers marched off to waiting ships, to be dispersed among British settlements, from Massachusetts to Georgia, many eventually reaching French Louisiana, where they became known as *Cayun* (from Acadian to Cadjun). A number escaped to Quebec and some went on to France. Their confiscated lands were in due course allocated to British loyalist settlers. The entire operation had lasted from early August to November. More than 8000 were deported in this early instance of ethnic cleansing. The episode, known to the locals as *le grand dérangement*, made a lasting impression on French opinion – and, after independence, on American consciousness. It was the subject of Henry Wadsworth Longfellow's famous poem 'Evangeline' (1847) with its resonant first opening line: 'This is the forest primeval'. One of those emotionally affected by the Acadian tragedy was Louis de Bougainville, who endeavoured after the war to assist some of the refugees.

But the dismal year of 1755 had not yet exhausted its grim surprises. In late October and November, without any warning, the British seized 300 French vessels, merchantmen and fishing boats in the Atlantic and the Channel. The ships were taken away as prizes, and some 6000 French sailors were taken prisoner, some even being pressed into service on British vessels.

And still France did not declare war.

Louis XV was not inclined towards war, glory and conquests. It might be going a little far to agree with the historian Pierre Gaxotte that 'No sovereign was more sincere in his pacific intentions, more sparing with the blood of his subjects',[2] but it is true that, after the Battle of Fontenoy, Louis commented, 'The blood of our enemies is still the blood of men; true glory lies in sparing it.'[3] He had no wish to imitate Louis XIV and wage a long series of wars. He had no need to: for centuries French rulers had fought back seemingly endless invasions to build up and strengthen their nation. The aim had always been to create a French state that could shelter within logical geographical boundaries. Apart from the indefensible low country to the north-east, France was now relatively safe behind the Pyrenees, the Alps and the coastlines. Internal disruption could be minimised by ridding the country of religious dissidents, such as the Huguenots, and enforcing royal rule against troublesome nobles. There was no point in ruinous wars of conquest and expansion.

Louis did, though, have to preserve the balance of power in Europe. Much of France's foreign policy was directed at building up a complex series of alliances with other European countries. When this balance was threatened, as it was during the crises that followed royal successions – in Spain, and in Austria – war ensued. Britain, on the other hand, was an island, much less anxious about foreign invasions, but with a lasting interest in overseas trade and eager for commercial bases in distant countries. Colonial enterprises followed, fostered by the emigration of religious dissenters, Quakers and others, and situated in climates where Europeans could feel comfortable.

France, as a continental power, felt little need for colonies. They were costly to settle and to maintain, but they could be useful, as long as they did not cause problems. This was one reason why France did not want religious dissenters to play any role, as they were doing in British North America. In line with this policy, the French administrators in Canada took good care to ensure that the settlers kept to their old religion. This is why, when the French Protestant Huguenots lost their political rights in France, they emigrated mostly to Holland, Britain and northern Germany, but not to Canada or the West Indies.

French people had no real desire to move overseas. The islands of the West Indies were useful from the commercial point of view, providing fruit, sugar and rum, but they had little to offer to European immigrants. Voltaire's much-quoted dismissive comment that Canada was only 'a few acres of snow' and not worth fighting for, reflected not only ignorance about that country's potential, but a state of mind that was prevalent among the French. Culture radiated from France towards all of Europe, through literature, art, music and philosophy. What was the point of building up new satellite countries in distant places that had nothing to offer in return? Britain could therefore make advances in North America and extend her influence on the Indian subcontinent without French public opinion becoming overly concerned. The French government took little action even when Britain's peacetime behaviour became aggressive and insulting. Isolated incidents caused indignation, but not war.

Furthermore, France's financial position was grim. Louis XIV's wars had been appallingly costly. Scotsman John Law's 1717–21 efforts to create a national bank and a major trading and colonising company, which had begun in a wave of enthusiasm, had ended in disaster. The more recent War of the Austrian Succession had made matters worse. Attempts to impose an income tax on the tax-exempt nobility led to an uproar and threats of boycotts against the entire political and administrative structure. National bankruptcy was an ever-present and increasing threat.

Early in 1756, however, the European balance of power was upset. Frederick II of Prussia signed what became known as the Westminster Accord and moved over to the British side. To restore the balance, France decided to ally herself with Austria, by means of the Treaty of Versailles, and then with Russia. These changes caused uncertainty and fear throughout the continent. The troubles and clashes in Canada had only been a sideshow: now all of Europe was affected. Britain finally declared war on France on 18 May 1756. Shortly after, Frederick sent his troops into Saxony. A bitter conflict had started. It would last seven long years.

Louis de Bougainville could have stayed with Chevert, following him through the various manoeuvres and campaigns of the war in Europe. Instead, he had already decided to join the French forces in Canada. His time in England had made him aware of British ambitions in North America and elsewhere. If Britain controlled the distant shipping lanes, she could soon achieve global domination. This would have far greater consequences than the possible successes of Britain's allies on the European continent. Louis's patrons arranged for him to be appointed as aide-de-camp to the Marquis de Montcalm, the commander of the French forces in Canada. There is little doubt that his uncle D'Arboulin and the Marquise de Pompadour helped in this respect, but his father may also have called in a few favours.

As he surveyed his family's fortunes and his sons' careers, Pierre-Yves had every reason to be satisfied. Despite continuing poor health, Jean-Pierre was now permanent secretary to the *Académie des Inscriptions et Belles-Lettres*. Louis-Antoine seemed set for a successful career in the army – and the looming war would be no more dangerous for him in North America than it might be in Europe. The boys had broken with the family's traditional occupations in the law and local administration, but they certainly were helping the Bougainvilles to climb the social ladder. And so, in late March 1756, Louis set out for the port of Brest to sail for Canada.

Part 2

WAR IN CANADA

4. Crossing the North Atlantic

March–May 1756

'How long did the journey from Paris take you?' asked La Rigaudière.

They were watching the misty grey coast of Brittany fading away in the distance.

'Two days,' replied Louis.

'That was good. I've often taken three, sometimes longer, especially at this time of the year.'

Leaving the capital under the grey skies of a late winter, Louis had passed through silent, sodden fields and surly towns, before entering a Brittany that had formally been French for a couple of hundred years, but where the Breton language still prevailed. It was an enigmatic world of small enclosed fields and grey granite villages, through which the stranger passed silently and often with a sense of insecurity. When finally the coach rattled over the cobblestones of Brest, he felt he was entering a different universe.

The bustling port throbbed with activity. Sailors, soldiers, traders and prostitutes – *les filles de joie* – crowded the narrow streets; shouts, calls and curses filled the air; carts trundled past, laden with produce for the waiting ships. A small forest of masts crowded the harbour, barely swaying in a mild breeze. Along the quays, sailors and convicts carried supplies along wooden gangplanks, threading their way between heaped-up crates, wicker baskets, tethered cattle, caged poultry and pigs waiting to be dragged on board some vessel, where they would eventually provide the only fresh food the crews could get on the long journeys.

Bougainville had boarded the *Licorne*, warmly welcomed by her captain, *Lieutenant de vaisseau* Chevalier Michel Froger de la Rigaudière, who took him below deck and showed him to the dark, cramped cabin that would be his home for the next five weeks. Louis's only experience of sailing had been two short crossings of the English Channel. Everything around him looked unfamiliar: the officers who greeted him with a studied look of appraisal, the petty officers shouting orders, the men at their various tasks, sometimes hurrying, mostly laughing among themselves and talking a language he could not understand. The ship seemed so small, the smells so strange, the companionways so steep and narrow.

After a day or two, the pace of life on board slowed down. They were to accompany the transport ships *Léopard*, *Illustre* and *Héros*, and they could not sail until all three were ready. He watched the soldiers marching into the ships, laughing and jostling each other. But still nothing happened: they had to wait for a favourable wind. This came at last on 3 April. There was a flurry of activity – men hauling on cables, then climbing with astonishing dexterity into the rigging, and a deafening yelling of instructions – before the *Licorne* started on her way into the Atlantic.

The Brest roadstead was smooth, scarcely ruffled by the breeze. The outlying islands gave a little more protection, but even the open sea was welcoming, with a light breeze and blue springtime skies. As ship life began to settle into a normal routine La Rigaudière offered to teach Bougainville the art of navigation. He would be the first of several sea captains who answered the young man's eager questioning, and helped to transform the army officer into a naval commander. 'M. de la Rigaudière, knight, is most amiable and an officer of the greatest distinction. He has promised to teach me as much about naval matters as will be possible during the crossing.'[1]

La Rigaudière's role as a mentor extended even further, for he had links with the Pacific. His father had been one of the French captains who had sailed into the ocean during a relatively short period when Spain had allowed some of her ally's ships access to South American possessions. In 1706, he had gone in a fast frigate, the *Aurore*, to discuss the future of the colonies with the local authorities and urge them to prevent any form of disaffection among the Spanish settlers during a particularly troubled period. He had brought back to France a detailed chart of the South Seas, which he presented to the Secretary of State for the Navy, 'having corrected on it the errors that have been made on previous ones'.[2] Consequently, his son was able to discuss with Bougainville the relative difficulties of sailing through the Strait of Magellan as against rounding Cape Horn, as well as the potential value of the Falkland Islands and the vast prospects for exploration and trade offered by the Pacific.

Louis spent much of his time during the crossing watching the officers calculating the ship's position according to the old painstaking and often unreliable methods. They observed the height of the sun to work out their latitude, and did their best to assess the distance they had travelled from France. As he knew from his discussions with scientists and mathematicians at Royal Society gatherings in London, pinpointing a ship's position at any one time was far from easy. Accurate calculations were essential, but experience and, to some extent, luck were also important. Fortunately, as the captain pointed out, the route from Brest to Quebec was fairly simple. There was little difference in latitude, so all a ship really needed to do was to sail west until a coastline and familiar, identifiable landmarks appeared. The main danger to the *Licorne* and the accompanying transports was the presence of British warships that might suddenly pounce on them.

A wild storm struck the ships as they neared North America, driving away the *Héros* and forcing the *Licorne* onto a southerly course to avoid the mountainous seas ahead and the ever-present danger of icebergs. The storm in time subsided and finally, on 12 May 1756, the French entered Quebec Harbour. The crossing had lasted thirty-eight days. La Rigaudière, helpful as ever, had taken the trouble during the storm to explain the moves needed to ensure that the ship coped safely with the dangers they were facing. Louis would long remember his initiation into maritime life by this kindly man. La Rigaudière soon met a tragic end. Promoted *capitaine de vaisseau* (post captain) in September 1756, he was accused a little later of not coming to the aid of another warship during a sea battle off Louisbourg, Cape Breton Island. He was ordered to report to a court martial but hanged himself in November.

5. Noble Savages

June–July 1756

Bougainville was welcomed to Canada by a distant cousin, De Vienne, a local government official. Louis stayed with him for a couple of days, and together they strolled about this Quebec he had heard so much about. With an estimated 6000 inhabitants, it was a sizeable settlement, larger than inland Montreal, but it nevertheless reminded him of a French provincial town, with narrow winding streets and grey stone houses, severe but quite homely inside. It was a lively place, prosperous, with the usual throng of sailors and soldiers, traders shouting their wares and fishermen bringing in their latest catch.

Louis parted with Montcalm, who was going to Montreal by coach to meet the Governor, Marquis de Vaudreuil. The young man had found Montcalm 'friendly, witty, frank and open-minded … keen to put my services to use',[1] and their friendship did not lessen over time, in spite of the difficult times both experienced.

Montcalm was indeed a charming man. Handsome and dignified, now in his forty-fourth year, Louis-Joseph, Marquis de Montcalm de Saint-Véran, belonged to the old nobility. Although he was sailing to a destiny that many would view as glorious, he was a reluctant warrior. He had joined the army at the age of fourteen, served with distinction during the War of the Austrian Succession, but had eventually gone back to his estate at Candiac, near Nîmes, with the firm intention of ending his military career of more than twenty-two years. However, he had been called back to take over the Canadian command: it was a duty he could not shirk.

De Vienne also warned Louis about the rivalry between the native French Canadians and the administrators and military commanders Versailles kept sending to New France. The situation was unlikely to be made any easier by an administrative complication – Montcalm and the army were answerable to the Secretary of State for War, the Comte d'Argenson, while Vaudreuil was answerable to the Secretary of State for Marine, the Marquis de Peirenc de Moras. Louis left Quebec on 22 May, travelling up the St Lawrence River to Montreal, where he met up with Montcalm. Together they called on Vaudreuil, and soon had experienced at first hand the tension between the colonists and the administrators.

Pierre-François de Rigaud, Marquis de Vaudreuil, was the son of a previous governor, a true native of New France with all the inbred resentment the locals felt at the French political appointees. He had hoped to be given command of the troops, so that he could combine this with the governorship, but Versailles had chosen Montcalm instead. For his part, Montcalm had expected to be in charge of all the French forces in Canada, but Vaudreuil controlled the militia and some of the marines, and had no intention of transferring them to the new arrival. This would create confusion and uncertainty in the chain of command, and contribute to the eventual loss of French Canada.

The first meeting between the two men was marked by the traditional formalities and courtesies of the eighteenth century. Bows and protestations of mutual friendship and devotion punctuated the occasion, so that Montcalm was able to report back to the Minister of War, 'M. de Vaudreuil overwhelms me with civilities.' But he commented in a letter a week later: 'I am on good terms with him, but not in his confidence, which he never gives to anybody who comes from France'.

They discussed the situation and pored over maps. Both agreed that aggressive moves against the British were out of the question: the French could pursue only a defensive strategy. They had to hold Quebec, which stood at the end of the lifeline with France. It must be protected against attacks from the sea, but also from the British colonies to the south. Although its main purpose was to maintain the link with Europe, Quebec also served to close the St Lawrence River to enemy ships and thus shield Montreal on the eastern side. Indeed, the St Lawrence was crucial to the defence of the whole colony. The French needed to keep both banks, including a deep strip along the south bank, to protect the waterway from British attacks. Montreal also had to be protected against attacks coming from a valley that led, by way of two narrow lakes, George and Champlain, from the Hudson River right up to a wide plain that stretched for miles along the riverbank. But Montreal was also vulnerable from the west, along the St Lawrence, from nearby Lake Ontario. It was important to prevent the British from massing on the American side of the lake, crossing to its northern shore and launching a two-pronged attack on the capital.

Vaudreuil stressed that Lake Ontario needed securing and that this was a good time to mount a counter-blow to growing British activities along its southern shore. Montcalm was less sure, but he bowed to the governor's greater knowledge of the country, and appreciated that Vaudreuil had been planning an offensive in the region for over a year. It was both politic and courteous to accept his views. In spite of some private reservations, Montcalm had to admit that Vaudreuil could well be right, and that cancelling his plans would be both costly and unproductive – as well as causing a serious clash between the two men.

First, however, he carried out a speedy inspection of French forts to the south: Fort Saint Frédéric on Lake Champlain and Fort Carillon at Ticonderoga, at the southern end. Satisfied with the condition of these important defensive outposts, and with the spirit of their garrisons, he returned to Montreal where Bougainville was carrying out mainly administrative duties.

Louis now had his first encounter with an Indian tribe. To a young Frenchman, especially one associated with the world of writers and *philosophes*, this was an important occasion. Were these indeed examples of the 'Noble Savages' so many people in Europe had argued about? (The term *sauvage* had not yet acquired its modern flavour of brutishness. It came from the Latin *salvaticus*, meaning forest- or countryside-related, denoting a person who lived close to nature.)

Back in 1703 the *Voyages* of Louis-Armand de Lahontan had begun a controversy over whether 'uncorrupted savages' might be found in North America. The early French settlers had spoken of 'Hurons', referring to tribes of Iroquois Indians found in the regions around Toronto. The argument was that, somewhere, native peoples could be found living at an earlier stage of development, unspoiled by the ownership of private property – which bred greed – and the privileges that went with inherited wealth and noble birth – which led to oppression. Indeed, Lahontan's book included a *Dialogue curieux entre l'auteur et un sauvage* (or Huron, meaning one who leads a rough life). As more became known about the tribes of North and South America, however, this theory came under strong attack; but its supporters, their position strengthened by the writings of Jean-Jacques Rousseau, still believed that, somewhere, societies living in an ideal, primitive state would one day be found and would provide evidence of the corrupting effects of modern civilisation. Rousseau's *Discours* on the effects of the sciences and the arts had been published in 1750, and a second essay, on the origins of inequality, four years later. In simple terms, Rousseau argued that mankind had been corrupted by the ownership of property, which led to greed, jealousy and social oppression.

Bougainville's detailed account of the meeting was included in his memoirs on Canada and later used for a lecture, *Notice historique sur les sauvages de l'Amérique septentrionale*, which he gave at the National Institute many years later, in 1799. The Indians, a sub-group of the Algonquins known as *Folles Avoines* (Wild Oats), came up to Montreal on 3 July in five canoes, bearing six scalps and bringing a small group of British prisoners. They landed and walked up to the castle in a double file, on each side of their hapless and frightened captives. The latter were then made to sit in a circle, while their captors made a speech and began to dance around them. Although terrifying for the victims, to Bougainville:

the strange spectacle [was] more likely to terrify than to amuse, yet nevertheless interesting to a philosophe desirous of studying human nature, especially in its most primitive state. These men were naked save for a piece of cloth in front and behind; their faces and bodies were daubed with paint; feathers, signs and symbols of war adorned their heads; in their hands they held tomahawks and spears … No one could have a better ear for music than these people. Every movement of their bodies synchronises perfectly with the rhythm. Their dance is similar to the Pyrrhic dances of Ancient Greece.[2]

These comments contain many of the elements that would later appear in the account of his Pacific voyage. Here were men who could still be regarded by contemporary social analysts as primitive, but there was little about them that could arouse the admiration or envy of an educated European. The exception was their sense of rhythm, which he would also find among the islanders of the Pacific. The comparison with the Greeks of the classical period would be applied to the islands of the South Seas, when Bougainville selected the name of a Greek island, Cythera, for Tahiti, and used other names from the Aegean Sea for other islands and archipelagos.

The British prisoners in Montreal were spared, taken away by French troops 'to save them from being knocked on the head by the Algonquins and Iroquois'.[3] This fate would later befall others, in scenes of horror Louis would find hard to forget.

6. LAKE ONTARIO TO QUEBEC

July 1756–February 1757

THE FRENCH KNEW the British were building up their forces on the southern shore of Lake Ontario. Vaudreuil's plan to forestall an advance on Montreal was sound, and Montcalm accordingly set off on 21 July down the St Lawrence valley, making for the French post of Fort Frontenac. Situated in the area known as the Thousand Islands, where Lake Ontario pours its waters into the St Lawrence River, it was an important defensive and, in this case, offensive outpost. In fact, the British had long been planning to gain control of Lake Ontario and seize the French forts along it. Shirley had started drawing up plans for such a campaign back in December 1755, well before the war had officially begun. What he had outlined at a Council of War in New York had been approved in principle, but carrying it out meant supplying men and money. He got no help from the administrators of Pennsylvania and Virginia, but the British Cabinet did make a grant of £54,000 towards Massachusetts' expenses. However, Shirley was about to be replaced and his influence was rapidly waning. The most that he could do at this stage was to strengthen the troops defending Fort Oswego on the southern shore of the lake, which was now being harassed by French troops and their Indian allies.

As Montcalm and Bougainville made their way down by canoe from Montreal the young man commented on the beauty of the banks of the St Lawrence, with trees coming down to the water or opening out to present the travellers with a vast panorama. 'What a shame that such a beautiful land is uncultivated!' he exclaimed.[1]

Their first major stop was the French mission station and fortified post of La Présentation, now the town of Ogdensburg, in the State of New York. It had been founded six years earlier by the Abbé François Piquet, who combined the role of successful missionary with that of soldier and patriot. He had converted a number of Indians and brought them over to the French side. He entirely agreed with Bougainville that Canada offered vast prospects for development, and proudly pointed out to him the impressive vista of meadows and forests, as well as the abundant game and fish that provided an easy living for the Iroquois.

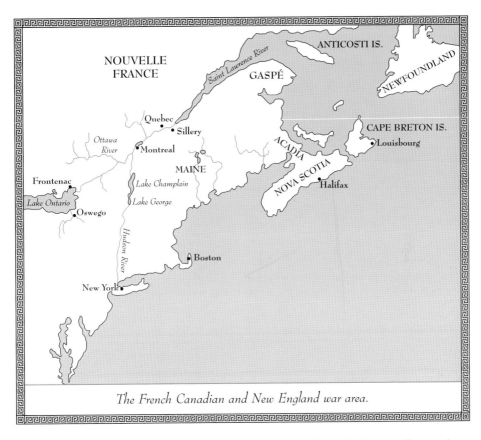

NOUVELLE FRANCE

ANTICOSTI IS.

Saint Lawrence River

GASPÉ

NEWFOUNDLAND

Quebec

Sillery

CAPE BRETON IS.

Ottawa River

Montreal

Louisbourg

MAINE

ACADIA

Frontenac

NOVA SCOTIA

Halifax

Lake Ontario

Lake Champlain

Oswego

Lake George

Hudson River

Boston

New York

The French Canadian and New England war area.

Montcalm held the usual ceremonial meeting with the Indians, offering them wine, tobacco, pigs and the necklaces of coloured snail-shells they called porcelain. Once again, Bougainville recorded his impressions of the native people, and especially the apparent equal role played by women in the deliberations. 'They have,' he wrote, 'the same standing among the Indians as that of the matrons of old among the Gauls and the Germans.' Montcalm was more interested in the military intelligence provided by the Indians on the state of the British defences around Oswego. He moved on to Frontenac (present-day Windsor), which was to be the main staging post for the French troops gathering for the attack on Oswego.

By 4 August, the French were ready for the attack. Some 3000 men had been gathered from Frontenac down to Niagara and were advancing, in shore-hugging boats and on land, towards the British positions. The first post, Fort Ontario, fell on the 13th; further defences were taken during the next few days and on the 19th the British capitulated.

Since he spoke English quite fluently, Bougainville was sent to negotiate the terms of surrender. It had been a relatively bloodless battle: the British lost an estimated fifty men, the French close to half that number. The fort was destroyed, as were the nearby vessels and much of the powder and provisions. Father Piquet set up a large cross over the ruins, with the motto '*In hoc signo vincunt*' ('In this sign they conquered'), close to a large pole bearing the arms of France and a motto reputedly provided by Bougainville: '*Manibus date lilia plenis*'. It is indeed likely that Louis suggested this, as it is a quote from the *Aeneid*, a work he knew well and would use on other occasions in his journal and elsewhere. It translates as 'Scatter lilies with generous hands'. It can be regarded as a message of peace and reconciliation, although he may have wondered about its appropriateness when he witnessed his Indian allies mutilating and killing a number of the British survivors. It was not their custom to spare prisoners.

Louis then started back for Montreal to bring news of the victory. France was now in control of Lake Ontario, having cleared the enemy from the southern shore, and would need only small garrisons at Niagara and Frontenac to guard Montreal's western approaches. He wrote to his brother Jean-Pierre, 'I have tasted the pleasure that a first victory brings.' When he arrived in the administrative capital, however, he found that the French already knew about the victory. There was a victory march when the bulk of the army arrived with Montcalm, the captured flags were hung in churches and a *Te Deum* sung – but Vaudreuil had already written to Versailles, claiming the victory for himself.

Admittedly, it was his plan, an idea he had cherished and nurtured for a long time, and one Montcalm had been unsure about, but the actual campaign had been carried out by the military commander, not the civilian governor. However, Vaudreuil's report and subsequent letters to France were punctuated with *I* and *my* – 'The measures I took …', 'I cannot congratulate myself enough …' and 'my orders …'. Montcalm's own report followed a few days later, and it was left to their respective ministers to reach their own conclusions. Relations between the two men were now truly soured, with the locals and the officers ranging themselves according to whether they were Canadian-born *habitants* or French natives.

Bougainville recorded his own opinion of the tension, resorting as he so often did to classical parallels:

One must be blind not to see that we the French regular forces are treated as the Spartans treated the Helots. The Marquis de Montcalm does not receive the honour of being consulted and it is generally through public rumour that he hears of M. de Vaudreuil's military plans … When [Vaudreuil] produces an idea, he falls in love with it, as Pygmalion did with his statue. I can forgive Pygmalion, because what he produced was a masterpiece.[2]

Montreal was now well protected against any attack from the west. The south was another matter. The French controlled a considerable tract of land, but it was exposed to attacks from English colonists and troops from New York State, especially along the border with Vermont (or New Hampshire), with Lakes Champlain and George running south to north. The French had a well-fortified strongpoint in Fort Carillon to the south of Lake Champlain at Ticonderoga; the British held the southern tip, defended by Fort William Henry. In between lay a semi-wilderness of forests and hills, with a few farming settlements, through which roamed Indians supporting either the French or the British. Reports on raids by these war parties make sad reading. They talk of scalpings, and the torturing and killing of prisoners, including the hapless settlers whose farms were attacked and burnt down.

At the beginning of September, Bougainville left Montreal for Ticonderoga, to assess the progress made on new defence works and to obtain first-hand information about British activities further south. The rivers and the lakes were particularly exposed. Indian scouting parties were sent on this reconnaissance work with firm instructions to bring back prisoners alive so that they could be questioned.

British parties were doing much the same on their side, sometimes with dire results. On 19 September, some fifty men led by Captain Hodges were ambushed not far from Fort William by French Canadian and Indian forces, Bougainville among them. It was impossible to restrain the warriors who, almost naked and daubed in war paint, led the attack. They were, Louis reported, 'insolent' and usually took little notice of the officers. When they returned, they boasted of their victory in terms that appalled him:

The very recital of their cruelties is horrible; the ferocity and insolence of these black-souled barbarians makes one shudder. It is an abominable kind of war; reprisals as a system are terrible and in such an atmosphere callousness is infectious.[3]

A medicine man had stayed behind at Ticonderoga and began incantations to ensure the success of the raiding party. Louis once again had recourse to classical parallels:

The lodge shook, the sorcerer sweated beads of blood and the devil came at last and told him that the warriors would return with scalps and prisoners. A sorcerer in the medicine lodge is exactly like the Pythoness on the tripod or the witch Canidia invoking the shades.[4]

But time was passing and the approach of winter made a showdown between the French and the British forces unlikely. A bitterly cold wind was sweeping down from the hills, rain showers were increasingly mixed with sleet, the last leaves were dropping from the trees. Montcalm and Bougainville set off for Montreal on 26 October, both men nearing exhaustion.

Montcalm allowed Louis to go to Quebec, where he stayed with De Vienne and wrote long letters to Jean-Pierre (their father had recently died). He was utterly worn out:

Since I arrived in Canada, I have travelled close on 500 leagues. The continuing travel, the poor food, the frequent lack of sleep, the nights spent under the open sky in the woods, the expeditions with the Indians, have affected my chest a little. At the end of last month, I even spat blood. Diet and rest will set me up and make me fit to start anew in the spring … Let us hope that this campaign and the successes we have achieved in Europe will win peace for us! Here we desire it more than anyone. What a country and what people, my dear brother, and what patience is needed to put up with the dislike they are pleased to feel for us! … All I can say is that when the time comes to leave this country, we shall sing with all our hearts: *In exitu Israel*.

And to his *chère Maman*, Madame de Hérault, he described a period of recuperation marked by studious relaxation:

I spend my time reading, writing and meditating. Without Montaigne, without Horace, Virgil, Tacitus, Montesquieu and Corneille, without the companionship and sympathy of my general [Montcalm], weariness would have overcome me utterly.[5]

Louis spent part of his leave doing further work on his calculus treatise, writing up his notes on the Indians and on the French settlers, and preparing his *Mémoires sur l'état de la Nouvelle-France [à l'époque de la guerre de Sept Ans]* which he would later send to Madame de Hérault for transmission to the Minister of War.

Life, in fact, was not quite as austere as he made out. Quebec was a pleasant town, with the houses comfortably huddled together, cosy havens from the snow that blanketed the narrow streets and the few open squares. It was Montreal, though, that was the centre of French Canadian life – 'a sparkling fragment of the reign of Louis XV dropped into the American wilderness' as Francis Parkman puts it – and Louis soon made his way back there.

Whatever they may have privately thought of the officers and administrators who had come over from France, the *habitants* were more than happy to invite them to their homes. As a young man who had been received in the gilded apartments of Versailles and the literary salons of Paris, a protégé of the famous Marquise de Pompadour, Louis was welcomed by hostesses at dinner parties, balls and soirées that often went on till the early morning. He was charming, learned and witty, and more than a little glamour surrounded him.

The recent victories had lifted the settlers' mood. There was money around – he heard almost daily gossip about the profits made by wartime contractors and corrupt officials – and a great deal of gambling went on. Louis managed to keep his losses to a minimum, but he gained a reputation among the ladies, whom Montcalm described as *spirituelles* and *galantes*. According to one family tradition, Marguerite Gaultier, a well-to-do lady, not long widowed, fell in love with him and had hopes of eventually marrying him. However, the disparity in their ages makes this unlikely: he was twenty-eight and she was fifty.[6] To keep on side with local society, Montcalm was forced to give costly receptions: 'sixteen people at table every day … a dinner for thirty-six people … a ball … suppers three times a week'. These winter months were a drain on his pocket, and he was only too glad when Lent arrived, bringing with it a period of austerity. Spring was also approaching. The snow began to melt, the roads became passable once more. The St Lawrence flowed more freely and faster. It was time for the military campaign to resume.

7. From Victory to Defeat

1757–8

PLANNING FOR THE next southern campaign began in January. Montcalm was convinced that the British would use Fort William Henry, at the southern end of Lake St Sacrement, to launch a major offensive on Montreal. It must be captured as soon as possible. Vaudreuil shared this view, but kept his plan secret from the general. He made his own arrangements with his brother Rigaud – the younger Vaudreuil customarily used the minor patronymic and was usually referred to as 'Brother Rigaud'[1] – supplying him with locals and Indians, and spending lavishly on the preparations. Montcalm obviously knew that Vaudreuil was working on an expedition, but he did not fully realise what the governor was up to until late February, by which time Rigaud de Vaudreuil's force was on its way.

Although jealousy was a major motivating factor, Vaudreuil's plans were not unreasonable: Montcalm's French troops had no experience of the harsh Canadian winter and were ill equipped for a march through the snowbound countryside. Vaudreuil, on the other hand, had provided his brother's men with moccasins, snowshoes, sledges, heavy overcoats, blankets and bearskins. They were to make their way as quickly as possibly to Fort William Henry, then held by a winter garrison of fewer than 400 men. Rigaud's force, including soldiers he picked up at Fort Carillon, totalled close on four times that number.

Rigaud hoped to surprise the British, but his force was sighted on 17 March. When he launched his attack the next day, the defenders were able to hold him at bay with well-directed gunfire. Some English boats and sheds were set on fire, but the fort still held. The attackers were clearly superior in numbers, but it was obvious to the British that there were few professional soldiers among them. When, on the 20th, Rigaud dispatched an officer to negotiate British terms of surrender, the English commander, Major Edward Eyre, sent him packing with a curt refusal. Rigaud's men then spent a couple of days destroying and burning the outer buildings, storehouses, huts, a sawmill and a hospital, plus a few more boats and boatsheds, but he made no direct attack on the fort itself. Then he turned back to Montreal.

This was far from the victory his brother had hoped for, but it was nevertheless a strong blow to British military positions. The British had suffered severe damage, although they had had enough time to remove the ammunition from their outlying store, thereby retaining precious gunpowder and weapons and saving the fort from a disastrous explosion. If a more disciplined and less confident force had led the assault, Fort William Henry might well have fallen. As it was, the Vaudreuil brothers were forced to save face by claiming that the operation had been a mere exploratory raid, and as such had been a success.

Montcalm meanwhile had been working on his own plans. When Rigaud de Vaudreuil arrived back in April 1757, he felt somewhat reassured about any immediate threat from the south. Fort William Henry could be taken by a properly mounted campaign, and the danger from the south eliminated, as he had done the previous year with the threat from the west. A more immediate danger, however, was looming from the east.

News had been received that a large squadron was being readied in various English ports, soon to sail for Canada. This implied a threat to Quebec, as the British ships might be strong enough to force their way into the mouth of the St Lawrence. It was no time to deplete the defences of Quebec and Montreal by sending a large military force towards Fort William Henry. As it turned out, the British intended simply to secure the French sea fortress of Louisbourg on Cape Breton Island. Once they had done this, they could start massing their forces for an advance on Quebec.

Montcalm waited to see whether Louisbourg would hold out, and whether the French squadrons sent to defend it would arrive in time. Fortunately, the British fleet, consisting of fifteen ships of the line and three frigates, with 5000 troops on board, did not set out until mid-May. There were further delays, giving enough time to marshall the French forces. When the British were finally ready to attack, they realised that they were outnumbered. They gave up – and then a number of their ships fell victim to a wild storm. Louisbourg was saved, for the time being at least.

So by July Montcalm felt confident enough to order his 7000 troops and allies to march south. Like Bougainville, he was uneasy at having to cope with his Indian allies, now numbering several thousand and eager to accompany him. They could not be disciplined or used in military manoeuvres as regular troops could be, but he could not send them home either. Summer was well advanced and time was pressing. They crossed the St Lawrence, marched south to the Richelieu River where they embarked in boats for Fort Carillon and continued by boat and through the forest to Fort William Henry.

In his journal, Bougainville wrote a detailed account of the attack and of its controversial aftermath:

1 August. The army embarked at 2 p.m. in the following order: the Queen's
Brigade, followed by Courtemarche's militiamen, then foot supplies, the
field hospital, a detachment from the Royal Roussillon. Mr Jacquot's vessel
led a fleet of 250 sails. Halt at 5 p.m. four leagues from Fort Carillon
[Ticonderoga], above Bark Island where the Natives who were waiting for us,
having left the day before, took the lead in 150 bark canoes. The scene was
strange for a soldier used to European armies who cannot imagine the
spectacle of some 1500 Natives naked in their canoes.[2]

The total French forces, estimated at 7000, outnumbered the British who could
only muster some 2370 men, including the garrison of the fort itself which did not
exceed 500. Montcalm did all he could to conceal his advance from the enemy, but
this was impossible, with constant raids by the Indians who were keen to take
prisoners. Although it was often difficult to save the lives of those who fell into their
hands, the capture of prisoners was important because it enabled the French to
obtain information about British defensive measures. Saving their lives was not
simply an act of mercy; it was a military necessity. One of the numerous skirmishes
resulted in the capture and killing of a messenger.

[The Indian chief] came back today. He had come upon three men, one of
whom was captured, another killed and the third escaped. He brought the
prisoner back here as well as the coat of the man he had killed. In the lining
we found a letter General [Daniel] Webb had written to Lieutenant-Colonel
Monroe or alternatively to whichever officer commanded Fort William
Henry. He advised him that he could not come to the assistance of the fort
until he had received the colonial militiamen he had instructed to join him
without delay (and that he understood the French force numbered 11,000
men, with powerful artillery support and was surrounding the fort on all
sides over a depth of five miles), and that if the militia he had asked for did
not arrive in time the commander should obtain the best conditions he could
for a surrender.[3]

This led Montcalm to hasten his preparations. Artillery fire began on the 5th,
lasting most of the day. Then, on the morning of the 6th, Montcalm sent
Bougainville to the fort with the captured letter in the hope that this would cause
the British to accept their position was hopeless. But it was too soon, and
Bougainville met with a courteous refusal:

An officer, having blindfolded me, led me firstly to the fort, then to the
fortified area where I handed to the commanding officer the letters of Mr de

Montcalm and of General Webb. Great expressions of thanks for this French courtesy, expressions of joy at having to deal with such a generous enemy, such was the gist of Lt Col. Monroe's reply to Mr de Montcalm.[4]

The exchange of courtesies was all very well, but clearly the hostilities had to proceed. The battle resumed. By the morning of the 9th the British had come to the conclusion that honour had been saved, but that nothing further could be done, and the white flag was raised. Colonel Young brought Montcalm a proposal for surrender, which seemed reasonable, and agreement was reached. Bougainville drew up the formal document and went around issuing instructions to the French troops. Montcalm then called the Indians together, read out the agreed terms and asked them to observe them.

It was agreed that British troops should march out with the honours of war and be escorted back to Fort Edward, further south, but take no part in any further military activities for eighteen months; French prisoners held in America were to be returned; all the remaining stores and munitions would become French property.

At midday, the outer fort opened its gates, but the Indians began looting almost at once. 'We had great difficulty in saving the food and munitions.' By evening, calm seemed to have been restored, and Bougainville set off for Montreal with news of the victory. This saved him from witnessing the scenes that began soon after and that have left a black cloud hanging over a victory of major strategic importance. Later, however, he collected sufficient information from others to detail the 'misfortune we feared' in his journal:

At daybreak the English, who were terrified by the sight of the Savages, wanted to leave before our escort had been properly assembled. They abandoned their trunks and all the other heavy luggage that the lack of carts did not permit them to take away and they set out. The Savages had already massacred several of the sick in the tents that served as hospitals.

The 'turmoil' was started by the Abenaquis from Penwamesko, who claimed the most recent ill-treatment by the British.

They shouted out their war cry and threw themselves at the rear of the column, which was just setting off. The English, instead of showing a bold front, were terror-stricken and fled helter-skelter, throwing down their weapons, their luggage and even their clothing. Their fear emboldened Savages from every Nation who began to loot, killing a dozen soldiers and carrying off five or six hundred.

Louis noted that the French escort did its duty and that a few grenadiers were wounded. 'The Marquis de Montcalm, who had run up when he heard the commotion, Mr de Bourlamaque and several French officers, tearing the English from the hands of the Savages, risked their lives, for in such cases the Savages respect no one.'[5]

Montcalm, who had tried to save lives by rushing into the fray and shouting 'Kill me, but spare the English who are under my protection', eventually succeeded in buying back 400 prisoners, whom he sent under escort to Fort Edward. He also sent a letter of explanation to General Webb, outlining the events and the efforts the French had made to bring the incident to an end.

By then, however, Indians had taken 200 English captives to Montreal, where Vaudreuil endeavoured to buy their freedom in exchange for brandy. His endeavours met with limited success. Atrocities that appalled and shocked Bougainville 'to the core' were committed, including torture and cannibalism. '*Heu fuge crudeles terras, fuge litus iniquem,*' he wrote, quoting once again from the Latin ('Alas, let us flee from these cruel and nefarious shores'). The number who lost their lives is not precisely known. Some fled into the forest, where most of them probably died of hunger and exposure; others were caught and murdered by bands of roaming Indians. Possibly fewer than fifty were killed in the first onslaught. According to Vaudreuil, the number was no more than five or six, but Jonathan Carver, a colonial volunteer and author of the influential *Travels*, said they numbered close on 1500. Both reports were biased and have been discredited.[6] What mattered was the massacre of unarmed prisoners and how politicians on both sides later used the incident for their own ends.

Louis was physically and mentally exhausted. It had not been a bad year strategically – French Canada was now safe from any threats from east, west or south – but he was depressed. He had set out for North America with great hopes and in good spirits. Montcalm had befriended him and it looked as if his career would prosper. But New France was a hotbed of jealousies, intrigues and corruption. Vaudreuil had again been prompt to claim the credit for the recent successes, writing to Paris about '*my* capture of Fort William Henry', and trying to take the credit for what he called his 'generous procedures' towards the British prisoners, some of whom he had ransomed by bribing the Indians with brandy.[7]

As for the corruption, it was so widespread that Bougainville would include in his *Mémoires sur l'état de la Nouvelle-France* a section entitled 'Mémoire sur les fraudes commises dans la colonie'. Not only official contracts and supplies of goods to the troops were affected; there was also profiteering on daily consumer goods. The war had brought about a sea blockade which, although it did not totally block supplies coming from France, created serious shortages. Wine and other goods were in short supply, and even meat and flour became harder to obtain, because of widespread disruption across the country and the need to feed the large number of men under arms. Beef especially was in short supply and was replaced by horsemeat. This led to riots by locals who protested at the killing of man's animal friends, some claiming it was against religious tradition to eat them. The governor threatened the crowd with imprisonment or hanging, but the protesters moved on to the barracks, inciting the soldiers to join them. A near-mutiny was avoided by a mixture of firm action and conciliation: the Chevalier de Lévis, left in command by Montcalm, assured the crowds that he ate horsemeat daily. It was indeed nothing unusual in France.

Bougainville's memories of the local tribes were not all bad. He had earlier, with a touch of reluctance, been adopted by an Iroquois tribe – with some unexpected consequences, as he had reported to his *chère Maman*:

I have added considerably to your family and, without boasting about it, I have given you some fairly unpleasant relatives. The Iroquois of Sault Saint Louis have naturalised your adopted child and named him Garoniasigoa, which means 'Great Angry Sky'. So my celestial looks have an evil appearance? My new family is the Tortoise, in the second rank for warlike qualities, coming behind the Bear, but well ahead in advice and eloquence.[8]

Whether this ceremony was then consummated in the arms of a young Indian girl, and whether their union was fruitful, is a rumour that cannot be substantiated. Years later, a French traveller reported meeting an Indian chief named Lorimier who claimed to be Bougainville's son, but the evidence for this is slim indeed and nothing more substantial has come to light.[9] The adoption was meant to honour one of the leaders of the French campaign, whose skill and bravery had been noted, and to conciliate a young Frenchman who had been shocked by the behaviour of France's allies in the field. It did soothe his feelings, but he always found it hard to banish the murderous scenes from his mind.

He spent only a short time in Montreal, going to Quebec immediately he was freed from his duties. Winter soon blanketed the port, but he found it a friendly town, with a number of welcoming acquaintances. He needed a rest in quiet surroundings after the rigours of the campaign. He wrote to Madame de Hérault: 'I am, to tell the truth, very tired. I spent twenty nights without undressing, poorly fed and with the earth as my bed.' He was becoming increasingly weary of New France and began to hint that he would appreciate her help in finding a different theatre of war:

Will my exile last long? In the name of the friendship you have always been kind enough to show me, do your best, *chère Maman*, to see that, should the war last, my next campaign will be my last in this country. Whether I am promoted or not is all the same to me, so long as I see you and France again.[10]

Later, in early November, he admitted to her that he had been going through a period of depression:

Already this unhappy country has been snowbound for a week and soon frost will be added to the other hardships we must expect in a winter that lasts eight months … These natural surroundings, so apt to engender and maintain a melancholy temper, the moods that follow one another, always sad and at times hideous and even horrifying; the very nature of this cruel country, and yet still more the disposition of those who live in it … what a field for melancholy, what a setting for regrets and fond desires! At the very thought of some day leaving this exile, one's mood seems to brighten and cheerfulness returns, but this illusion quickly fades and the present stern reality obliterates all that the future may offer. That, *ma chère Maman*, is your child's present condition – a kind of crisis that requires a truly stout heart.

Quebec society, though, helped him to recover his spirits. There were still parties and receptions, although on a lesser scale than at Montreal where most of the army contractors and manipulative administrators lived. Here the mood seemed more relaxed, with books and literary discussions, music – Bougainville played the lute – a little flirting and a great deal of card-playing. The food situation was no better than at Montreal but, as Montcalm wrote to Lévis with a touch of humour, horsemeat seemed more acceptable there: it was served 'in Spanish-style patés, as peppered steaks, with bread crumbs, as stewed tongue, as boiled beef, as a special recipe, as a cake'.

In March, Montcalm and Louis moved back to Montreal, which the younger man found more dreary. The commander worked on plans for the coming campaigns, but noted that his aide-de-camp seemed bored and listless. A visit to his Iroquois 'brothers' was something of a distraction, but it was still hard for him to forget the aftermath of the Fort William Henry capture.

They were waiting for the first signs of spring and, with them, mail from France. When news did arrive, it was both good and bad. The British had triumphed in India and enjoyed a number of naval victories. There had been complex changes in European alliances: Russia had allied herself with France and Austria, then invaded eastern Prussia, while Sweden had joined the Russian side. Frederick II of Prussia, after some initial setbacks, had defeated the Austrians at Prague and the French at Rossbach. William Pitt was taking over the British war effort and shoring up his Prussian ally with substantial cash subsidies. There was no indication that the war was about to end or that the future of French Canada was in any way secure.

For his next campaign, Montcalm required information about the activities of the British. On 10 April, he wrote to the Minister of War, 'I am endeavouring to obtain "live letters" – prisoners – to discover British intentions.'[11] There was broad agreement among the French that, if they launched an attack on Schenectady by way of Lake Ontario and the Mohawk River, they could secure the entire area south-west of Montreal. This would open the way to Albany and the Hudson Valley. Bougainville drew up a detailed itinerary in May and approaches were made to the Iroquois to join in a major offensive to the south and south-east.

In June, just as the French forces were being readied for these operations, rumours came about of a new British advance on Lake George and thence towards Lake Champlain: it was clear that they were planning to recapture the positions they had lost the previous year. They had learnt a great deal from their previous setbacks. General James Abercromby had at his disposal almost 15,000 troops, including 9000 militiamen, who were now advancing towards a French force less than a quarter as strong. And whereas the unfortunate Braddock's officers had marched proudly in resplendent uniforms, boldly leading their men as though they were on a barrack square, Abercromby had dressed his soldiers in drab clothing, leggings and cloaks suitable for the forests and the clinging briars, and far less visible to the defenders. Their moves were not totally hidden – it would have been impossible for a force that size to advance without some scouts noticing them – but it made them more difficult targets for marauding Indian bands or French colonial snipers.

They progressed with few obstacles until they reached the shore of Lake George where hundreds of small boats and flat-bottomed barges were used to ferry them north. It was 5 July, a fine day that lifted the spirits and justified later British historians describing the scene in lyrical terms:

> The spectacle was superb: the brightness of the summer day; the romantic beauty of the scenery; the sheen and sparkle of those crystal waters; the countless islets, tufted with pine, birch and fir; the bordering mountains with their green summits and sunny crags; the flash of oars and glitter of weapons; the banners, the varied uniforms, and the notes of bugle, trumpet, bagpipe and drums, answered and prolonged by a hundred woodland echoes.[12]

On that morning, Bougainville had been given the rank of assistant quartermaster, raising him from the role of senior planner and aide to that of an active soldier. Montcalm needed every man available to take part in the defence of Ticonderoga, down by Lake Champlain. Fortunately, reinforcements reached him on the evening of 7 July, just in time for the major engagement. And the leader of the attacking British forces, Lord Howe, was mortally wounded in an early skirmish, leaving his forces disorganised, with Lord Abercromby several miles away. The balance between attackers and defenders had suddenly changed.

Throughout the day, the French held against several waves of attacking British, and avoided becoming encircled. Attempts to penetrate the French left flank failed. 'A murderous fire' greeted every English advance, wrote Bougainville.[13] Then the Chevalier de Lévis led a counter-attack. As night fell, Abercromby's men gave up and retreated back to the south.

The attackers had lost almost 2000 men, killed, wounded or taken prisoner; French losses amounted to 372 soldiers and a couple of dozen Canadians. Among the wounded was Louis himself, although his injury was not serious and he was soon well enough to travel to Montreal with details of the battle and later go down to the British camp to negotiate an exchange of prisoners. There was no doubt that the French had scored a remarkable and even unexpected victory, and Montcalm celebrated it with a fine flourish. On 12 July, his troops sang a *Te Deum* and a commemorative cross was erected with a rather lengthy message in Latin crediting the success to God's help: '*Deus hic, Deus ipse triumphat.*'

But Montcalm was unwilling to risk his troops any further. According to Vaudreuil, he should have followed up his victory by marching south and driving the beaten enemy all the way back to the Hudson River. Montcalm, however, knew his troops were outnumbered; and he would be marching towards forces that were now regrouping and preparing to defend their own positions, where they had good reserves of food and munitions. His own troops, on the other hand, had only a week's supply of food and their lines of communication were stretched to the limit. Although some reinforcements were arriving, with munitions, there would still not be enough to give them a clear advantage over the British. Furthermore, Montcalm had instructions that required him to avoid unnecessary or generalised campaigning.

Vaudreuil was irate at what he considered timidity, if not downright cowardice. He expressed his anger in a letter to the minister in France, using terms such as 'infamous conduct' and continuing: 'I should be wanting in my duty to the King if I did not beg you to ask for his recall.' In fact, Montcalm's view of the overall situation was quite realistic. 'The situation of the colony is becoming increasingly critical,'[14] he wrote, aware that the British were once more getting ready to attack Louisbourg in the east and at the same time advancing towards Fort Frontenac to the west.

Bougainville was in a more ebullient mood. He was far younger than Montcalm and not a little exhilarated by the recent victory. When he went off to discuss the exchange of prisoners, he presented a bold front to the British. They boasted to him that the French fortress at Louisbourg would soon fall, causing the French to lose the control of the St Lawrence estuary, but he retorted that the British Navy had failed in 1757 and would do so again. He agreed to wager two cases of champagne against two crates of English beer that Louisbourg would still be holding out by mid-August. Lord Abercromby accepted the bet. Discussions went on in an atmosphere of increasing courtesy and friendliness – indeed, with some touches of joviality. Both sides agreed to hold a banquet on an island in Lake George when peace was signed, which they all felt confident would be soon.

On 3 September, Abercromby's nephew sent Bougainville a newspaper report announcing the fall of Louisbourg: it had taken place on 26 July. Louis was crestfallen. This was real cause for concern: the centre had held triumphantly at Ticonderoga, but French Canada's eastern defences were being forced back. A little later, the French received news of the fall of Fort Frontenac by Lake Ontario on 27 July. French Canada was now in real danger.

Overall, 1758 had not been a good year. When information was received suggesting that the British were preparing a new attack on Fort Carillon, it looked as though it might end in disaster. Louis was put in charge of restoring and strengthening Fort Carillon's defences – 'using our skills to make up for what we lack in numbers'. His aim was to prepare a base near the head of Lake George, where a small force could outflank any attackers. He even offered to head this force, of about fifty men, determined to hold the position at all costs. He also wrote a letter intended for Vaudreuil, setting out a plan for a French winter or early spring campaign that could at least delay what was feared would be a major advance on French Canada. There was evidence that the British were already progressing along the St Lawrence valley and threatening Fort Duquesne – which the French would soon find impossible to hold because their own defeated troops were continuing on their retreat from Frontenac.

Bougainville's plans were not accepted – they were more heroic than practicable. It was now autumn, and both Vaudreuil and Montcalm were hoping that an early winter might bring a temporary halt to British moves, and give the French a breather to prepare for a likely major British onslaught.

On 6 September, Louis made his way to Montreal with Montcalm. They arrived on the 9th and at once joined Vaudreuil in an emergency meeting. They found the citizens close to panic. They had accepted Vaudreuil's confident assurances that everything was under control; now they were shocked by the losses of recent weeks. The mood was not helped by messengers from Fort Carillon announcing that the British were approaching the fort. Montcalm and Bougainville rushed back to Lake Champlain. Fortunately, it was a false alarm: boats had been seen making their way along the lakeshore, but they were more intent on reconnaissance than assault. Louis remained at the fort until 18 October. He then returned to Montreal to prepare for a major mission: he was being sent to France to seek reinforcements and other help.

8. Return to France

December 1758–March 1759

BOUGAINVILLE LEFT MONTREAL on 3 November – not an ideal time of year for a trip down the St Lawrence. He went in a small boat that was also taking five British officers down to Quebec. Not surprisingly, the journey was neither comfortable nor safe. They were wrecked on a rock cluster, and forced to spend the night on a low shelf, before swimming ashore in icy cold water.

Luckier was the commissioner, André-Jean-Baptiste Doreil, who was being sent to France in support of Bougainville's mission. To ensure the two men were not lost together at the start of the voyage, he was told to make his way separately to Quebec.

They found the townsfolk as gloomy as their fellows in Montreal, although their situation was made a little safer by the approach of winter, when vast fields of snow would surround the city. A few early flurries had already fallen, and the river, as Bougainville had learnt to his cost, had become a dangerous waterway. This reduced the likelihood of a sudden British raid. They were worried, however, about the shortage of food and ammunition.

> The condition of Canada was indeed deplorable. The St Lawrence was watched by British ships; the harvest was meagre; a barrel of flour cost two hundred francs; most of the cattle and many of the horses had been killed for food. The people lived chiefly on a pittance of salt cod or on rations furnished by the King; all prices were inordinate; the officers from France were surviving on their pay; while a legion of indigenous and imported scoundrels fattened on the general distress.[1]

Bougainville was welcomed, since most of the residents believed that their salvation would have to come from France. They were keen to help him to find a passage to Europe, but there was little to choose from: the only available ship was a privateer from Saint-Malo, the *Victoire*, which would be accompanied by a merchant vessel, the *Hardi*, and a storeship, the *Outarde*. Bougainville boarded the *Victoire*. They sailed at midnight on the 11th.

The captain of the *Victoire* was Nicolas-Pierre Duclos-Guyot, who was to play a major role in Bougainville's life. The Duclos-Guyots were long-time residents of Saint-Malo, but Nicolas and his brothers were the first sailors in the family. Born in 1722, he had gone to sea on a French India Company vessel at the age of twelve. By 1744, he had made eight voyages to India, and risen steadily through the ranks to the grade of lieutenant. By then, the War of the Austrian Succession had broken out and he served on a number of privateers. This widened his range of experience, taking him, among other places, to South America. With the outbreak of the Seven Years War, he continued this service, taking part in numerous seafights and developing valuable links with the French Navy. On 18 December 1756 he had received a warrant of captain, taking command of the *Victoire* shortly after. He occasionally teamed up with his brother Alexandre, commander of the *Port-Mahon*, and acting together or singly they had captured seven prizes, including two English privateers based on the island of Guernsey.

The *Victoire* was then formally transferred to the navy, Duclos-Guyot receiving a commission of *lieutenant de frégate* for the duration. In late April, he was sent to Canada with a cargo of flour, troops and silver. As British warships massed for the attack on Louisbourg and the subsequent fall of the stronghold, the French needed the services of experienced privateer captains, with their fast vessels able to avoid patrolling enemy ships. The capture of Louisbourg severely hampered his movements: he had been in Quebec since the beginning of July, waiting for orders to set off on his return voyage to France.

Duclos-Guyot belonged to the lower category of naval officers, known as 'the blues'. Like so many aspects of life in the Old Regime, the navy was subject to a rigid class system. Professional officers were accepted only if they belonged to the nobility. They formed the upper category known as 'the reds', after the predominant colour of their uniform, and jealously defended their privileges. Families whose sons wanted to join the service sometimes had to make special efforts to provide clear evidence of their nobility: to this end they often bought a small estate for their offspring so that the boy could adopt the title that went with it. Thus the family name of the famous navigator Jean François La Pérouse was in fact Galaup; his second name was that of a fairly modest country estate. In wartime, however, the navy was forced to call on the services of officers in the merchant service. As in the case of Duclos-Guyot, they were given temporary commissions. Only very exceptionally were these converted into permanent appointments that led to a transfer into the royal service.

But no one could challenge Duclos-Guyot's experience. It outclassed anything most 'red' officers could claim, and Bougainville drew on it freely, during this and subsequent voyages. Nicolas, something of an old salt at the age of thirty-six, would prove a willing and helpful mentor. Compared with his earlier voyage with La Rigaudière, however, Louis had few opportunities to learn the finer points of navigation during this crossing. As the ship sailed down the river, he made a few notes, listing in particular points and coves that needed fortifying to help protect Quebec from the expected British onslaught – Cap Tourmente, Pointe aux Bouleaux, La Prairie. This was to be part of the defensive programme he was preparing and would submit to the military authorities in France.

But as soon as the *Victoire* emerged from the Gulf of St Lawrence, a fierce storm assailed her, driving her off course and making life on board both dangerous and miserable:

> The despotic rolling of the ship dominates our lives like a tyrant, and not only our lives, but also our movements, our attitudes, our rest; we must struggle against it with every mouthful we want to eat and whatever need we have to satisfy … We suffer in this wretched machine beyond anything words can express. The rolling is horrible and unceasing. Our cattle and poultry are dying in droves …

But even in the harshest circumstances, he could not resist using classical Latin and French allusions:

> Ah! How right was Horace when he said: *Illi robur et aes triplex circa pectus erat, qui fragilem truci commisit pelago ratem* ['His heart was mailed in oak and triple brass, he who was the first to commit a frail bark to the rough seas'] … And how right Pantagruel when he exclaimed: 'Oh thrice or four times happy is the gardener who is planting cabbages, for he always keeps one foot on the ground'.[2]

Less classically minded, the sailors around him took a vow to go on pilgrimage, barefoot and wearing only shirts, if only the Virgin would bring them safely to harbour.

The mountainous seas moderated only two or three times during the fifty-two days it took the *Victoire* to struggle across the Atlantic. And even more danger threatened: the ship's compass proved defective and, instead of sailing into the English Channel to reach Saint-Malo, they found themselves entering the Bristol Channel, a nest of English privateers and cruising warships. Luckily, they recognised their situation in good time and were able to round Land's End and make for Morlaix, then a major port for French India Company ships, where they anchored on 20 December.

Within hours of his arrival, Bougainville was on his way to Paris, to his brother Jean-Pierre and Madame de Hérault. Then followed a round of visits and dinners, some to friends, others to acquaintances who might be useful to his mission. They included the Maréchal de Belle-Isle, former Secretary of State for War; Lieutenant-General de Crémille, a highly respected officer; the influential but ageing Prince de Conti, no friend of the Marquise de Pompadour but once mentioned as a possible ruler of Poland and currently, although this was not known for certain, a senior member of the *Cabinet Noir* or *Cabinet Secret*, which advised Louis XV on political and international matters and ran what was in fact a royal secret service. Others close to the king included the Marquis de Chauvelin, a former ambassador to the Genoan Republic and soon to be appointed Master of the King's Wardrobe, and the Comte de Noailles, Governor of Versailles. The Marquise de Pompadour's circle included Monsieur de Baschi, who was related to her by marriage, and the recently widowed Maréchale de Mirepoix, whom Bougainville had met briefly when he had gone to London as part of her husband's embassy.

There were other, more personal calls to be paid, to relatives of his fellow officers and especially to the dowager Marquise de Saint-Véran, Montcalm's mother. Bougainville had been entrusted with a very personal mission by Montcalm, namely arranging the marriage of his children. It was usual, in the eighteenth century and earlier, for fathers to arrange the marriages of their sons and daughters or, at the very least, to approve or prevent the matches the young people might have in mind. A marriage, as Montcalm put it, could be 'romantic and chimerical' or 'good and practicable'. Bougainville, being younger and unmarried, believed this distinction to be less important. He was somewhat relieved when Madame de Saint-Véran told him a wedding had already been arranged – and celebrated – between Montcalm's daughter and the quite suitable Marquis d'Espineuse. He also discovered that discussions had begun for the marriage of the young Comte de Montcalm to a pleasant heiress of sixteen.

These delicate matters settled, Louis turned to the true purpose of his voyage, the future of Canada and the assistance the colony so badly required. France was settling down after a period of disruption and manoeuvrings brought about by an attempt on Louis XV's life. The culprit, a hapless and confused individual named Damiens, had been dealt with in accordance with the brutal criminal code of the Ancient Regime: the verdict of guilty but insane was unknown at the time, and Robert-François Damiens was slowly put to death in the Place de Grèves. But Louis XV believed for a time that the wound Damiens had inflicted might prove fatal. It certainly unsettled him. The possibility that he might well have been killed on that fateful day, and consequently would have died unshriven, preyed on his mind. He withdrew from public life, leaving the dauphin to govern the state.

Repentance in the face of death and the final judgement required him to mend his ways and break up with Madame de Pompadour, whom the crowds outside the palace were blaming for both the state of the country and the attempt on the king's life. Indeed, some of her supporters, ministers such as Machault, urged her to leave Versailles and move to her country estate. Madame de Mirepoix and a couple of others talked her out of it, and she eventually went to see Louis and persuaded him that Damiens was a lunatic and that his actions were of little significance. Once back in favour, she rid herself of Machault, a former Minister of Finance and Secretary for the Navy, and of D'Argenson, Secretary of State for War.

This had happened in 1757, a year also marked by military disasters. Although the balance of power at Versailles had been restored, the overall situation was far from rosy. The main problem was, as always, lack of money. Everyone Bougainville talked to complained that the war was proving ruinous. The uncertainty created by the Damiens affair was now being replaced by a growing despondency over the cost of the war.

François-Joachim-Pierre de Bernis, the Secretary of State for Foreign Affairs, loudly publicised his own worries:

> Trade at a standstill, no money left … the treasury empty, not a penny to be got from Montmartel [one of the government's bankers], no uniforms for the troops, no boots for the cavalry, a navy that lacks sailors … I have no strength or spirit left to carry the burden of public affairs … I am continually depressed by the consequences of this war …[3]

Louis XV, taking back the reins of power from the dauphin, dismissed Bernis just as Bougainville was preparing to sail from Quebec, but Bernis did represent the mood of the times. The new minister, Etienne François, Duc de Choiseul, did his best, but the war had been a costly and wearying conflict, and it showed no signs of ending.

Gloom did not eliminate the traditional courtesies. Everywhere he went, Bougainville was made welcome. Ministers, officials, courtiers displayed the utmost politeness towards him. Versailles and the Paris salons were delighted to hear his tales of distant lands. He felt a surge of optimism that his mission would be successful, especially when he received, not just fulsome praise, but promises and assurances. But promises cost nothing and the assurances of help were never specific. It took him a little time to realise that the public and the court, tired of the seemingly unending war, were not concerned about a distant, snowbound colony. Possessions such as the French West Indian islands brought in sugar and rum; India had held the promise of a lucrative trade; islands in the Indian Ocean had strategic value. Canada, however, had little hold on the general imagination. 'France can be happy without Quebec' became a widely quoted comment when the time came to write off New France.

When Louis began to detail his requests for assistance, Nicolas-René Berryer, a former lieutenant of police and now Minister of Marine, expressed the opinion of most government ministers: 'Sir, one does not try to save the stables when the house is on fire.' It led Louis to hurl back at him a retort that has endured: 'Well, sir, at least, they cannot say that you speak like a horse.'⁴ French society, as ever, enjoyed good repartee, but by and large it shared Berryer's views. Madame de Pompadour had laughed when Bougainville told her of his retort, but she had also hastened to soothe the feelings of the powerful minister, who had been infuriated by Louis's witticism.

With the doors of officialdom closing on him, Bougainville turned to the marquise for help. She knew how to bypass the official channels, and he submitted to her a new plan he had drawn up. He had not come merely as Montcalm's representative, begging cap in hand for help: he had his own proposal. She appreciated such initiatives, liked his idea and was only too willing to assist her protégé.

He did ask for more troops – approximately 1500 men – and supplies to defend the mouth of the St Lawrence, but he also proposed a diversionary move against North Carolina. It was a bold, almost a desperate plan. He knew that once the British heard that transport ships had left France, they would naturally expect them to make straight for the St Lawrence River, and would mass their troops in anticipation. His idea was that a substantial proportion of the convoy would veer south towards Carolina, where they could catch the British unawares. Bougainville further argued that the settlers of Pennsylvania, who were mostly Quakers and pacifists, were unlikely to support the British, that many of the colonists were Germans who could be talked into declaring their independence from London, and that the Cherokee Indians, who were already disaffected, could easily be persuaded to side with France. Four thousand men landing in North Carolina could alter the balance of forces in America and win a great psychological victory.

Madame de Pompadour arranged for the plan to be passed on to the council of ministers and ensured that they approved it. Bougainville was succeeding beyond his wildest dreams – until he realised that approval had once again been given only in principle. They liked the idea, applauded him, and took no further action. The lack of money, men and equipment was still the insuperable obstacle. The marquise did her best to find the funds, to the extent of two million *livres*, even pledging some of her own money. It was all in vain.

Honours and promotions, on the other hand, cost nothing and could bestowed as some form of consolation prize. Louis was raised to the rank of colonel and given the Cross of St Louis, a rare double honour which the king himself had requested. 'I did this intentionally,' he told Bougainville. Louis was still only twenty-nine. Montcalm was made a lieutenant-general, Lévis a major-general, Vaudreuil received the Grand Cross of St Louis. There were rewards for all the other senior officers. Their king was indeed grateful for their valour and their devotion. That he could not do anything tangible to help them as the grim year of 1759 loomed ahead was regrettable, but inevitable.

Bougainville had not failed: circumstances had failed him. 'A lawyer, mathematician, soldier and courtier, he stood revealed as a star of the first magnitude in the firmament of diplomacy.'[5] He took his leave from his friends, embraced his brother and his *chère Maman*, and made his way south to Bordeaux for the return voyage to Canada. There, on 15 March 1759, he met up again with Duclos-Guyot, now captain of the frigate *La Chézine*. His mission had not been entirely fruitless: he was bringing with him some 300 to 400 recruits, 60 engineers, sappers and artillerymen, along with supplies of gunpowder, weapons and provisions. This was scarcely enough to save the colony, but it would help to boost morale.

The *Chézine* sailed a week later from Blaye, a busy small port on the Gironde estuary, a picturesque place with a citadel, impressive fortifications and remains of old castles testifying to a colourful past. Here, according to tradition, lay the remains of Roland, the legendary knight who had accompanied Charlemagne across the Pyrenees. But Louis had little time for sightseeing. The *Chézine* left for Quebec on 20 March.

The crossing took fifty-one days, but it was less stormy than the *Victoire*'s, four months earlier. There was far more time to spare to learn the finer points of navigation from Duclos-Guyot, to discuss his voyages to India and China and, above all, the recently published *Histoire des navigations aux terres australes* of Charles de Brosses. Jean-Pierre de Bougainville had bought an extra copy of this important two-volume treatise when it came out in 1756, so that he could give one to his brother. They had time to discuss it before Louis had to return to Canada, but now he had the leisure to study it more closely and to obtain Duclos-Guyot's reactions to it.

Charles de Brosses was a magistrate from Burgundy, a well-to-do senior member of the regional *parlement*, and a leading figure in the respected *Dijon Académie littéraire*. He had already established his reputation as a Latin scholar when he turned to the systematic history of Pacific voyages. He drew from primary sources as much as he could, avoiding the later and often error-laden printed accounts.

At a time when Versailles and Paris seemed to be the cultural centres of Europe, with serious research and publications disseminating knowledge through the work of the *philosophes* and the encyclopaedists, it might be thought that someone living more than 180 miles from the capital at a time when communications were slow and unreliable would be somewhat ignored. But in fact, many figures of the day lived outside Paris: Rousseau, Voltaire, Montesquieu and others worked in the provinces and spent much time travelling abroad. And the Dijon literary academy was no collection of dilettante amateurs: it was the leading provincial academy, affiliated to the prestigious *Académie Française* itself.

De Brosses and his father were both shareholders in the French India Company. Such investments were often made grudgingly, as a matter of duty, by people who held official positions. But they no doubt helped to arouse in any shareholder with an enquiring mind an interest in distant and little-known regions. This interest had crystallised in May 1752 when the astronomer and mathematician Pierre de Maupertuis read a paper he had recently forwarded to King Frederick of Prussia. Entitled *Lettre sur le progrès des sciences*, it drew that monarch's attention to the still unexplored parts of the southern hemisphere.

De Brosses composed a *mémoire* enlarging on Maupertuis's speculations and making use of the writings of the navigators Sir John Narborough, Jacob Roggeween and William Dampier. The French, not the Prussians or the British, should turn their minds to the Pacific Ocean.

The naturalist Buffon, who had already speculated in his *Histoire naturelle* on the possible existence of new species in the undiscovered areas of the Pacific, urged De Brosses to enlarge on his ideas, to stimulate French interest in the region. This was of special importance at a time when 'a neighbouring power is visibly assuming a universal command of the sea'.[6] Everyone knew that this neighbouring power was Britain.

It was this aspect of De Brosses's motivation, more than any other, that caught Jean-Pierre and Louis's attention. Louis had realised the extent of the British drive for naval supremacy and further exploration when he was staying in London. Not merely politicians and geostrategists, but scientists and traders had this goal firmly in their sights. The Canadian situation, which he knew could only get worse, had provided more evidence: if France did not take steps to ensure her own place, Britain would dominate the sea routes of the world, control the major naval bases and gain an unassailable position. Versailles, too preoccupied with European politics, was overlooking the world that lay beyond – the Americas, Asia and the vast Pacific.

The *Histoire des navigations aux terres australes* suffered from the fact that it had grown up from De Brosses's original *Mémoire*, itself a reaction to Maupertuis's *Lettre*. De Brosses encased the story of the voyages of discovery between a long essay on the advantages to be gained from further exploration and an actual plan for a voyage and a settlement. The history proper is in three sections – one for the sixteenth century, one for the seventeenth and one for the eighteenth. This arrangement is not as tidy as one might expect, given the title of the book, but it is the first thorough survey of Pacific knowledge in either French or English.

Collections of voyages had appeared before, but none dealt exclusively with the Pacific. De Brosses's opinions and comments can indeed be viewed as pleas for France to become active in the Pacific – so much so that when an English edition of the book appeared a few years later, it was easily turned by the translator into a reasoned case for English exploration: wherever De Brosses used '*français*' it was translated by 'English'. And there was no clear mention of De Brosses's name.

The book seemed almost as if it had been designed to respond to the Bougainville brothers' secret concerns. De Brosses placed the emphasis on trade, rather than mere conquests, which were costly and achieved little in the longer term. However, to foster commercial enterprises, France would need staging posts and establishments abroad, as well as a strong navy – 'for he who is master of the sea is master of the land'. Bougainville read and reread the *Histoire* and quoted it to Duclos-Guyot as the *Chézine* settled down to the routine of an Atlantic crossing. Between the technical and practical tuition he was asked to give to this likeable army man who yearned to become a seaman, Duclos-Guyot discussed with Bougainville the voyages he had already made and the countries he had visited.

De Brosses's book reminded him of his brother Alexandre, who had sailed as an officer on the *Lion*, leaving Cadiz in December 1753 for Tierra del Fuego and Staten Landt. The *Lion* then rounded Cape Horn, and sailed up to Valparaiso, Callao and Juan Fernandez Island. Back in Valparaiso, she once more rounded the southern tip of America, but in a low latitude that eventually brought her to an unknown group of islands the Spanish named San Pedro; it was South Georgia.

They described it as 'a land some 25 leagues long, running NE and SW, and topped by steep mountains, so frightful in appearance and so high that we could hardly discern the summits, although it was more than six leagues away. This land was covered in snow.'[7] South Georgia would be useless as a base or a colony – the climate was bleak, the seas around it rough – but further north and closer to the coast of South America there lay an important (and uninhabited) cluster of islands. The English called them the Falkland Islands; the French knew them as the Malouines, 'the islands of Saint-Malo', on account of the many sailors from Saint-Malo who had sighted them or actually called there.

Bougainville stored all this information away for a future that increasingly included voyages of exploration into unknown seas and a search for French bases. But he kept his plans to himself, sharing them only with Jean-Pierre.

More immediate concerns faced him. They had to make it safely into port in Canada and endeavour to bring some little cheer to the beleaguered colonists. The *Chézine* sailed into the St Lawrence on 10 May 1759. Two days later Louis stepped ashore in Quebec, a town 'where they were dying of hunger', and announced that about seventeen ships, large and small, were on their way, bringing supplies and some reinforcements. 'Never was there a greater explosion of joy,' wrote Foligny, one of the officers in charge of the city's defences. 'It revived the courage of an entire population that, during one of the harshest winters ever known, had been reduced to a quarter-pound of bread and half a pound of horsemeat.'[8] The next day, Bougainville left for Montreal to report to Montcalm and Vaudreuil.

9. Quebec Falls

May–September 1759

THE MONTREAL WINTER had been harsh, but the snow and the biting wind had given the Canadians a sense of security and protection in gloomy times. Now, with spring melting the lakes and rivers, and freeing the countryside from its cover of snow, that sense of security was fast ebbing. Although Bougainville brought some promise of help from France, the gradually improving weather revived the overwhelming sense of foreboding. As Montcalm had written to his wife, 'Can we hope for another miracle to save us? I trust in God.' But since a miraculous intervention from any of the saints the population prayed to daily seemed unlikely, the commanders prepared for the inevitable onslaught.

Vaudreuil had taken a census of the three administrative areas of Montreal, Quebec and Three Rivers. It revealed that the French defence forces consisted of about 30,000 troops, plus a few new volunteers, some irregulars from Acadia, the militiamen, the trappers or *coureurs des bois* and a few thousand Indians. The British were believed to be marshalling some 50,000 for the campaign. In reality, the British commander, James Wolfe, had far fewer troops, but they were well trained and disciplined, and supported by a fleet of over sixty vessels, warships and transports.

Vaudreuil's favoured strategy was to hold the Acadian territory along the south bank of the St Lawrence. Montcalm pointed out that much of it was open country offering few obstacles against invaders coming up from the south. Patrolling that area meant spreading French troops too thinly: he preferred to concentrate his forces for the defence of Quebec and Montreal against British attacks expected to come from the east and west. He was convinced that Quebec held the key to survival: 'Once Quebec is gone, New France is gone'.[1]

He now held overall command, thanks to a recent decision from Versailles, largely the result of Bougainville's pleading. Vaudreuil's standing was considerably reduced, and he had to concede, with some reluctance, that the St Lawrence River held the key to Canada's future. Keeping the British out of the river was of paramount importance. It was known that a British fleet had sailed from England in February and had reached Halifax in Nova Scotia at the end of April. It was now moving to Louisbourg at the mouth of the river, where final preparations would be made for the coming onslaught. Every rumour that reached French headquarters from the south and west spoke of troops being gathered for a major advance against Quebec and of negotiations with Indian tribes to try to get them to side with the British or at least declare their neutrality.

Montcalm, Vaudreuil and Bougainville went to Quebec to organise the defence. Montcalm set up his headquarters on a plateau some distance upriver from the town, but overlooking the St Lawrence. Bougainville's camp was to his right, while the left flank was held by the Chevalier de Lévis. This enabled them to keep watch on the movements of the enemy, and to co-ordinate the defence.

A rough fleet of fireships was assembled to keep the British at bay. They were small sloops armed with a single gun, and *cageux* platforms – structures used to guide rafts of logs down rivers. Packed with anything flammable, from oil to dried branches, they could all be floated towards the advancing British vessels, and, it was hoped, set on fire. The target was to gather 100 or so of these craft, manned by a total of 300 men. The cost in lives could be high, as those who manoeuvred these floating pyres had to jump overboard and swim to shore to escape the inferno they had created. In addition, a line of bonfires was set up as a signalling system along the banks, ready to be lit the moment any enemy ships were sighted. The first of these flared up as early as 25 May, when the first British vessels were seen downriver.

While Bougainville and others worked feverishly at strengthening such defensive structures, the British fleet was already making its way into the St Lawrence. The last ship of the fleet sailed from Louisbourg Harbour on 6 June, 'the troops cheering and the officers drinking a toast to the coming hoisting of British colours on every French fort, port and garrison in America'.[2]

Bougainville was dividing his time between erecting earthworks and destroying the steps that had been cut by boatmen at various places along the high riverbank – these had to be sacrificed as they could easily provide access to enemy troops. He also supervised the making of the *cageux*, and the placing of heavy log booms across small waterways, to impede any British boats trying to sail into them.

What could not so easily be prevented was the occupation by the British of the south bank of the St Lawrence. The few defenders and the isolated French farmers who remained were driven away. The same soon happened to the *habitants* on Orleans Island in the middle of the St Lawrence. Then General Wolfe occupied land on the north bank, not far from the French encampment commanded by Lévis, on the other side of a stream called the Montmorency.

By late June, the British ships were in full view, sailing upriver towards Quebec in a double file. It was time to use the *cageux*. On the 27th Bougainville went down to supervise their night-time launching. A procession of rafts and other crafts was towed by six boats manned by men in blue uniform, invisible in the darkness. When they neared the first English vessels, they fired a number of rockets, this being the agreed signal for setting the *cageux* alight. A sixty-four-gun ship and three transports caught fire, and the lines of vessels broke up in disorder. The British were not caught entirely unaware: they had 100 or so small boats ready, manned by sailors armed with grapnels to turn away the burning rafts and send them drifting away downstream.

Day by day, the British stranglehold on the St Lawrence waterway tightened. The shelling of Quebec began on 9 July, continuing intermittently over the days following. The cathedral and several houses caught fire. Wolfe then decided to attack, marching towards the city and taking on the forces of the Chevalier de Lévis. The French held their position, soon strengthened by men from the regiments of the Royal Roussillon, Guyenne and Languedoc.

The weather, which had impeded Wolfe's men on a previous occasion, once again favoured the defenders, as torrential rain fell.

'We could not see half way down the hill,' says the Chevalier Johnstone, who was at this part of the line. Ammunition was wet on both sides, and the grassy steps became so slippery that it was impossible to climb them. The English say that the storm saved the French; the French, with as much reason, that it saved the English ... Wolfe saw the madness of persisting, and ordered a retreat. The rain ceased, and troops of Indians came down the heights to scalp the fallen.[3]

This French victory cost the English 443 men, the French 70. It was only one gratifying incident in a campaign that included many setbacks, but it cheered Vaudreuil who began to feel that Wolfe could be held back.

In the meantime, though, the English were advancing on several other fronts. Lévis had to be withdrawn from his command to defend Lake Champlain, which the English were threatening. Fort Carillon, or Ticonderoga, the key strongpoint between Lakes George and Champlain, soon fell to forces advancing under General Jeffrey Amherst. The next defensive point was Fort Niagara, which was under siege from late July. It, too, fell after a series of bitter engagements, and the English began to prepare to march on north towards the banks of the St Lawrence.

The weather held up this advance. Lévis was able to bring up another 800 men, which more than made up for the losses his forces had suffered. Amherst realised that he was not ready for further advances: his earlier optimism had led him to neglect some of the essential preparations. Autumn was approaching, and by the end of September he decided to give up. Wild storms were blowing in and some early frosts made it clear that he would be courting disaster if he attempted to move any further into French-held and well-defended territory. Holding back Amherst, or at least causing him to hesitate, helped to cheer up the French who were holding the southern front – but by the time they could be sure that they would be safe until the spring, Quebec had fallen and Montcalm was dead.

Back in Quebec, Bougainville had spent the month of August foiling a whole series of attempted landings, the first on the 5th. Then, on the 8th, 1200 British soldiers landed at Pointe-aux-Trembles. La Roncière describes what happened:

A hundred Scotsmen sheltering behind a line of rocks open fire, while Admiral Holmes shoots back at the floating batteries anchored in the narrows of Red Cape. But where are the cavalrymen in blue uniform the English had seen through their spyglasses? Bougainville had made them dismount and lie down flat next to a detachment from Languedoc and 150 Canadians. The hurricane of bullets and shrapnel passed above Bougainville's men, as well as over those of La Rochebeaucour and Saint-Martin, and they now fired back. Bougainville then attacks, with the help of Indians shouting their war cries. The English, forced to re-embark, try to make a comeback at high tide, a league away. They are again driven back, to the astonishment of Wolfe, who had arrived in the corvette *Hunter* to supervise the operation ...[4]

During the night of 19–20 August, 1000 British troops suddenly attacked Duchambault, burning down a store containing uniforms. Bougainville rushed down to deal with this. Then, on the 29th, he raced on to Saint-Augustin to deal with an attempted landing. Two days later, he was back at Pointe-aux-Trembles. Vaudreuil and Montcalm sent Bougainville extra men – 'grenadiers, volunteers, Canadians and Indians'.[5]

Both sides knew that the best of the summer had already gone. Once September set in, cooler weather and storms were likely. The French began to plan moves that would further slow down the attackers. Wolfe, knowing this, wanted to avoid having to remain camped along the outer defences of Quebec. His lines of communication were stretched as it was, supplies were becoming scarce, and a Canadian winter would mean acres of snow, impassable tracks and the likelihood of stretches of the river freezing over, cutting or at least impeding his lines of communication with Louisbourg and Halifax.

His attempts to advance on Quebec from the east were being frustrated time and again, more often than not by Bougainville and his troops. What he had to do – and soon – was to get his men upstream, past the city, in order to attack it from the west.

This was by no means easy: the French guns could easily be trained on the river and, together with log booms and the usual fiery rafts, could create havoc among his vessels.

However, Wolfe learned from two deserters that a convoy of supply boats was expected, coming down the St Lawrence. On the night of 12 September, under cover of darkness and using a Scottish officer who spoke good French, he sent his troops along the river. When challenged, the officer replied that they were the expected supply vessels. Meanwhile, diversionary gunfire, which seemed to herald a major attack from the British shore camp to the east, kept the French occupied.

Wolfe's troops, some 4500 men, climbed up the steep banks, the famed Heights of Abraham, that led to the plain of the same name. They were then arranged in battle formation and marched towards Quebec, no more than a mile away. The British were faced by an equal number of French defenders but the latter were a less cohesive and disciplined force, and in retrospect Montcalm was unwise to send them in military formation against the solid line of redcoats. The British held against their first onslaught, then counter-attacked with muskets and bayonets. The French line eventually broke, and some started to retreat in disorder towards the city. Wolfe was killed on the battlefield; Montcalm was grievously wounded and died the next day. 'All the better,' he said when told that he did not have long to live, 'for I shall not see the British in Quebec.'[6]

Bougainville was at Cap Rouge, nearly 15 miles away on the other side of the city. He had been deceived by the diversionary sound of gunfire from downstream and believed that a British attack was imminent from that quarter. News of the redcoats gathering on the Plains of Abraham reached him at 8 a.m. He collected all the men he could safely gather, 900 grenadiers and cavalrymen, and sped to join in the coming battle. A stone farmhouse on the way had been captured by British troops, and attempting to recapture it delayed him somewhat. The battle had begun at 10 a.m. and by the time he reached the battlefield, the French retreat was already starting. He turned back to secure the area of Cap Rouge and Lorette, which had been his responsibility, so that he could at least protect the supplies stored in those settlements and help prevent any other British advances.

Quebec surrendered on 18 September. The British entering the city were struck by the damage it had suffered. 'The ravages are inconceivable … Those houses that are still standing are all holed by our cannon balls,' wrote John Knox in his journal, and indeed Quebec was nothing but a shapeless mass of ruins.[7]

Bougainville had led his troops to Lorette. From there, he negotiated the exchange of the prisoners and wounded with General George Townsend. Even in these bitter times, the courtesy common among officers remained, and in a series of letters exchanged from late September to mid-October they politely discussed the condition of the wounded and their need for supplies. Townsend had known

Bougainville in London and he held the younger man – who, after all, was a Fellow of the Royal Society – in high esteem. Louis therefore was an excellent choice for the negotiations and the period of settling down that followed the fall of Quebec.

It was a particularly sad time for him. Not only had Montcalm, a man he respected and liked, died in battle, as had several of his fellow officers, but he also received news from France that his closest friend, Jean-Baptiste Hérault, had been fatally wounded in August at the Battle of Minden. He died on 19 August. Jean-Baptiste was *chère Maman's* only son, and a kind of stepbrother to Louis. Heartbroken, Madame Hérault withdrew from Paris society to look after her widowed daughter-in-law and her only grandson, born just two months after Jean-Baptiste's death. This boy would become a famous political figure during the French Revolution, the *conventionnel* Marie-Jean Hérault de Séchelles, but would be executed during the worst days of the Terror.

The French officers retired to Montreal for the winter. It was more bitter than usual, the hardships it brought accentuated by the shortage of supplies. The French did not, however, sink into inaction. With the death of Montcalm – and the rumours now flying around that he had sent a lengthy report to Versailles on corruption among the Canadian administrators and army contractors – Vaudreuil had become more conciliatory. The Chevalier de Lévis, who had taken over as military commander, decided to harass the British forces as much as was practicable in the harsh winter conditions.

In November, some French ships managed to slip past occupied Quebec with supplies and men for Montreal. Four ran aground and were set on fire, but eight succeeded in sailing past the English batteries. In the same month, rumours began to spread throughout Quebec that the French were planning to attack with a force estimated at 15,000 men, intending to recapture the city while it was still isolated by the weather and unlikely to receive help from other British positions. Nothing happened, but in December news raced around Quebec that Lévis's men were advancing and that he was planning to celebrate Christmas inside the city walls. Once again, these rumours proved unfounded.

Isolated groups of French regulars, Canadian militiamen and Indians did appear in January and February, attacking the few British outposts that had been established around Quebec. These were well fortified, but nevertheless exposed. There were several other serious incidents in late February and March, with considerable casualties on both sides.

Lévis and Vaudreuil made the British garrison in Quebec feel as uncomfortable and uneasy as possible. The British sentries and work parties suffered from frostbite and getting around the city streets and courtyards was hazardous. When a fierce sleet storm struck the city in early January, a number of broken limbs were reported. Little provision had been made for winter clothing, and the men were forced to improvise, as John Knox recorded:

> Our guards on the grand parade make a most grotesque appearance in their different dresses; and our inventions to guard us against the extreme rigour of this climate are various beyond imagination. The uniformity as well as the nicety of the clean, methodical soldier is buried in the rough, fur-wrought garb of the frozen Laplander; and we rather resemble a masquerade than a body of regular troops, insomuch that I have frequently been accosted by my acquaintances, whom, though their voices were familiar to me, I could not discover, nor conceive who they were. Besides, every man seems to be in a continual hurry; for instead of walking soberly through the streets, we are obliged to observe a running or trotting pace.[8]

The Scottish Highlanders found their traditional uniform particularly uncomfortable – kilts offered little protection against a Canadian winter. 'A detachment of these breechless warriors being on guard at the General Hospital, the nuns spent their leisure in knitting for them long woollen hose, which they gratefully accepted.'

If life proved harsh in Quebec during those bitter months, it was only marginally better in Montreal. Bougainville and most of the officers and soldiers were totally exhausted by the recent campaign. Louis looked so stressed that Vaudreuil ordered him to his bed and the young man did not argue: 'I have spent close on eighty nights without sleep,' he wrote to Madame de Hérault. 'I have endured indescribable fatigues and gone through miseries of a kind unknown in Europe.'[9] He gradually recovered and made a number of calls on his acquaintances. They all welcomed him and tried to cheer him up with a semblance of salon life, but the mood was far more subdued than during the previous winter. Food was scarcer and correspondingly dearer. Prices in general were fast becoming exorbitant. As ever, the poor suffered the most, but everyone had a pinched expression and even at the highest levels the cost of food, clothing and heating was a regular topic of conversation.

There was extra unease and foreboding among Montreal society. The future of the colony looked bleak enough. Almost everyone believed that the southern bank of the St Lawrence, the shores of Lake Ontario and key points around the estuary would remain in British hands after the war, but only a few pessimists thought that the whole of French Canada would be annexed by Britain. The sooner the war ended in Europe, the better the peace terms would be – but the great powers were giving no sign of ending their struggle. On the other hand, many of the officials and traders feared that the corruption and dishonesty that had been such a feature of

Canadian life during the war would cost them dearly once peace came. They might fare better under British rule than under severe administrators sent over from France to reorganise the colony.

The Chevalier de Lévis was determined to turn the tide against the British. Holding the two main cities until peace was signed back in Europe would help to ensure the survival of New France. After a few short days of rest, he drew up his plans for the recapture of Quebec as soon as the weather allowed. By mid-March, all his preparations were completed. Quebec would be in French hands again before the British had had time to bring in their much-needed reinforcements. But he had to be patient, for spring that year was slow in coming.

10. The End of French Canada

May–September 1760

LÉVIS'S RESOURCES WERE relatively small, but adequate as long as the Quebec garrison remained isolated. But the same weather that kept the British holed up in Quebec made his own advance difficult. There was still too much snow and mud for his 6000 troops to march across the country, so the bulk of them travelled in various types of river boats. Ice was still clinging along the banks, but they managed to clamber ashore, and were soon joined by garrisons from various French outposts. They were supported by a small flotilla led by Jean Vauquelin, consisting of the *Atalante*, the *Pomone* and the *Pie*. It was a hard, slow struggle in conditions of extreme discomfort.

They trudged along valiantly until 27 April, when they reached the village of Sainte-Foy, now held by a small detachment of British troops. General James Murray, the British commander at Quebec, was forced to send his men hurrying out to hold back the French. The weather was frightful: there was a bitingly cold wind, with drizzling rain, at times turning to sleet, and occasional flashes of thunder. Fierce fighting began. Murray lost over 1000 men, killed, wounded and missing.

Lévis lost 800. It was a victory of sorts and he pressed on towards Quebec, but it was too dangerous to attempt a frontal attack on the city. He began to dig trenches, in anticipation of a siege which he hoped would contain the British until French reinforcements arrived. He had so little left in the way of ammunition that he was forced to ration each gun emplacement to no more than twenty shots a day. Meanwhile, the British fire grew more fierce by the day, until some 150 guns seemed to be constantly vomiting murderous iron upon the French. For all that, the strange courtesies of war did not cease. Lévis sent Murray some spruce boughs, to be made into beer. Murray responded with a Cheshire cheese. Lévis's rejoinder was a brace of partridges.

Both men were waiting for help from outside. Lévis had sent a request to France months earlier for at least one transport with munitions and siege guns. He hoped that, once navigation became again possible on the river, this ship and at least one other he knew had wintered at Gaspé would reach him in time. Murray, for his part, prayed that both would be intercepted and that a British vessel would soon arrive. Murray's prayers were the first to be answered. On 15 May, a ship of the line, accompanied by a frigate and two other vessels, appeared, all flying British colours. A great cheer went up in the besieged city as they started to attack Vauquelin's small flotilla. Lévis was forced to retreat. The siege of Quebec was lifted.

Bougainville had not joined Lévis at Sainte-Foy, but had gone to the Isle-aux-Noix, a small island in the Richelieu River, five miles north of Lake Champlain. It was a highly important strategic post, defending Montreal against any advance from the south. Its commander had been François-Charles Bourlamaque, but he had been transferred to Montreal after the death of Montcalm to serve as Lévis's second-in-command. Louis was now French Canada's third most senior officer.

The island had been well fortified, but even more needed to be done in anticipation of the British attack. Bougainville directed the work with all the energy he could muster. On 16 June, he wrote to the Maréchal de Belle-Isle in France: 'We will defend the colony to the very last. I am endeavouring to make up for what we lack in numbers by the works I am having carried out day and night, wonderfully assisted by the officers and soldiers.'[1] But there was little he could do when the assault finally came. All he had at his disposal was some 1700 men, a dozen guns and limited ammunition. Brigadier William Haviland was leading 4000 men, who came in view of Isle-aux-Noix on 9 August. It was part of a concerted advance against Montreal, which included Amherst marching up from Lake Ontario with a force of 10,000, and Murray, who had recovered from the defeat at Sainte-Foy, coming up from Quebec with approximately 4000 soldiers.

Haviland started shelling the Isle-aux-Noix. Casualties began to mount, but Bougainville held on, in accordance with a plea from Lévis to hold up the British advance for as long as he could. On the 21st, he reported that there was nowhere left for the men to shelter. 'There is no place that the guns cannot reach … I am not intimidated by the attacking army, but I must admit that we are far from impregnable.'[2] A week later, he learned that the British had destroyed what few vessels the French still had left. Vaudreuil instructed him to leave the island and join the forces defending Montreal.

Bougainville hesitated: Vaudreuil was the civil governor, whereas Lévis was his military commander. But if he stayed any longer, his men would run out of food. In a compromise, he decided to leave behind the sick and wounded, with a tiny handful of men whose task was to give the impression that the French were still holding on. Meanwhile, he set off with the rest of his force in an arduous night march towards the St Lawrence and Montreal. Firing guns and making as much noise as they could, the weary and invalid remnants of the fort managed to hold

Haviland and his troops at bay for another week. Bougainville joined up with Jean-Georges Roquemaure at Saint John, 12 miles from the Isle-aux-Noix, but they were soon forced to retreat further north. Amherst and Murray were advancing steadily, capturing any remaining French outposts they found on their way.

On 6 September, all the senior officers, Bougainville included, were called to a meeting where each was asked for his opinion on what was to be done. It was unanimously agreed that a last stand would be fruitless and merely a waste of lives. As a result of their losses in casualties and prisoners, and desertions by some of the local militia, the French could marshal little more than 2100 men. 'It was better to arrange a capitulation that would be advantageous to the people and honourable for the troops, who would thus be saved for the King, than continue a stubborn defence that could only postpone by a few days the loss of the country,' reported Bougainville. Vaudreuil had drawn up a proposal for surrender, which he read out to the assembled officers. It was endorsed without dissent and, once again, Louis was to carry the document to General Amherst. The French had asked for honours of war, namely to be allowed to leave the city in regular formation and under their officers. Amherst flatly refused: the troops must surrender as prisoners and would never again be allowed to serve anywhere against Britain.

Lévis and some of the other officers rejected this humiliation, preferring to fight to the end. Bougainville took their appeal to Amherst, who bluntly rejected it. The Englishman blamed the French for atrocities committed by their Indian allies, and insisted on the humiliating surrender. Bougainville returned. Vaudreuil decided to accept Amherst's conditions, but Lévis and Bougainville broke their swords rather than give them up, and Lévis ordered his officers 'to burn their colours and so escape the harsh conditions which demanded their surrender to the enemy'.[3]

The formal surrender document was signed on 8 September. On the 14th, Bougainville was taken to Quebec, followed by the French troops marching dispiritedly in scattered groups. English transport ships took them to France, Bougainville and Bourlamaque supervising their embarkation. The senior officers were released on parole, and once the troops had been seen to and the final negotiations completed for the surrender of the whole of French Canada to Britain, Bougainville was allowed to sail for France. Weary and despondent, he arrived in Europe in December 1760.

Part 3
CREATING A COLONY

11. SOCIETY AND SCIENTISTS

1761–2

'MONSIEUR LE COLONEL Louis-Antoine de Bougainville.' The lackey, dressed in royal blue with white breeches and a white wig, did not raise his voice unduly above the gentle hubbub of the drawing room, but Louis's arrival easily caused a flutter of interest among the guests. The men turned towards him, bowing slightly; matrons exchanged glances and whispers behind their fans, their daughters watching him from under lowered eyelids.

Basing his description on an early portrait, the French historian J.E. Martin-Allanic conjures up a man in his prime, 5 feet 5 inches in height, with powerful shoulders, a complexion weathered by campaigning in Canada and by months spent at sea, and a slight ironical smile that suggested someone sure of himself and not depressed by the reverses he had suffered. The onlookers knew Louis as a hero, still young, unmarried and with good prospects. He had earned his compatriots' respect; he was well connected and charming.

The war in North America was only of slight interest. When Bougainville returned to France, he found that public opinion was rather more concerned about the cost of the war than the loss of any overseas territories. Everyone knew things had been going badly in India and in Canada, but more worrying was the continual seesawing of France's fortunes in Europe.

Ferdinand of Brunswick had won a brilliant victory at Warburg at the end of July 1760, driving the French back towards the Rhine, but he had been defeated at Kloster Kamp in October. This was gratifying to national pride, but the original setback and the later compensating success had cost thousands of lives. The troops were as weary of marching back and forth across Europe, as the civilians back home were of endeavouring to identify which side was winning and where the battles were taking place. And almost no one bothered to count the casualties among the peasants whose villages were pillaged by advancing and retreating soldiers.

Across the Channel, the British were equally affected by the cost of the war and depressed by the defeats their allies suffered on the continent. Both sides consoled themselves by glorying in tales of individual heroism or tragedy. The death of General Wolfe was seized upon by writers and painters – even though Benjamin West's planned canvas depicting Wolfe outside Montreal caused an uproar when it was discovered that he intended to show the various characters wearing contemporary dress instead of the classical Graeco-Roman trappings then *de rigueur* for all heroic subjects. The French had not only Montcalm's tragic death to arouse their sentimental pride, but the heroism of the Chevalier d'Assas at Kloster Kamp. Trapped in an ambush by an advance party creeping up to the French camp and threatened with death if he called out, Assas shouted a warning that became famous: 'Help me, Auvergne. These are enemies.' Upon which he was immediately killed.

Men like Voltaire and many of the *philosophes* saw little sense in seeking consolation in romantic scenes of heroism, and even less in pursuing a ruinous war. The middle class, with its merchants and traders, shared his view for a different reason: the treasury was empty and increased taxes were predicted. Their British counterparts were similarly worried, and in 1761 they forced Secretary of State William Pitt to resign. There was general concern throughout the country about the cost of the war and the increase in the national debt had begun to worry his colleagues, and they got rid of him. The Seven Years War had so far cost the Exchequer over £160 million, a substantial proportion of which had to be raised on the expensive money markets.

In France, many people blamed the Marquise de Pompadour for helping to prolong the conflict. The accusation, like others levelled at her, was probably unfair, for Europe had become locked in a conflict with so many different war aims that finding a way out often seemed impossible. By the time Louis returned to France, however, discreet negotiations between the various powers were slowly beginning.

Louis stayed for a short while with Madame Hérault, but soon found himself a suitable house in Rue Neuve-des-Bons-Enfants, near his brother Jean-Pierre, who lived in Rue du Croissant in the parish of Saint-Eustache. This was the house where their father had retired shortly before his death. With Jean-Pierre, whose health was steadily worsening, lived their aunt Charlotte de Bougainville, both waited upon by an elderly servant, Balthazar Guillaume.

Once he had settled in, Louis began to visit old acquaintances and patrons. His first call was on the Marquise de Pompadour. She welcomed her protégé as one who had fought to the last with Montcalm and continued the struggle after the marquis's death. He next obtained an audience with the Duc de Choiseul, who was rapidly becoming one of France's most powerful politicians. Once again, he was well received. Choiseul shared many of Bougainville's views about the need to counter

Britain's ascendancy in the post-war years, and he invited him to join his inner circle.

Étienne-François de Stainville, Duc de Choiseul, was a man of great talents and a perfect courtier. He was short of stature, with plain, even ugly features, but a great wit and fully at home in the *salons* of his time:

> Kind, noble, frank, generous, gallant, magnificent, liberal, proud, bold, lively, fiery even, he made one think of those French knights of old, but to these qualities he also added several of his country's weaknesses: he was light, indiscreet, presumptuous, libertine, prodigal, petulant and proud. But never have I known a man who could spread more delight and contentment among his acquaintances. When he came into a drawing-room, he dug into his pockets and seemed to bring out an unending stream of witticisms and jollity.[1]

He had long gained the favour of the Marquise de Pompadour, who had obtained for him the post of French ambassador to Rome back in 1753, and four years later that of ambassador to Vienna. He was made Duc de Choiseul shortly after this, and began to accumulate government appointments, taking over successively foreign affairs, the war ministry and the navy. He became effectively Prime Minister of France, and was to hold power for a total of twelve years. He played a major part in the restructuring of the army and navy after the Seven Years War, helping to restore France's status among European powers.

With him rose his cousin, César-Gabriel de Choiseul-Chévigny, who took over the embassy in Vienna when Stainville left it. He took over foreign affairs in 1761 and then the navy from his cousin. Like him, he was raised to the rank of duke, becoming the Duc de Choiseul-Praslin. Choiseul-Stainville, however, remained the dominant partner, keeping relations with Spain for himself. Both men negotiated an end to the disastrous Seven Years War, and then together reorganised as much of the administrative, military and naval services as the fiercely conservative nobility and upper middle class allowed them to.

The cousins were members of a leading noble family from Champagne, with extensive – and invaluable – connections through marriage and kindred. Choiseul-Praslin had a true courtier and politician's self-assurance, and a charm that fascinated people and inspired confidence. His household was enlivened by two remarkable women: his wife, the charming Louise-Honorine Crozat du Châtel, and her sister, the imperious Duchesse de Gramont, both friends of Madame de Pompadour.

Bougainville was made welcome by this circle, hailed by the Marquise de Pompadour and her friends who introduced him to a wider group as a hero of the

Canadian war. Many of the colony's civilian administrators, including Vaudreuil, had been brought back to France in disgrace, and some of them were imprisoned in the Bastille, to await trial for corruption and fraud, but Louis received only praise for his actions in North America, and commiseration for the sad outcome of the various campaigns.

> He stood out among the guests, being of a somewhat above average height, with a noble bearing, and an ease of manner. He enjoyed in this high society the reputation of a man of wit and obtained every benefit from it. Of an obliging nature, he could never refuse his services to anyone who found himself in need of them; he was sometimes generous to the point of excess.[2]

Nevertheless, he was still formally a prisoner of the British, who had been allowed to go home on parole, having given his word that he would take no further part in the war. This restriction irked him – he did not want to turn into a dilettante, whose main activity in life was frequenting the salons. He soon began to write to acquaintances in London, asking to be freed. He wrote to William Pitt in March 1761 for permission to serve in Europe, and asked for the same favour on behalf of the Chevalier de Lévis. He sent his request by way of Charles Townshend, a senior political figure he had known during his time in London. The refusal, which came promptly, was cleverly and courteously couched, but it was a curt rejection nonetheless: 'Kind and generous friend: our court is much too aware of the talents which both of you possess to agree to place you in a position where you could use them against it.' So Louis instead devoted himself to his brother. Together, they reconsidered the plans they had discussed over the years. They could affect the future, not only of France but of the Bougainville family as well.

Jean-Pierre de Bougainville had written a number of works on voyages of exploration and conquest in antiquity. He had then turned to more modern voyages, analysing the wealth of available material with his usual meticulous care and attention.

Voyages to the southern seas, including those by French explorers, went back a long way and were far more extensive than many realised. Back in 1504, a vessel from Honfleur, in Normandy, had been blown off course near the Cape of Good Hope and had reached what became known as Gonneville Land. This, many believed, was part of that great southern continent cartographers had long speculated about. Paulmier de Gonneville's landfall was actually South America, but this was not discovered until the middle of the nineteenth century. Occasionally, travellers had returned to France, bringing back exciting tales of fabulous kingdoms in the Far East and in the Pacific Ocean. They included Pierre-Olivier Malherbe, a Breton expatriate, who, after years in Peru, Mexico, China and India, had finally returned by way of Marseilles in 1608. Later, French buccaneers joined up with English and other raiders, and sailed into the Pacific, adding their tales of the fabulous South Seas.

Then, towards the end of the seventeenth century, political circumstances enabled French ships to enter the Pacific, a region dominated by Spain and so jealously guarded that it was eventually known as the Spanish Lake. The first Frenchman to lead an expedition towards these waters, Jean-Baptiste de Gennes, sailed in 1695 with six ships, but got no further than the Strait of Magellan. However, he did blaze the trail for others, and over the next 20 years an estimated 168 French ships entered the Pacific, traded with the Spanish settlements along the American seaboard and began to cross the ocean to trade with China and India.

All these expeditions vastly increased interest in the South Seas, strengthened by the published experiences of some of the naturalists who had joined the voyages, notably Louis Feuillet, whose *Journal des observations* appeared in 1714, and Amédée-François Frézier, whose *Voyage* came out two years later. Louis could add to all this information: during his time in London he had met a number of scientists and naval captains. The chief among these was George Anson, whose voyage round the world in 1741–2 had added nothing to knowledge of the Pacific, but had aroused wide interest and wider discussion.

Compiled by Walter Richard, the account of Anson's expedition, *A Voyage round the World*, was published in 1748, and appeared a year later in a French translation. It included details about the rounding of Cape Horn and the value of the Falkland Islands as a base. It referred to the superiority of the British Navy over all others, and urged Britain to use her advantages and extend her activities into the Pacific Ocean. It was 'a classic story of adventure at sea, and a reasoned plea for the expansion of British power and commerce in the South Sea; and in both respects it retained the interest of the British reading public for the rest of the century'.[3]

Anson himself was highly influential. Raised to the peerage in 1748, he became First Lord of the Admiralty in 1751, a position he held almost without interruption for another eleven years. Not satisfied with urging his fellows to look to the Pacific, in January 1749 he began to plan a full voyage of discovery to the southern latitudes. The plan was curtailed to an expedition to the Falkland Islands, to avoid alarming the Spanish who, quite rightly, saw in his wider proposal an attempt to challenge their monopoly over the Pacific. Eventually, Madrid's concerns forced the British government to shelve even the Falklands plan, although Anson apparently attempted to revive it later. The outbreak of the Seven Years War not long after and Anson's death in 1762 pushed the idea well in the background, but the English sailor's intentions and the rationale behind them led Bougainville to think about France's position and to hold long discussions with his brother.

The two brothers pored over maps of the South Seas. French cartographers had taken over the dominant role once played by the Dutch mapmakers. Philippe Buache redrew the map of the southern hemisphere issued back in 1714 and added to it the Cap de la Circoncision sighted by Bouvet de Lozier, the possible link to the rumoured southern continent. His chart, published in 1755, was particularly timely in view of Buffon's 1749 speculations on the existence of an unknown continent as large as Europe, Asia and Africa combined. The English cartographer John Green was equally prominent in this period. He endeavoured to reconcile the accounts of early Spanish navigators with more recent knowledge of the Pacific, reflecting the view of many when he said, 'There are doubtless many large Countries or Islands in this part of the South-Sea.'[4]

The mapmakers' interest and speculations were matched by similar concerns among naturalists and various *philosophes*. Buffon, in particular, always fascinated by the possibility that new animal species might be discovered in as yet unknown lands, continued to advocate the serious exploration of the southern ocean by French navigators.

Pierre de Maupertuis's famous *Lettre sur le progrès des sciences*, although written back in 1752, remained a frequent topic of discussion. Maupertuis had addressed it to Frederick II of Prussia, urging him to turn his attention to matters of importance to the human race as a whole, and suggesting that the exploration of the unknown austral lands was essential to scientific progress:

> Everyone knows that there is in the southern hemisphere an unknown area where might lie a new part of the World larger than any of the other four. And no prince has been curious enough to promote research that would determine whether land or sea fills that space, and this in a century when the science of navigation has reached such a high state of perfection.[5]

Although he was a patron of writers and *philosophes*, Frederick was more interested in military conquests than naval exploration; Voltaire had then fallen out with Maupertuis and poured ridicule on his writings and his scientific reasoning. However, even after his death in 1759, Maupertuis's influence remained strong – De Brosses had developed his ideas – and many geographers and scientists continued to discuss and expand his ideas.

At Versailles, or at receptions given by the Marquise de Pompadour or the Duc de Choiseul, Louis met mostly members of the nobility, political figures, artists, with a sprinkling of thinkers and writers. But there were other salons in Paris where leaders of the literary and *philosophes* gathered, and where he was always made welcome. These were run by so-called 'blue-stockings', intellectual women derided by Rousseau, who once said, 'A blue-stocking is the scourge of her husband, children, friends, servants, and every one.' At most of these gatherings, the conversation dealt with serious questions, social, economic and literary, even though a good turn of phrase and an easy wit – both attributes Louis possessed – were always welcome.

The *philosophes* Louis met in these salons were interested in the 'savage' or uncorrupted societies that might be found on distant islands, or in forms of civilisation that might have developed without European influences. They were men who endeavoured to analyse the society around them – early sociologists and social historians – and physiocrats like François Quesnay, who can be called the founder of economic science. All listened with interest when Bougainville began to talk of the need for new and more thorough voyages of exploration.

Among the most celebrated hostesses was Madame Marie du Deffand, who was blind; Madame Marie Thérèse Robet Geoffrin, renowned for not suffering fools gladly; and Julie de Lespinasse, the friend of Jean d'Alembert, a noted *philosophe* and early collaborator of the encyclopaedist Denis Diderot, who would one day write a famous tract on the inhabitants of Tahiti, entitled *Supplément au Voyage de Bougainville*. There was also Madame Anne Catherine Helvétius, wife of the controversial *philosophe* Claude-Arien Helvétius; and the Baron Paul Henri d'Holbach, author of numerous articles on metallurgy and mineralogy, himself a host of some renown, famed for his lavish dinners.

Jean-Pierre de Bougainville, his health steadily worsening, seldom ventured out. He was happier in his book-lined study than in these sparkling assemblies. Somewhat unprepossessing in appearance, and shorter than his brother, he was ill at ease in salon company. There were too many hangers-on, eager to shine by their wit, but with little else to contribute. He sought the company of serious-minded colleagues and savants. He waited with ill-disguised impatience for Louis to return from the dinners and receptions where he hoped his brother would have discussed matters relating to the southern continent and the South Seas, now the subject of their almost daily conversations. Often, he would send Louis off with questions for some of the *philosophes* and savants he expected him to meet. Then the brothers would spend long hours studying texts and charts, planning the expedition they had thought about for so long:

These detailed studies, these learned disputations, these burning evocations of the past and the present, was it not made to arouse a vocation in the mind of the younger Bougainville? His brother was driving him towards it with all his soul … He had prepared him for this glorious role since his early days. The boy he had guided since his college days was now a thorough man, ready to carry out his grandiose dreams.[6]

It is all too easy to visualise Louis-Antoine de Bougainville at this period as a pleasant, but earnest and rather serious young man, calling on society people and scientists with equal ease, then burying himself in Jean-Pierre's study – and also occasionally fretting over his inability to take an active part in the war that was continuing in Europe and elsewhere. But that would be a false picture. Back in Canada, he had enjoyed society life in Quebec and Montreal. He had been a popular guest at dinners and receptions, and more than welcome at the gaming tables; Montcalm had sometimes felt compelled to keep an eye on him to ensure that his losses did not mount up unreasonably. Louis had been the target of many amorous glances from ladies, single and married. There had been rumours, not all of them unfounded, of a number of affairs. Paris offered far more attractions than Canada and Louis led an enjoyable life, as several police reports record.

Inclusion in police files did not imply any criminal activity. Police surveillance of individuals went back to 1667 when Nicolas de la Reynie was appointed Lieutenant-General of Police in Paris. Keeping an eye on areas of possible disaffection, and on potential troublemakers and bothersome clerics, was an important part of police activities. Information on a wide range of people, even minor titbits about their behaviour, was stored away, just in case it might come in handy one day. Gentle blackmail could always be used to persuade an awkward citizen to change his behaviour or his allegiance. La Reynie placed informers in public places, such as cabarets, gardens, squares and street corners, with orders to listen to what people were saying about the king and current events. Known popularly as *mouches* (flies on the walls) they sent regular reports to the Lieutenant General of Police, who then, in his weekly visits to the king, kept the monarch informed about the current climate. The system had been useful for Louis XIV, who in the early part of his reign had faced two successive periods of rebellion against royal absolutism. Louis XV maintained the practice and extended the network of informers to other areas of Paris where libertarian nobles and intellectuals might gather: 'the Palais Royal, the Tuileries gardens, the forecourt of the Palais de Justice, and also a number of more or less notorious taverns and, more rarely, a few tollbooths and barriers at the edge of the suburban "liberties". These observers were supposed to write a report once a week.'[7]

These police records, known as *gazetins*, and covering mainly the period 1724–81, include a wealth of information about public reactions to the events of the day, and a great deal of gossip about the people of Paris, both low and high born. They contain details about Louis's private life between 1761 and 1763. He had attracted the informers' attention when he began an affair with a 'person of importance', unnamed but in all probability the wife of a nobleman. They reported on his gambling and on the length of time he spent in backstreet gambling dens. However, he does not appear to have had a true gambling problem, and their attention soon turned to his mistresses: at least three were recorded. 'Mademoiselle Dumirey, a dancer at the Opera … had replaced in his affection another dancer, Miss Arnould.'

> A fine crowd! One claims to feel nothing towards the so-called marquis, 'a kept woman being a jewel that lends itself to a rich man'. The other, 'dark-complexioned and unfeeling, always has her mouth filled with saliva, which means that she shoots the cream of her speech into your face'. Hence a third affair with a Miss Reybbres, from Düsseldorf, whom Bougainville set up in a very fine apartment in Rue Neuve-des-Petits-Champs, with a view over the Palais Royal, paying her, like a great lord, an allowance of 60 *livres* a month and providing for her at his banker's, for the duration of his absence, the sum of 12,000 *livres*.[8]

The accuracy of these backbiting, gossipy reports is open to question – this account goes on to state that Bougainville was about to sail to Guadeloupe, in the West Indies – but they do indicate that, with time on his hands, he found some solace in Parisian life.

The peace negotiations proceeded slowly. In 1761, the Duc de Choiseul-Praslin was selected to lead a delegation at a conference at Augsburg, and he appointed Bougainville to accompany him. Louis's knowledge of English and his experience with negotiations in Canada would prove invaluable, and he looked forward to returning to some form of active life – but the Augsburg Congress did not eventuate.

He would have liked to go to Malta, which was threatened by the Turks, or to join the Chevalier Charles d'Arsac de Ternay, who was leading an expedition to Newfoundland, but the terms of his parole prevented him from taking part in anything that might involve military action. He could not even travel to Brittany, where the French were mounting an expedition – futile, as it turned out – to recapture the offshore island of Belle-Isle, recently captured by the British.

In 1762, however, Louis's situation began to improve. Choiseul and his British counterparts had begun to negotiate in earnest. In this context, concessions had to be made on both sides. Releasing Bougainville from his parole was a small favour to ask. On 8 March, he was at last advised that his freedom was granted, on condition that he served only in Europe. In July, Choiseul sent him with confidential instructions to the Maréchal d'Estrées and the Maréchal Benjamin de Soubise. After this, he served for several weeks as aide-de-camp to the Comte de Stainville. He took part in an engagement against a mixed English and German corps at Hirschfeld, and was slightly wounded. Stainville then sent him back to Versailles to report on the state of the army in Germany.

He found on his return that attempts had been made to undermine his position.

During my absence, I had been the victim of some appalling vexations within the duc de Choiseul's household. The pretext was a relationship considered too intimate with a person of importance. The Duchesse de G. received me with marked ill-will and she never thereafter allowed me to recover from this disfavour. I decided thenceforth to visit the Minister only as other callers did, with no special connection.[9]

The identity of the 'person of importance' remains a mystery, but the 'Duchesse de G.' can be identified as Choiseul's sister, the Duchesse de Gramont. A lack of fortune and mediocre looks had made it difficult for her to find a suitor, and she had spent some years in a convent, waiting for her brother to rescue her. He had arranged a marriage with the wealthy but fairly dreary Duc de Gramont, who was not attracted by her. After a brief period she had left him to join her brother's household. 'Though not so pretty, and not nearly so nice as her sister-in-law, she was more amusing and had more influence with Choiseul. The courtiers soon found this out, so that, while Madame de Choiseul was admired but neglected, Madame de Gramont was disliked but courted.'[10] She was a dangerous woman to cross – as Walpole noted, 'She is extremely pleasant when she wants to be. She is a devoted friend, but a harsh and insolent enemy'[11] – and Louis somehow got on the wrong side of her. He may have allowed some witticism about her looks or character to slip out and, as was almost inevitable in the corridors of Versailles, it had been reported back to her. Henceforth, he took good care to avoid social functions at the Choiseul home and kept his relationship with the duc on a more formal business footing.

Choiseul, however, liked Bougainville and he did not let such pettifogging matters interfere with his plans. As soon as peace had been negotiated, he intended to develop some of France's remaining colonies and restore the power of the navy, substantially increasing its budget immediately the country's finances permitted it. Bougainville's own views about British ambitions overseas and the need to counteract them fitted in perfectly with Choiseul's. The peace negotiations were entering their final stage. The Duke of Bedford came to Paris to discuss peace terms; the Duc de Nivernais went to London to settle details, and a preliminary peace treaty was signed on 3 November 1762. Bougainville now had to see to his own future. There were few prospects in those immediate post-war years for an army colonel. Some other position would have to be found.

The first task Choiseul thought of for him was administering the parlous South American colony of French Guiana. A backwater few even knew about, it had been a French settlement, based essentially on the seaport of Cayenne, since the early seventeenth century. Lost to Holland in 1667, but reconquered ten years later, it was underpopulated, with an estimated 6000 inhabitants, including some 500 Europeans. Some time earlier, Choiseul had received a proposal from a resident of Cayenne, who planned to develop an 'equinoctial France' in Guiana. Three earlier attempts had been made, during the seventeenth century, to build up a solid French settlement, but they had all failed. The new plan was more detailed and more carefully drawn up. Its proponent, Bruletout de Préfontaine, asked that the French government first of all send out a reliable governor-administrator. The appointee would need the full backing of the government, and should possess the skills and experience to lay the foundations for a colony and supervise its development.

Louis was nominated for the position of Governor of French Guiana. At first, he was tempted to accept, even though, with a formal peace treaty not yet signed, he suspected that the British authorities might put a number of obstacles in his way. He also had reservations about the scheme, and secretly believed that it might hamper his future career. The colony might fail, as several government advisers believed, and this would be a black mark against his name. On the other hand, if it succeeded, he might become buried in the dull administrative work of running a distant outpost, and get forgotten. His brother Jean-Pierre was opposed to the idea. He had set his heart on Louis undertaking the voyage of exploration he had dreamt of for years. Nevertheless, Louis set himself the task of learning more about Guiana and collecting the uniforms and supplies he would need. When the political situation caused a postponement of the plan, he asked to be refunded for his expenses. Choiseul granted him 3000 *livres*.

The Guiana settlement was attempted a little later, but in an over-optimistic and ill-planned manner and, as the pessimists had predicted, it was a dismal failure. Some 12,000 volunteers were sent out, but with little in the way of supplies for the early stage of development. They soon found themselves short of food and even of drinking water, and succumbed to fevers and starvation. By 1765 fewer than 1000 remained alive. Préfontaine's plan for a governor to come out first with a small force to lay the foundations for the colony was proved right. Earlier delays meant that Bougainville had been saved from getting involved in a disastrous venture.

The formal peace treaty between France and Britain was signed in February 1763. Choiseul once again asked Bougainville whether he wanted the governorship of Guiana, but Louis submitted an entirely different programme: the colonisation of the Falkland Islands, combined with a voyage of exploration across the Pacific.

12. THE FIRST EXPEDITION

January–August 1763

WHEN THEY LOOKED at the history of world exploration, people like Choiseul, De Brosses and the Bougainville brothers came up against a simple, but embarrassing situation. Christopher Columbus, an Italian in the service of Spain, had discovered America. Vasco da Gama, a Portuguese, had pioneered the lucrative route to India and the Far East. Ferdinand Magellan, also Portuguese but working for Spain, had been the first to cross the Pacific Ocean, and the Spaniard Alvaro de Mendaña had discovered the Solomon Islands, possibly even the southern continent itself. The Dutch had sailed along the west coast of Australia, and the Dutchman Abel Tasman had discovered New Zealand. Britain could take pride in the voyages of Francis Drake, William Dampier and George Anson. What did France have to glory in? A number of voyages to the East and along the Pacific coast of South America, with a few crossings of the Pacific Ocean – but by merchants, few of whom had made any significant discoveries, or if they had no one had taken much notice of them. National pride called for some major undertaking. And so did the scientists and the strategists – increasingly loudly. France could not be left out.

The obstacle, as always, was the cost. The Seven Years War had been so expensive and so unproductive that there was widespread unrest throughout the kingdom. This was not Bougainville's concern, but it was Choiseul's. In the post-war period, a minister had to be realistic and cautious. He did not discourage Bougainville. Quite the opposite: he was prepared to support him – when the time was right. Bougainville went ahead with a first proposal 'to undertake the discovery of the Southern Lands or to establish a settlement in the South Seas, to the north of California'. It was relatively brief. The aim was to make sure that Choiseul read it and realised at a glance what was involved. Three vessels would be dispatched in May: 'one of them of thirty guns, one of twenty, and a coastal vessel or ketch of twelve. These vessels will call at Saint Catherine Island or at Rio-Janeiro.' After a rest, they would sail to the Malouine (Falkland) Islands to establish a settlement. 'This establishment (which Admiral Anson urged so strongly in the account of his voyage) will serve as a supply store for the later sequence of discoveries.' The expedition's commander would send a small ship back to France, to report on the first stage of the plan and bring back munitions and men. Once the Malouine settlement was established, the commander would follow the east-south-east route, 'endeavouring to discover land in that area and to reach, by going on eastwards, Cape Circumcision, discovered in 1739 by Mr Bouvet'. Should the 'Southern Land' be discovered, the French expedition would 'establish a settlement there and endeavour to found, in a stable manner, a colony with the assistance the Minister will have sent to the Malouine Islands base and some new reinforcements that will enable France to maintain an establishment that would be so beneficial to her navy, her trade and her renown'. If no southern continent were discovered, the expedition would return to the Malouine Islands base, to rest, recruit men and load the supplies sent from France. Then, 'choosing the most appropriate time of the year', the French ships would round Cape Horn and set up an establishment to the north of California, 'and the Minister will endeavour to establish lines of communication between that establishment and Louisiana'. Louis concluded:

> The benefits these two undertakings would be likely to bring about will not be outlined here. His Lordship the Duc de Choiseul is well placed to realise at a first glance what they would be. If the proposal seems likely to be accepted, full details will be provided on the fitting out of the vessels, the route to be followed and the settlements to be established.[1]

This document is unsigned and undated. It is written in Bougainville's own handwriting, but it looks like a fairly early document, possibly drafted after the first offer of the Cayenne governorship.

For one thing, Louisiana was no longer going to be a French possession: it was in the process of being transferred to Spain by a secret treaty signed in 1762. Then a substantial portion, east of the Mississippi River, was lost to Great Britain as a result of the French–British peace treaty. These complex and somewhat confusing manoeuvres would lead to considerable unrest, until the return of Louisiana to France in 1800, followed by its formal cession to the United States in 1812. But Bougainville seemed unaware of this situation, which suggests that his proposal was written in late 1762.

Choiseul did not reject his proposal outright. Louis's plan was overambitious for the time, but he was attracted by the possibility of a base at the Falkland Islands. He referred the report to a senior adviser at the Ministry for the Colonies, Jean Augustin Accaron, who had already examined the plan for the French Guiana settlement and reported adversely on it, considering it too limited in scope and offering too few prospects. He felt better disposed towards Louis's plan. It was far broader in outlook, contained elements that could be developed further and fitted in well with Choiseul's own views for France's future.

Accaron invited Louis to meet him, and soon took a liking to him. An able administrator, and well regarded by his minister, Accaron had a promising future – but also three daughters of marriageable age, for whom he was anxious to find suitable husbands, men who would help his family to progress further up the social scale. Bougainville, a personable bachelor in his early thirties, at ease in every kind of company, charmed the young ladies and gave at least one of them the impression that his flirting was based on deeper feelings. When Accaron's report was completed and Louis began preparations for his first voyage to the Falklands, his visits came to an end. The Accaron girls did not forgive him, and one of them, who later made an excellent marriage and became the Comtesse de Grasse, turned her husband against him for years to come.

During his discussions at the ministry, Bougainville met other officials, including Accaron's assistant at the time, Pierre-Paul Le Mercier de la Rivière de Saint-Médard. His record was as impressive as his name: he had been a counsellor at the Paris Parlement until 1759 when he was appointed administrator of the French West Indies. Recently returned, he was marking time until peace would enable him to return and take over the administration of the island of Martinique. He would go on to a long and impressive career and Louis would meet him again on numerous occasions.

Bougainville discussed with him approaches to colonial settlements. Le Mercier was a supporter of the writer and jurist Charles de Montesquieu, who had favoured such establishments as bases for trade with neighbouring countries – bases were all that France was left with in India and the Indian Ocean after the 1763 peace treaty. Le Mercier believed that colonial settlements were rather similar to the French provinces, and should be closely linked with the home country: 'What we call the State is a political body formed by the union of several bodies of a similar nature: the provinces are the main limbs of this body, and the colonies are like provinces.'[2] Bougainville felt that this could result in restrictions on free trade, preventing the overseas settlements from dealing with other countries in their region. His view reflected the growing eighteenth-century trend towards more liberal trade, and shows him as favouring the economic theories of Pierre Quesnay, soon to be known as 'Physiocracy'. Le Mercier was more influenced by the imperialist model, descended from the days of the Roman Empire, under which overseas settlements should be viewed as part of the metropolis. This structure has been carried through to modern times: such territories as Martinique and Guadeloupe in the West Indies became French overseas departments with representatives elected to both houses of the French Parliament.

These discussions were interesting, and relevant to Bougainville's proposal to take French settlers to the Malouine Islands, but his heart remained set on a voyage of exploration. As far as he was concerned, the Malouines would be essentially a place of call for French ships on the way to the South Seas. Colonisation was a means to an end. Following a preliminary examination of his first plan, he was asked to draw up a more detailed proposal that could be submitted to the king – after being vetted by Choiseul and his advisers. He had to be sure that his ideas would find favour with Accaron and Le Mercier, whose endorsement would be the first step in the process of approval.

Bougainville began work with his cousin, Michel François Bougainville de Nerville. His brother Jean-Pierre had done as much as he could do to help and had retired to Loches, in the peaceful district of Touraine, to stay with their sister Marie-Françoise and her husband Louis de Baraudin who was *lieutenant du Roi*, in charge of the local châteaux and townships.

Bougainville de Nerville was a barrister, but he was no keener on practising law than Louis had been. First, though, he needed to widen his fairly scanty knowledge of the Pacific Ocean and its mysterious islands. He turned to Charles de Brosses's *Histoire*, but Accaron introduced both men to his ministry's archives. In all those dusty boxes and files were reports few had ever bothered to read.

There, they discovered a proposal prepared by a descendant of a native brought to France by Paulmier de Gonneville in the sixteenth century. He had never returned to his native land, but settled in Normandy. He told his children and grandchildren about his distant homeland whose inhabitants knew nothing of Christianity. The descendant, Jean Paulmier de Courtonne, had taken holy orders, and in 1665, eager to see missionaries sent out to remedy the situation, he submitted a *Mémoire touchant le dessein de la découverte des Terres australes, dites inconnues, et celuy d'y establir une mission chrétienne et une habitation française*.

Also in the colonial archives was a second document by Paulmier, entitled *Pour les Terres australes: État des choses qui sont attendues de la piété du Roy*. It listed what would be required for the rediscovery of the so-called Gonneville Land, and for the settlement of a small colony to support the missionaries bringing Christianity to the natives. The Abbé Paulmier had also approached Rome through the papal nuncio in Paris, in the hope of getting himself appointed as first vicar-apostolic of the southern lands:

At a General meeting of the Evangelisation Congregation held on 25 February 1666 in the presence of Pope Alexander VII in his Quirinal Apartments with fourteen cardinals present, Gianbattista Cardinal Pallotta addressed the pope as follows:

By means of a printed memorandum Your Holiness is asked by the Reverend Jean Paulmier, a French priest, to grant him the apostolic blessing and faculties to go as a missionary to the unknown Australian Land, from where he says he has his origin.[3]

Pallotta was able to answer questions about the project, drawing on yet another lengthy document by Paulmier, entitled *Mémoires touchant l'établissement d'une mission chrétienne dans le troisième monde, autrement appelé la Terre australe, méridionale, antarctique et inconnue.* The request was well received, although difficulties arose from the abbé's suggestion that the island of Madagascar should be the main base for the undertaking. This created difficulties with the Capuchin and Vincentian orders, both of which had their own plans for the evangelisation of the region. Paulmier went around Paris, calling on the heads of these orders, while waiting for a decision from Louis XIV. He made little progress and the proposal was eventually dropped.

Louis de Bougainville and his cousin studied these documents with growing fascination. They soon realised, however, that the Abbé Paulmier had only the vaguest notions of where his ancestor's Gonneville Land might be situated. They then met an officer of the French India Company, Antoine-Jean-Marie Thévenard, a man who was to go on to a remarkably successful career in the French Navy and whom Bougainville would come across several times in later years. Thévenard was convinced that the land Bouvet de Lozier had sighted was part of the southern lands, and that his discovery, rather than Gonneville's, deserved further investigation. He favoured a base on the Falkland Islands, although he did not share Bougainville's view that this meant France had to establish a colony there.

Louis was now in a position to write up his new report, to be submitted through Accaron to the Duc de Choiseul and, he hoped, the king. An expansion rather than a modification of his first proposal, it took into account the consequences of the recent peace treaty and dropped all references to Louisiana and northern California, while stressing in several places the importance of countering British dominance. He began by describing the commercial and strategic advantages France could gain by creating a colony in the southern lands, and added:

To these, one can add political motives of equal importance: the whole of North America now belongs to the English; there is no doubt that, since they have sought a passage to the Pacific Ocean by the north of Hudson's Bay, they will endeavour to make further discoveries to the west of the Canadian lakes, where they will set up settlements.

They will also try to open up a passage to the South Seas by way of the south. Anson, in his *Voyage*, stressed the importance of a settlement on the Malouine Islands or on the coast of Patagonia. Should that enterprising nation discover a port in the northern Pacific Ocean, Anson's advice to them would acquire even greater importance. It is consequently of utmost urgency, both for the safety and the range of French navigation, to forestall the English by establishing a settlement, if that is possible, on the Southern lands.[4]

He then asked for four ships, one of which would promptly return to France with details of the Malouines settlement, while the other three would sail east to rediscover Bouvet de Lozier's landfall, which he had named Cape Circumcision. He mentioned specifically that the colonists should include a substantial number of French Canadian refugees, or Acadians, while the crews should consist mostly of sailors with experience of Newfoundland and Greenland waters and some who had previously sailed to Brazil. He admitted that it was difficult to predict what would be needed for a colony on the southern land, since it had not yet been discovered and no one really knew what it was like, but he provided considerable details on the history of the Malouines – although he made a fairly gross error in referring to Falkland as an English navigator, whereas the islands were named in honour of Lucius Cary, second Viscount Falkland, who was killed at Newbury in 1643.

Accaron broadly supported the proposal, but he considered it too ambitious in view of the impoverished state of the treasury. He recommended that the expedition 'should be reduced to sending only three vessels and merely to the colonisation of the Malouine Islands'.[5] Choiseul invited the cousins to come along and discuss their plan in detail. He told them that he was prepared to accept it with a few modifications in line with Accaron's own recommendations. He felt confident that Louis XV would endorse it, but he did point out two major difficulties: first, the kingdom's finances were in too parlous a state to meet the whole or indeed the main cost of such an expedition, and second, political difficulties were likely to arise from Madrid. Spain had long staked her claim to the islands and, although they remained uninhabited, she would probably raise strong objections to the French colony.

Bougainville had anticipated the financing problem. The solution, worked out with his uncle Jean-Potentien d'Arboulin, was to set up a private company, with themselves as main shareholders. The company would meet most of the costs, in exchange for the income the colony was expected to produce. The king, for his part, was asked to pay for the fitting-out of the ships, the equipment and supplies needed for the voyage and the guns and munitions required for the defence of the settlement. The treasury would also provide the pay for the officers and soldiers sent to the Malouines for their defence – if these men remained in France, Bougainville and his cousin pointed out, the Crown would still have to pay them. As for the colonists, if, as Louis suggested, they were displaced Acadians, they were already being helped financially by the government. If the state continued to pay them the same amount, they would not represent any increased burden on the treasury.

Louis was quite eloquent in putting forward this argument, which he knew was in line with Choiseul's own concerns. The minister had set aside a village for these refugees close to his own château at Chanteloup, and only a few months earlier he had appointed a government servant, Antoine Lemoyne, to supervise and assist the various 'Acadian and Canadian families scattered in various places and ports of the kingdom'. Choiseul had also already written to the administrators of the ports of Rochefort and Saint-Malo, asking them to encourage these unfortunates to emigrate. He explained that the king would continue to pay the '6 sols per person they were granted' for the first quarter of 1763. After that, they would be offered the chance of settling in various French colonies, and if they accepted they would continue to receive their allowance and be provided with other small grants, including a fitting-out grant for each family before their departure. They would receive a free passage and free food until they reached the colony. It would be simple enough, Louis pointed out, to add the Malouine Islands to the list of colonies, and obtain an adequate number of settlers for the isolated outpost.

The second problem was more delicate. The islands were claimed both by Spain (who called them the Malvinas) and by England. Madrid's claim was based partly on their geographical proximity to the South American continent, and on the line of demarcation that Pope Alexander VI had drawn up in 1493 to prevent disputes arising between Portugal and Spain. This, the so-called Treaty of Tordesillas, was no longer recognised by England, which had long since broken with Rome and rejected papal authority, or by France, which had settled in Canada since the beginning of the sixteenth century. When Spain's Charles V had objected to French encroachments on what were considered Spanish territories, Francis I had replied, 'The sun shines for me as it does for others, and I would dearly like to see the clause in Adam's will that excludes me from a share of the world.'[6]

But Spain also had claims based on prior discovery. This was not easy to argue impartially, because the early discoverers of the islands had not brought back much reliable information. Louis, with Nerville listening and backing him from time to time with his trained lawyer's mind, outlined the various claims. Choiseul needed to be aware of the full picture – and it was a complex one.

Amerigo Vespucci was possibly the first to have sighted the islands, in 1502, but he was an Italian. He could, and should, be kept out of the equation. Magellan probably saw them in 1519, but he was a Portuguese, although he was working for Spain. A stronger claim for discovery could be put forward on behalf of a Spaniard, Alonso de Camargo, in 1540. One of the ships from his expedition, which had been sent out by the Bishop of Plasencia, may have sailed close to the archipelago and may even have sent some men ashore, for the accounts, although confused and confusing, contain descriptions of the shore, birds and seals that corresponded to those of the Falklands. Nevertheless, the Spanish had not bothered to revisit the islands or ensure that they were legally incorporated into their South American possessions: 'Not until the exploits of British navigators in these waters had awakened in the Spanish an understanding of the importance of controlling the southern passage to the Pacific were fleets again fitted out to perfect and strengthen the Spanish hegemony'.[7]

The first of these English navigators may have been John Davis, who sailed from Plymouth in 1591 with Thomas Cavendish, became separated from him and eventually was 'driven in among certain Isles never before discovered'. Then, in 1594, Richard Hawkins reached the Patagonian coast and recorded that he subsequently discovered an unknown land which he named Hawkins' Maiden Land, in honour of Queen Elizabeth. Although British writers were prompt to claim that Davis and Hawkins had come upon the Falkland Islands, their vague descriptions make this hard to accept. The only undisputed first sighting of the archipelago by an Englishman was that of John Strong who, in 1689, spent six days among the islands and went ashore in what he named Falkland Sound, the name later applied to the entire group.

However, it already had a name – the Sebald Islands, after the Dutchman Sebald de Weert, whose *Geloof* reached the western islands of the archipelago in 1600. They appeared under this name on Dutch maps, and their existence was confirmed in 1614 by the expedition of Willem Schouten and Jacob Le Maire. There could be no doubt about their existence – nor indeed about their barrenness and their uninhabited state: for years, navigators viewed them only as useful seamarks or places suitable for a brief call.

A number of countries could therefore lay some claim to the archipelago under the heading of first discoverers: Spain, Holland, Britain, and even Italy and Portugal – although the last two claimants might be stretching things a little.

Then came the French. At the beginning of the eighteenth century, an extensive series of French voyages to the South Pacific began. In 1701 Jacques Beauchesne-Gouin landed on an island that became known – and remains known – as Beauchesne Island. Others soon followed. They reported that fresh water was available, and countered the general impression that the archipelago was a bleak, windswept and inhospitable group on which nothing much was likely to grow, apart from rank grass and stunted shrubs. This widening knowledge and these encouraging reports would, in time, reassure Bougainville and his partners.

French voyages to the Pacific ceased around the 1720s. It was becoming evident by then that the Spanish empire was weakening, and that Madrid's monopoly in the Pacific was coming to an end. France and Britain were cautiously manoeuvring to fill the resulting vacuum, and the Falklands would play a significant role.

Anson's 1740–4 South Seas expedition, though plagued by various failures, had succeeded in capturing rich prizes at the expense of Spain and in sacking the Peruvian port of Paita. More important in the present context was Anson's suggestion that Britain secure a base for future operation in the south-west Atlantic. He hesitated between Pepys Island, which English explorer Ambrose Cowley had described in glowing – and quite misleading – terms, and the Falklands, but he urged his government to send out an expedition that would survey both groups: 'If, on examination, one or both of these places should appear proper for the purpose intended, it is scarcely to be conceived of what prodigious import a convenient station might prove so far to the southward, and so near to Cape Horn'.[8]

When this was published, with the likelihood that the British Admiralty would support the idea, the Spanish ambassador to the Court of St James lodged a strong protest, stressing that this would infringe Spanish rights over the islands. The Spanish foreign minister made a similar protest to the British ambassador in Madrid. Since Britain did not then wish to upset relations with Spain, Anson's proposal was dropped. In 1750, however, new rumours arose of British preparations for an expedition to the Falklands. This led to another flurry of protests. There was no expedition, but Madrid had a new occasion to complain in 1753, when a chart, published with the Admiralty's endorsement, showed the Falklands as a British possession.

The Seven Years War soon followed this period of pinpricks, so the matter of the Falklands dropped out of sight altogether, and in 1762 Anson died. Britain had other problems to deal with, including absorbing into her overseas empire a number of territories captured during the war.

The situation changed a little in 1761 when France and Spain signed the Family Compact, binding the two Bourbon-ruled countries to pursue the war together and defend their joint interests. This spirit of co-operation continued after the war ended. Consequently, when Bougainville put forward his Malouines plan, Choiseul did not feel that the Spanish king would raise any strong objections to their colonisation by his French cousin. After all, Bougainville was planning to establish a small colony on uninhabited islands that Spain had never really had any use for. Choiseul was sufficiently convinced by these arguments to seek Louis XV's approval, but he did tell Bougainville to observe the utmost discretion and keep his preparations as secret as possible. There was no point in alerting the English, and even less in disturbing the good relations Choiseul was endeavouring to maintain between Madrid and Paris. Once the colony was established, the British and Spanish might accept the inevitable. *Un fait accompli* is, after all, a French expression.

Bougainville was told to restrain his enthusiasm and place a limit on his ambition, at least for the moment. Bases overseas would be useful, but he had to remember that the navy was in a depressed state and ill-equipped to sail to colonies and protect them. 'Before annexing continents and islands, one needed to build up one's seapower. In 1763, we had no more than 40 ships, in a poor condition.'[9]

Bougainville then wrote a revised proposal, which he sent to Choiseul through Accaron: 'My lord Anson, in the account of his voyage around the world, urges the English on several occasions to form an establishment to the south of Brazil, claiming that the nation that sets up such an establishment will control trade in the South Seas'. He could have added: 'and trade in the Indian Ocean'.

Accaron explained that 'Mr de B.' was seeking the ministry's permission for just such an expedition, 'at his own cost and that of his close relatives'. A twenty-four-gun frigate and an eight-gun ketch would leave in August, taking food supplies to last fifteen months. 'They would first of all look for the Malouine Islands, situated some 150 leagues south-east of the River Plate. They would spend two months acquiring a detailed knowledge of them.' Then they would search for the southern land, 'believed to be situated approximately 3 to 400 leagues south-south-east of the Malouines Islands'.[10] Accaron (and Louis) stressed that a settlement, 'either on the Malouine Islands, or in the part of the southern land they are confident to discover, would be of immense benefit to France'.

And Louis went on to list the advantages: a safe port of call for ships engaged on the India trade and a valuable base in wartime, great opportunities for whale and seal hunting, a healthy climate, comparable to Canada's, consequently offering valuable facilities for agriculture and forestry, and an invaluable training ground for sailors. If France wished to keep these discoveries secret, this would present no problem. In this respect, Bougainville was rather optimistic: nothing is more difficult than preventing sailors or indeed their officers from gossiping once they have returned home.

Choiseul was satisfied that it would be possible to keep the plans a secret until after the expedition had sailed. On 10 May 1763, he wrote on Accaron's accompanying report: 'Approved. Let Mr de Bougainville receive by way of loan, against his receipt, all that he requires in the way of military equipment.'[11] The expedition Louis and his brother had been thinking about for years, and which he had planned in detail with his cousin, was now turning into reality. It had taken almost six months, from the time of his first proposal to the final acceptance.

Bougainville now wasted no time. He needed a second-in-command with a sound knowledge of navigation. He had already approached his old mentor Duclos-Guyot, who had agreed, and recruited his brother Alexandre, who had considerable experience in southern waters. Together, they had obtained a new frigate and a small corvette, which were being completed in Saint-Malo. Things could now go ahead, and Bougainville wrote to the *intendant* at Brest, who had responsibility for most of the shipyards in Brittany, asking him to provide the brothers with everything they needed to complete the work. To command the second ship, Louis approached Antoine Thévenard, with whom he had discussed Pacific exploration. But Thévenard refused. He was not in favour of setting up a colony on the Malouines and he preferred to wait until the go-ahead could be given for a voyage to the South Seas, which he hoped to lead.

Louis then had to formalise the financial arrangements. As promised to Choiseul, a *Compagnie de Saint-Malo* had been set up, with a capital of 200,000 *livres*. He contributed 95,000 *livres*, his cousin Bougainville de Nerville 70,000, his uncle Jean-Potentien d'Arboulin 31,000 and a friend of the family, Claude Henri Feydeau de Marville, 4000.

The two ships had to be named. It was decided that the frigate would be called *L'Aigle*, the Eagle. This had been the name of Bouvet de Lozier's ship and it was also the French translation of the Dutch *Arend*, Roggeween's ship on his 1722 voyage across the Pacific. It was also a good choice because the Bougainville family's arms included an eagle. For the second ship, the name *Sphinx* was selected. It was intended to symbolise the secret aims of the expedition, which were not to be divulged.

To captain the *Sphinx* Duclos-Guyot suggested François Chesnard de la Giraudais, a man of thirty-four who had been at sea since the age of five, when his father took him on his ship. He was widely experienced, having crossed the Atlantic on a number of occasions and served in both the War of the Austrian Succession and the Seven Years War. He had particularly distinguished himself during the Canadian conflict. In 1760 he had commanded the *Machault*, the last vessel to bring a convoy of merchantmen into the St Lawrence estuary, and returned to France after the fall of Montreal with Vaudreuil's final reports.

What Bougainville and his fellow shareholders now needed was a clear understanding with Choiseul on what the *Compagnie de Saint-Malo* would pay for and what the government would provide. This required yet another formal document, a *Mémoire sur différents objets relatifs à l'expédition des navires* L'Aigle *et* Le Sphinx, *actuellement en armement à Saint-Malo*. It contained six different sections, each one carefully highlighted: permission to bring back a cargo of coffee and other items from the Indian Ocean, which currently fell under the monopoly granted to the French India Company; a request that the maritime authorities recruit 'men of good will' for the expedition, without letting them know what the aim of the voyage really was; a request for the king to supply some forty men, half of them soldiers, half of them Acadians, and the secondment of a young officer named Charles-Denis de Saint-Simon, who had served with distinction and initiative in the Canadian conflict; and the appointment of a young engineer-geographer for survey and cartography work, and of a botanist with medical training. The government would also provide medical supplies, some light guns, as well as a number of books and maps relating to the route around Cape Horn.

The fifth section requested temporary naval and other commissions for several of the officers: for Duclos-Guyot, the rank of fireship captain; for La Giraudais, a similar appointment, or at least the rank of frigate lieutenant; for Thisbé de Belcour, who was to command the troops, the rank of army captain; and for Saint-Simon, the rank of army lieutenant. Bougainville himself asked, in the final section, for the rank of *capitaine de vaisseau*, the nearest equivalent to the army rank of colonel, which he had reached in February 1759.

Choiseul approved all these requests, with the exception of the appointment of a captain to command the troops: 'I am not aware that troops are to be part of this expedition. It is not a question of conquering, but of discovering.'[12]

Things were now moving quickly. Louis went up to Saint-Malo and stayed with Duclos-Guyot, who took him to the shipyards and showed him the work in progress. He was welcomed everywhere: his reputation had preceded him and his links with the Minister of Marine and other personalities in Paris opened every door for him. His closest friend, 'Maman' Hérault's son Jean-Baptiste, had married a daughter of the Magon family, one of the most influential in the district. Although she had withdrawn from society, her relatives did everything in their power to assist him.

Louis sat down to write a detailed letter to his brother, keen for Jean-Pierre to share his excitement. But when Louis reached Paris on 24 June he discovered that his brother had died two days before. The funeral had taken place at Loches even as Louis was travelling back to the capital. He was deeply affected by this loss. Jean-Pierre had been his close friend and collaborator, and now he could not even give him a last report on the great undertaking. His brother had made sure that his death would not cause Louis to delay his departure to help deal with his estate: knowing that his end was near, he had ensured that his will was up-to-date and that all his affairs were in order.

In spite of his poor health, Jean-Pierre de Bougainville had built up a solid reputation among the writers and academics of his day. He did have his enemies, however. Voltaire, for example, wrote of him: 'This Bougainville was a wretched individual, a paltry fellow known only for the dull translation of a dull poem.' Others dismissed his death as no loss to the French Academy – 'a gap that will soon be filled'.[13] Behind these comments lay the struggle between the pro-church party and the largely anti-clerical *philosophes*. Jean-Pierre belonged to the former grouping. He was a retiring, devout man, something of a semi-puritan Jansenist, as well as a supporter of the Queen's party. One might say today that he was a traditional conservative by nature, disliked by a growing party of free-thinking liberals.

Bougainville spent the month of July in Paris, with the exception of a brief visit to Compiègne where the court was spending part of the summer. He spent most of this time finalising the various appointments.

Choiseul had found him Lhuillier de la Serre for the position of engineer-geographer. He was a talented young man of around thirty, who had drawn maps of Touraine, but had been transferred to the army during the recent war. He had been badly wounded, but recovered sufficiently to serve under the Maréchal de Soubise who thought highly of him. There was no problem with Saint-Simon, 'a six-foot tall Colossus', although he still had unfinished business in Canada, where he planned to return. Given the option of going back to Canada or joining the Falklands expedition, he decided on the latter. He was appointed second-in-command to Bougainville de Nerville, commanding officer in the Malouine Islands. De Belcour, who had served under Bougainville in Canada and 'shown both bravery and intelligence',[14] was only too glad to be offered a new position as officer in charge of the small detachment of troops. He had gone briefly to Newfoundland with the Chevalier de Ternay, and he was able to join an expedition to Rio de Janeiro when the war had ended. Since then, he had been largely unemployed and 'was perishing of destitution'.

Louis had no one especially in mind for the post of naturalist. At his wife's suggestion, Choiseul put forward the name of Dom Antoine-Joseph Pernetty, a Dominican monk and an acquaintance of Madame du Deffand. He was talented and popular, an artist, well learned in the natural sciences, and he could double as the expedition's chaplain.

Pernetty was also rather an oddball. Not only had he written a *Manuel bénédictin* and a *Dictionnaire portatif de peinture, sculpture et gravure*, but also *Fables égyptiennes et grecques dévoilées*, a work on the link between Egyptian and Greek fables, in which he put forward the theory that Homer had travelled to Egypt to study alchemy, and that the *Odyssey* and the *Iliad* could be regarded as allegorical works on alchemy and the occult. He believed in ghosts, was working on a *Dictionnaire mytho-hermétique*, and carried a tooth, set in gold, which was said to have belonged to Heloïse, the lover of the hapless Abélard. He was, however, a pleasant companion to have on board and would prove to be a keen observer and commentator. Admittedly, some of his speculations about what he saw were a little peculiar: he wondered whether the porpoise had evolved from the whale, whether the Persians might not have descended from the Patagonians, and whether Laplanders were descendants of the Persians.

He had little connection with the sea and, according to one story, he had been lured by Bougainville on board his ship and held there until dinner was over and the vessel was well out to sea. This is quite improbable, as the ship would have been in Saint-Malo at the time and Pernetty lived near Paris. The tale may, however, have originated with Pernetty himself, on some occasion when friends or colleagues asked what on earth could have induced him to join an expedition to some bleak and scarcely known archipelago in the distant South Atlantic.

Everything was now in place. Louis had gone to Compiègne at the beginning of August for a final meeting with Choiseul. They settled the few outstanding points, and agreed on the final instructions. Then Choiseul took him to call on Louis XV, who handed him a letter formalising the arrangements:

> Mr de Bougainville, I am writing this letter to inform you that my wish is that you should proceed to Saint Malo to take over command of the frigate *Aigle*, in which you will embark, and of the corvette *Sphinx* commanded by Lieutenant de La Giraudais, to sail for the regions mentioned in your instructions and carry out the observations I have requested you to make. And these presents being for that purpose, I pray God that He will keep you, Mr de Bougainville, under His Holy Protection. Signed at Compiègne the 14th August 1763.[15]

13. A Settlement on the Malouines

September 1763–March 1764

On 25 August 1763, Louis de Bougainville arrived back in Saint-Malo, and went at once to see his ships. The preparations for departure were almost complete. The *Aigle* was a fine frigate of 300 tons, solidly built, part of the naval expansion programme that Choiseul had already set in motion. Duclos-Guyot showed Louis around and introduced other members of his family. Louis had already met Pierre-Nicolas's elder brother Alexandre; now he was presented to his two sons, Pierre and Alexandre, who held the rank of ensign. One of the apprentices, the youthful Michel Seigneurie, was also a member of the Guyot family.

Another apprentice was the promising young Charles Fesche. The lieutenants were Michel Sirandré and Chesnard de la Giraudais's cousin, Marin-Éloi. The second lieutenants were Pierre Marie Lavarye-Leroy and Antoine Semon, the third ensigns were the Breton René-Jean Hercouët and Guillaume Bombard, the clerk René-André Oury, and the ship's surgeon Pierre Montclair. Four men, civilians or army personnel, were also included: Bougainville de Nerville, Thisbé de Belcour, the geographer Lhuillier de la Serre and Dom Pernetty, 'employed by the King to carry out observations'.[1] There were also a group of twenty Acadians, mostly artisans who could double as a garrison if needed, and three Acadian or Canadian family groups totalling fifteen people.

The total complement of the *Aigle* was 132, less one sailor who deserted before the ships left port. This compared with a total complement of thirty-six on the *Sphinx*. Again, members of the captains' families were on board: the senior lieutenant, Henri Donat, was a relative of La Giraudais, as was Joseph Donat, a second lieutenant, while Jean-Baptiste Duclos-Guyot was another son of the *Aigle*'s captain. The *Sphinx*, a 125-ton corvette, was a smaller vessel, carrying a mere eight guns, compared with the *Aigle*'s twenty. Saint-Simon sailed in the corvette: he held the rank of infantry lieutenant, but Bougainville had promised him the eventual rank of captain.

A naming ceremony was necessary for the two ships. Bougainville chose the

Feast of Saint Louis, 25 August, which was his name day – his *fête* – and the king's. It was carried out, as Pernetty recorded, 'with all the pomp that is customary in such circumstances, and during Mass the two ships fired two general salvoes, one in honour of God and the other for the King'.[2]

There were a few more preparations still to be made. The crews, soldiers and passengers settled on board during the next few days, and the ships were ready to sail by 1 September. But there was a further delay as Bougainville and Nerville had some last-minute financial arrangements to settle. Papers had to be signed and some documents had to arrive from Paris. This took another week – and then there was the usual wait for a favourable wind.

These delays gave Bougainville an opportunity to meet an old naval personality, retired in Saint-Malo, Bénard de la Harpe. The old man had sailed to Peru sixty years earlier, and he had even married there. On the way back, he had rounded Cape Horn, passed by the Falklands and gone on to Mauritius in the Indian Ocean. He had reservations about the existence of a southern continent south and east of the Cape of Good Hope; his time in Peru had convinced him that the southern land lay somewhere in the Pacific Ocean, and he had on several occasions endeavoured to persuade the French authorities to back a voyage of exploration in the South Seas. La Harpe played a significant role in sowing doubts in Bougainville's mind about the direction he should take once the Malouines colony was settled. The Indian Ocean route might be far less productive than he had once imagined: the Pacific Ocean might well offer far more.

Finally, during the night of 9 September, the two ships set off. But what Duclos-Guyot had taken for a favourable breeze proved unhelpful the moment they reached the open sea, and they were forced to shelter in one of the nearby bays. It gave time for Louis to head up and begin his shipboard log:

> Journal of my campaigns at sea during the years 1763–1764 and 1765, commanding with the warrant of captain the frigate *Aigle* and the corvette *Sphinx*, built and fitted out at my expense and that of Mr de Nerville, my cousin, who sailed with me, and Mr D'Arboulin, my uncle, and taken into the King's service without cost to us.[3]

There was little else to record yet. There had been a few problems on board, partly due to inaction, personal problems and probably boredom. An Acadian family asked to be put ashore. Bougainville allowed them to keep the money they had been given in expectation of their settling in the Falklands. The ensign Bombard, who was ill, was also sent ashore, and Lhuillier de la Serre's servant was dismissed for laziness and incompetence. It was not until 22 September that the breeze finally veered in their favour and the ships could begin their journey.

For people unaccustomed to long sea journeys, like Pernetty and Nerville, the departure from France opened up a new world. Once the coastline had vanished in the distant horizon, they found themselves totally isolated from the rest of humanity.

They were living in cramped conditions that would have been fairly familiar to the lower classes, used to living in small farm cottages or shared tumbledown houses in the cities, but were a rude shock to those who lived in substantial homes or abbeys. Even so, unlike the sailors and the soldiers, they had their own cabins, tiny and uncomfortable though they were. Even less familiar was their separation from the world they had known. Unable to communicate with anyone outside the confines of the ship, they had no idea of what might be happening elsewhere. For all they knew, Europe could again be at war, and any ship they might meet could be an enemy. Pestilence and famine might be spreading through the lands they were sailing to, or revolution might have broken out.

On 2 October, three ships hove into sight, one of which had clearly suffered storm damage. Bougainville came up within hailing distance and asked whether she needed help. The vessel, which had just hauled up Dutch colours, shouted back that it came from Curaçao and expected to be able to make a French port without difficulty, since it had already sailed across much of the Atlantic with its makeshift masting.

A few days later, the French ships were sailing in waters where pirates from the Moroccan port of Sale were known to operate. The appearance of a suspicious vessel on 5 October worried Bougainville sufficiently for him to plan a defensive strategy in case of attack. The *Sphinx* would hoist English colours and pretend to be fleeing from the *Aigle*, which was to fly the French flag. They would manoeuvre around the possible enemy, and when they were both in position the *Sphinx* would haul down its English ensign and raise the French colours. There was little gallantry in flying false flags, but it was by no means unusual. As it turned out, the stranger flew an English flag. Shouted questions in French got no response, whereupon Thisbé de Belcour, who spoke adequate English, called out in 'maritime English'. The stranger replied that they had just left Lisbon and were on their way to the Azores. The alert passed off without any further incident. However, Bougainville decided that it was unwise to keep too close to the African coast, and a few days later they veered south-west to cross the Atlantic.

Working out one's position at sea was another mystery for Pernetty and his friends.

Bougainville explained to them in layman's terms what he himself had learnt on his crossings of the Atlantic. It was not too difficult to find a ship's latitude – the distance north or south from the equator. This was worked out by calculating the sun's altitude at midday or observing known stars. Longitude was another matter. This is an imaginary line that runs down from the North Pole to the south. Allowing for the earth's rotation, one can estimate the distance east or west from one's point of departure or, more usually, from Paris. By comparing the local time with that of Paris, one could estimate fairly accurately a ship's longitude. The point of intersection of a ship's latitude and longitude gave you its position.

The problem was knowing what the time was back in Paris, something that was possible only if one had a clock that worked properly on board a ship. The pendulum clocks of the period were hopeless on a vessel that rolled and pitched with every wave. The general alternative was a sandglass that took half an hour to empty. Eight turns of the glass equated to a four-hour watch, which was adequate – except that sailors, being human, often shortened their time on watch by upturning the glass before it was empty. It was possible to rectify the position by checking the log against the midday sun, but clouds do not always part at the required moment. Thus it was that in 1713 the Saint-Malo privateer René Duguay-Trouin found that his ship's time was eleven hours fast after only eight days.

During his time in London, Bougainville had heard many discussions about the problem of timekeeping at sea. Back in 1714 the British Parliament had offered a large sum, £20,000, to anyone who could solve the problem. Yorkshire watchmaker John Harrison claimed in 1735 to have built a new watch, a 'chronometer', that could resist the movement of a ship and the expansion of metal parts caused by changes of temperature. Tests over the following few years seemed to back his claim, but not all scientists and seagoing captains were convinced.

Although Harrison had produced a much improved model in 1761, it had not yet been fully tested and was not available in France in 1763 when the *Aigle* and the *Sphinx* sailed from Saint-Malo. Calculations remained complex and unreliable and, as Bougainville explained to Pernetty, early navigators often had no idea of the distances they had travelled. This had resulted in many inaccuracies on sea charts, including reports of legendary islands in the Pacific and elsewhere. These, he pointed out, could include the mysterious southern continent. But there was no need to worry about the voyage to the Falklands. Bougainville was a skilled mathematician and Duclos-Guyot an experienced seaman, and together they were confident that they were making good progress along a route which, after all, was not unknown.

Food was another problem. When the capricious winds command, one cannot estimate the length of a voyage. To be safe, captains crammed food and water casks in every possible nook and cranny. Live poultry, pigs and cattle were tethered or placed in crates on deck and elsewhere. These, with the stock of spare ropes and sails, the passengers' luggage and the sailors' few belongings, as well as the material and supplies needed to start a colonial settlement on an uninhabited group of islands, crowded the ship to such an extent that those not needed to sail the ship did not know where to spend their days.

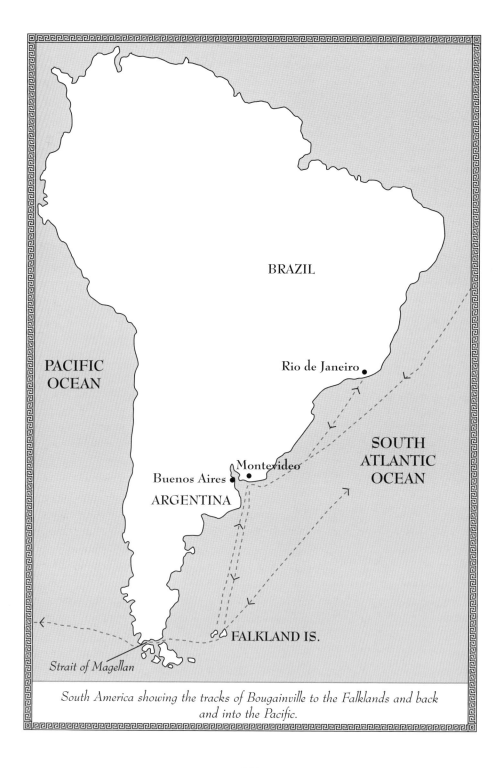

South America showing the tracks of Bougainville to the Falklands and back and into the Pacific.

To make matters worse, the food soon began to go bad. Men like Duclos-Guyot and La Giraudais had enough experience to make sure that they were not cheated by suppliers – who, knowing that a vessel would be away for many months, increased their profit by loading cheap and bad food whenever they could get away with it. Even so, after a few weeks, often after the livestock had been killed and eaten, it was discovered that the flour and grain were going bad. Comments by a nineteenth-century admiral show how bad life on board could be even a century after Bougainville's time:

> The biscuit has been invaded by myriads of larvae and insects. The cakes, riddled through, crumble into dust as soon as we touch them. These microscopic insects have become horribly troublesome; they fly about everywhere, and one cannot breathe without the risk of absorbing some through the mouth or the nostrils. To this plague another, no less unpleasant, has been added. The cockroaches have multiplied with such fertility that the corvettes became infested with them in a very short time; the rats for their part have multiplied with no less success. All these animals cause a nauseating smell inside the ships.[4]

Things did not improve until François Appert discovered the process of food canning at the beginning of the nineteenth century. Until then, captains had to rely on finding a place of call where fresh fruit, meat and vegetables might be obtained, and the water casks cleaned and refilled. These searches for 'refreshments' were often dangerous, as the locals, indigenous or colonists, were suspicious of strangers and often attacked them.

The bad food situation that developed on so many ships a few weeks after leaving port was the cause of the diseases that often affected crews and passengers: dysentery, fevers of various kinds and, above all, scurvy, which had been a plague of mariners since ancient times. Throughout the sixteenth, seventeenth and eighteenth centuries, when long-distance navigation became possible, an estimated three million sailors worldwide developed scurvy, and about a third of them died of it. It even affected convicts in prisons and soldiers on long campaigns. It was the result of an insufficiency of vitamin C, but this was not known until the early twentieth century. Although people were aware in Bougainville's day that a poor diet was an important contributing factor, the prevalence of scurvy among sailors gave rise to the belief that sea air was the main trouble; hence the care taken by captains to provide frequent opportunities for the crews to take exercise ashore. This had obvious beneficial effects – because it coincided with the purchase of much-needed supplies that included greens and fruit – and so the view that 'land air' was the best cure was reinforced.

Walks ashore were certainly better than the bleedings and purgatives used by eighteenth-century doctors, which rarely had any beneficial effect on the weakened crews. If anything, they hastened their deaths. There would be little improvement until well into the nineteenth century, as is made clear from a graphic report by a ship's surgeon, a member of Nicolas Baudin's 1800–4 expedition to Australia:

> The number of sick was increasing every day. Swellings covered by black scabs appeared on various parts of their bodies, the skin revealed small wine-coloured stains at the root of the hairs; their joints stiffened, their flexor muscles seemed to shorten and held their limbs half bent. But nothing was more hideous than the appearance of their face: to the leaden expression of victims of scurvy was added the prominence of gums jutting out of the mouth, which itself showed ulcerated spots. The sick gave out a foetid smell, which, when you breathed it, seemed to attack the very root of life.[5]

Responsible captains did whatever they could to preserve their crew's health, and Louis earned a reputation as one of the best of his time. They endeavoured to keep the areas below deck as clean as possible, sprinkling water and vinegar to reduce the stench and 'purify' the air, encouraged personal cleanliness and provided the men with opportunities to wash their clothes, and kept the hatches open whenever the weather permitted.

Accidents, however, could not always be prevented. The men had to clamber up the riggings and furl or unfurl the sails, whatever the weather. On 30 October, one of the *Aigle*'s boys fell overboard and, in spite of every effort, he vanished in the heaving seas. Pernetty recorded the scene that followed: the lad's few belongings were auctioned among the crew. Normally, the meagre proceeds would be kept, to be handed over in due course to his heirs, but in this case he had none: 'Mr de Bougainville bought almost everything and gave the proceeds to the poorest and most hardworking boys'.[6]

A little later, as the *Aigle* – the slower *Sphinx* had been left behind to catch up later – reached what was reckoned to be the equator, Pernetty witnessed another custom of the sea. He was so impressed by the jollity and buffoonery marking the crossing of the line that he devoted an entire chapter to it. Anyone, whether sailor, soldier, officer or passenger, who had not yet crossed the equator, was singled out for special treatment. The 'baptism' varied according to status: the rough handling, often close to bullying, meted out to the lower ranks had to be restrained when it came to their superiors. A gift of money made to the *Bonhomme La Ligne* – Old Man Equator – and his acolytes ensured a gentler approach.

The senior officers and passengers who had never yet crossed the line included Bougainville himself, Nerville, Thisbé de Belcour, Lhuillier de la Serre and Pernetty, as well as the Acadian families. A red ribbon was tied to their left thumb, which was fixed to a sounding-rope symbolising the line. The whole ship's complement gathered to witness the ceremony and to join in the fun as soon as the mock formalities were over.

A decorated crate served as the throne. It was placed next to a large vat filled with seawater used for the baptismal ritual. Then *Bonhomme La Ligne* appeared, announced by a herald accompanied by the ship's boys who were baptised with bucketfuls of water. One of the apprentices, who had upset his fellows in some way, was thrown bodily into the vat. All were adorned in a burlesque manner, with a proliferation of feathers, animal skins and paint. Louis went through the ceremony in good humour, taking the required oath to respect the wives and girlfriends of sailors the world over, and to ensure that he would allow the same ceremonial to be carried out whenever a ship under his command crossed the equator. This done, he was sprinkled with a little water on the forehead and he dropped his offering into the collection plate. The day ended with much throwing of water and traditional sailors' songs and dances.

Pernetty could not help himself from speculating about the tradition. He put down its origin to Vasco da Gama's voyage of 1497 and explained that 'it lessened the boredom that develops during any lengthy navigation', and that it 'arose from a certain republican attitude of mind that is present in all small societies'.[7] This latter comment, with its undercurrent of sociology, was fairly typical of the *philosophes*, and would reappear in later years, when Bougainville was faced with the theory of the noble savage.

The voyage continued without incident for the rest of November, with still no sign of the lagging *Sphinx* and only one sail appearing briefly along the horizon. Although Louis considered the French charts unreliable, he was gradually coming up to the coast of Brazil, and on the evening of the 29th he sighted an island that was soon identified as Santa Catarina, just off the coast of Brazil, which was then a Portuguese possession. The crossing from Saint-Malo had taken ten weeks.

Relations between France and Portugal had been fairly strained over the centuries. The French were currently allied to Spain, a situation which, with some fluctuations, had lasted for most of the century. Portugal, on the other hand, remained suspicious of Spain, by which it had been taken over for some sixty years – from 1580 to 1640. Portuguese trade had become closely linked with England, France's traditional enemy, and back in 1710–11 the French had launched serious attacks against Brazil, the second of which, by René Duguay-Trouin, had resulted in the capture of Rio de Janeiro. Things had calmed down over the years, but there was often a feeling of unease or uncertainty when French ships approached a strategic outpost such as Santa Catarina. Louis need not have worried: the reception he received could not have been more friendly.

As the *Aigle* approached, Louis sent off a boat to discuss with the commander of the fort the important matter of gun salutes. This was always an essential aspect of international etiquette. It reflected the state of relations between two countries – or a local port captain's attitude towards a foreign power – and it often led to prickly negotiations and lengthy arguments. In this case, there was no problem. Bougainville offered to salute the fort if the commander agreed to respond with an equal number of shots – anything less could be regarded as an affront. The commander replied that he would respond shot for shot, because the visitor was on a royal mission. This settled, the *Aigle* fired nine shots, and received a salute of nine guns in answer.

These courtesies were followed by official visits to the port commander and to the island's governor. Formal dinners were arranged, with the usual sequence of toasts. The governor offered to provide the French with all the supplies they might require, and placed a large house at their disposal, to act as a base during their stay and to provide a home where the Acadian families, unused to long sea voyages, could rest and recuperate. 'All the Portuguese made us as welcome as we could have wished,' Louis wrote in his journal, 'and our country can only praise the manner in which we have been made at home during this stay.'[8]

The stay lasted a fortnight, with growing cordiality, daily visits and exchanges of gifts. The governor sent cattle and goats to the *Aigle*, as well as 'twenty-six local ducks with large red crests, multicoloured and talking parrots, two Portuguese hunting dogs, and other gifts including some dried toucan skins still with their feathers on'. Bougainville in return gave him 'a large box full of fans and snuff-boxes'. Dom Pernetty was invited to say mass ashore – 'High Mass, followed at midday with a dinner that was as splendid as circumstances allowed'.

Language difficulties did restrict the conversation somewhat. Alexandre Duclos-Guyot was the only officer who spoke adequate Portuguese. Several of the French managed a smattering of Spanish and Portuguese, and most of the Portuguese had some knowledge of French. This, with the plentiful food and flowing wine, ensured a convivial atmosphere. Pernetty met a Franciscan priest and sat next to him at dinner, intending to have a long talk in Latin. Unfortunately, the Portuguese knew very little Latin beyond what his religious duties required, and he fled from the table as soon as he could.

On 15 December, the *Aigle* was ready to sail. It was agreed that, since the decks were now crowded with fresh supplies and livestock, the traditional gun salutes would be omitted. The Portuguese were satisfied with the mutual waving of hats and an exchange of shouted hoorahs between the shore and the deck as the vessel made for the open sea. The time spent in Santa Catarina was fondly remembered by the French, especially as the reception they found in Montevideo was, at least initially, much cooler than they expected.

The crossing took only a week, but a violent storm assailed the ship and prevented a satisfactory landing until the 28th, when it was possible to anchor outside the city. The governor was courteous, but suspicious of French intentions. He was afraid that they might been planning to start trading, which would be a breach of local regulations, and he ordered guards to follow the French wherever they went. A boat was lowered to go fishing: Spanish dragoons followed it and attempted to confiscate it. Bougainville went to complain to the governor and pointed out that the *Aigle* was a naval vessel sent out under the king's authority, and not a merchantmen looking for a trading opportunity. It took him some time to get his argument over, but the potential breach was patched up.

At the time, the Spanish were at loggerheads with the Jesuits, who controlled large missionary estates in South America. This became evident when senior Jesuits began to approach the French. Louis thought it wiser not to get involved. The Jesuits invited Dom Pernetty to meet them, but he was a Benedictine, an order that was not kindly disposed towards Jesuits. The invitation was declined. Then the Jesuits asked Thisbé de Belcour to take over command of their forces in Paraguay. Belcour refused to break his agreement with Bougainville, whereupon – at least according to Pernetty – they attempted to carry him off by force.

Bougainville had really come to Montevideo to await the slower *Sphinx*. He did obtain flour and rice in exchange for French wine, but only with difficulty, and he was greatly relieved when the *Sphinx* finally appeared on the horizon on 31 December and came to anchor near the *Aigle*.

It was time for the New Year celebrations. There was a dinner at the governor's, attended by both captains and all their officers. Relations between the Spanish and the French had greatly improved, and further visits were made during the following fortnight, as well as excursions on horseback in the surrounding countryside. These social exchanges provided an opportunity for Pernetty to observe the young city – Montevideo had been founded less than forty years earlier – and its inhabitants. Drawing also from the observations of earlier visitors, he wrote a lengthy chapter on the colony for his *Histoire d'un voyage*:

> The Spaniards of Montevideo are very lazy ... The men who are not involved in business get up very late, as do their wives. They then spend their time with their arms folded until they feel like going to smoke a cigale [sic] with their neighbour. You often see four or five of them standing in a doorway, smoking and talking. Others go on horseback, not for a ride in the country but for a saunter around the streets. If they feel like it, they get down and join those they meet, chat without saying anything in particular, drink maté tea and get back on their horse. Very seldom does a Spaniard go on foot and, in the streets, you meet as many horses as men.

As for the women, they spend long hours sitting down, playing the guitar or some other instrument, singing or drinking maté.[9]

Pernetty was fascinated by the cigars, which, apparently, he had not heard of before. 'They do not smoke pipes in Montevideo or in the Spanish colonies in America. They smoke lengths of tobacco, which they call cigars, or *cigals* or *sigares*. These are small cylinders six or seven inches in length and about an inch in diameter, made up of tobacco leaves rolled together.' Although not fond of the Jesuits, he got on well with a Franciscan who was tutoring the governor's son and with whom he discussed physics and philosophy. Unlike his Portuguese counterpart, this friar spoke fluent Latin.

On 17 January, the two ships sailed for the Falkland Islands. They carried livestock for the proposed settlement – horses, cattle, even a tame tiger, although what might be done with it when the French built their settlement was not clear. As it turned out, it did not settle easily on the deck of the *Aigle* and had to be put down a week later.

Land was sighted on 31 January. Islands, large and small, came into view, as well as fierce-looking reefs the French took special care to set down on their rough charts. Their cautious approach was not made any easier by a succession of calms that made it difficult to manoeuvre. On 3 February, it was possible to go ashore and begin exploring. The area was bleak: bare land, dank grass, and marshes into which the French sank down to their knees. 'Fortunately,' wrote Pernetty, 'we had brought some small bottles of brandy and a few ship's biscuits, which helped us greatly to face the heat and the weariness.'[10] The bay into which they had sailed was named Luxembourg, after the Maréchal de Luxembourg, and the inner cove Baie Accaron, after Choiseul's helpful and knowledgeable adviser.

It was not until 17 February that Bougainville found a suitable location for a settlement. He was in what is now known as Berkeley Sound – he named it Baie Saint-Louis – on East Falkland, just north of the present capital, Stanley.

I decided to set up the establishment at the back of the bay we had entered. The season, already well advanced, did not allow me to search any longer. On Friday 17th I landed with tents, the families, the cattle and part of the crews, the ships having moved that same day to seek an anchorage within the shelter of the islands. I set up camp by a stream, on a slope sheltered from the prevailing winds. I ordered Mr Lhuiller, the engineer, to draw up plans for a building that would take 30 people as well as the material needed to set up a colony … On the 19th we began to break the ground. On the 24th, five days later, we found a layer of highly combustible peat. I tried it out on a forge erected nearby.[11]

The building was to be a substantial structure, flat-roofed, some 160 feet long and 140 feet wide, built of timber, clay and turf. It would eventually be surrounded by a number of turf huts, built by the colonists, and defended by a small fort. 'The foundations of the fort and some other buildings are still visible.'[12]

Ceremonies were needed to take formal possession of Saint-Louis and indeed of the entire archipelago. Bougainville was setting up what he intended to be a true French colony, a port of call for ships on their way to the Pacific and Indian Oceans. Simply raising the flag was not enough. So on the 26th, when the construction of the fort had progressed sufficiently for him to bring up fourteen guns, he laid the foundations for a commemorative obelisk. On the eastern side, he proposed to place a medallion with the effigy of Louis XV; on the western side would go the French coat of arms.

He then decided that the structure should be topped by a bust of the king. This was not as simple as it sounded: there was plenty of good clay around, but no one had sufficient skill to model Louis XV's features – only Bougainville knew what the king looked like. Describing the royal features to the would-be artist was far from easy. Several attempts failed to produce the desired result, as Dom Pernetty narrated with ill-concealed glee:

> The head, heavily pockmarked, looked like a lump of earth, the body much the same. It was set up on the quarter-deck for a couple of hours, by which time the head had sunk through the body. So that, instead of the intended bust, a double fleur-de-lys was placed on top.[13]

The medallion and the arms presented fewer problems, being carved out of wood by the *Sphinx*'s carpenter. A silver medal, a little under 3 inches in diameter, was then sealed into the monument's base between two sheets of lead. On it had been engraved a long and somewhat pompous message, well summarised by the Latin motto it included, '*Conamur tenues grandia*' (Though small, we attempt mighty tasks). A bottle was then buried by the plaque, containing the list of the officers and men, and of the settlers.

Further work was carried out during March and early April, and supplies were landed for the colonists. It was felt that all this progress should be marked by yet another ceremony, which took place on 5 April. It began with a twenty-one-gun salute, followed by the firing of a few rockets. All the officers in full uniform, as many of the crews as could be spared, and the settlers all gathered for the solemnity. There was another gun salute, then Dom Pernetty began to say High Mass at an altar specially built for the purpose next to the obelisk. This was somewhat spoiled when a strong gale blew up, forcing Pernetty to curtail his service, which amounted largely to the singing of the *Te Deum*.

The medallions were then unveiled, the flag raised over the fort to yet another salvo. There was time for another hymn, followed by 'Long live the king' shouted in unison no fewer that seven times by all the participants. Then the guns once more resounded over the bay. This time, it was the signal for the *Sphinx* to sail out on a voyage to Guadeloupe in the West Indies, where she was to take surplus stores and trade them for needed supplies and for cash.

Louis handed his cousin Nerville the royal warrant appointing him commander of the new colony. This was followed by a formal dinner, during which a succession of personalities in the island and back home were toasted, with yet more firing. The ceremonies came to an end as the sun was setting, marked by the day's fifth full gun salute.

It was now important to report to Paris, so that the authorities could be advised of the expedition's success. Louis would also have to discuss the next stages of the project. The *Aigle* raised anchor on 9 April, leaving twenty-nine people behind, including Bougainville de Nerville as commander and two families of settlers. The voyage was speedy and relatively uneventful. On the 25th, the frigate was in sight of the island of Batz, off the Brittany coast. Louis had himself rowed ashore to Morlaix, then set off at once for Compiègne, where he arrived three days later. He could now report to the minister on the new colony he had created for France.

14. Interlude in France

May–October 1764

When Louis arrived at court, he had been without news of France for almost eight months. There was so much to catch up on, so much whispered gossip he had missed.

The present king's grandfather, Louis XIV, had moved to Versailles from the Louvre in Paris, partly to get away from the sometimes unruly mobs, partly because of his love of the country. He had expanded Versailles into a royal residence, with large reception rooms, as well as apartments for officials and courtiers. In 1682, it became the seat of government. Ironically, he often felt the need to get away from it, going to Compiègne, a peaceful spot north-east of Paris, with acres of forest, quiet rivers and sleeping lakes.

Louis XV was even keener on Compiègne, where he increasingly sought refuge during the summer months – and everyone had to go.

> The royal family, courtiers, Princes of the Blood and ministers got on to the road; followed by the state papers, archives and a great deal of furniture, silver and linen. The whole thing entailed enormous trouble and expense. The King fixed the dates for these journeys at Christmas and nothing but death could alter them.[1]

Somewhat ironically, Louis XV had the château enlarged so that, in time, it resembled a mini-Louvre. In 1751, an elaborate 'grand project' was started under the architect Jacques Gabriel. This was still proceeding when Bougainville visited, and it would continue off and on until the revolution of 1789. Still far smaller than Versailles, Compiègne enabled the king to enjoy a more relaxed atmosphere, surrounded by the officials he needed and by selected courtiers.

The major item of news that greeted Bougainville was the death of the Marquise de Pompadour. She had been unwell for some time and had died on 15 April. The question on everyone's lips was whether this would lead to significant changes in the

French establishment. So many people owed their position to her, among them the Duc de Choiseul and Bougainville himself. As yet, however, nothing had changed. Choiseul was as powerful as ever and Louis XV seemed happy enough to let him retain his influence. There were other problems to deal with, including the ongoing struggle between the king and the local *parlements*, led at the time by Louis-René de la Chalotais, a senior magistrate of the Breton assembly. Because Bougainville had arrived at the beginning of the summer season, things were relatively quiet, but by 7 October Brittany would be in almost open revolt against the royal authority.

In a promotion, Accaron had been moved from his position at the ministry, but he was still able to deal with the question of the Malouines, and Bougainville went to see him almost at once. Together, they worked on finalising Louis's report, which was ready to submit to Choiseul within a couple of days. It was fairly brief, summarising what Bougainville had achieved and putting a number of suggestions: once the king had formally approved the annexation of the Falklands and the Spanish authorities had been notified that this action was in no way a challenge to their South American empire, the islands should be strengthened – further Acadians would be dispatched and new fortifications would be built.

Bougainville and Accaron's report embodied everything that Choiseul had hoped for. Forestalling the British in the South Atlantic was becoming increasingly important. The second stage of their plan – sailing into the Pacific – was not forgotten either. He handed Bougainville a copy of the *Gazette de Hollande* of 15 June featuring a report on preparations being made in England for a small squadron intended to circumnavigate the globe and carry out observations. This was a first indication of the voyage of Commodore John Byron. It added a note of urgency to the French plans.

Telling the Spanish about the occupation of the Falklands was another matter, requiring a tactful approach. Although Choiseul was not Minister for Foreign Affairs – that position was held by his cousin Praslin – he had retained for himself the part of the portfolio that dealt with relations with Spain, partly because of the implications for French world strategy, partly because of the Family Pact linking the two branches of the Bourbon family.

Choiseul and Bougainville consulted the Abbé Augustin de Beliardi, an Italian in the French service who had great experience of the intricacies and subtleties of papal and Spanish politics. He knew how to make his way through the labyrinth of Italo-Spanish relations. Choiseul explained to him that it was becoming urgent to keep the British out of the way. France was Spain's friend and ally, so the occupation of the uninhabited Falklands was in no way a threat, but rather a necessary and friendly move, beneficial to both countries. France was not being greedy, but helpful. For his part, Bougainville stressed that the Spanish clearly had never had any use for the islands, and no real claim to being their first discoverers.

Beliardi smiled at arguments that he considered ingenuous. Playing the role of devil's advocate, he pointed out that Spain did not really consider France her long-term ally: the friendship between the two countries was based on expediency. The Spanish viewed all foreigners in their colonies as intruders who should be kept out at any price, whatever nation they belonged to. It was true that French merchants had been allowed to carry out some trade in Spanish waters at the beginning of the century, but this was viewed as purely temporary, caused by war and soon over. And could one not argue equally plausibly that a true friend would not try to take over the other's territory? As for discovering the Falklands, it was unwise to push that theory too far, for France's own claim was quite thin, and the British and the Dutch could equally well make a similar assertion. Having said all this, Beliardi, with consummate diplomatic tact, offered his services to assist Choiseul in any way he could.

The three men began work on a memoir summarising France's actions and intentions, which Beliardi, who held the rank of consul-general, would personally take to Madrid. It stressed England's designs on the South Seas trade, reminding Spain that these went back to the days of Sir Francis Drake and Sir Walter Raleigh, and that if a British outpost was ever established along the sea route to the Pacific Ocean it would threaten all the South American colonies. The interests of Spain and of France could be safeguarded only by a close co-operation:

> These considerations – and the certainty that the English now wanted to set up an establishment within reach of the South Seas – decided His Most Christian Majesty to forestall them and establish, within reach of the Indian and Southern Oceans, an observation post and to put an end to all the moves made by those ambitious traders.[2]

France then asked for Spain's help in developing the Malouines settlement, undertaking to allow only French or Spanish ships to put into the port that France intended to develop and fortify with Spanish assistance. Choiseul added an important final note that would allow Beliardi more leeway in his negotiations, and give him a line of retreat in the face of possible Spanish intransigence. 'Furthermore,' he wrote, 'France can absolutely not give up this outpost unless she is sure that Spain will settle there in a serious manner.'[3] As it turned out, this would be the solution Madrid eventually favoured.

But before Beliardi could leave for Spain, the Spanish ambassador, the Count of Fuentes, arrived at Compiègne, seeking an urgent meeting with Choiseul. The date was 6 July. The Governor of Montevideo, he told Choiseul, had advised his superiors in Madrid of the arrival of the *Aigle* and the *Sphinx*. Bougainville had told him that they were on the way to the East Indies, but the governor had found this

115

quite puzzling: such a route was very unusual. The King of Spain hoped, Fuentes said, that French captains would be told quite clearly that South America was out of bounds, and that the sensible way to the East was by the Cape of Good Hope. He also reported that rumours had begun to circulate about some takeover in the Malouines.

Choiseul needed all the finesse he could muster to deal with Fuentes's official protest. He gave the ambassador a written reply to the points he had raised, stating that bad weather had forced Bougainville to put into Montevideo. He asked for his thanks to be sent to the governor for the help he had given to the distressed Frenchmen. When Fuentes pressed him about Bougainville's real mission – he must have known that Bougainville was in France – Choiseul added in confidence that there had been hopes of finding some uninhabited island in the South Atlantic that French ships might use as a place of call. Fuentes, well disposed towards France, agreed to Choiseul's request to soft-pedal the issue of a French settlement until Beliardi could explain the situation in person to the court at Madrid.

Within a few days, as Beliardi was travelling to Madrid, new rumours began to circulate in Paris, this time about a colony on the Malouines. On 13 July, the *Gazette de Hollande* published a fairly accurate report of Bougainville's activities, adding the comment that a settlement on the islands was all the more justified in that the 'name of these islands, which are totally deserted, indicates that they were French and that consequently he could take possession of them, as much because of this as being their first settler and that he was to land people of both sexes to set up a colony'.[4]

This comment suggests that the rumours were not simply the result of gossip or careless talk by Bougainville and others, but a news item carefully leaked to a journalist, so that both Spain and Britain would be faced with a *fait accompli*.

Arguments could now be left to the officials and diplomats. Preparations for a return voyage, with supplies and new settlers, were put in hand. Bougainville met Louis XV on 1 August. The king thanked Louis for his work, accepted the formal grant of the new colony and confirmed Nerville's appointment as its administrator. The explorer pushed his luck a little at this stage by asking for permission to undertake the voyage around the world he had always had in mind once the Malouines colony was established. To his delight, his request was accepted, and on 5 August Accaron started work on the necessary arrangements.

Bougainville drew up a formal request for one frigate and two corvettes, to take supplies and men to the Malouines, but also to be available for a lengthy voyage thereafter. His request was promptly acted upon, and Accaron was assured that everything would be ready for a departure date in early October. Choiseul issued instructions for additional settlers and provisions for the Malouines colony.

Bougainville found it less easy to obtain funds for his purchases. An instruction personally issued by the minister to the colonial treasurer for the sum of 10,000 *livres* revealed the parlous state of the government's finances: the money simply was not there. Local borrowings patched the situation up somewhat, but by 14 August it had become clear that a voyage of circumnavigation could not be financed.

Choiseul must have known this. The circumnavigation had now been approved in principle at the highest level: that was the first stage, and he had won it. He knew that the country's finances would not allow the expedition to go ahead at this stage, but it could wait. In the meantime, Louis could get on with consolidating his settlement on the Malouines. As a bonus, he could at least carry out an exploration of part of the Strait of Magellan, where much-needed timber could be obtained. That would be of help when the expedition was finally able to make for the Pacific.

It fell to a senior official, Jean-Baptiste Du Buc, to tell Bougainville, possibly with some satisfaction, as there was some rivalry between the two, that Accaron's attempted arrangements for a lengthy voyage were premature. There was scarcely enough money to pay for the Malouines enterprise. Louis had gone to Saint-Malo on 16 August. A few days after he arrived, the *Sphinx* came into the port – to be put up for sale in order to recoup costs already incurred and to provide funds for refitting the *Aigle*. He then returned to see Choiseul, who by now was back in Versailles, to discover what could be done about the final arrangements. There was sufficient money at least for the voyage to the Malouines. This came from the sale of the *Sphinx*, but also probably from his uncle D'Arboulin and from several other participants in the enterprise. Choiseul felt that Bougainville should sail without wasting any more time. The sooner he left the better, for there were now indications that the British were beginning to challenge French claims to 'their' Falklands.

This was made clear in a 'report from London' published in the *Gazette de la Haye* on 13 August and in the *Gazette d'Amsterdam* the following day, rejecting any claim by the French to have been the first discoverers of the archipelago. The English had been the first to report its existence, followed by the Dutch. 'Captain Hawkins called it Maidensland, the Dutch ... gave it the name of Statenland. The English Captain Sharpe, on his way back from the South Sea in 1681, sailed around it and called it Albermarle, and finally the Dutchman Roggewyn named it Belgia Australis.'[5]

Choiseul could ignore these arguments, which had been planted in the Dutch newspapers, but there was one last-minute hitch. Officials from the Ministry of Foreign Affairs were creating difficulties about formalising Bougainville's Act of Possession. They could find no satisfactory precedent for his actions. It took a little pressure by Choiseul on his cousin for the matter to be finally settled.

On 6 September, Louis once again called on Choiseul. They had details to settle about the colonial settlement, the financial arrangements needed to be confirmed, and even the layout of the proposed town and port required approval. After a final audience with Louis XV, Bougainville was ready to set out for Saint-Malo. There were brief visits and farewells to relatives and friends in Paris, and on 22 September he was back in Saint-Malo, ready to take over the *Aigle*.

She was to be commanded once again by Alexandre Duclos-Guyot; yet another brother, the young Baptiste-François, served as first lieutenant. Returning to the Malouines were Thisbé de Belcour, Denis de Saint-Simon and the engineer Lhuillier de la Serre. Newcomers were a military officer, Captain Joseph des Perriers, and a geographer and engineer, Charles Routier de Romainville. Dom Pernetty was not sailing back: he was replaced by the Abbé Desertos-Duguérard, a local priest from Saint-Malo. Bougainville, unimpressed by him, wrote that 'he is a drunk and a fool'.[6] The first colonists were to be strengthened by some fifty workers, including a dozen stonemasons and several hopeful settlers. In all, the *Aigle* carried a total complement of 116 men and women.

The checking and loading of supplies, passengers and crew took five days. The frigate was ready to sail on 27 September, but then came the inevitable delay while Duclos-Guyot waited for a favourable wind. This did not eventuate until 6 October.

The voyage was relatively speedy and uneventful. The *Aigle* made for Madeira, continued south to the islands of Cape Verde and on to the Falklands. Bougainville had hoped to come upon Pepys Island, allegedly discovered by Ambrose Cowley in 1684 and the existence of which Anson had planned to check. It could become a useful staging post for French ships but, alas, as Guyot confirmed, it did not exist:

> This Englishman [Cowley] must have allowed his imagination to become over-heated by some fanciful ideas when he wrote such a pompous account of it in his journal … We cannot allow ourselves to doubt that this island is fictional, after all the manoeuvres we carried out to find it, and we can find in none of the reports of those who mention it and who made endeavours similar to ours any indication that anyone has seen it, other than our Mister Cowley.[7]

There was no point in wasting any more time. The *Aigle* went on her way, sighted the Falklands on 3 January 1765 and two days later anchored outside the small French settlement. 'As we were tacking to enter the bay,' Bougainville recorded in his journal, 'the commander sent us a boat from which they called out that everyone was in the best of health.'[8] Soon after this, the shore battery fired a gun salute. The anchors were lowered. The voyage was over. 'That night, I slept on land,' wrote Louis.

15. A First Look at the Strait of Magellan

January–August 1765

BOUGAINVILLE WAS DELIGHTED to find the colonists well and in good spirits. Only one had died, lost during a hunting expedition, presumed to have fallen in one of the baleful marshes that seemed to swallow their prey in stagnant silence. But, on a brighter note, there had been one wedding and two christenings.

It had not been a bad winter in the bleak country around the little settlement. All the cattle had survived, and there was no lack of fish and game. It was still too early to give a verdict on the ground crops, but it was clear that the soil would need a great deal of fertilising before wheat and oats could flourish. Bougainville de Nerville confirmed these verbal reports in a lengthy letter to Dom Pernetty, who had asked to be kept up to date on developments:

The winter we have spent here has not been a harsh one; never a snowfall heavy enough to cover the buckle of one's shoes; no more ice than would support a stone the size of one's fist; and if it had not been for the rain that went through our covers as through a sieve, we would have needed very little in the way of furs. You would not have recognised the colony if you had come back with Mr de Bougainville. You would have been struck by how plump and fat we were … By our reckoning, we have shot more than 1500 bustards during the season … Our crops give us the highest hopes. All the vegetables have done well … the wheat in the land we burnt produced some good ears, but no grain. Our soil being virgin soil needs to be worked over more and even improved with good manure. The animals we have are not sufficient for our needs. Four of our heifers and our three horses are still in open country: we were never able to catch them, but their wandering life had taught us about one of the great advantages of this country – beasts can stay out in all seasons, outside day and night, where they find both feed and litter.[1]

Nerville's optimism was justified. When Charles Darwin visited the area in 1833, he found impressive numbers of wild cattle and horses: 'The island is abundantly stocked with animals – there are about 5000 wild oxen, many horses & pigs'. He added: 'Horses fond of catching cattle – aberration of instinct'.[2] This visit led him to 'read Bougainville', which enabled him to expand on the origin of the horses when he wrote his *Narrative* of the voyage in 1839:

> These animals, as well as the cattle, were introduced by the French in 1764, since which time both have greatly increased. It is a curious fact, that the horses have never left the eastern end of the island, although there is no natural boundary to prevent them from roaming. The cattle ... seem to have increased in size; and they are much more numerous than the horses.[3]

The archipelago, although rather windswept and with a relatively high rainfall, would eventually sustain a population of a couple of thousand, not counting the British garrison, and a profitable sheep industry. Its problem was the lack of trees, which meant a shortage of timber, both for building and for firewood. Louis planned to sail to the Strait of Magellan as soon as possible to bring back timber for his colonists.

First, however, he had to oversee the landing of the supplies he had brought, settle in the additional recruits he was bringing for his colony and have a small boat built for coastal exploration. The stores were all landed within a few days, and work began on the construction of a small schooner from material brought by the frigate. While this was going on, Bougainville decided to visit East Falkland Island and determine its size: there were so many inlets and indentations that it had not been possible for the settlers to complete a circumnavigation.

On the 11th, he sent one of the *Aigle*'s boats around the coast and into a deep, wide opening that seemed to suggest they could row right around the island. At the same time, he went off on foot with four others, intending to meet the crew on the southern shore. There was, as the colonists had suspected, a narrow strip of land, 'one side being within range of a rifle shot from the other', barring what would have been an easily navigable east to west strait. They thus proved that East Falkland was a substantial island. They climbed a nearby hill and deposited a sealed bottle containing a note of their presence, and began their journey back. Bougainville and his companions returned overland, covering, in all, a distance of some 60 miles. The expedition, which he found pleasant and rewarding, took just over a fortnight. By then the *Aigle* was ready for the voyage to the Strait of Magellan.

The boat returned to Fort Saint-Louis a day after Bougainville. The men reported that they had seen two ships towards the north, which seemed to be making for the French settlement. Then they disappeared. Alexandre Duclos-Guyot thought they could have been sent from France with more supplies or colonists, as had been promised, and that they were now sailing around the islands looking for the French settlement. Louis, however, knew this was not likely, as France had no money for any further voyages; he believed that the ships were English, 'part of an expedition that was being readied as I was leaving, in order to set up some outpost in the South Sea'.[4]

It was indeed the expedition of John Byron, who had sailed from Plymouth on 3 July 1764 with the *Dolphin* and the *Tamar*, later meeting up with the storeship *Florida*. Byron's instructions, surrounded by secrecy, were to look for Pepys Island, proceed to the Falklands, sail through the Strait of Magellan, then go up to the Pacific coast of North America and sail home either by way of a north-west passage into the Atlantic or by China or the Dutch East Indies. The aim was less exploration for its own sake, than 'the advancement of trade and navigation … to attain a perfect knowledge of the distant parts of the British Empire'. The expedition embodied everything that Choiseul and Bougainville had feared from Britain after the end of the Seven Years War. Bougainville sent one of his officers, Lavarye-Leroy, on a reconnaissance mission in one of the few fishing boats the settlers possessed, but there was nothing to be seen. The English had gone.

Byron had not found any trace of the French settlement on the Falklands, either then or on an earlier quick reconnaissance. The inlet Bougainville had called Port de la Croisade Byron named Port Egmont, and he gave the title Cape Dolphin to the northernmost headland of East Falkland, and Cape Tamar to another nearby point. And he took formal possession of the islands, just in case anyone challenged earlier British claims to the archipelago:

> The surgeon of the Tamar mad[e] a pritty little Garden near the Watering Place, for the benefit of those that may come next. I took Posession of this Harbour & of all these Islands for His Majesty King George the Third of Great Britain & His Heirs, tho' they had been before taken Possession of by S[r] Rich[d] Hawkins in the Year 1593.[5]

Louis was sure that the British ships were on their way to the Strait of Magellan and he decided to follow them as quickly as possible in order to ascertain their route. Weather conditions prevented an immediate departure, but on 2 February he was on his way in the *Aigle*. He spent a day on a fruitless search for Pepys Island, which he had already looked for in December; he found nothing and became finally convinced that it did not exist.

Commodore Byron had wasted almost a fortnight looking for Pepys Island, and this enabled Bougainville to catch up with him at the entrance to the Strait of Magellan. It was dawn on 15 February. There was no breeze and Byron's three vessels were trapped by the lack of wind off Dungeness Point. 'They seemed quite embarrassed to find that we were following them and that the calm weather was preventing them from crowding on sail in order to avoid us.'⁶ Embarrassed was hardly the right word for it – Byron was irritated and worried, as he noted a couple of days later:

I was in great hopes she would have run ashore upon one of the Banks between Point Possession & the first Narrow, for the Navigation is extremely difficult to those who are not well acquainted. But the misfortune was, the Storeship kept so far a Stern that she served as a Pilot to the Stranger … but seeing the Stranger get under way & working up towards us, I run [*sic*] directly over into Gregory Bay & broᵗ my Ship to an Anchor with a spring upon our Cable & got all our Guns over on one side.⁷

As it turned out, it was the *Florida* that ran aground on a sandbank while going through a narrow channel. Bougainville, described as 'very officious', to use Byron's term, promptly had one of his boats lowered, loaded with a spare kedge anchor and a length of cable, and sent over to assist. By then, the tide had risen sufficiently to free the storeship and Louis's help was not required. He was thanked for his intended assistance and sent back. The four ships had entered the first bay, Possession, the shores of which seemed no more attractive or wooded than parts of the Falklands. The *Aigle* accordingly went on her way, as it was known that the forested part of Patagonia began further along the strait.

The next day, it was the turn of the French to touch bottom. The *Aigle* was successfully towed off by her boats and continued her route towards Cabo Negro, on Brunswick Peninsula, north of present-day Puntas Arenas. The forest now made its appearance, but Bougainville decided to travel further, to look for a better anchorage and also to keep a watch on the English ships:

The three English vessels had anchored in this bay [Port Famine]. I decided to continue on my way in order to avoid the quarrels and indiscretions that might arise if we anchored so close to each other. Anyhow, by going further into the Strait I would be in a position to find out whether they were passing through in order to reach the South Sea, or whether they were only coming to get timber for some new settlement in the Atlantic, and I left them unsure of my own destination.⁸

Past Cabo San Isidro, the French found an attractive bay they named after the *Aigle* – the name has remained to this day as Bahia del Aguila. Louis explored it by boat and went as far as another bay, which he identified as French Bay, so named by Jean-Baptiste de Gennes who had struggled this far in his unsuccessful attempt to sail through the strait in 1696. But on the way Louis discovered a deep bay 'enclosed like a box, a good anchoring place where I decided to go and collect my cargo of timber ... this bay to which the crew has given my name'.⁹

Bahia de Bougainville was a deep, well-sheltered bay, forested along its shores, and with a clear running stream that proved invaluable for refilling the water casks. Across the strait, a mere 6 miles or so wide at this point, they could see to the south what they believed to be Tierra del Fuego, but what were actually a couple of deeply indented islands, Capitán Aracena and Clarence. They spent a week felling and cutting the timber, then had a break on the 24th, which was a Sunday. They spent the day doing their laundry and fishing, but thought it wiser to row around to French Bay for these activities, because they had discovered evidence that Bahia de Bougainville was normally inhabited and they did not want to be accused of interfering with the locals' food supplies.

On the Monday, they saw two of Byron's ships sailing past, on their way to the Pacific Ocean. They waited for the third vessel to appear, but there was no sign of it. The *Florida* had turned back to make her way to England, bearing a report from Byron to Lord Egmont, First Lord of the Admiralty, which included a section on the presence of the French.

It was several days before any Patagonians showed themselves. No doubt they had been observing the French for some time from the forest, but they did not venture anywhere near until they felt reasonably confident that the strange visitors meant them no harm. Their confidence grew when the French started loading up the *Aigle* on 22 February: this indicated they would not remain long. A few men appeared, but they did not approach until mid-March, when the French were clearly getting ready to depart.

Louis decided to leave the Patagonians gifts in a tent he had had erected along the shore and covered with bark, to store tools and implements in case of rain. He chose a selection of clothes, kitchen utensils, woodworking tools and cinnabar, from which vermilion powder was made, 'which is greatly prized by the natives of this country'. Near the tent, he planted a white flag. On 16 March, everything being ready for departure, he went for a final row around the headland and into Port Famine. There he saw smoke rising along the shore. 'We went towards it and had the satisfaction finally of seeing several families of Patagonians whose canoes, 5 in number, lay nearby at the mouth of a small river. I gave them food and clothes and we parted good friends. Their height is ordinary, and their colour is bronze. Their weapons are bows and arrows.'¹⁰

Sirandré, the first officer, confirmed that they were of average height: 'the tallest of them, in a group of about forty, was no more than five foot 7 inches ... the women are shorter'.¹¹ References to their size are important because at the time a controversy had arisen over the 'Patagonian giants'. François Froger's account of his voyage with De Gennes, published in 1698, had reported nothing unusual about their height, but from the time of the first encounter, with Magellan back in 1520, it had been widely believed that the Patagonians were enormous. 'We reached only up to his waist,' wrote the chronicler of the expedition, Antonio Pigafetta. The name *Patagones* which the Spanish gave to these men actually means 'big feet', a term that referred more to the splayed toes of people who often walked barefoot or wore roughly made moccasins. The Patagonians may well have appeared remarkably tall to Magellan and his men, there may even have been one or two of a truly unusual height among those they met, but later travellers, like Froger, and John Narborough in 1670, had their doubts, confirmed by Bulkeley and Cummins who, in 1741, wrote of 'People of a middle Stature and well-shaped … being in general from five to six Feet high'.[12] In 1767, Bougainville himself would note that the tallest Patagonian he encountered 'scarcely attained a height of 5ft 9in'. Several were only 5 foot 6, as he was.

Byron revived the old belief when, in the report he sent back by the *Florida*, he enthused over 'one of the most extraordinary Men for Size I had ever seen till then … People who, in size, come the nearest to Giants of any People I believe in the World.'[13] The London Royal Society took up the issue with enthusiasm, its secretary, Dr Matthew Maty, becoming a champion of the giantism case and writing to his counterpart in Paris, Lefrançais de Lalande, to acquaint scientists of this new supposed evidence. The French heard the news with scepticism. The Duc de Praslin drily commented that Byron must have been looking at the Patagonians through a microscope. The naturalist Charles Marie de La Condamine wrote in the *Journal Encyclopédique* that the whole thing was a fable.

The argument rapidly developed into a bitter dispute between the British and the French. Not unreasonably, the latter accused the British of trying to conceal the real purpose of the Byron expedition with spurious facts about a search for giants. Dom Pernetty, always quick to embrace unusual theories, tended to accept reports of giants, even when Bougainville ridiculed the whole idea. Scientists did not want to dismiss the theory, but needed more evidence before they would adopt it. It took years for the controversy to die down and for the *Patagones* to be restored to an average human size. Even so, reports of giants trickled in from captains and sailors until almost the end of the eighteenth century.

Bougainville had done everything possible to befriend the locals. Once they had overcome their fear of the French, they gladly exchanged gifts over a period of several days, when fierce and contrary winds prevented the *Aigle* from setting off on her voyage back to the Malouines. Louis spent about three hours with them on the 18th. An excited crowd of natives came down, bearing gifts of animal skins and receiving in exchange more items of clothing, axes, knives, cooking pots, mirrors and the ever-popular vermilion. The clothes in particular were popular as 'they were partly naked, having only animal and penguin skins to cover their nudity'.[14] This was always a matter of astonishment, as the climate, even in summer, struck the French as cold and harsh.

The winds briefly veered in the favour of the French and the *Aigle* began her return journey, but she was soon forced to put into Port Famine, where Bougainville met more Patagonians. This time half a dozen were persuaded to come aboard, where they were fed and clothed. On the way back to shore, the French sailors shouted, '*Vive le Roi* which they repeated quite well'. When the boat that had brought them on board returned to the *Aigle*, 'they hailed us with *Vive le Roi*' and danced around a flag the French had erected on the shore.

Bougainville noted that Byron's men had been cutting timber along the shore, presumably for heating and grass for their animals. Port Famine was not an unattractive place, despite its bleak name. Back in 1581, Pedro de Sarmiento had attempted to set up an outpost there, both to assist Spanish ships on their way to the Pacific coast and to keep out strangers. It was a dismal failure: the small garrison was ridden with disease and dissensions, and the men eventually died of hunger. But Byron had put twice into the bay, finding 'wood enough for a thousand Sail … fish enough every day for both Ships … as many Geese and Ducks as they please'.[15]

Finally, on 22 March, the French were able to sail, although not to make quick progress, towards the open sea. It took them a dreary four days to reach Cabo de Virgenes and to set off for the Malouines. They reached Port Louis on the 30th and began at once to unload the timber they had collected. They also brought with them thousands of seedlings and small trees they hoped might grow on the Malouines, since the island climate seemed as good as, or better than, that in the strait. Unfortunately, the thin soil and the fierce westerlies were too much for the plants and practically all of them died out within a few weeks.

Once the unloading had been completed, the *Aigle* began to take on supplies for the return journey to France. Louis had every reason to feel satisfied with his young colony. The population, men, women and children, now totalled 75. 'A few days before my departure I married the two sisters of the woman called Malivilain, also known as Boucher, and three women are pregnant.'[16]

He sailed on 27 April, but it was to prove a slow and tedious voyage. He had wanted to leave all the supplies he could at the Malouines, which meant that meat and vegetables on board soon ran out. 'All we have is bread, wine, brandy and a little butter. The allocations must be cut down right away.'[17] Not surprisingly, scurvy began to affect the crew. Held back by contrary winds, the *Aigle* struggled towards the Azores. By 11 July, in 'Damned weather, especially as we are down to bread and water with a little wine. The latter will not last long.'

It was not until 18 July, two and a half months after leaving the Malouines, that they managed to drop anchor off Angra, on the south coast of the island of Terceira. The French had to wait until port officials had been to inspect the ship. The port captain and his health officer had to satisfy themselves that the sailors were suffering from nothing worse than the non-contagious scurvy. It was then a question of settling the matter of etiquette, in particular the official salutes that ship and shore would exchange. Bougainville sent Captain Belcour ashore to call on the French consul, who introduced him to the local commander. It was agreed that the Portuguese would render to the king's emblem the courtesy it was owed – the *Aigle* would fire a twenty-one-gun salute, and the fort would return the salute in full. This done, Louis went ashore, visited the commander, and received a personal salute of nine guns, which the frigate returned in full. The French could now buy all the supplies they needed and load them without delay.

The Portuguese Azores were then under British influence, but although Portugal was closely linked with Britain the locals expressed a clear dislike of Britain. 'The Secretary of Finance and the *Corregidor* assured us that the Portuguese deeply resented the yoke under which England kept them.'[18] Louis later discussed with Choiseul the strategic importance of the island group, the effective if unofficial control Britain maintained over it and the consequent importance of ensuring that the French settlement on the Falklands was strengthened and expanded.

The local authorities expressed their views in a practical manner: they provided Bougainville with everything he asked for – cattle, sheep, pigs, poultry, maize, wine and firewood. The sailors enjoyed plentiful meals, and their health was soon restored. In fact, to make up for those who still needed time to recover, eight Portuguese sailors came to assist with the loading and the manoeuvres.

The *Aigle* sailed on 26 July. There were the usual contrary winds and calms to cope with, but progress was being made. The island of Ushant came into view on 10 August. Two days later, the frigate dropped anchor in Saint-Malo, 'greeted by the cheers of a large crowd'. On Tuesday 14 August, Bougainville left for Paris 'where I arrived on Friday evening 17 August, having left last year on 18 October'. He stayed with his uncle Jean-Potentien d'Arboulin. The Duc de Choiseul was away in Flanders, so Louis went as quickly as he could to Versailles to hold discussions with officials from the various ministries. He needed to tie up some loose ends following the voyage of the *Aigle* and to make arrangements for further supplies and, he hoped, for additional settlers to be sent to the Malouines. But 'Nobody was prepared to say anything precise; it was as though they were whispering around a corpse. It seemed to Bougainville as if the Malouine affair was dead and they were merely waiting for his return before burying it.'[19]

16. THE END OF THE MALOUINES VENTURE

September 1765–October 1766

LOUIS HAD COME home to become entangled in the complexities of international diplomacy. The Duc de Choiseul was a good patron, well disposed towards his plans, which helped to counter the ideas – 'schemes' is the word they would both have used – of the British. But he was not having everything his own way.

Both Choiseul and Bougainville had done their best to blur the issue over the settlement on the Falklands – just like the British, who were endeavouring to conceal the true aims of the Byron expedition – so it had been something of an embarrassment when the *Gazette d'Amsterdam* had published a detailed article about the Malouines colony on 26 July 1764. The Spanish found all their suspicions confirmed: France had been encroaching upon its South American possessions. Within a week, the First Secretary of the Spanish Foreign Affairs Ministry, Augustin de Llano, had received a full report from one of his officials, summarising the situation and its implications for Spain. Nothing would now stop the French from developing a contraband trade with Chile, it pointed out, and even if this could be contained, the settlement at Port Saint-Louis was bound to attract the attention of Britain. France had just lost a number of her colonies after the Seven Years War. She could easily lose another war, and such a defeat would inevitably mean the surrender of the Malouines to Britain. Spain would be the loser, even if she did not take part in that future conflict. The thought caused the official to wax lyrical:

> And then farewell to a direct route to the Philippines, farewell to the South Sea and its maritime provinces, farewell to Spain's trade with these various regions, farewell to the fisheries, our sole resource, and farewell too to Buenos Aires if the Malvinas should become an enemy settlement, well placed, on account of its short distance, to turn against Rio de la Plata! How indeed could we resist a seaborne invasion from that quarter, while another was being mounted at the same time, by land, from the Brazilian side?[1]

The official, Pedro Pablo d'Aranda, was in fact pro-French and he had no wish to cause a strain between his country and France, but Spain's interests had to come first. The affair should be solved in an amicable way. Spain had to put an end to French activities on the Malouines, but also thank the French for holding the British at bay and thereby encouraging Spain to do the same and more. And getting the French to leave did not mean banning them altogether from the archipelago: they would be welcome to call there – on their way to the East Indies. This, ironically, had been the original reason Choiseul and Bougainville had given for the presence of the *Aigle* and the *Sphinx* in the Falkland Islands.

Llano agreed with Aranda. Neither wanted a clash with Versailles over the isolated colony. But their Minister of State, Géronimo Grimaldi, and eventually the king, had to be told. And the French should not be allowed to prevaricate any longer: Grimaldi wrote to the Spanish ambassador in Paris, instructing him to see Choiseul without delay. Diplomatic courtesy was to dominate the interview. The Count de Fuentes was to express surprise and hurt that Spain had not been informed of French actions, but 'Let this comment be made in a friendly tone'. At the same time, Grimaldi asked the French ambassador, Pierre Paul, Marquis d'Ossun, for an explanation. 'France seems to be planning to occupy the Malouines … These islands would be of no use as a port of call for ships on their way to the East Indies or China.' So what was France's long-term plan?

Ossun promised to ask Choiseul for an official reply. But his Spanish counterpart in France, Fuentes, did not call at once on Choiseul: he was ill and only later, on 13 December, was Grimaldi's request passed on, and even then it was by the embassy's first secretary, Fernando de Magallon. It was a tricky interview for an ambassador's stand-in, and Magallon raised the key issue only when he was about to leave. Choiseul told the official to put the Spanish case in writing, but this was merely a delaying tactic, which Magallon courteously but firmly swept aside. Choiseul then pointed out that the islands were French and that what France did in the Malouines was its own concern. Magallon replied that this was a claim, not a fact. The arguments went to and fro, the exchanges becoming quite tense, especially when the secretary began to hint that France could easily lose the islands to some third power in a later war. Choiseul did not take kindly to the suggestion that France might be the loser in any future war.

Overnight, Choiseul calmed down and decided to call on the ambassador himself: although ill and about to go on sick leave, Fuentes was still available. He was conciliatory, but he repeated Spain's disappointment that France had not thought fit to tell her ally of her actions in the Malvinas. He almost smilingly swept aside the suggestion that Bougainville had been surveying a group of islands few people knew anything about, and that this was tantamount to the actual discovery of a hitherto unknown archipelago. It was a little too far-fetched. If that was the case, said Fuentes, one would have thought that France would have been only too glad to publicise the fact, and claim full credit.

Choiseul changed the subject, turning to the settlement of the islands, an action largely aimed at excluding the British. Spain, after all, had no settlement or outpost of any kind there, nothing to indicate that this was Spanish territory and that Spain wanted it. Finally, Choiseul agreed to close down the French settlement on condition that Spain agreed to replace it with one of her own. His argument, that France was trying to keep the British out, had, in a way, rebounded against him – if the Spanish took over that task, France would have to agree to bow out.

This was the situation in late 1764, when Bougainville was about to land at Port Saint-Louis with the *Aigle*, quite unaware that France was intending to give up the colony. Choiseul had been forced to conclude that Madrid was truly upset about the French settlement. The lack of communication between the two countries over the settlement could be interpreted as evidence of bad faith and of France's unease about the real worth of its claim to the islands. Maintaining good relations was more important than a small colony on some faraway island group. Conciliation was the only solution.

The King of Spain endorsed the compromise finally agreed upon by the diplomats: France would vacate the islands and Spanish colonists would be brought in. Choiseul was thanked for his co-operation, his 'docility' as Carlos III put it in a letter asking Fuentes to express his gratitude.

But Choiseul did not want to sacrifice Bougainville. What could be done to soften the blow? Fuentes suggested that, when he returned from the Malouines, Louis should go to Madrid, where he would be more than welcome. The situation and all its implications should be laid out before him, with proper compensation for the setback that was being forced upon him.

By early February 1765 the whole matter was settled, but Louis did not arrive for another six months – and by then a new factor had come into the discussion: the English had formally restated their claim to the Falklands and, as far as anyone could tell, were actually settling on the islands.

Consequently, when Louis reached Paris, on 17 August 1765, the situation looked dismal. Not a single official was willing to talk to him. Only Choiseul could explain to him what had really happened. But the minister was out of town and Louis spent a week visiting relatives and friends, and meeting Charles de Brosses, who was also in the capital.

Choiseul arrived a week later. Louis met him on the 25th, to be told that the whole matter had been settled with the Spanish and that his colony was to be handed over. As soon as he had had a chance to rest, Louis should go to Madrid to make the final arrangements – most amicably: there was a great deal of goodwill towards him at the Spanish court. Choiseul gave him the gist of his discussions with the Spanish ambassador: it did look as though Spain had a valid claim to the islands. French sailors may well have discovered them and visited them on a number of occasions but France had not occupied them until Bougainville's recent effort. And, finally, the Spanish were worried that they might become a base for contraband with their South American colonies. After all, Choiseul reminded Louis, when French ships had been allowed to sail to Chile and Peru earlier in the century, they had constantly engaged in smuggling and illegal trade.

Louis was not going to give up without a final effort. He came back the very next day with a lengthy three-part memoir on 'the reasons for the French settlement, the benefits that would result from it both for France and for Spain, and the weakness of any claim the Spanish might be now making'.[2] He pointed out that the Malouines would be a defensive outpost against British imperialistic moves, a base where sailors and navigators could be trained, and a resting place for whalers, sealers and others. Merchantmen engaged in trade with the Indies could use the islands to refresh their crews and repair their ships, as could explorers setting off on voyages of discovery, opening the way towards the Antarctic and 'the immense continent' that still had not been found. Choiseul wavered, then came down on Louis's side: the islands would remain French after all.

Choiseul has been criticised by some historians as a man who tended to change his mind, to the irritation and bewilderment of friends and foes alike. But he was a shrewd politician who knew that nearly every situation remains in a state of flux until the truly inevitable has to be faced. Things were not quite the same in August 1765 as they had been back in February. It was worth having another try. On 2 September, Choiseul told the Spanish chargé d'affaires that the question should be re-examined.

Bougainville now pressed his advantage. He provided Choiseul with an analysis of various treaties signed by Spain and England over the previous 100 years, which laid the basis for co-operation between the two powers and excluded France. The possibility of Spain eventually allowing the British to use the Falklands as a base could not be excluded. Neither Madrid nor London could really be trusted. The minister kept the report and told Louis that he had already raised that issue with the Spanish court.

Louis then suggested that the Malouines settlement should be strengthened and given much-needed supplies. He handed over a formal request, which he had prepared earlier, to send Chesnard de la Giraudais to Rochefort, where he could be provided with a transport vessel to take food and other goods to the colonists. The *Aigle* would similarly be readied for a return voyage to the Malouines. Choiseul promptly agreed and ordered his officials to press on with all the necessary arrangements.

A storeship of 450 tons, the *Étoile*, which the government had bought in 1762, was quickly loaded with supplies. La Giraudais received instructions to take command and sail to the Malouines, then go without delay to Bahia de Bougainville in the Strait of Magellan. There he would take on all the timber his ship could carry, return to the Malouines, unload and return to France. The preparations for the *Aigle*'s voyage took somewhat longer – she needed some repairs and refitting, and this involved Bougainville travelling to Saint-Malo to expedite matters. Her captain was to be Alexandre Duclos-Guyot, who received his instructions direct from Bougainville. The *Étoile* sailed on 9 November, the *Aigle* on 25 November.

In the meantime, the international situation had become strained. In mid-September, the French chargé d'affaires in London told Choiseul that the British had asked for details of Bougainville's activities in the Malouines, 'islands that have been known for a long time and visited by subjects of Great Britain, from what they claim, and to which they give an English name'.[3] The diplomat had gained time by replying that he knew nothing about the matter, but now it was over to his minister.

Fortunately for France, there was growing tension between Britain and Spain over an unpaid ransom for the port of Manila, which had been captured by Brigadier William Draper in 1762. The presence of Byron's expedition in the Strait of Magellan and his entry into the Pacific had now become known, and was regarded as another threat to the Spanish colonial empire. The crisis might lead to hostilities, even if only within a localised area. All this could change Spain's attitude towards the French holding the Falklands and helping to keep out any passing British ships. Carlos III sent a message to Choiseul, effectively asking his advice over his dealings with Britain.

Choiseul's view was always that the best way to avoid a war, or to make it successful, was to prepare for it promptly and efficiently. He did not believe that the Manila affair was very serious, but he used it to delay sending Bougainville to Madrid. Maintaining the status quo in the Malouines was the better policy until things quietened down.

Nevertheless, the Spanish chargé d'affaires in Paris, Magallon, still had his instructions, which were to arrange for Bougainville to travel to Madrid without delay. He had several lengthy discussions with him in late September and early October. Nothing much came out of them and no date was fixed for Louis's departure – he was more concerned with going to Saint-Malo to supervise the outfitting of the *Aigle*, although he took good care not to mention this to Magallon.

In his report to Madrid, Magallon supplied an interesting, if not particularly friendly, portrait of the Frenchman:

He is a young man of some thirty to thirty-four years, impressively intrepid and intelligent, capable of carrying out the most difficult and boldest of tasks, filled with a deadly loathing towards the English, against whom he would like to see war declared without delay. He claims that he could draw up a defensive and offensive plan against them that would not fail to give results. His hatred and natural ardour prevent him from being held up by any of the thoughts usual in those who do not want to take the risks caused by undue haste, especially when one has not examined and weighed out all one's resources and made all one's preparations, which requires more time and a less exalted imagination.[4]

Magallon met Choiseul late in October. It resulted in the usual stalemate as the French continued to mark time. The minister was courteous and friendly, but supremely evasive.

Back from Saint-Malo, Louis started working with Choiseul, helping him to draw up a plan of campaign, just in case war did break out with England. They also discussed a matter that had become a general topic of conversation in Versailles: the health of Louis XV's only son, Louis. A serious young man, but suffering from tuberculosis, he had been involved in the plans of a number of ambitious politicians and courtiers, especially those who supported the Jesuit Order. Choiseul did not get on well with him, and he knew that if Louis XV were to die, with the crown immediately passing to the dauphin, his career would be at an end. By October 1765, however, it was becoming evident to everyone that the heir apparent was dying. Next in line would be Louis XV's grandson, a boy of eleven – which could mean that, if anything happened to the king, a regent would take over. Modern politicians examine public opinion polls to assess their future; in earlier times, they studied the health of the royals.

The dauphin died on 20 December. The court went into immediate mourning. There were a few changes in the royal household and at Versailles during January, and affairs of state were put aside for a while. As the Spanish ambassador realised, it was not a suitable time to discuss the Falklands with Bougainville and even less so with Choiseul. Nor was it, as it was courteously pointed out to him, a good time for Louis to travel down to Madrid, as the route would take him through the snow-covered Pyrenees and along the similarly snowy and slushy roads of central Spain. No doubt in the spring, the question of his visit to Spain could be raised again?

Then, on 7 April 1766, the Duc de Choiseul passed the portfolio of the navy to his cousin, the Duc de Praslin, keeping foreign affairs for himself. Ever since the end of the war, Choiseul had devoted himself to the task of rebuilding France's naval strength. Shipbuilding was going on apace in the reorganised naval yards of Brest, Rochefort and Toulon; plans were on hand to restructure the Marseilles and Lorient shipyards. He had reformed the classbound and highly conservative navy, as he was doing for the army, although his attempt to break down the barrier between the 'reds' and the 'blues' had led to such howls of protest that he was forced to draw back. His energetic reforms would count among the finest achievements of his long ministry. They continued, under his indirect supervision, when his cousin took over.

Now, with the period of mourning over, the weather improved, the tense situation with Britain easing and Choiseul personally responsible for foreign relations, Bougainville's departure could no longer be delayed. Somewhat craftily, Choiseul sent Louis off to Madrid on 9 April, ostensibly to take the war contingency plans they had worked on during the previous few months. These were highly confidential and needed to be handed to the Spanish government by an able and respected courier. The matter of the Falklands would also be discussed, naturally, but almost as a secondary issue, out of courtesy, with Louis explaining to the officials why France should retain possession.

He arrived in Madrid on the 18th, so exhausted by the journey that the Abbé Beliardi saw him to his hotel, told him to rest and undertook to arrange, on his behalf, appointments with the French ambassador and Grimaldi, the Minister of State. Beliardi and Bougainville got on well: they had friends in common in Paris, including Louis's *chère Maman*.

Louis and Beliardi went to meet the French ambassador on the 26th. Ossun asked for a summary of the Falklands question, which he could present to Grimaldi. This was promptly completed. It was a tactful overview of the position, but concluded with the suggestion that France would be the most appropriate country to protect the islands against expected British encroachment, 'as she considers herself better placed to supply colonists and troops and to fortify that outpost than Spain, which already has immense areas to defend'.[5]

At this point, Grimaldi did what politicians usually do when faced with an awkward situation: he set up a committee to report on Bougainville's report. Not unexpectedly, the committee concluded that the islands should be Spanish – indeed that they had always been Spanish. It was not likely that Grimaldi, who was Italian by birth and not particularly popular with the people of Madrid, would reject the committee's findings and risk recommending to Carlos III that the Malvinas should be handed over to a foreign power. His attitude was uncompromising: Bougainville should give up his settlement.

To add salt to the wound, the Secretary of Finance, Miguel Muzquiz, pointed out that, since Bougainville had established his colony without Spain's authority, any costs he had incurred should be paid back to him by France, not Spain. 'One should not erect buildings on someone else's land. Let your king, who employed you, refund your expenses.'[6] Louis had not only failed to save his colony – he was now facing ruin.

Ossun came to his assistance. A proud nobleman with a superior manner, he felt in no way responsible for a mere lawyer's son, but Louis had been recommended to him by the Duc de Choiseul, he was well regarded by Louis XV and Ossun knew of his fine military record in Canada. He decided to go over Grimaldi's head and talk to Carlos III direct.

The king agreed to his suggestion that the entire affair should be settled amicably. The islands were to be formally returned to Spain, Bougainville would supervise the handover, and since the buildings and farms could be used by the Spanish, Bougainville's costs ought to be refunded. Furthermore, he agreed to grant Louis an audience.

This took place on 10 May in the presence of both Ossun and Grimaldi. Upon entering the chamber, Bougainville knelt down, but Carlos stepped forward, giving him his hand. They talked freely about the international situation, agreeing that the British presented a danger to both realms. The king then asked Louis about the Malvinas and the Strait of Magellan, including his opinion on the famous Patagonian giants. Before he left, Carlos III asked Bougainville whether he was satisfied with his time in Madrid, 'because he was anxious to ensure that justice was done'. Louis bowed his thanks. As they parted, the king assured him of his goodwill and asked to be remembered to Choiseul. It had been a long and altogether successful meeting. As he took his leave of them, Grimaldi and even Muzquiz promised that there would be no difficulty with the reimbursement of all his expenses. On 17 May, Louis left for Paris; he arrived there on the 29th.

On 4 June, Bougainville called on the Duc de Praslin, the Minister of Marine, who had a new proposal for him. The French islands of the Isle de France (present-day Mauritius) and Bourbon in the Indian Ocean, the Mascareignes, were being reorganised, and a governor was required. Praslin favoured Bougainville for the position, and Louis accepted the offer. But there remained the matter of the Malouines.

On the 9th, Choiseul asked him to call. He had received two letters, one of them from Ossun. To expedite the settlement, Grimaldi was authorising Fuentes to make all the necessary arrangements direct with Bougainville. The second letter came from France's ambassador in London, announcing the return of Byron's expedition. There were still no precise details about the voyage, but there was a feeling abroad that the British were looking for a suitable site for a settlement 'for when war is renewed or even before'.

Fuentes met Bougainville a little while later, and urged him to finalise all his accounts, so that the financial side of the transfer could be cleared up. Louis did not have all the papers he needed for a balance sheet, as he was still waiting for statements and receipts from Saint-Malo. He asked for a little more time, but the

Spanish were becoming increasingly impatient. Placing a Spanish garrison on the Falklands was becoming urgent in view of suspected British activities. Fuentes's next point made it clear that Louis could not accept the offered governorship of the Mascareignes in the Indian Ocean: the Spanish insisted that he go to the Falklands without delay to oversee the handing over. Choiseul shared their opinion. It was Praslin, less aware of the complexity of the negotiations over the Malouines, who had thought an appointment to the Isle de France was possible in the near future.

Louis's future would not lie in Mauritius and the neighbouring islands, but what was he to do once the Malouines colony was no more? He reintroduced the idea of a voyage of exploration in the Pacific. Choiseul had earlier approved the idea in principle, and France's finances had improved over the intervening three years.

And now, almost providentially, Byron's voyage had come into the equation. The Comte de Guerchy, France's ambassador to London, returned on leave at the beginning of July, bearing important information. Back in London his chargé d'affaires, Durand de Distroff, was busying himself with obtaining additional details and getting copies of documents through an agent in the Admiralty, and by bribery. Choiseul thus received a world map on which Byron's route had been drawn, and a copy of the log, obtained from one of the expedition's officers, a draughtsman or artist. He had further copies made, some of which he forwarded to Madrid.

He showed them to Bougainville and together they discussed their implications. The documents may not have been entirely reliable, but they were enough to alarm both the French and the Spanish. Britain was not only challenging the Spanish policy of exclusiveness in the Pacific, but also beginning to claim total dominance over world sea routes:

> We shall give to the Spanish court all the advice the circumstances require. For our part, we are going to carry out the most thorough investigations on the rights, which I believe belong to Spain, of exclusive navigation in the South Sea. Mr de Rockingham [Prime Minister at the time] is surely not trying to persuade the other trading nations of Europe that the English are the Masters of the sea. If that were so … they would soon become masters of continents in every part of the world, and the phantom of a universal Monarchy would assume reality in their favour.[7]

Concern grew when Durand reported on 17 July that a new expedition was being organised in London. Byron was helping with its planning, although it seemed unlikely that he would command it. However, the general belief was that its aim was to occupy the islands discovered by Byron. The Prime Minister, William

Pitt, and the First Lord of the Admiralty, Lord Egmont, were both directly involved. The first place of call was to be the Malouines:

> From various comments made by Admiralty people, it has been learnt that Captn Byron had first of all urged the Office to give preference to the settlement envisaged for the Byron Islands, situated near the Philippines, on account of the beauty and extent of the harbour discovered there, but that after full consideration it had been decided to settle on the Falkland Islands, now that a safe route has been discovered through the Strait of Magellan.[8]

Choiseul and Bougainville pondered the location of these so-called Byron Islands, which represented an additional threat. It was not just the loss of the Malouines they were facing, but of a promising route through the strait. And there was the threat of new British outposts in the western Pacific. Britain controlled North America and India; soon it would be the turn of the Pacific Ocean and the Philippines. Not unexpectedly, Durand's regular dispatch of rumours and gossip contained false information, some of it intentionally planted by the Admiralty, but his reports could not be swept aside.

Byron had not followed his original instructions, which had been to sail to the north-west coast of America, look for the elusive North-West Passage and proceed across the northern Pacific to 'Asia, China, or the Dutch settlements in the East Indies', returning home by way of the Cape of Good Hope. He had in fact sailed across the central Pacific, towards the Tuamotu Islands and the Tokelaus, then veered north towards the Marshall Islands, east around the Philippines and down to Batavia. In other words, he had travelled right across the Spanish area of exclusivity. In all likelihood, Britain was planning to establish a settlement somewhere in those seas, although it was not clear where this might be.

Bougainville summarised the voyage and the contraband log in a brief report for Choiseul and Praslin. Apart from the interesting but minor question of giants living in Patagonia, two main issues stood out. One was the threat to the Malouines and the other the discovery by Byron of islands in the Pacific, which would be of interest to geographers, but even more so to British politicians.

Durand kept up a flurry of letters, adding urgency to the situation. The ship *Dolphin*, which he called *Dauphin*, was in Deptford, being readied for what would obviously be a long voyage. On 25 July, he advised that the *Dauphin* was about to sail for the Falklands, accompanied by the *Swallow*, currently at Chatham. Two additional ships were to leave shortly after: the *Swift*, a sloop from Woolwich, and the *Roy*, from Norwich. The commander of this small fleet would be a 'Capitaine Vallas' – Samuel Wallis. By the end of June, therefore, the French – and very soon the Spanish – were made aware of Wallis's expedition. There was no time to waste.

The Malouines would have to be transferred to Spain without further delay, so that the two Bourbon kingdoms could present the British with a united front. Fuentes met Bougainville in mid-August to discuss the final details.

Fortunately, a political crisis in London gained them time. The First Lord of the Admiralty, Lord Egmont, favoured the immediate dispatch of a force to take over the Falklands. The First Lord of the Treasury, the Duke of Grafton, worried that this could bring about early hostilities with Spain and France, opposed the plan. A clash over the Falklands might compromise Wallis's voyage, which was to include further exploration in the Pacific. There was a split in the Cabinet. Egmont and several others resigned. Following this political stoush, apparently, the original orders were changed: 'When Captain Wallis – whose ship, the *Dolphin*, together with the *Swallow* and the *Prince Frederick*, storeship, was by now riding at anchor in Plymouth Sound – received his sailing orders on August 20, they did not call for him to sail to the Falkland Islands'.[9]

The French plans emerging from private discussions between Bougainville and Choiseul – with the Duc de Praslin kept advised in confidence – were closer to those the British had originally worked out: Louis would go to the Falklands and then begin a voyage around the world. The broad lines of his project were soon worked out, the details gradually settled as the days went by. In one respect, likely objections from the financial administrators were rapidly minimised by the fact that the Malouines handover had already been agreed upon. This meant that the cost of the first part of the voyage would have to be covered anyhow – and Spain had agreed to make a substantial contribution.

Choiseul, as he so often did, was juggling with various issues at the same time. The Spanish were to get the Malouines; the results of Byron's voyage were to be analysed in detail, from its strategic as well as its geographical aspects; and Spanish supremacy in the Pacific Ocean was to be tactfully challenged by a French circumnavigation. While the British would be partly placated by closing down the Malouines settlement, their expansionary aims would be at least partly neutralised. Most importantly, a major French voyage of exploration was being prepared, although this was to be kept in the background for as long as possible.

The nagging concern over the Byron Islands near the Philippines led to the revival of a somewhat strange proposal Choiseul had briefly discussed earlier in the year: the purchase of one of the Philippine islands by France. Originally, the aim had been to make an offer for one of the southern islands, but now that Spain was embroiled in a dispute with Britain over the Manila ransom, he could envisage the transfer of a much larger area. A neat little scheme was developed: Bougainville would hand over the Malouines to Spain, and then sail across the Pacific to acquire the Philippines, in part or altogether, for France. A letter from Choiseul to the

French ambassador in Madrid shows that he still thought the purchase of the Philippines could be arranged:

> I do not know whether the indifference which Mr de Grimaldi revealed in connection with the retention of the Philippines is real or not. It is true that they are of no value whatsoever to Spain, whether for her trade or the security of her other possessions, and that they cause her fairly considerable outgoings. And if she was agreeable to their passing into English ownership without any real feeling of distaste, it would be far more natural to transfer them over to ourselves … This transfer, which would be most advantageous for our navigation in Eastern seas, would present no disadvantage whatsoever for the Spanish. In that case, we would see to the payment of the [Manila] ransom to the English.[10]

Meanwhile, there were more realistic matters to settle. The summer recess was coming to an end, government offices were reopening and the matter of the Falklands had to be settled once and for all. The Spanish were becoming truly irritated about the slowness of the French. Louis would have to go back to Madrid as soon as possible to fix up the final details.

He left on 2 September. The journey, on horseback as before, took him ten days. He immediately called on the Marquis d'Ossun, handed him the various items of mail that Choiseul and others had given him and asked the ambassador to organise the meetings he was to attend. A couple of days later, during a private conversation, Louis told Ossun about his proposed circumnavigation. In return, the ambassador updated him on the exchange of notes between Madrid and London, and the growing Spanish anxiety about British activities and in particular Wallis's expedition.

On 15 September, Ossun took Louis to meet Grimaldi, who told him that Carlos III was pleased that the Malouines transfer was in its final stage. The target date was to be 1 January 1767. Louis, by way of confirmation, gave Grimaldi a copy of Choiseul's letter to his cousin, Nerville, in which the minister gave him formal instructions to hand over the settlement to the Spanish officials who would be arriving with Bougainville.

Soon after this, news arrived from French and Spanish sources of another British expedition to the Falklands. They already knew about Wallis's voyage, but this was a different matter altogether. It was a clear attempt by England to settle on the Falklands. Captain John McBride had been sent out in the *Jason*, had apparently landed on the archipelago and established a colony. Wallis, it was believed, was going out to strengthen it. Furthermore, added Fieschi di Masserano, Madrid's ambassador in London, there were rumours of British 'plans to set up establishments in other parts of South America', in the South Seas and possibly in the Strait of Magellan.

All this incensed the Spanish. Fuentes, in Paris, was instructed to approach Choiseul and obtain his approval for a joint protest to London, which was to contain the words 'England will be held responsible for any consequences if she persists in these endeavours'.[11] This sounded too close to an ultimatum for Choiseul – and for Louis XV, who had no wish to get embroiled in another war. The terms of the protest were toned down. The French were not even sure that it should be sent at all, as information recently received in Paris indicated that Wallis was not going to the Falklands, and that McBride's so-called colony was little more than a move to warn off the French.

The instructions McBride had received from the Admiralty did not even mention a French settlement, let alone require him to set up a colony. They suggested simply that he should carry out a general reconnaissance and show the British flag:

> If any subjects of a foreign Power were found to be settled at any point in the Islands, they were to be visited and informed that the Islands belonged to Great Britain, and that, since His Majesty had given orders for the settlement thereof, the subjects of no other Power were entitled to reside there without the King's permission. Any such persons were to be offered transport on His Majesty's ships to some port in the Dominions of the Power to which they belonged.[12]

McBride had sailed from England on 26 September 1765. He intended to check on the settlement Byron was reported to have made, and which the French and the Spanish had taken to be the implantation of an actual colony. It was in fact no more than the 'Pritty little Garden' laid out by the *Tamar*'s surgeon. McBride had reached the islands on 8 January 1766, cleared a patch of land at Port Egmont, 'weeded Byron's vegetables', but he had not yet found the French colony. He did little more than erect a small fort, but in September, having climbed a hill, he came across a bottle containing a message in French, presumably the one left by the *Aigle*'s survey party. Thus alerted, McBride at last discovered the Saint-Louis settlement and promptly sent the French a note asking by what authority they had erected a settlement in the Falklands.

Nerville was able to gain time by replying that he could not read English and so could not understand the Englishman's message. McBride largely ignored this – it was not his role to argue with the settlers, but to warn them off. He sent a small party ashore, taking a formal warning to Nerville to remove his colony. This done, the *Jason* sailed back to England. McBride had not presented any immediate threat to the French, and the British left no lasting trace of their passage, but the *Jason* expedition clearly indicated that Britain was not about to allow the islands to fall into Bourbon hands – and McBride had made it quite clear that they would return before long.

The lack of precise information about British activities and the constant flow of rumours helped Louis, ensuring that the Spanish remained anxious to settle the Malouines affair as quickly and as amicably as possible. Carlos III and Grimaldi remained well disposed towards him, smoothing away all arguments about the amount of compensation he might receive, and softening the attitude of nationalistic Spanish ministers and officials. His second voyage to Madrid therefore went smoothly. He had made a number of friends on his previous visit – he was still the polished courtier, full of charm, who had set hearts aflutter in Montreal and Versailles – and they were all eager to help. The financial settlement he negotiated was favourable, the circumnavigation – which he could not conceal much longer from his hosts – seemed to present no danger to the Spanish empire, and they did what they could to help him.

The king counter-signed the order to pay Bougainville and the *Compagnie de Saint-Malo* the sum of 618,108 *livres*, 13 *sols*, 11 *deniers*. Louis signed the formal handover document the next day. This did not mean that he admitted the islands truly belonged to Spain – he never held that view – but it closed one chapter of his life, and opened a new and far more important one.

On 6 October 1766, he left Madrid for Paris. The long dreary months of tortuous diplomatic negotiations were finally at an end. Now, he could embark on his great adventure.

Louis de Bougainville as a young man (pastel, artist unknown).

The city of Quebec in the eighteenth century (engraving).
Bibliothèque Nationale, Estampes.

The French settlement in the Falkland Islands in 1763–4 (drawn for Dom Pernetty's *Voyage*).

No drawing of the *Boudeuse* appears to exist, but it would have been similar to this eighteenth century French frigate.

The arrival of the *Boudeuse* in Tahiti, as imagined by a later painter, Albert Brenet.
Musée de la Marine, Paris.

Bougainville and his officers receive gifts from the Tahitian islanders (pastel, artist unknown).
Rex Nan Kivell collection, National Library of Australia, Canberra.

VOYAGE

AUTOUR DU MONDE,

PAR LA FRÉGATE DU ROI

LA BOUDEUSE,

ET

LA FLÛTE L'ÉTOILE;

EN 1766, 1767, 1768 & 1769.

A PARIS,

Chez SAILLANT & NYON, Libraires, rue S. Jean-de-Beauvais.

De l'Imprimerie de LE BRETON, premier Imprimeur ordinaire du ROI.

M. DCC. LXXI.

AVEC APPROBATION ET PRIVILEGE DU ROI.

The title page of the first edition of Bougainville's journal of his voyage around the world.

A formal portrait of Bougainville in later life (oils, artist unknown).

A contemporary photograph of the inauguration of the Bougainville memorial in Tahiti, 1909.

The fort at Brest is now a museum.

Part 4
Sailing Around the World

17. FINAL PREPARATIONS FOR A CIRCUMNAVIGATION

October–November 1766

BOUGAINVILLE REACHED PARIS during the late afternoon of 15 October. The journey from Madrid, whether by coach or on horseback, was always a strenuous and at times dangerous undertaking. With short stops at roadside inns for an indifferent meal, or an overnight stay in uncomfortable rooms, one inevitably reached one's destination grimy and exhausted. Louis could not, however, allow himself the luxury of even a few days' break. His uncle D'Arboulin was anxiously waiting for him, as was Chesnard de la Giraudais, back from the Falklands and waiting to report on his voyage and the conditions in the colony.

Nor could reporting to Choiseul be delayed. Bougainville had letters and papers for him, which he handed over the day after his arrival, as well as mail for the Spanish ambassador, Fuentes, and some private correspondence for the daughter of the Comte d'Ossun. He saw to this on the morning of the 16th, arranged for a meeting at Versailles the next day and hurried back to talk to La Giraudais.

It was a lengthy discussion. La Giraudais had left in the *Étoile* in the previous November and reached the Malouines in mid-February. He had found the settlement in a good condition, the colonists' morale high, in spite of their concern about a possible British intervention. But La Giraudais knew that the islands' future was uncertain, and that both Spain and Britain were putting pressure on Bougainville to bring the whole undertaking to an end. Tactfully, La Giraudais had done his best to evade some of the questions the settlers levelled at him. There was no point in lowering their morale any further.

He had unloaded the supplies brought from France and was getting ready for a brief expedition to the Strait of Magellan, when the *Aigle* arrived with Duclos-Guyot. Both ships made for the strait in late April, not a good season for such an undertaking, entering it on 3 May. There were a number of friendly meetings with various groups of Patagonians, and the usual exchange of gifts. Some of the French even went riding at the invitation of the Indians.

The weather was not as bad as had been expected. More troublesome was a period of recurring calms that meant the ships could not sail to Bahia Bougainville, as planned. The two vessels put into a small bay, where the felling of trees proved easy, and on the way back encountered large crowds of Patagonians – some 800 of them. The encounter caused some anxiety among the French, who found themselves swamped by a flood of shouting, singing, clamouring natives. In one incident, possibly an attempt to steal the sailors' possessions or even to kidnap some of them, a party of men from the *Aigle* was attacked and several were wounded. The ships made their way separately back to the Malouines. The *Étoile* promptly unloaded her timber and was readied for the voyage back to France, sailing on 3 July. She had arrived at Rochefort on 2 September.

La Giraudais had reported to Choiseul and to Fuentes, shortly after his return, while Bougainville was still in Spain. He had lent a copy of his journal to Fuentes, so that it could be sent to Madrid. The ambassador had asked him whether he had seen any sign of a British presence in the Falklands – or, as the copyist spelled it, 'the Flacklan'. La Giraudais was adamant that no one had come across any British settlement, and that this had been confirmed by a survey of the coast, carried out in June in a locally built schooner, the *Croisade*, by Joseph des Perriers and by Lavarye-Leroi, port captain of Port Saint-Louis. The odds against a British presence in the Malouines were a thousand to one, he told Fuentes. This was important information for both the Spanish and the French, and at a later meeting Fuentes asked La Giraudais to confirm his views in writing.

> I could not positively assert that the English are not there … because they may be deep in some harbour where they might not have been seen, and as this possibility is of major importance I will not deny it. If I were asked for my personal opinion, I would wager my life that they are not there, for it is not possible for that nation to have come unnoticed in boats and overland to explore the place where we have lived for the last four years, something which they certainly knew.[1]

Bougainville had his reservations about this. The possibility of some outpost could not be ignored, but it was something that would have to be dealt with in due course by the Spanish.

He had more pressing matters to see to, all related to his proposed voyage. His time in Paris and Versailles was hectic, with little time to rest and almost none for socialising. On 17 October, he hurried to Versailles for an early meeting with Praslin and Choiseul. Both men received him warmly, for he had handled the delicate Spanish situation with tact and skill, and had earned respect on both sides of the Pyrenees. The king was pleased with him, Choiseul told Louis, and everything was being done to ensure that the great voyage could proceed without further delay. It was also necessary to proceed quietly. A number of influential Spanish officials had been suspicious of France's actions in the Falklands, never totally convinced that Bougainville and Choiseul had truly believed that the islands were available for colonisation by anyone who could muster the resources. They would be even more unhappy to learn of a French expedition looking for likely outposts in the Pacific.

Fuentes, whom Bougainville visited on the 18th, was anxious to complete the agreed refund of his expenses in the Falklands, while making it quite clear that Spain was paying only for the cost of the failed colonisation. Nothing in the agreement could imply that France was selling the islands to Spain, as this would suggest that the original Spanish ownership was in doubt. Fuentes was even uneasy about the mention of the *Compagnie de Saint-Malo* in the receipt Louis gave him. To reassure him, Bougainville came back on the 20th and offered to write out a new receipt along lines that would ease his qualms, but Fuentes finally declared himself satisfied.

The transaction included the sale of the *Aigle*. The *Sphinx* had already been sold and was excluded from the deal. The Spanish were not interested in the *Étoile*. She had originally been intended for the repatriation of the Acadians, but Spain had now undertaken to see to the return of those settlers who did not wish to stay under Spanish rule. This meant that the *Étoile* would be available to Bougainville for his circumnavigation, once the Malouines handover was complete.

The main vessel, the *Boudeuse*, was already being refitted for the strenuous circumnavigation – Praslin had been seeing to that in Louis's absence, and the work was well advanced. Nicolas Duclos-Guyot, appointed second-in-command to Bougainville, had already left for Nantes to supervise the work and the loading of supplies. Meanwhile, La Giraudais, who was to command the *Étoile*, was in Rochefort, carrying out similar work.

Bougainville's tasks in Paris, apart from settling financial matters with the Spanish ambassador, included recruiting officers and other personnel for the voyage, obtaining additional equipment and supplies, and discussing the text of his official instructions. Praslin and Choiseul were preparing these, so that they could be submitted for Louis XV for his final approval.

Praslin had earlier instructed the seamen's commissioner in Saint-Malo that the petty officers and men he was recruiting there and at Nantes should be selected, as far as possible, from those who had already sailed to the Falklands under Bougainville. They were not to be told, however, the real destination of this particular expedition.

Louis himself was approached by a number of people while in Paris. Some wanted to recommend a friend or relative; others had problems to settle in connection with the proposed voyage. Any discussions he had were complicated by the need for secrecy.

Pierre Poissonnier, a medical consultant and inspector of naval and colonial hospitals, who was supplying medical supplies for the expedition, including some powders to combat scurvy, was having problems with Duclos-Guyot. The latter was reluctant to accept a distilling machine, a cucurbit, that Poissonnier had devised in 1762 and that was now gaining wide acceptance in the navy. It involved taking additional supplies of coal and firewood, and Duclos-Guyot considered the machine a fire risk. Bougainville agreed that it could be placed on the deck of the *Boudeuse*, and promised to supervise its operation. It turned out to be invaluable when the frigate sailed through the Pacific Ocean, converting sea water into much-needed drinking water.

At the same time, Poissonnier suggested the appointment of Philibert Commerson as the expedition's naturalist. Commerson, who was then in Paris and unemployed, had a number of friends in scientific circles, who had put his name forward for the voyage. The scientists Bernard Jussieu and Lalande, and Pierre Poivre, the recently appointed administrator of Mauritius, all warmly endorsed this nomination, which Bougainville accepted.

Commerson was a gifted but erratic and sometimes difficult character. He had qualified as a doctor at the University of Montpellier, but his real passion was botany. He was a widower, aged thirty-nine, with a young child who was being cared for by his brother-in-law, a priest. He had nothing to hold him in France, apart from his housekeeper and mistress, Jeanne Baret. This problem was soon solved when the pair decided that Jeanne would sail with him, disguised as a male servant. No one guessed her sex when she boarded the *Étoile* or until many months later. Her presence, however, would create a number of problems during the lengthy voyage.[2]

Bougainville needed a fully qualified astronomer, especially as he would be entering relatively unknown waters. Lefrançais de Lalande, the astronomer royal, suggested Pierre-Antoine Véron, a brilliant student of his, who had been serving on naval ships since 1761. Now aged thirty-three, Véron was a Norman of modest origins, the son of a carpenter. He worked as a gardener until the age of twenty, when he moved to Rouen and eventually was able to study mathematics and in time to travel to Paris. Lalande had arranged for him to sail on the *Diadème* in 1761 and on the *Sceptre* in 1762; there he had met Charles François Charnières, a young officer who was working on the problems of determining longitudes at sea. Véron and Charnières had become close collaborators. The minister endorsed the nomination, but Véron was appointed to the storeship *Étoile*. He proved to be an able and hardworking member of the expedition.

While in Paris, Bougainville was invited by the Comte de Maurepas to a dinner where he met a young nobleman, Charles de Nassau-Siegen – or, to give him his full name, Charles-Henri-Nicolas-Othon de Nassau-Siegen et d'Orange. Born in

Sénarpont, in northern France on 9 January 1745, he was well connected, with a lineage that included members of the Hesse and Hohenzollern families. His mother had died when he was only a small child, and he had been brought up by his grandmother, Charlotte de Mailly, Marquise de Nesle, a member of the Coligny family. He had served during the Seven Years War from the age of sixteen, but once he returned to civilian life he had little to do apart from attending receptions and gambling. The police spies drew up their usual lurid reports on him, mentioning his mounting debts and the women of doubtful character he consorted with: 'This state of idleness, added to the credit one earns from the title of prince and the name of Highness used with tradesmen, resulted in a prodigious amount of debt'.[3] Rumours of an affair with the opera singer and actress Sophie Arnould increased the concerns of his relatives, who decided to have him removed from temptation. What better than a ship sailing to distant seas? Even though he would have to pay his own way during the voyage, this would be a mere fraction of what he was squandering in Paris and Versailles.

Bougainville found Nassau-Siegen charming, quite well educated and by no means as superficial as his critics were alleging. He seemed genuinely interested in the planned voyage, about which he had been told in confidence, and eager to be part of it. Louis took to him – his conversation was delightful and witty, and he possibly also saw in the prince a younger version of his own, at times philandering, self. He gladly accepted him as a member of the expedition, officially as a passenger in the *Boudeuse*. It was a decision he never regretted.

Nassau-Siegen then asked whether Bougainville could also accept a friend of his, Henry de Fulque, Chevalier d'Oraison. Born in Aix-en-Provence on 16 January 1739, D'Oraison had joined the cadet corps, the *Gardes de la Marine*, at Toulon at the age of eighteen and served in a number of ships, taking part in several campaigns and being captured twice. After the end of the Seven Years War, he had been sent by Choiseul to 'visit' naval shipyards and port installations in England, Denmark, Sweden and Russia, a mission he had carried out with discreet efficiency. This had earned him promotion to *enseigne de vaisseau*. Bougainville granted the request, subject to Choiseul's approval, which was promptly forthcoming.

Other nominations were made by Choiseul and Praslin, although they referred the proposed appointments to Bougainville for confirmation. Five officers, D'Oraison included, had joined the navy by way of the *Gardes*, a training school founded by Jean Baptiste Colbert in 1670 and reserved for members of the aristocracy.

This connection marks an important distinction between the officers of the *Boudeuse* and those of the *Étoile*. The former was a frigate, part of the French Navy, and it was essentially the preserve of aristocratic appointees. The latter was a storeship, carrying supplies for the expedition, a former merchant vessel staffed by officers who could not claim the aristocratic background required for entry into the king's navy. Fulque d'Oraison provides a good example of the class of noble youths who were entitled to enter the *Gardes*. He belonged to one of the oldest families of Provence, tracing his lineage back to the twelfth-century noble Hughes d'Oraison Clumanc. The Oraisons had ruled the district for 500 years, and had been raised to the rank of marquis by Henry III in 1588. The Fulque family became linked with the estate at the beginning of the eighteenth century and built an imposing castle in 1740.

Bougainville had many pressing matters to see to while he was still in Paris. His schedule was crowded, his days filled with meetings and hurried visits to officials and acquaintances. The minister, in particular, demanded his attention. There were calls to make on the Spanish ambassador, on administrators at various ministries and on scientists and friends. Everything seemed to be proceeding at last, but at an exhausting and frenzied pace.

On 19 October, he met Praslin to whom he outlined his broad proposals for the voyage and the type of officers he wanted to appoint. Praslin had his own opinion and the discussion went on in a friendly manner for some time. On the 21st, Louis went back to see him and introduced Commerson and Véron, whom he proposed to take with him on the expedition. Praslin accepted these nominations, appointing Véron as royal pilot and observer, and determining his salary. He also confirmed Commerson's appointment as royal botanist and informed him of his quite substantial salary, which delighted the naturalist. As he wrote to a friend, 'They have allowed me to take a valet.'[4] This, of course, would be Jeanne Baret.

Praslin then invited the botanist to submit 'a summary of the observations he planned to carry out in the field of natural history'.[5] Commerson's reaction was typical: working feverishly practically day and night, he drew up a seventeen-page document that he presented to the minister three days later. It was largely impractical, but it did impress Praslin, who agreed with Bougainville that the man would be a great asset on the expedition.

The next day, the 25th, Louis brought the draft instructions that Praslin has asked him to prepare. Following the transfer of the Malouines to Spanish sovereignty, he planned to sail to China by way of the Strait of Magellan, with the option, if the weather made it preferable, of sailing round Cape Horn. During the crossing of the Pacific, he would look for various little known or merely suspected land, such as 'Diemen's Land, New Holland, Carpentaria, the Land of the Holy Spirit, New Guinea, etc'.[6] He would have the option of taking possession of any empty or new land he came across, 'being careful to erect poles bearing the arms of France' but not to leave anyone behind to man an outpost. He was to look for some island close to China, where a trading post might be set up by the French India Company.

Praslin endorsed this broadly worded proposal, but referred it to Choiseul for his opinion. His cousin found no problem with the draft, which he sent on to his officials to be rewritten in a final form the king could sign. Bougainville then hurried back to tell Nassau-Siegen, Véron and Commerson that their departure was now imminent. There remained one minor problem – finding a chaplain.

Philibert Commerson had earlier put forward the name of his younger brother, Georges-Marie, who was a priest at Châtillon. The minister had no objection, but the idea did not appeal to Father Commerson, and the proposal was dropped. He rejected the invitation because of the short notice given and the upheaval that a prompt departure would cause in his parish. There was also a small provincial priest's lack of interest in travel to distant and frightening parts of the world. His strong disapproval of Philibert's affair with Jeanne Baret may also have been a factor. It was altogether an odd suggestion – it is hard to fathom why Philibert would have wanted his brother on board when he had Jeanne sharing his cabin.

Georges-Marie Commerson's refusal forced Bougainville to call in haste on the Archbishop of Paris. Fortunately, someone was available, an unattached and rather impoverished Franciscan priest whom officials had been trying to place in a suitable position. His availability meant that he could leave at once. He had few demands to make of the organisers – all he asked was 'that on his return to France, he would be guaranteed adequate means of sustenance'.[7]

Father Jean-Baptiste Lavaysse or Lavaisse (the archives list him as 'Lavoys', which would be pronounced much the same in the eighteenth century) came from Autun – not far from Jeanne Baret's birthplace. He remains a fairly shadowy figure, but he had apparently already sailed as a ship's chaplain, which made him particularly suitable for the Bougainville expedition. He carried out his functions on the *Boudeuse* quite satisfactorily, but landed at the Isle de France, his health somewhat impaired. He returned to France in 1769, ill and unfit for any further naval service. The promises made to him in Paris do not seem to have been carried out, for he was simply handed over to the care of his local diocese. He was still alive and in fairly penurious circumstances around 1787, but nothing more is known of him.

Having settled the matter and arranged for Father Lavaysse to travel to Nantes and join the *Boudeuse*, Louis returned to the pressing matter of his final instructions. The king had promptly given his agreement, signing the final version of the instructions on 26 October. Choiseul then handed them over to Bougainville. They allowed Louis considerable latitude. The *Boudeuse*, under Louis's command, would leave Nantes first and sail to the River Plate 'to join two frigates which H. Catholic M. [the King of Spain] has sent from his European ports, that are to wait for him there'. Bougainville would then take the Spanish ships to the Malouines and formally hand the islands over to Spain. Then, once the *Étoile* arrived, the two

French vessels would 'sail for China by way of the South Sea'. Louis would be free to cross the Strait of Magellan or round Cape Horn 'according to what the time of year and the winds dictate'. During the crossing, he was to 'examine in the Pacific Ocean as many as possible and as best he can the lands lying between the Indies and the western shores of America of which several were sighted by navigators'. Since knowledge of these islands or continent was 'very slight', it was worth improving. And 'as no European nation has any establishment or claim over these lands', it could 'only be in France's interest to survey them and take possession of them should they offer items useful to her trade and her navigation'. Because the area was known to contain 'rich metals and spices', Louis was to 'examine the soils, trees and main productions' and bring back 'samples and drawings of everything he may consider worthy of attention'. He would note possible ports of call for ships and record 'everything relating to navigation'. As soon as he landed anywhere, he must erect 'posts bearing the arms of France' and 'draw up Acts of Possession in the name of His Majesty'.

He was to leave China at the end of January 1768 at the latest, as the monsoon would not allow him to depart after that date. He would be allowed to call at the Philippines if necessary and could, if appropriate, take his two vessels there as well as to China, or he could send the *Étoile* by a different route. Bougainville was to establish whether there was 'an island within reach of the China coast that could serve as a depot for the India Company to trade with China'. Since he was not to be longer than two years, and since 'events during his campaign may require him to make straight for the Isle de France', he had the choice of landing or not landing on the China coast. In any case, Bougainville should do 'everything in his power to call at the Isle de France in order to find out whether the state of peace has been maintained or whether we are at war with some nation and whether H.M. has despatched any instructions concerning some particular destination for the two vessels'.

If it should prove absolutely necessary, Louis was authorised to separate his two vessels, and to burn one if, 'in unknown seas, the deteriorating health of his crews or some accident made it impossible for him to sail with the two ships'. Otherwise, he could sell the surplus ship.

During the voyage Bougainville was to pay 'bonuses either in cash, or in clothes and other items taken on the said vessels to petty officers and sailors who deserve them and to increase their ration if he considers it necessary and to effect such changes as may be required by the health of the crews'. At the end of October, Louis received a set of supplementary orders, covering matters of discipline and relations with other ships or the commanders of foreign ports.[8]

Choiseul now asked Bougainville to advise Fuentes of these arrangements. He did not want the Spanish to feel that the French were acting behind their backs, as they accused them of having done with the Malouines settlement. Nor did he want to give them the impression that he was using the transfer of the islands as an excuse for breaching their monopoly of the Pacific. Choiseul's concerns were justified. Fuentes read Louis's copy of his instructions with growing disapproval. All this was new to him, and if his government had suspected that Bougainville planned to open up a new route to the East by way of the Pacific, his reception in Madrid might have been much less friendly. The ambassador was not mollified by Louis's reply that Madrid knew he was planning to travel to the Philippines and that there had been no objection. Fuentes merely agreed to keep an open mind until he had discussed the matter personally with Choiseul.

This was a serious setback, threatening to delay further the departure of the expedition. Louis hastened back to Praslin's home, where he found Choiseul. Both cousins reassured him: they could handle Fuentes. As it turned out, Praslin had invited the Spanish ambassador to dinner that very evening; Choiseul met him the next morning. Their interview was not an easy one: Choiseul needed all the tact and the finesse for which he was so renowned. Fuentes left, only partly convinced. Bougainville saw Choiseul almost immediately after this meeting. The minister suspected that Fuentes would feel obliged to report to Madrid, but he also knew there would be no reply for at least two or three weeks, so he told Bougainville to leave without delay. It was, once again, the policy of the *fait accompli*.

Choiseul had, though, guaranteed that there would be no contraband, no illicit trading with any Spanish colony – Spain's monopoly would not be infringed. Bougainville had no intention of trading and gave his word to Choiseul. Since the *Boudeuse* was a naval frigate, her officers were forbidden to engage in any commercial transaction – and indeed for most of the 'reds' such activities would have been totally *infra dig*. The *Étoile*, however, was a different matter: although Bougainville did not suspect it at the time, some of the 'blues' had their own ideas about private dealings.

As it turned out, Fuentes did not send his report to Grimaldi in Madrid right away. He waited for Bougainville to come back to him after his meeting with Praslin and Choiseul, confident that they would take his reservations seriously. Then he could send a full report to his superior. He did learn that Louis had left for Nantes, but thought he had simply gone to check on progress and would come back to Paris to make his final arrangements. Then he heard that the *Boudeuse* had sailed. As he wrote to Grimaldi, he found all this 'quite strange'. Neither man felt there was much that could be done. Grimaldi did not even write back to Fuentes about Louis's unexpected departure until 20 January 1767. All they could do was to trust Choiseul and Bougainville's assurances that they had no intention of undermining Spanish rights, and that the real danger came from Britain.

Meanwhile, in Nantes, Antoine Lemoyne, the *Commissaire Général de la Marine*, had been supervising the preparations, buying supplies, and overseeing the recruitment of sailors and soldiers. Bougainville had left Paris on 30 October, taking Nassau-Siegen with him. On 1 November, he called on Lemoyne, who assured him that the *Boudeuse* was a fine ship, and that she was almost ready to sail. She was not, however, in Nantes, but in Paimboeuf, further down the Loire River, undergoing final preparations. During the next few days, Bougainville made final arrangements with Lemoyne, went with him to chandlers, and wrote reports and letters to Paris. Supplementary instructions were arriving from Versailles, including some concerning Starot de Saint-Germain, the expedition's clerk. He also received a long report from his cousin, Nerville, about the latest known developments in the Malouines.

Louis also met three young aristocratic officers who had just arrived from Brest: Bournand, Suzannet and Kerhué. Alexandre de Lamotte-Baracé (or La Motte Baracé), Chevalier de Bournand, born in the Anjou region in 1736, had joined the *Gardes* at Brest at the age of seventeen and a year later joined the *Lys*. He was one of those taken prisoner by Admiral Boscawen's squadron before the Seven Years War had actually begun. He was imprisoned in England and, later freed on parole, he had sailed to the Mediterranean to serve with the Knights of Malta, whose main function was to protect the island against possible Turkish attacks. He had then returned to serve in the French Navy after the war, sailing to Cayenne and the West Indies. His promotion to *enseigne de vaisseau* came about in August 1767 – during the voyage of the *Boudeuse*.

Jean-Baptiste-François de Suzannet was a native of Poitou. After his cadetship in the *Gardes* at Rochefort, he had served with distinction during the Seven Years War. He was at Brest with his friend Jacques-Marie de Cramezel de Kerhué, a Breton who had joined the *Gardes* at the same time. He had served at Louisbourg, then in various ships during the later years of the war. In 1765, he had been appointed to the *Étourdie* as the same time as Suzannet for a campaign to Saint Pierre and Miquelon, the remaining French possessions in Canada.

There were also newcomers to introduce to each other. On the 4th, D'Oraison arrived, with Du Bouchage. The former had been appointed at the request of Nassau-Siegen, and the pair went off together, visiting new acquaintances the prince had already made.

Jean-Jacques de Gratet, Chevalier du Bouchage, already knew the other young officers. Quite young, he had joined the *Gardes* in 1757, serving mostly in the Mediterranean until 1765. He had been appointed to the Bougainville expedition at the same time as D'Oraison and Bournand, so he had had time to renew acquaintances. The day after his arrival at Nantes, he was told of his promotion to the rank of *enseigne de vaisseau*. He was to die in Mauritius two years later.

Thinking that he should try to mollify Fuentes, Louis wrote him a courtesy letter, in which he omitted to mention the ambassador's basic concern about the voyage. He concentrated instead on the almost frantic pace of activities at Nantes and 'the multitude of matters' he had had to deal with. It was a tactful way of explaining why he had not reported back to Fuentes before hastening off to Nantes. All the work had kept him in Brittany and

> ... prevented me from expressing my gratitude for all your kindness. I am now in Nantes, merely awaiting a favourable wind in order to sail. My frigate is a very handsome ship and quite ready. You authorised me to write to you from Buenos Aires and the Malouines: I will report to you on our combined operations ...

On 5 November, Bougainville set off for Paimboeuf with Lemoyne. Nassau-Siegen stayed a little longer in Nantes 'where he had friends with whom he was enjoying a merry time'.[9]

18. A False Start

November 1766

IN PAIMBOEUF, BOUGAINVILLE was met by Duclos-Guyot and Saint-Germain. This was Louis's first encounter with Louis-Antoine Starot de Saint-Germain. There is a slight aura of mystery about that appointment. Saint-Germain seemed ill-suited for a long voyage around the world. He had studied law, but he did not belong to the naval administrative corps, and he seems to have had no particular desire to become a ship's clerk – an *écrivain* or scribe. Born in September 1731 in the Dauphiné region, he had first obtained a position as administrator of stores in Guiana, a post he held from 1763 to 1766. Back in France, he applied for a similar position in the French possessions in the Indian Ocean, but was instead appointed to the *Boudeuse*. Recently married and no seaman, certainly no intrepid explorer, he bitterly regretted having to embark on a lengthy circumnavigation. His journal, a valuable record in many respects, is peppered with acid comments: 'What is the use of such a voyage?' He was to be left behind at the Isle de France in a poor state of health and later made his way back to France.

The clue to his appointment may lie in the fact that Catherine-Éléonore Bénard, who was Louis XV's mistress around 1767, married the following year Joseph Starot de Saint-Germain, then aged forty, a relative of the *Boudeuse*'s clerk. Marrying off a middle-class mistress to a member of the minor – and often impoverished – nobility was a common practice at the time. It had happened with the Marquise de Pompadour. The Saint-Germains were obviously receiving signs of favour at the time and Choiseul would have considered the appointment to the Bougainville expedition of higher status than some obscure clerical position on a French Indian Ocean island.

Bougainville had a relatively brief discussion with Saint-Germain. His instructions were to provide the clerk with all the facilities he required, and to work in close collaboration with him. Accounts and statements required both their signatures: no one would ever be able to cast aspersions on the financial management of the expedition. They then went down to the *Boudeuse*, where the entire complement, officers and men, was waiting to greet him.

The brand-new frigate, one of three built in 1765–6, lay proudly at anchor, 125 feet long, 32 feet wide, 26 guns, beautifully carved fore and aft:

The eighteenth century was not the golden age for decorating ships. The luxurious styles had reached their zenith during the second half of the previous century. It had been realised that the cluttering of statues, stern-walks and sponsons, the castles decorated with sculptures, were harmful to the progress of the vessels. The trend was now for soberness, with only the figure head at the bow and a few decorations aft. Bougainville, in this respect, showed a seaman's understanding, rather than an aesthete's when, before the departure from Brest, he ordered the removal of the sculptures from the stern, as being 'a useless burden'.[1]

Piped aboard, Louis reviewed the officers, petty officers and men lined up along the deck, stopping to exchange a few words with those he had not met before, nodding to those he had. Everything around him was fresh: the odour of new paint still lingered in the air, mixed with the rising smell of tar from the freshly caulked decks. For most of those present it was a strange experience: an army colonel with little practical experience of navigation taking over command of a naval vessel.

Impressive though she looked, the *Boudeuse* would nevertheless provide little more than uncomfortably cramped accommodation for the 200 or so men who were to sail in her. This, too, was something an army man, a relatively well-to-do courtier, would have to get used to. Louis had crossed the Atlantic on several occasions in similar conditions, but the *Boudeuse* was to be his home for many months on end.

He went down to his own quarters. These consisted of a small recess, with a narrow bunk, and a small cupboard skilfully designed to use every inch of available space, where he could keep his personal possessions and his private papers. Adjoining it was the wardroom, which served as his sitting room and study. Twenty by twenty-two feet, it looked relatively spacious and well lit, but it was also the officers' messroom and meeting place, and in use for much of the day and part of the night, with charts and instruments spread over the table.

Around it were the officers' own cabins, small cubby-holes most of them, divided by canvas screens. Their size varied according to rank, but none could be called comfortable. The ship's surgeon and the chaplain each had their own cabin in the area of the quarterdeck reserved for petty officers: they measured six by seven feet.

The space below decks for the men afforded no privacy: it was merely the 'tween-decks area, no more than 5 feet 3 inches high. Tall men were fairly rare in the eighteenth century, but care was still required when walking along. The cramped conditions would have to be shared for months with cattle, sheep and pigs, since live animals were the only way to ensure fresh meat in the days before canning and refrigeration. The poultry, fortunately, was kept in cages on the quarterdeck. Sailors and soldiers could sing, dance, talk or, if they could find a free space out of people's way, sleep in part of the fo'c's'le area, by the main mast.

Further down, in the orlop deck, were stored the mass of supplies required for long voyages: flour, hard tack or ship's biscuits, beans and other dried vegetables, casks of fresh water, spare sails and cables, pulleys, tools, powder and, tucked away in a corner, boxes of minor trade goods for eventual barter with islanders and other people encountered in faraway places.

Louis spent the afternoon talking with the few men he did not know. He had met them briefly during the welcoming review, but now wanted to find out about their backgrounds and their attitude towards the expedition. Dussine-Péan, who was to have the rank of *lieutenant de frégate*, had been recruited by Duclos-Guyot; he looked tired and ill-at-ease, and within a couple of days the surgeon would certify him as suffering from exhaustion and unfit for a lengthy expedition. He was accordingly discharged.

Josselin Le Corre, a 'blue' officer, had also been recruited by Duclos-Guyot, who had recently become related to him through marriage. Aged thirty-nine and an experienced seaman, Le Corre was to prove a considerable asset to Bougainville, who later recommended him for promotion in the naval service. Because he was a 'blue', however, there was no place for him in the navy and he returned to the merchant service. He later sailed in the expedition led by Marion du Fresne to Tasmania and New Zealand in 1771–2.

Father Lavaysse was a little more reticent. Knowing of Louis's connections with the modernist and often agnostic *philosophes*, he was unsure about the commandant's attitude towards the clergy, but he relaxed when he found that the expedition leader was friendly and welcoming. Louis asked Lavaysse about his earlier experiences in the navy, and kept away from discussions on religious matters. Laporte, the surgeon, was more open, and gave the impression of a knowledgeable and efficient medical man.

Charles-Félix-Pierre Fesche, the *volontaire*, Louis knew already. Now aged twenty-two, Fesche had sailed in the *Aigle* when only seventeen. With three voyages to the Malouines to his credit, he was now a seasoned seafarer and perfectly acquainted with the background of the French colony. He kept a journal during the expedition, probably in collaboration with Saint-Germain, which remains as an important source of information about the voyage and the places visited.

Finally, Louis was introduced to Duclos-Guyot's two sons Pierre and Alexandre, and to Denis Couture, chief petty officer, who was to prove invaluable on the voyage. He already knew his second, Germain Bonjour, who had been part of the crew of the *Aigle* in 1763. Another important member of the *Boudeuse's* complement was André-Philippe Ossere, the young sergeant in charge of the company of thirty soldiers. Ossere, born in the island of Ré, off La Rochelle, was a protégé of the Maréchal de Richelieu. He was still only twenty-one, but had a good record in the colonial defence service.

On 13 November, everything was readied for departure. The last loads of fresh food were brought up the gangway, a final roll call was taken, the last letters were written to the ministry, to family and friends. The next day, all leave over, duties were allocated, and the decks were cleared of everything that could be stowed below. Then on the 15th, the frigate sailed down the estuary of the Loire, on a westerly course.

The great adventure had begun.

On the 17th, however, a wild west-south-west storm blew up. During the night, the ropes holding the foresail snapped, and the topmast split; a little later, splits were also noticed in the main mast; then a studding sail and a staysail were torn. Bougainville held a brief meeting with his officers. It was too dangerous to sail to South America with these serious problems. He decided to make for the port of Brest for repairs. This was a big disappointment for him. The frigate was new, as were all the sails and the ropes, but in a way that was the problem – the *Boudeuse* had never undergone any of the usual sea trials, and had never ventured out into open water or faced bad weather.

When he reached Brest on the 21st, Bougainville discussed his problems with the port commander, Joseph de Roquefeuil, and the administrator, Jean Etienne de Clugny. He asked for major changes: the height of the masts should be reduced, and his 12-pounder guns exchanged for 8-pounders. This meant that most of the sails, including the spares, would have to be reduced in size. All this would take time. The departure of the *Boudeuse* was delayed for three weeks, but the news of this setback did not reach the Spanish or English authorities until much later. As far as they knew, Bougainville was on his way to the South Atlantic.

Louis began to wonder about a change of plans. The *Étoile*, he felt, would be more suited to his purpose once the Malouines handover was completed. Although his instructions had allowed him a fair degree of latitude, he felt he needed authority for this, so he wrote to the Duc de Praslin: 'I believe that the delay of a month forced on us by the accident we have suffered and my knowledge of this frigate, must lead to some changes being made to the plan of the voyage.'[2] He was forming the opinion that the *Boudeuse* would be 'totally unable to resist the squalls and seas of Cape Horn', so suggested that, once he had finished his work in the Falklands, he should send the frigate back to France with a reduced complement of 160 men. She would bring back with her the settlers who did not want to stay in the islands. He would then carry out the voyage of exploration in the *Étoile*, which had room for 140 men and enough supplies to last 18 months.

Praslin replied on 1 December:

> As for the plan you have in mind of giving up the command of the *Boudeuse* and take over the *Étoile* … the King leaves it to you in such a situation to act as you think best for the good of the service and the success of your mission. His Majesty however does expect you to make the best possible choice … His Majesty places his trust in your wisdom over this matter, and leaves you free to continue your voyage with both ships or with only one, as suits you best.[3]

This certainly gave Bougainville a great deal of freedom, but it also added the burden of a heavy responsibility: if he made the wrong decision, he would bear the blame. Praslin, however, had no choice. Louis had to be able to act on his own; otherwise it would take weeks, possibly months, to get approval from Versailles – and by then both Spain and Britain would have discovered France's real plans. It was best if no one knew anything until it was too late to raise objections.

The enforced stay in Brest allowed for some changes to the complement. Two men deserted and eleven were sent to hospital – some may have been suffering from venereal disease. Six men were taken on as replacements. On 6 December, the *Boudeuse* set sail. The great voyage had now truly begun.

Meanwhile, work was proceeding apace on the *Étoile*. Lemoyne had gone straight from Nantes to Rochefort to supervise the final arrangements. Dussine-Péan was leaving the *Boudeuse*, and Lemoyne had hoped that his son, Jean-Robert-Suzanne Lemoyne de Montchevry, born at Cayenne, Guiana, on 8 March 1750, might take his place as a volunteer. The youth had already been at sea as a *volontaire* in 1765. Lemoyne had little difficulty in obtaining the appointment for his son, but the boy failed to reach Nantes before the *Boudeuse* sailed. Fortunately, he had no trouble in getting an appointment to the *Étoile* and in Rio de Janeiro in July 1767 he transferred to the *Boudeuse* in exchange for Pierre Duclos-Guyot. He was promoted *garde de la marine* shortly after. He had a weak chest, however, and died at the Isle de France on 15 November 1768.

Chesnard de la Giraudais's second-in-command was a highly experienced officer, Jean-Louis Caro, who had served with the French India Company since his early youth and proceeded through all its grades, from junior apprentice to captain. He had obtained his first command, with the rank of *lieutenant de frégate*, on the *Fine* bound for the Isle de France. By 1765, he was sailing to China in the *Villevault* with the rank of second lieutenant. His appointment to the *Étoile* earned him a temporary commission in the royal navy as *lieutenant de frégate*. The careful, down-to-earth journal he kept during the circumnavigation gives the impression of a serious, practical officer who had little time for shipboard squabbles or the theories of the *philosophes*.

Four other 'officers of the blue' sailed in the *Étoile*. Joseph Donat was a relative of Chesnard de la Giraudais and the brother of Henry Donat de Lagarde who had sailed in the *Sphinx* to the Falklands. After his return to France in the *Étoile*, he is believed to have returned to the merchant service, but little more is known of his career. Details about Lafontaine-Villaubrun are equally sketchy. He was a fairly late appointment to the *Étoile*, replacing René Hercouet who had sailed on a previous voyage to the Falklands, but was unavailable to take up an offer to sail as second lieutenant. Lafontaine-Villaubrun was left behind at the Isle de France at the request of the local authorities, and some time later was commanding a merchant vessel in Indian seas.

Much more is known about Pierre Landais, born in Saint-Malo on 20 February 1734. He had first gone to sea at the age of eleven, sailing in a merchant vessel. He underwent his baptism of fire a year later during the War of the Polish Succession, but was taken prisoner soon after. He then returned to the merchant service, rising to lieutenant in 1752, but when the Seven Years War broke out he joined a privateer. He was taken prisoner in 1756. Freed, he returned to privateering in 1760, but later joined the navy with the rank of lieutenant. While serving in the *Zéphyr* in September 1762 he was wounded and for a third time taken prisoner. Peace was signed a year later, and he served, still as an officer of the blue, in the storeships *Garonne* and *Barbue* sailing to Newfoundland. This period of service ended in December 1764, and he was subsequently appointed to the *Étoile* with the rank of *lieutenant de frégate*.

Pierre-Marie Lavarye-Leroy, another native of Saint-Malo, was born in 1726. He served in the *Étoile* after the Malouines handover. He had entered the merchant service at the age of eleven and eventually rose to the rank of merchant captain. His record before joining the *Aigle* in 1763 was most impressive: he had completed twelve trading voyages to the West Indies, Africa, North America and the Indian Ocean, eight on privateers and three on naval ships. Bougainville saw him as an able and reliable officer, senior in experience and rank to most of the others, and considered him to be a suitable person to take over Port Saint-Louis in the Malouines. He was appointed port captain and later given a special bonus of 300 *livres* in recognition of this service. While in the islands, he had a small sloop constructed, *La Croisade*, which enabled him to survey some of the lesser known coasts and inlets of the archipelago. When the colony had been handed over to the Spanish authorities, he sailed to Montevideo with Bougainville, who then appointed him to the *Étoile*.

Another *volontaire* was appointed to the *Étoile* in addition to young Lemoyne,

Alexandre-Joseph Riouffe, born at Cannes in southern France, probably in 1750. Like Lemoyne, he had sailed for the first time in 1765, in the *Garonne* bound for Cayenne. The ship returned to Rochefort in June 1766 and in early 1767 Riouffe was appointed to the *Étoile*. He completed the circumnavigation and was back in France on 24 April 1769.

The clerk Michau (also Michaud, Michaux) was a land-based official whose only time at sea seems to have been his voyage in the *Étoile*. He had first worked in the artillery section of the Rochefort military college, and after serving there for ten years was transferred to the administrative side. He was probably in his mid- to late twenties when he was appointed to the *Boudeuse* in October 1766; he was transferred to the *Étoile* when Saint-Germain was given the main appointment. According to a report, he needed to save money, which may be why he sought this seagoing position – he would be housed and fed, however modestly.

The surgeon François Vivez (or Vivès) is far better known, not merely on account of the journal he kept in the *Étoile* but because of his outstanding career in the naval service, a milieu into which he was born and which he never left. He was a man of severe principles, devoted to his duties and expecting the same standard from others. He was born in Rochefort on 14 September 1744, the son of a naval surgeon. He had first gone to sea at the young age of seven in the *Formidable* with his father; he was enrolled as a pupil surgeon just before his twelfth birthday and qualified as assistant surgeon in May 1760. He worked from 1759 to 1762 at the hospital for the wounded at Rochefort, still under his father, then moved to Aix in 1763. He served as second surgeon in the storeships *Coulisse* and *Garonne* in 1764 and 1765, and joined the *Étoile* as medical officer in 1766.

The chaplain, Father François-Nicolas Buet, was a native of Quimper. A relatively obscure character, he met a tragic death when the expedition was in South America. The engineer cartographer, Charles Routier de Romainville, was appointed much later. Born in Paris in 1742, he joined the army in 1756. He served with distinction, but was wounded in August 1762 at the Battle of Johannesberg. Selected as engineer-geographer for the Malouines settlement, he had sailed in the *Aigle* on 6 October 1764 and was promoted lieutenant in November. On arrival in the Malouines, he drew up a plan for a new settlement, to be known as Ville Dubuc, and he remained in the islands right until the end of April 1767 when he embarked in the *Boudeuse* for Rio de Janeiro. The Spanish offered him a post with the rank of captain, but he refused, preferring to join the complement of the *Étoile* as cartographer and draughtsman. During the voyage, he drew a number of maps and some 'charming pen sketches', many of which have been lost.[4]

Some of these officers and men had already gathered at Rochefort and most of the others arrived during December. Commerson came on the 23rd, preceded by his reputation as a botanist of note. Chesnard de la Giraudais made him feel most welcome and gave him his own cabin, comparatively more roomy than the one originally set aside for him – so that he could provide space for his servant, 'Jean' Baret. The astronomer was Pierre-Antoine Véron, who had been recommended to Bougainville by Lalande. He was a gentle, unassuming man, and Commerson, who fell out with a number of his fellow voyagers, always remained on friendly terms with him. On his death Commerson named a plant after him, the *Veronia tristiflora*, 'a star-shaped flower that shows itself for only a few hours, and which against a dark background is spattered with tears'.[5]

Although Lemoyne felt optimistic about progress, he soon learned of delays. There were complaints about materials and supplies not arriving as promised. The blame seemed to lie with Charles Ruis-Embito, the port administrator. Some felt that his Spanish antecedents made him unsympathetic towards France's attempt to colonise the Falklands, but this accusation seems baseless: he was a fussy civil servant, legalistic and literal in carrying out his functions. He knew how to ward off complaints and he wrote to the minister, Praslin, that Lemoyne had been neither clear nor prompt with his requests. Part of the problem, he added craftily, was the late arrival of the Bordeaux wine requested by La Giraudais and Lemoyne.

There was another reason for the delay: officers were taking on board goods for resale in South America, a profitable sideline, although illegal once a ship was sailing under royal warrant. Some naval supplies were unloaded to make room for these trade goods, and the companionways and even the officers' mess and wardroom, the *grande chambre*, became grossly overcrowded. According to Vivès, 'one could scarcely go in' the wardroom and 'there was nowhere for our crew to sling their hammocks and they slept on the cables'.[6]

Philibert Commerson echoed these sentiments to the point of indignation – these, after all, were part of his own quarters and working space:

Trading for one's own account, on the King's ships, is absolutely forbidden. Nevertheless, one could close one's eyes to these abuses, if only they were tolerable; but to go as far as to unload quantities of needed supplies in order to take on bundles of trade goods, to crowd out the water and the food of the unfortunate crew, to prevent them from hanging a single hammock in their own part of the between-decks and force them to sleep here and there on badly secured bales, running the risk of being crushed at any moment, is an abuse that ought to be repressed, and it is one that lasted for 3/4 of our navigation.[7]

But finally, on 1 February 1767, the *Étoile* set sail. However, she would not go to the Falklands, but to South America.

19. Back to the Malouines

December 1766–April 1767

By and large, the *Boudeuse's* voyage to the Malouines was uneventful. Much of the equipment on board, particularly that replaced at Brest, was still being tested. Louis was happier than when the frigate left Nantes, but he still felt at the back of his mind that it might be wiser to sail into the Pacific in the *Étoile* and leave the untried *Boudeuse* to return to France.

On 8 December, he sighted a vessel coming from the opposite direction. It looked familiar, and he became convinced that she was the *Aigle* on her way back from the Malouines. Unfortunately, they were too far away and neither ship altered course in time to get within hailing distance, so he was unable to check. The *Aigle* had stayed back in the Malouines the previous July, unloading the timber obtained in the Strait of Magellan. The South Atlantic winter had been especially bitter, with a great deal of rain, cold, ice and snow. She had sailed for home on 7 September and was only now approaching the coast of Brittany. It was quite probable that this was the vessel Louis had sighted, so he missed out on getting an updated report from her captain.

The *Boudeuse* continued on her way, crossing the line on 7 January and observing the usual ceremonies, and sighting the American continent on the 29th. Two days later, Bougainville dropped anchor in Montevideo. It was still a new and fairly raw settlement, far from the bustling Uruguayan capital it would become seventy years later. Founded in 1726, it was a conveniently situated port in the outer estuary of the River Plate, built on a small peninsula and overlooked by a small mountain, the 'Hill of the Lookout', that gave the city its name.

Bougainville had been there before, in December 1763 with the *Aigle*, and he knew a number of the officials, who were happy to welcome him back. 'We have only praise for the manner in which we were received,' wrote Fesche in his journal. 'It would be difficult to be better treated; their homes became ours, and we often came close to abusing their kindness.'[1] The local hospitality filled a serious gap:

there was no inn of any kind in the town, not even an eating-house. Fesche was not impressed by Montevideo itself:

> The town of Montevideo is, in every respect, quite ugly; the houses are all very low-roofed and badly built. This is not because the country lacks the materials needed to build well and solidly, but because of the excessive laziness and sloth of its inhabitants. There is an abundance of fine, well-grained stone just outside the town, but it would be too much trouble to hew them. Furthermore, one would need mortar and lime, and this work is beyond them. They are satisfied with picking up the first stones they come across, to mix with water the soil lying around the spot they consider suitable for their structure, and this is what they use for mortar and cement … There are a number of these shanties built with a kind of brick, but they are held together in the same manner as the others.

The French spent a pleasant and restful time in Montevideo, but it was no more than a dependency of Buenos Aires. The local officials were largely port administrators and naval staff. To make the final arrangements for the transfer of the Malouines Louis needed to go to Buenos Aires, further up the river.

He left on 6 February, sailing into the estuary and across to the south bank of the River Plate in a small schooner, accompanied by the Prince de Nassau-Siegen and Saint-Germain. It was an uncomfortable journey, with heavy rain. They landed wet through, in the dark and at low tide. The Governor of Rio de la Plata, Francisco de Paula Bucareli y Ursua, sent his carriage to bring them up to town. He had only been appointed that year, and was to prove an amiable friend to the French. They found Buenos Aires far more attractive than Montevideo, laid out with impressive geometrical evenness. 'The streets are drawn in perfectly straight lines,' commented Saint-Germain. It had been founded in 1586 when Juan de Garay arrived with a small group of adventurers. In Bougainville's time, the population reached 15,000. Today, it exceeds 1.5 million.

An energetic man, Bucareli y Ursua was keen to settle the Malouines affair, and to promote the colony and develop its trade and agriculture. But he had other, more important matters to deal with, in particular the unpopularity of the powerful Jesuits whom he spent much of 1767 expelling and sending back to Spain. Even though it was a Sunday, he asked Louis to discuss the terms of the handover the moment he arrived. They got to work right away, and a memorandum of agreement was drawn up and signed within forty-eight hours. It covered the financial aspects of the transfer and the repayment of Louis's expenses. The French were also authorised to sell any trade goods they might have on board, and to purchase all the supplies they might need for the forthcoming voyage.

This done, the visitors had to cope with a busy round of visits and dinners. 'The bishops and all the town called on us,' wrote Nassau-Siegen. There were other functions that appealed rather more to the young prince: 'The ladies, who are very pretty here, sent us their compliments and offered all they could do to help. Several of them gave balls for us.'[2] However, they could only stay for a few days. Louis decided to return overland. This would give him a chance to see the countryside, and it was quicker than sailing down the estuary that was now being buffeted by a wild storm. They crossed over to the northern bank of the River Plate, near the island of Martin Garcia, but found that there was no formed road of any kind. It took them three days, struggling in rain and wind across prairies and marshlands, to reach Montevideo.

Ironically, when they were back on board the *Boudeuse*, cleaning up and resting after their wild journey, the weather began to improve. The little schooner soon arrived from Buenos Aires bringing the supplies they had bought, but there was still the livestock to board, and the Spanish officers and men who were to accompany the French to the Malouines were still not ready. 'We are wasting precious time,'[3] complained Bougainville, who was anxious to start his circumnavigation. He had to be patient, and try to cope as best he could with the easygoing *mañana* attitude of the Spanish colony. Finally, on 28 February, the *Boudeuse* was able to sail. She was to be accompanied by two Spanish frigates, the *Liebre* and the *Esmeralda*, and by a small craft, a tartane, the *Nuestra Señora de los Remedios*.

The men were ready to leave, but nature was not willing to let them go. A sea fog arose, keeping all ships at anchor. It cleared partially the next morning, whereupon Bougainville exclaimed that they were far too close to shallow water. He sent Bournand to the Spanish commander, suggesting that they sail cautiously, on short tacks, to get further out to sea. But the Spanish captains could not act without the permission of their river pilot, who was refusing to let them go. The *Boudeuse*, however, was under no such constraint and the Spanish suggested that he ought to sail alone as soon as he considered conditions to be right.

Accordingly, Louis raised anchor the next morning. The river pilot may well have been justified in his caution, because the moment the *Boudeuse* struck open water the wind rose and rapidly became a wild storm. The crossing to the Falklands took three weeks, in mostly rough weather, and the ship sustained minor damage. The Spanish frigate arrived a little later. She had struggled to catch up with the French, but had also suffered some damage.

The French settlers had been worried at first when a sail had appeared on the horizon. They were afraid that this might be a British frigate coming to carry out McBride's threat to have them removed from the islands. A great cheer went up when they saw the French colours. That evening, as they settled around the dining table in Nerville's humble residence, Bougainville was told in detail of the *Jason's* visit and the effect this had had on the colonists. Apart from that dark cloud – and the suspicion that, whatever action the British might take, the Spanish were also likely to intervene – the settlement was flourishing. They had by now adapted to their environment, the livestock had multiplied, even though some of the animals were running wild. Not all the crops had succeeded, but fish was plentiful and there was an abundance of seals and penguins. Louis could only confirm, however, that the colony as originally planned was coming to an end. A couple of days later, on 25 March, the Spanish ships arrived, and arrangements were set in hand to transform the French Malouines into the Spanish Malvinas.

On 29 March, a sunny, clear day, all the inhabitants gathered outside Nerville's house to hear the terms of what most called the surrender of the islands. Bougainville, flanked by the Spanish commander, Felipe Ruiz de Puente, and his cousin Nerville, read out Louis XV's letter authorising the transfer of sovereignty and of property. The settlers were given the option of staying, under Spanish sovereignty, or of returning to France. Louis spoke to each in turn, trying to persuade them to stay. Thirty-seven agreed, a sufficient number for the continuation of the colony. The others preferred to return to France, or to try their luck in the Spanish South American colonies. A few were taken on as sailors for the voyage around the world.

The pall of gloom that had settled over Port Saint-Louis was scarcely relieved by the official ceremonies of 1 April, when the French royal ensign was lowered, and of the 2nd when the Spanish colours were raised to the sound of a twenty-one-gun salute. Introducing the new governor, Felipe Ruiz de Puente, and his lieutenant, Antonio Catani, did little to raise anyone's spirits. The next few days were spent making a detailed inventory of the settlement, with the symbolic naming of the two main stores, now to be known as San Felipe and San Antonio, after the two administrators. The Spanish were disappointed by the rough, exiguous homes of the settlers, and by the absence of any chapel – this they decided to remedy as a priority. They found the Falklands cold after Buenos Aires, the houses damp: their only redeeming feature was that they had a fireplace: 'They have a chimney in the French style, fortunately, because one will be able to live in these places only by keeping close to the fire'.[4]

On 16 April, Nerville moved to the *Boudeuse* and handed over his residence to Puente. Antonio Catani described the house as having 'one octagonal room, a bedroom, a kitchen and some fairly small rooms for the servants, the whole built of stone mixed with lime and mud and covered with a thatched roof. The inside is well protected by some large linen curtains, blue with fleur-de-lys, that decorate the walls.'[5] Catani himself was given the house formerly occupied by Captain des Perriers, Nerville's second-in-command. It was hung with a wallpaper that Catani found 'horrible'. Des Perriers had it stripped off, much to Catani's satisfaction, who feared he might have to pay him for it as well as for the few fixtures the Frenchman was leaving behind.

Those colonists who had decided to leave now had to pack their meagre belongings and move out of their 'shanties' – as the Spanish called them. Their homes and the fields they had cultivated were valued, and the totals were added to the amount Bougainville was collecting on behalf of the Crown. Each family received a small capital sum; their passage back to France was supposedly being covered by Spain. Unhappily for most of them, it would not be easy to find a spare ship to take them back, largely because Bucareli had to repatriate the Jesuits who were being expelled from the Spanish possessions.

Catani's report on the islands, a fairly lengthy one sent to Bucareli, had little to say that was favourable. There were only half a dozen vegetable gardens in the entire settlement, and even then they were struggling to produce anything in the bleak climate. 'One must put this situation down to the fierce cold and the storms that prevent people from doing anything unless they are close to a fireplace.'[6] The hardy French colonists, many of whom had been used to even colder climates in Canada, laughed at the shivering Spanish.

All this boded ill for the future, as Louis commented: 'Now that they have [the Malvinas] I am certain that they will do nothing with them and that one day they will abandon them. I have seen what they have done at the River Plate, with the finest colony in the world; but they are very lazy ...' His suspicions were proved right. The Spanish did give up the settlement, whereupon the British moved in, succeeding in building up a viable colony, but triggering a conflict between the two countries that has lasted into modern times.

Bougainville had his own reports to write to Choiseul and Praslin. He also prepared one for the French ambassador in Madrid, the Marquis d'Ossun, who was to pass the information on to the Spanish court. The Spanish ships were getting ready to leave, providing the opportunity to send mail to family and friends back in France. He could also send on his report for Bucareli, to tell him that the handover of the colony had been completed without trouble. He praised the helpful attitude of both Puente and Catani, and asked him to extend his protection to the French colonists who had asked to be repatriated.

Puente also wrote to Bucareli, reporting fairly formally on the operations that had been carried out. Others, however, gave free rein to their dissatisfaction. Catani in particular wrote long letters of complaint to officials and colleagues back in Buenos Aires. The weather was appalling, with 'wild gales ... snow so that the paths are blocked ... the sun, when it shows itself, does not last two hours ... the weather is ever changeable, with rain or snow'. The islands were unattractive, 'without a single tree more than one ell in height ... there are approximately 36 houses, most of which do not deserve that name ... they all have thatched roofs. One can live in them only by being careful.' The French settlers who were leaving had been slow to vacate their homes: 'We had to stay on the frigates, we didn't know where to put ourselves.' The future was bleak indeed, and only supplies from the continent could keep the Malvinas going. He ended his letters with a plea to be allowed to leave – 'What I desire the most is to get away from here as soon as possible, and I shall not cease to pester those who have shown me their favour.'

Captain Felipe de Mena, the military commander, was even more insistent in an appeal to his protector, Don Domenico de Bazabilbazo: 'I humbly beseech you to use your influence and to plead on my behalf, stressing the extent of my sacrifice, and to obtain cautiously permission for me to leave this place of exile, as soon as you feel that H.M.'s wishes have been carried out …'.[7]

As the Spanish frigates prepared to sail, room had to be found for the departing French. A few of the lucky ones were allocated places – the only cabins available were those vacated by the officials who were staying behind. The others were told to find places for themselves, their families and their belongings below deck. There was not much room to spare. Des Perriers went on the *Esmeralda*, taking the various reports and letters to be sent on to France. With him went the colony's clerk Charles Martin, the port captain Lavarye-Leroi, the artillery officer Calamand, the pilot Saint-Mars, the assistant surgeon Macé Le Redde, and forty-six others. These included seven women and seventeen children. On the *Liebre* went the assistant medical officer Denis de Saint-Simon, the engineer Romainville, the surgeon Baslé, the chaplain Desertos-Duguérard, the clerk Oury, and thirty-eight others, including five women and eight children. In all, ninety-five people were leaving the former French settlement. The *Liebre* was expected to go to the River Plate and then on to France, taking the whole group with it. This hope would not materialise; some people did not reach France for several years.

The frigates left on 27 April. Bougainville remained behind with the *Boudeuse*, to wait for the *Étoile*, about which he was becoming seriously worried. Had she met with some disaster on the way to the South Atlantic? In his letter to the Duc de Praslin, he had expressed his growing anxiety:

I had reckoned that the *Étoile* had set sail from Rochefort around the 10 January. However, she still has not arrived here, and I do not know what to make of this delay … I shall wait here for the *Étoile* until the end of May. Beyond that time, the quantity of food we will have left will be no more than the absolute minimum required for the crossing to Rio de Janeiro … Apart from the fact that it is essential for the King's ships to gain knowledge of that town, I will gain a month's sailing by going there rather than to the River Plate, where both entry and exit are difficult, lengthy and very dangerous especially in winter. I cannot say, my Lord, how despondent we shall all be if the *Étoile* does not come.[8]

He wrote along the same lines to the Duc de Choiseul: 'I do not know what to think of the *Étoile*'s delay, but I shall be inconsolable if she does not arrive; never was a crew in better condition or showing more zeal and good will.' His anxiety was justified: without the supplies the storeship was expected to bring, the expedition to the South Seas could not proceed. He did secretly suspect, however, that the *Étoile* had not come to grief, but that La Giraudais had decided, rightly or wrongly, to put in at a South American port. He took the precaution of handing letters to both Nerville and Martin, each one addressed to La Giraudais in case they found the storeship at Montevideo. If he was there, there was now no point in his coming to the Falklands: Louis instructed him to proceed forthwith to Rio.

To while the time away, he went exploring with Nassau-Siegen and the younger officers. They spent a week, from 9 to 17 May, going to a small inlet which the settlers had named Drunkard's Cove after one of their number who had died there after a drinking binge, and to Beauport, which he had visited back in 1764, the place where Port Stanley would one day be built. The trip confirmed his view that the Falkland Islands had a future if only a real effort was made to develop them. He was sure that a cattle industry could flourish there, that a whaling station should be established, as well as a base for deep-sea fishing and for ships to call on their way to the Pacific or the Indian Ocean. When he got back to Port Saint-Louis, he told all this to the Spanish, showed them charts, pointing out the proximity of Buenos Aires and the value they could gain from it. But the newcomers, shivering in the unaccustomed cold climate and fearful of the approaching winter, merely nodded and prayed for an early end to their exile.

The days passed slowly, still with no sign of the storeship. Louis decided to prepare for departure. There was really no point in wasting time in the Falklands, waiting for a ship he now hoped would not arrive, because he had no need for it. The Spanish had some wheat they could spare, so he bought 150 hundredweight from them. He invited Ruiz de Puente and his fellow officers to a farewell dinner. Then on 2 June, exchanging the usual gun salutes, the *Boudeuse* sailed for Rio de Janeiro.

Fesche expressed the general mood of gloomy uncertainty: 'I have no idea whether we are going back to France [or] what will happen if the *Étoile* is not in Rio de Janeiro; it may well turn out that she is there.'[9] The weather reflected their feelings: 'Squalls, rain, hail, rough seas.' When the wind dropped, fog fell. The frigate rolled and pitched. The sky cleared for a few days, then the bad weather returned. 'Fog, rain, calms, light airs. [Then] the winds came from the SE to SSE with storms, squalls, rain.'[10] There was no improvement until the 19th, when land appeared in the distance. They were nearing Rio.

20. MEETING THE *ÉTOILE* AT RIO

June–July 1767

WHEN THE PORTUGUESE port pilot came on board the *Boudeuse* on 21 June, he told the French that there were a number of foreign vessels in the roadstead: a Spanish warship, two British frigates and a French storeship. 'I am in no doubt that this is the *Étoile*, which received Mr de Bougainville's instructions, sent by means of the Spanish frigates that sailed from the Malouines,' wrote Fesche.[1] That evening, La Giraudais came aboard. 'I am happy that we have found the *Étoile*,' exclaimed Fesche, 'so that we can continue our voyage around the world.' Without the storeship, the expedition to the Pacific would have had to be aborted, and all their efforts reduced to naught. Everyone gathered round to find out why she had not joined them at the Falklands.

As we have seen, there had been delays at Rochefort. Then, La Giraudais explained, there had been damage during the crossing, especially as the *Étoile* neared the South American continent. This had forced him to alter his route, and to sail to Montevideo for repairs. He omitted to mention that going to the River Plate suited the officers much better, since it ensured that Bougainville would not discover how crowded the ship was with private trade goods. Having explained the change of route, he went on to give his report on the crossing itself.

The *Étoile* had finally sailed from France on 1 February 1767. The sea was particularly rough, and many on board had been seasick, but by the 4th, the number affected had dropped by half and soon only Commerson was still unwell – 'I am ashamed of being the only one who is not getting his sea legs'.[2] It took him another week to recover, during which his faithful 'valet', Jeanne Baret, cared for him. She shared his cabin, a fairly unusual practice for any servant, but this was explained away by his indisposition and the crowded conditions. In time, however, other comments were made, the most unkind being by the surgeon Vivès, whose journal is shot through with innuendoes and barbed shafts. 'The special care she took of her master did not seem natural for a male servant,' he wrote, adding that time passed quickly for them in 'this quiet period of enjoyment'.[3] His recollections

– not confirmed by anyone else on the ship – were that Baret's gender came under suspicion after only a month, once Commerson had recovered and was taking an active role in the ship's activities. A 'little murmuring' arose from the crew 'about, they said, the presence of a disguised girl on board ship. Without hesitation, eyes turned towards our little man.'

None of this sounds convincing. Vivès was writing with hindsight and he was embroidering the facts. It would have been quite normal for a male servant to spend a great deal of time attending to his sick master, and it was not surprising, given the congestion in the ship, that he continued to do so once Commerson had recovered. The naturalist had suffered a bad accident while botanising some years earlier, and a further mishap during the voyage from Paris to Rochefort. His leg was to trouble him for the rest of his life, and on the crossing to Montevideo it became badly ulcerated. He needed his servant's help to make his way up the companionways and along the unsteady deck. It was only much later that speculation arose about the remarkable devotion 'Jean' showed to his employer. Nevertheless, sooner or later, Jeanne's skin, with no hint of a five o'clock shadow, her voice, somewhat high for a male, and her practice of keeping herself to herself, especially for her private ablutions, would cause tongues to wag.

For the captain, the presence of a woman on board would have been a matter of discipline. It was a serious infringement of quite specific naval regulations. For the ordinary sailors, however, the concern was the superstitious belief many held at the time that a woman on a ship, except in vessels specifically catering for passengers, brought bad luck. And for those who were not so superstitious, a female on board suggested the possibility, if not the likelihood, of enjoyable night-time adventures. But because the log of the *Étoile* has never been found, there is no record of any action La Giraudais may have taken.

Where servants slept at night was not a matter La Giraudais would concern himself about. It was difficult enough for the sailors to find somewhere to sling a hammock or lie down. The ship was so badly overcrowded that the cooks complained they could not get access to some of the food stored below deck. The men who were caring for the few heads of sheep and cattle on board could not get to the hay, so that a number of the animals died. The weather did not improve until the *Étoile* approached the Canary Islands, late in February. And then, calms and light airs led to slow progress. The storeship did not manage to reach the equator until 22 March.

Commerson did not try to get out of his 'baptism' by Father Neptune and he could not entirely shield Jeanne Baret from the attentions of the men. However, the payment of a coin by way of tribute minimised the roughness of some of the theatricals, which often included a ducking in a vat filled with seawater, kitchen refuse – and urine. Jeanne Baret clearly managed to avoid stripping to the waist –

or stripping altogether, as the young sailors and servants often did. 'We did not wish to refuse the lavabo,' Commerson wrote, adding the significant words, 'and had prepared for this', implying that bribery had ensured that both he and his servant were not roughly treated. He wrote a lengthy account of the event in his journal.

The *Étoile* passed several ships sailing towards Europe, but only one came close enough to be identified. This was on 5 April, but as the ship was Portuguese, the language difficulty got in the way and all they could do was to exchange good wishes. Thus, as the French neared the South American continent, spotting Cape Frio, north of Rio de Janeiro, on 9 April, their isolation remained complete.

The sight of Cape Frio on 9 April caused spirits to rise. La Giraudais was still writing that he planned to sail to the Falklands, 'neither having instructions nor any wish to sail to Montevideo'.[4] But more patience was needed: the winds were not favourable and a series of gales damaged the ship. Broken spars and unsafe masting, combined with a lack of drinking water – only twenty barrelfuls remained – 'forced the captain and all the officers to call at Montevideo on the 30th of the said month at 4 p.m. in order to repair as quickly as possible all the damage sustained by the ship during this bad weather', as Caro noted in his journal.

Other commentators were more caustic. 'The sailors were weary of having to sleep on cables and ropes,' commented Vivès, while Commerson blamed the strain that was developing between him and several of the officers on 'the self-interest that had made it an original sin for me to occupy fifteen to twenty cubic feet in a ship that seemed to those unbridled traders to have been solely intended to make them wealthy'.[5]

Their month's stay in Montevideo was pleasant – and presumably profitable. The Spanish governor extended the same courtesies towards La Giraudais and his men as he had to Bougainville. The French invited the governor to a dinner on board, together with a number of his officials, most of them accompanied by their wives. This was reciprocated, but La Giraudais's main concern was to cover himself against any criticism for his failure to sail to the Falklands. He got Michau to draw up a list of the damage suffered by the *Étoile*, which was counter-signed by all the officers and petty officers. A copy was sent to the Duc de Praslin; another was kept for Bougainville to read. In a later letter to the minister, La Giraudais stressed that he fully intended to go on to the Falklands as soon as his ship was ready: 'I would already have sailed from here, My Lord, if the winds, which are continuing to be unfavourable, had not prevented me, but I plan to take advantage of the present fine weather to make for the Malouines, where I believe Mr de Bougainville has gone.'[6]

A couple of days later, however, on 18 May, the two Spanish frigates arrived with the colonists from the Malouines, and La Giraudais was handed Bougainville's instructions to sail for Rio de Janeiro without delay. It took him another ten days to get organised. The *Étoile* left on the 29th and reached Rio on 12 June. The *Boudeuse* arrived a week later. Louis accepted La Giraudais's explanations and report without apparent demur. He came on board the *Étoile*, was shown traces of the damage the storeship had suffered, and inspected as much of the area below decks as he felt was necessary – or wise. The trade goods had now gone and Louis did not delve too deeply into La Giraudais's reasons for the change of itinerary.

The French were now in Portuguese territory and the authorities were both unwelcoming and unco-operative. The governor, Antonio Alvaro da Cunha, refused to guarantee that the traditional gun salute given by a naval vessel on arrival would be returned. 'When you meet someone in the street,' he replied, 'you take off your hat to him without previously enquiring whether this courtesy will be returned or not.'[7] This was a specious argument: he knew perfectly well what naval etiquette required him to do. If the port authorities did not reply, this was normally taken as a slight to one's flag. Bougainville had a great deal more experience than the governor in dealing with smart remarks. He replied: 'If someone does doff his hat to you, and you do not respond, it will be taken as a sign of ill-will,' but he decided that 'It is better to avoid the possibility of any such insult' – the *Boudeuse* would not give a salute. When Louis and some of his officers called on Da Cunha, he was told that the governor could not see him, as he was unwell. This may have been true, for a few days later the gun salute was settled, the proper number of guns fired and acknowledged. Then Da Cunha came on board the *Boudeuse* with 'a fairly large suite'.

This helped to mend relations, which improved during the next few days, but only moderately. The *Étoile*'s chaplain, Father Buet, had been murdered while ashore, but little effort was made to find the culprits. The situation became a little more strained when the captain of a Spanish ship, the seventy-four-gun *Diligent*, which had been held up for weeks trying to get material and men to help with repairs, asked Bougainville for help. Louis promptly came to his aid. The Portuguese made their displeasure quite clear: the French were interfering and assisting another country while they were guests of Brazil.

There were a number of reasons for the unfriendliness of the Portuguese. The French were seen as allies of Spain, and had been sailing down to the South Atlantic on a mission that could only strengthen that country's position. To make matters worse, hostilities had recently broken out between Portugal and Spain in the Rio Grande, south of Rio. The Spanish had not respected the Treaty of Paris, which required them to hand the southern shore of Brazil over to Portugal. Arguments had been dragging on for some years, until the Portuguese, weary of the interminable dispute, decided to drive the Spanish out of the northern region. At the same time, by troop movements, they threatened Spain's hold on the southern territories. Bougainville found himself caught in this conflict, but felt 'duty bound to help his

King's allies'. The difficulties encountered by the sailors and officers in the port area show that the locals shared the governor's surliness.

It was not all bad. Da Cunha had already tried to mend matters when he visited the *Boudeuse* and in a gesture of goodwill invited the French to come up to his palace. 'He even announced that he was organising supper evenings by the water, under arbours of jasmine and orange trees, and booked us a box at the opera.' The musical evening was a notable occasion, reported by Louis in a manner than reflects the antagonism between the parties: 'In a fairly attractive hall, we were able to see the works of Metastasio presented by a cast of mulattos and those divine pieces of the great Italian masters played by a bad orchestra conducted by a hunchback priest wearing clerical dress.'[8]

Visits to the town brought more mixed comments from the French. 'The town is most attractive, a business centre, and full of interesting sights.' Most considered it 'large, fairly well built. Its streets are well paved, the churches opulent, but lacking taste.' The inhabitants, on the other hand, were less appealing. 'This magnificent place is the home of hypocrites and barbarians … hypocrisy rules to the highest degree in this nation which is worse than the Spaniards,' wrote Vivès. 'Morals are appalling in Rio Janeiro, not merely on account of the immorality of the women, which is extreme, but no form of virtue is known: it is a mere assemblage of religion and villainy,' commented Nassau-Siegen. This was a fairly strong judgement, coming from someone whose adventures with ladies of light virtue were known to everyone in Paris society.[9]

The murder of the *Étoile's* chaplain had certainly shocked the French. Whether Da Cunha would have discovered the chaplain's killers is open to argument, and if Commerson's account is to be believed the priest may have been at least partly responsible for his own demise:

> One should not hide the fact that the unfortunate priest brought about this catastrophe through his own actions. He was a Breton, he was inebriated and behaved in a manner that would have caused him to have been as easily knocked out in our French ports as in Rio de Janeiro. One should in fairness put both sides of the case forward.[10]

It is not clear what the priest's Breton background had to do with the case, but he was possibly more used to drinking cider than the Spanish wine he was offered ashore. According to Commerson, he had gone to visit some of Rio's churches with a young pilot named Constantin. While they waited for a boat to row them back to the *Étoile*, he had an argument with some local blacks who sought revenge and gathered a group of friends together to attack him. They knocked him out with their oars and held him down in the water until he drowned. Constantin escaped by shamming death. If Commerson is correct, then Da Cunha, concerned with the developing conflict with the Spanish in Rio Grande, had little time to waste investigating the death of a French priest who had possibly spent much of the day carousing.

In spite of all its architectural attractions and Rio's status as an administrative centre, murder was almost a daily occurrence. It was a noisy enough place to live in, with church bells that seemed to peal at all hours of the day or night, open-air stalls with merchants shouting out their wares, and a constant flow of wide-wheeled carts loaded with merchandise or military stores creaking over the roughly paved streets. Brawls between soldiers and civilians, and between sailors and soldiers, regularly occurred right in front of the vice-regal palace which lay across the square from Nuestra Señora de Lapa and the church of Santa Cruz, either of which Father Buet may have been visiting. All of these were within a stone's throw of the Fish Wharf and the line of landing places that stretched along the waterfront to the Customs House. It was an obvious route for the priest to take on his way back to the ship, but it was next to a warren of dingy streets lined with taverns, where thieves and smugglers were waiting for a chance to make a little money.

There may, though, have been a more personal motive for Commerson's unkind comments about the unfortunate priest. Father Buet had taken the place of his brother, Georges-Marie, and, as has been suggested, the priest was possibly unsympathetic towards Philibert Commerson. And, in any case, the naturalist was given to making caustic comments about most of his companions on the *Étoile*.

In spite of his patent dislike of the Portuguese, Bougainville was forced to draw on the resources of Rio and its naval yards. Both his ships needed repairs and fresh supplies before they could start on their epic voyage across the Pacific. Sails had to be repaired, new rigging had to be bought, specialist caulkers were required to ensure there were no leaks and the keels themselves had to be cleaned. He also needed to buy flour and dried meat and get them properly stowed away in the hold.

He spent three weeks at Rio, most of the time fuming against the Portuguese governor's lack of co-operation. He wanted to buy a small snow – a type of brigantine – but Da Cunha cancelled the sale. The same happened when he tried to rent a house, the very one that John Byron had briefly occupied a few years earlier when preparing for his voyage around the world. Louis was just about to sign the short lease with the owner, when the viceroy ordered the cancellation of the agreement. A number of other 'vexations', chronicled by Bougainville and others, revealed the strain that existed between the French and the Portuguese officials. Louis also recorded that Véron 'obtains very little help from the viceroy to carry out his astronomical observations, and Mr Commerson, a celebrated naturalist … sent out by the King to enrich his knowledge of natural history, is meeting similar problems'.[11]

In spite of all these difficulties, and warnings about the danger of venturing into the countryside, Commerson and Baret were remarkably successful on their botanising expedition around the city. One of Commerson's achievements has led to the immortalisation of Bougainville's name. The naturalist had found a vinelike shrub blossoming in profusion in the countryside and in a few gardens. It covered fallen trees and walls with a mass of vivid red flowers. He brought several specimens back, proudly labelled them '*novissima planta*' and carefully recorded his discovery in July 1767: '*E. Brasilia. Rio de Janeiro et locii vicini, julio 1767*'. He named the discovery after the expedition's commander: bougainvillea. It would not reach Paris until after Commerson's death in 1773, part of his still largely uncatalogued collection of more than 6000 specimens, but within a few years it appeared in the official records of the Paris Museum of National History and gradually became known to plant lovers in Europe and North America. It is now widely cultivated wherever the climate is mild enough for it to flourish.

Early in July, Bougainville, La Giraudais and Du Bouchage held a meeting with Da Cunha, to discuss a number of problems that had recently arisen. Louis was particularly upset by the governor's change of mind about the snow, but there was also the business about renting a house. The conversation, polite and formal to start with, degenerated when Louis complained that Da Cunha was behaving in an unfriendly manner and that he seemed to find the presence of the French in Brazil quite shocking. At this, the governor rose in fury and ordered Bougainville to leave. 'I let him give way to his bad temper, and as soon as we have concluded our business here, we shall leave.'[12] Martin-Allarnic suggests that Da Cunha may have misunderstood the French. 'It is probable that, instead of "*choquions*", referring to the behaviour being found shocking or upsetting, the viceroy, whose understanding of French was limited, believed he had heard another word that sounded much like it, *cochon* [pig], which would explain his fury.'[13]

Either way, the remainder of the stay in Rio was most uncomfortable. 'Orders were issued to arrest any of the French found in the streets after eight o'clock at night, and some were taken to prison that very evening and the following day,' wrote Nassau-Siegen, a comment confirmed by Fesche. The officers thought it wiser not to attend the opera any more, even though Da Cunha had not taken away their private box and actually advised Bougainville that the curfew did not apply to senior members of his staff – just how senior could be a matter of dispute and they did not want to take the risk of some Portuguese officer arresting them first and arguing later. It is possible, though, that the governor was truly concerned that any sailors found in the port, especially in the taverns, might be set upon by Portuguese ruffians.

But there were other signs of animosity: a Portuguese cavalry officer who had befriended Nassau became *persona non grata* in Rio and was sent 'as though exiled' to his estate at Santo. Women 'who visited some of our gentlemen' were imprisoned. Commerson's excursions in the countryside, and Véron's astronomical observations, were viewed with suspicion as possible spying, and the two men were firmly told to bring their work to an end.

On the other hand, Bougainville received an unusual request. 'A Portuguese sergeant came to ask whether we would be willing to receive him and offered to get all his regiment to desert. The uniform is blue, with white facings. They are residents and workers in this country, all forcibly conscripted.'[14] It was hardly an offer that Louis could accept. It would have been impossible to ensure total secrecy: the sergeant would have to arrange for his men to make for the ships and even invite others in the force to join them. Nothing would have provided Da Cunha with greater proof that the French were a menace than a planned mass desertion, especially as Bougainville was about to leave for Spanish-controlled Buenos Aires. The sergeant was given a glass of wine and sent on his way.

The next day, Louis sent an officer to the governor, giving formal notice of his impending departure. Final preparations were then made, and the officers entrusted their mail to Francisco de Medina, the commander of the *Diligent*. Both Bougainville and Saint-Germain dispatched their official reports to Choiseul and Praslin by this intermediary. Early on the 15th, and without any regrets, the French sailed away from Rio. It had been a disappointing and indeed a frustrating visit, and they all looked forward to a happier time in Buenos Aires.

21. Farewell to Montevideo

1 August–14 November 1767

As they made their way south towards Montevideo, Bougainville began to realise that the *Étoile* was a slow, clumsy ship in need of repairs. He completely changed his mind about using her for the circumnavigation and sending the *Boudeuse* home. He was far more satisfied now with the frigate than he had been when he first sailed in her. 'She is causing us to lose a great deal of time,' he grumbled about the *Étoile* a mere week after leaving Rio. It was a complaint he would make time and again during the circumnavigation. He found on the short voyage to Montevideo that she was leaking and needed a careful survey and a substantial refit. This would take time, but he consoled himself with the thought that it was now wintertime in the southern hemisphere, not a season for trying to find one's way through the Strait of Magellan.

A stay in Montevideo could be pleasant as well as useful. What mattered was how well the local authorities would co-operate. The Spanish, fortunately, were much better disposed towards the French than the Portuguese.

No sooner had he dropped anchor than an officer arrived on board with greetings from the governor, Don José de Viana. The next day, Bougainville himself went ashore and called on a number of local notables before getting ready to travel to Buenos Aires and pay his respects to the governor. He caught up with recent news, getting a Spanish perspective on the hostilities against the Portuguese. According to his new hosts, Da Cunha's men had marched by night, 600 of them, to capture a Spanish outpost across the river. They had given no warning of their plans, but they were seen by a Spanish patrol boat, which fired on them. This unexpected reaction to what they planned as an unseen advance caused panic among the would-be attackers. They then got caught up in some shallows and started floundering about, which gave their opponents ample time to organise their defence and bring up their troops. One ill-defended Spanish advanced post, however, did have to be abandoned, justifying Da Cunha's claims of early successes. By and large, the whole affair could be regarded as a stalemate.

An even greater topic of conversation was the expulsion of the Jesuits, who controlled much of the countryside. It was a complex task, requiring careful planning to avoid pockets of resistance building up, especially among some of the Indians, many of whom were grouped in mission stations run with a mixture of kindness and firmness. Those who disliked the powerful Jesuit order – Bougainville among them – had little time for the priests' authoritarian rule; others considered the expulsion an anti-Christian move, the consequences of lay political interference in church matters. The same differing points of view existed among the Spanish colonists, causing an unease that could easily develop into civil unrest and even local uprisings.

The task of removing the Jesuits had fallen on the shoulders of the region's governor, Francisco de Paula Bucareli y Ursua, who had been appointed, some said, partly because he had displayed considerable zeal in opposing the powerful clerics when he was in charge of the island of Majorca. He was also pro-French, and had welcomed the *Étoile* on her previous visit. The Spanish king had signed the decree outlawing the Jesuit order on 2 April 1767, and the instructions reached Buenos Aires in June. The French listened to the various accounts the Spanish gave them about the arrest and deportation of the missionaries and Vivès wrote down some of the details he heard, including the dawn raids that resulted in the arrest of all of Buenos Aires' Jesuit priests.

Of greater concern for Bougainville, however, was the repatriation of the French settlers. He travelled upriver to Buenos Aires on 9 August, arriving a couple of days later. He paid the required visits to local officials, and made arrangements for the purchase of supplies for both his ships. This done, he raised the issue of the unfortunate Malouines colonists:

> I submitted a memoir to M. de Bukarely [*sic*] for the departure of the French families on the ships that were ready to sail. There are five of them … The need to send back almost 200 Jesuits, and the officers and crew of the *Aventurier* [a small ship recently wrecked on a sandbank] will allow Mr de Bukarely to send back on this occasion the staff and the unmarried people from the Malouines.[1]

The affair dragged on for months. Louis had to ensure that the family heads at least received some regular grants for their subsistence, but there was little he could do about their lodgings, which were far from comfortable. Bucareli, for his part, felt they were no worse off than they had been in their Falklands homes, about which he had received only complaints from the Spanish left in charge there. Indeed, he referred to what had been Port Saint-Louis as 'Puerto Soledad', Port Solitude.

Nevertheless, the unhappy French colonists had much to complain about. Even for the lucky ones who had been selected to sail home in the first contingent, conditions were unenviable: 'They are crowded into those ships, already overfilled with the Jesuits. I shall draw the General's attention to this in line with the dictates of humanity.'[2] Less than half the evacuees formed part of this first group. They put up with the discomforts of the ships because they believed they would be going home – but, as it turned out, they were going to Spain. The others, a total of five families and twelve individuals, had to wait their chance, either in the small port of Encenada or, exceptionally, in Buenos Aires. For sustenance, they depended on the local authorities' cash handouts – and the fact that almost none of them spoke any Spanish did not help matters.

Bougainville was also concerned about the condition of the *Étoile*. Montevideo lacked the facilities for the major repairs required; indeed the anchorage itself was not safe when storms arose. While Louis was away in Buenos Aires, 'a furious westerly' caused a nearby Spanish vessel to drag on its anchors and collide with the *Étoile*, smashing her bowsprit and causing other damage. 'We have to work the pumps every hour.' She would have to be moved to La Encenada de Baragan, on the south bank of the River Plate. She also needed to be lightened as much as possible, by transferring part of the cargo to the *Boudeuse*. This task was not made any easier by a second wild storm that assailed them on 31 August. 'A fierce hurricane blowing from the NE, which lasted the entire day with rain, hail and thunder.' It was no better during the following days. 'The weather is very bad, very cold, rain, high winds and changeable.'

They finally dropped anchor in the Encenada roadstead on 10 September, and with the help of a pilot supplied by the port commander they entered the port. It was not an impressive place: 'A rough village of huts with thatched roofs, no store, no landing place.' There was more disappointment: the promised facilities were minimal, and materials had to be brought from Buenos Aires. And the weather still did not improve. Bougainville's daily log desperately records a succession of heavy showers, wild winds, thunder and lightning. Fortunately, there was plenty of time: it was not safe to sail for the south until at least November.[3] There were a few moments of relaxation. Louis went to Buenos Aires on a number of occasions, on business admittedly, but also to enjoy the dinners and receptions Bucareli and others gave for him.

Commerson went with him and he stayed to meet local residents who were interested in natural history, and to go off botanising. On one occasion Louis decided to accompany him – to look at some 'bones of giants'. Rumours about the size of the Patagonians in the southern provinces kept on circulating, and this was a chance to view some real evidence. But the bones brought out for their inspection did not provide the required evidence:

They are not the bones of men. In general, all these bones they bring forth in various places as being such do not indicate a connection with the human species, as a skull would do, for example. They show us bones that all belong to quadrupeds as much as to men. It seems that those we saw are the bones of elephants. Some have been found in Canada at Belle Rivière and in the Dauphiné. Elephants do not exist in those countries, but the world has undergone many changes.[4]

Apart from mammoth bones, there was the oldest man in the province, who was said to be 114 years old. He was blind, but his hearing was good and he could still walk. He was certainly elderly, but he did not look much more than ninety. Louis commented, in a somewhat deadpan sentence, 'I have not seen his certificate of baptism.'

There were also celebrations to attend. The feast of Saint Louis, France's national day during the Ancient Regime, was marked by a solemn mass in the Montevideo parish church, with a dinner and ball to which the entire garrison was invited, complete with gun salutes, fireworks and illuminations. Unhappily, a gunner was too slow in removing his rammer from the gun and had his arm broken by a cannon ball. 'His hand had to be cut off above the wrist. He will survive.' These were days when anaesthetics were unknown: the man was sedated with a stiff dose of brandy and told to clench his teeth while the surgeons worked on him as fast as they could with knives and saw.

Later came the fiesta of the blacks, which Louis attended in Buenos Aires:

On their feast day, the blacks elect 2 kings and 2 queens, one Portuguese, the other Spanish. Two large groups, well dressed and armed, set off in a procession behind the kings, marching with crosses, banners, Dominican priests, masks, instruments. They dance, sing, mime battles and recite litanies. The fiesta lasts from morning till night and the spectacle is quite pleasing.[5]

Others also enjoyed their time in South America. Nassau-Siegen, when not charming the ladies at a reception somewhere, went on excursions into the countryside. With D'Oraison, he rode out towards the north-east, into country that was, he was warned, inhabited by Indians and infested by bandits and tigers – presumably jaguars. They left on 9 September and spent three weeks away, part of the time accompanied by soldiers on their way to Maldonada and the Rio Grande. The prince came across a 'tiger', and stayed in an Indian village, but saw no bandits.

As well as botanising, Philibert Commerson had an opportunity to practise medicine, and the welcome he received sparked his usual irrepressible enthusiasm:

'If I had not been attached to my homeland and to my duties, I could make my fortune here in less than three years. I was paid thirty piastres for one consultation (and a piastre is worth five livres and five sous in our currency).'[6]

Bougainville, knowing he would enjoy Commerson's company on the voyage, offered him a place on the *Boudeuse*. The frigate was a more suitable ship for someone with the resounding title of king's naturalist but Philibert refused, arguing, with some truth, that his spacious quarters on the *Étoile* were more suitable for his growing collection of specimens than anything Louis could offer him. And staying on the storeship would ensure that the commander did not see too much of 'Jean' Baret or upset the pair's cosy arrangement.

Some changes, however, were being made. The astronomer Véron accepted Louis's invitation to transfer to the *Boudeuse*. Lavarye-Leroi joined the *Étoile*. Charles Routier de Romainville, the engineer-cartographer, who had been working in the Malouines, refused repatriation to France and was gladly accepted for the *Étoile*. The young volunteer Lemoyne de Montchevry was transferred to the *Boudeuse*, enabling Pierre Duclos-Guyot to join the storeship, a move that separated him from his brother Alexandre who stayed on the frigate.

The surgeon Vivès had been unwell as the result of a boating accident early in the stay, and Bougainville considered replacing him with Guillaume Baslé (or Ballet), the former medical man on the Malouines. Vivès, reported Louis, 'had been declared consumptive and affected by scurvy'.[7] Vivès himself felt that he had been 'at death's door', but he recovered sufficiently to return to his post and complete the long voyage around the world – he would live on to the ripe old age of eighty-three.

But Bougainville de Nerville had no intention of joining his cousin's expedition. He loathed the sea, and had suffered from seasickness when he had travelled down from France, and even during the relatively short crossings from the Falklands to Rio and from Rio to Montevideo. He had made up his mind to go home. He was farewelled, not without emotion, by Louis and his other friends. His troubles were not at an end, however: he does not seem to have reached France until 1769.

There were other losses: a dozen sailors and soldiers deserted, a couple of others were allowed to leave on grounds of ill-health to make their own way back to France, and two carpenters not fit enough to face the long voyage had been sent ashore. Men taken on in the Falklands and at Montevideo made up these losses.

It was time to leave. The farewells were marked with some sadness. Louis was sad to leave Nerville; Nassau-Siegen, Commerson and others parted with regret from the numerous friends they had made during the long winter months. The Spanish officials, from the governor down, organised a series of receptions so that everyone could exchange final messages. 'We shall miss the dear inhabitants of this little place, who have been most kind during our stay and have made life easier for us through their glorious generosity,' commented Vivès.[8]

Finally, on 14 November 1767, the two vessels weighed anchor. Everyone felt excited at the prospect of the great voyage beginning at last, but reality soon intervened: bad weather assailed them the moment they reached the open sea. They struggled on, and within a few days Louis was writing in his journal: 'Deplorable weather ... [which] tests the most Christian patience'. The circumnavigation would be no leisurely cruise, even though the ocean they were making for was called Pacific.

22. THROUGH THE STRAIT OF MAGELLAN

November 1767–January 1768

THE 'DEPLORABLE WEATHER' continued for over a week but, as November came to an end, Bougainville was able to record enthusiastically: 'The finest weather in the world, as warm as in France'. It was a fair comparison, since November in the southern hemisphere corresponds to May in Europe – but he was sailing south, daily coming closer to colder latitudes, and as the French approached the Strait of Magellan the temperature dropped.

When the third of December dawned, they sighted Cabo Virgenes, or the Cape of the Eleven Thousand Virgins, which guards the entrance to the strait and is a welcome landmark. It had received its somewhat unusual name from Magellan, who had sighted the headland on 21 October, the feast of St Ursula, the reputed leader of a large group of pious virgins martyred in Cologne in the third or fourth century. But it was several days before the *Boudeuse* and the *Étoile* were able to enter the strait.

This was the real beginning of the voyage of exploration. The South Atlantic was fairly well known, though few ships ventured into this bleak south-western corner, but now the French stood in the very doorway to the great South Seas.

It was worth marking the occasion with a Latin tag. Louis was always fond of sprinkling Latin quotations in his journal, even if at times he misquoted the original. For this occasion, he chose a line from Virgil's *Aeneid*, clearly his favourite poem and one well known to his eighteenth-century readers: '[We enter] the homeland of the clouds, a region pregnant with raging south-easterlies'. It was reasonably dramatic, and quite apt – like the Greek hero Aeneas roaming the Mediterranean, the French were entering dangerous and unwelcoming waters.

They sailed through the first set of narrows, the Primera Angostura, into San Felipe Bay. Then, just past Cabo Orange, they dropped anchor. A family of Patagonians lit a fire along the shore, and not long after they raised a white standard, not a flag of surrender, but the pre-Revolution French national emblem. The natives belonged to the Aonikenk or Southern Tehuelche, one of several tribes struggling to survive in this bleak part of the world. They knew the French from their previous visits, and the flag they were showing was one given to them by Chesnard de la Giraudais in June 1766.

Louis went ashore and was soon surrounded by a happy, jostling crowd:

[They] gaily and confidently marched towards us, shouting *Chaoua, chaoua.* We made a great fuss of them; in the two hours we spent ashore their number grew to 30. I had bread and biscuit given to them … They were extremely welcoming in their gestures, clutching us in their arms and expressing the greatest joy at seeing us … They all asked for tobacco, and the colour red seemed to please them greatly.[1]

There would be a number of meetings with the Patagonians during the coming weeks, all of them friendly, although some Indians, possibly remembering a clash with earlier visitors, usually Spanish, were a little more suspicious of outsiders.

The scenery was grandiose or depressing, according to one's mood. On a fine day – and these were relatively rare – the waters of the inland bays were calm, with long, slow ripples, surrounded by dark-green hills and a background of high snowy peaks. Waterfalls could be seen between rocky outcrops, and here and there stretches of low tussocky land led north towards the inland plains. But channels and inlets, many of them dead-ends, were conduits for bitterly cold winds that often turned into gales, lashing the surface of the waters into foaming waves, bringing sleet and at times snow from the Antarctic.

The two ships made their way slowly through the tortuous strait in December and early January, stopping to explore or to shelter from the weather, and to gather firewood – a necessity when canned food was still unknown and the stove was the only means of cooking, whether baking or making a stew or a fish soup. The various stages of this struggle through Magellan are all detailed in Bougainville's shipboard journals, which are peppered with complaints about the 'dreadful' weather: stormy westerly gales, squalls, rain, hail, snow. Not surprisingly, Louis added, 'My God! How much patience does this navigation require!'

His health, like that of many of the others, began to suffer and his comments shed an interesting light on contemporary medical practices: 'I was affected by a severe sore throat, for which I was bled three times. Several of our men are also affected. If one did not die of sickness in this cursed climate, one would die of impatience and boredom.'[2] And for good measure he threw in a line from Virgil: 'May the day dawn when this plight shall be sweet to remember!' This was early summer; how did the Patagonians, and especially the Fuegans, survive in such a climate when the winter came? All those they met, however, seemed cheerful and relatively healthy. Commerson and Nassau-Siegen, in particular, had been welcomed by them:

They took the Prince de Nassau for a woman, on account of his youth and his handsome features. A red coat I was wearing attracted some attention and caused me to be offered a girl ... I embraced one of these Patagonians, who was young and had attractive features. He did not leave me, and seeing that I was collecting plants, he began to do the same and offered them to me.[3]

All the French were amazed by the hardiness of the inhabitants. They were nomadic hunters in a region that seemed to harbour few quadrupeds, and fishermen who often cheerfully stepped up to their knees in freezing water. Most of them wore furs and seal or horse skins, but often they were only partly clad and sometimes went about almost naked. They cleaned and protected their skin by smearing it with fish oil, so that they exuded a pungent smell the French found offensive. Some of these tribes have now vanished and their survivors have adapted to more modern lifestyles, so the detailed descriptions given by Bougainville and other members of the expedition have left valuable information for modern ethnologists.

The features of these Americans are not harsh, and some are pleasing to look at. Their face is round and flat, their eyes bright, their teeth extremely white. They wear their black hair long, tied up on the top of the head ... they paint their bodies. They wear the skins of various animals ... a great cloak of guanaco and small lizard skins tied around them reaches down to their heels. They have a kind of leather riding boots open at the back. A few wore copper rings around their legs ... These people lead a life similar to that of the Tartars. Roaming across these enormous South American plains, on horseback, men, women and children, tracking game, using skins as clothing and for shelter ... Several used a few words of Spanish, such as mañana, muchacho ...

Others, especially those from Tierra del Fuego or from further down the strait, made less of an impression: 'These are generally smaller than the French, with unpleasant features and very thin. They all have rotten teeth.'[4] Although they seemed 'nice enough', Bougainville thought them 'small, ugly, knock-kneed and the most wretched of men ... they go about naked, wearing nothing more than a scruffy skin that can hardly cover them.' There was no doubt in Bougainville's mind that there were at least two distinct groups of Patagonians. Those he met along the northern shores, particularly in the east, were stronger and healthier, a consequence of their nomadic life as hunters and horsemen in the Argentinian plains. The Fuegans were clearly battling much harsher conditions, barely surviving on shellfish and whatever they might be able to find in the cold southern inlets.

The French named one group the Chaouas, from a word they often heard them use. The others they called Pêcherais, for the same reason. They took *chaoua* to mean 'friend', but *pêcherais* to mean 'us'. This latter opinion was strengthened when one of the visitors was shown a mirror and, on seeing himself reflected in it, exclaimed '*pêcherais*'. In fact, what he thought he was seeing was someone else, and he shouted out *pektewé*, a local term for an outsider. Ironically, therefore, the French were calling the locals the 'outsiders'.

The slow and painful progress through the strait provided opportunities for Commerson to go ashore and collect botanical specimens. He was sometimes accompanied by Nassau, but more often by Jeanne Baret, who climbed up steep and slippery escarpments to bring back plants that had caught the botanist's eye. His leg was still troublesome and prevented him from venturing up slopes, especially when these were covered with snow or ice. Jeanne's energy and the hard physical work she undertook laid at rest much of the suspicion that had begun to arise in recent months. No mere woman, surely, would have the strength to undertake some of the things she did. People began to refer to her as Commerson's 'beast of burden', a change from whispers about 'Jean' Baret being an effeminate or even a female valet. The officers, accustomed to salon society or middle-class ladies or their attendants, were more convinced she was a man than some of the men, whose mothers or wives belonged to the hardworking lower class. Even Vivès, who disliked Commerson and filled his journal with sarcastic comments about the pair, was forced to recognise her energy and her strength: 'I have to add in her praise that in general she surprised everyone by the tasks she undertook.'

In early January, the ships dropped anchor in an inlet and found traces of a foreign presence. A few lengths of rope and some fresh timber offcuts lay around on the shore. Some words roughly carved on tree trunks made it clear that Bougainville had been preceded by an English expedition on its way to the Pacific. It was led by Philip Carteret, who had sailed in the *Swallow* from Plymouth in August 1766, accompanied by Samuel Wallis in the *Dolphin*. Louis would continue to find traces of them, notably of Wallis in Tahiti and Carteret in New Ireland. He had long suspected that the British were sending or had already sent an expedition 'to establish a post in the South Sea'. He was wrong: this was a voyage of exploration just like his, its geographical and political aims much the same.

A few days later, tragedy struck, casting a deep gloom over the French. They had given some mirrors and glass to a group of Patagonians:

> Their custom is to hide lumps of talcum at the back of their mouths and up their nostrils. They no doubt wanted to do the same with the glass. A child of 10 or 12, with interesting features, became the victim. He swallowed some

glass. His tears, the blood clots he was spitting out frightened the natives. Two jugglers wearing a ceremonial hat took over – jugglers are the natives' doctors and you will notice that doctors are the same everywhere. They pressed down on his stomach enough to hurt him, with a number of incantations … I went ashore with our medical officers to take him some milk and an emollient infusion. The mother and the father's pain, their tears, the keen interest shown by the entire group … the child's docility in accepting the remedies, made a most moving spectacle.[5]

The child died during the night, and by morning the Patagonians had vanished. 'They flee from nefarious strangers whom they believe have come only to destroy them.'

The French struggled on along the strait, mostly in appalling weather, cold and damp with frequent sleet. They felt increasingly depressed. Their rudimentary maps were of little help, and they needed to take the greatest care as they wound their way past islands and rocky outcrops. Bougainville sent Landais in a boat to check that a channel ahead of them was safe enough to enter. It ended in ice floes and a bleak-looking shore. To make it worse, a bank covered in shellfish lay across it, with waves angrily breaking over it.

At last, on 26 January, he sighted Cape Pilar. It signalled the end of the stretch of land they had been following for the previous few days, called appropriately enough Desolation Island. It was also the end of the strait. It had taken almost two months to navigate it. Magellan had been luckier: it had taken him a mere five weeks. Ahead lay the Pacific Ocean, promising warmth and adventure.

23. ACROSS THE PACIFIC FROM EAST TO WEST

January–June 1768

AFTER THE STRAIT, sailing into the Pacific was like beginning a cruise. The sun was shining; the sea, although not smooth, was as peaceful as Magellan had found it when he gave it its name. The sailors could relax, wash their clothes and hang them up to dry, or simply lounge in the hot sun. Even climbing into the rigging to fix up a sail was a pleasure. There was no land in sight. Bougainville had given up any idea of calling in Chile, even for a brief rest and fresh supplies, or putting into the Juan Fernandez Islands. He had wasted too much time as it was, and there were discoveries to be made.

Or not. One of his first tasks was to see whether there was any sign of an amazing island known as David's (or Davis) Land. It had supposedly been discovered back in 1687 by a group of English buccaneers – 'a small sandy island', they had said, with 'a long tract of pretty high land' to the west. No one had seen it since, but mysterious islands acquire a special value through their very mystery. It might be, its discoverers suggested, the famous missing continent, 'the Coast of Terra Australis Incognita'. Later commentators accepted their guess as true: here at last was the great land mass so many believed existed. It was embellished over the years, especially with assurances that there would be gold and silver mines there, the kind that had made Spanish South America such a source of wondrous wealth. David's Land lay not far to the west of Peru and in the same latitude, so the rich veins of metals might well extend that far. Might? Many were soon convinced that they did. But no navigator had come upon the 'tract of pretty high land', and by the time the *Boudeuse* sailed, most people had stopped believing that David's Land had ever existed. Bougainville put an end to any further argument, by sailing right across its assumed location.[1]

There were more positive discoveries to make, though they took a while. For weeks, the French saw nothing around them but open sea. It was pleasant, restful, but unrewarding. Finally, on 21 March, land appeared along the horizon.

They sailed towards it, and saw small, low-lying islands, most of them surrounded by reefs, with a stretch of calmer water behind, and a shimmering sandy beach backed by coconut trees. They seemed to offer a promise of fish and coconuts, possibly of other fruits, but there were no apparent gaps in the reefs and they seemed uninhabited.

The French were about to sail away when men appeared, coming out of the woods, shouting and waving long pikes. Who could they be? How had they reached such isolated islands so far from anywhere? Were they castaways and, if so, of what race? As Caro, the lieutenant of the *Étoile*, put it in his journal: 'Who the devil has placed them on a little sand bank like this?'

Louis named the first island Island of the Lancers and the succession of atolls they were sailing past the Dangerous Archipelago. They were the Tuamotus of the south-east Pacific. Like Caro, he pondered about the islands and their inhabitants. 'Is this extraordinary land in the process of being born, or is it in ruins?' He admired the courage of the islanders, fearless men 'if they live with no worry on their stretches of sand that a storm could at any moment bury below the waves'.

The origin of the Polynesian people would remain a subject of sometimes heated debate for centuries. Had they come from Asia, or from South America? Had they in fact migrated from the Middle East, from Egypt for instance, or were they part of the lost tribe of Israel? No one at the time suspected that the Polynesians had developed superior navigational techniques, and that their canoes, often very large ones, could cover remarkably long distances. Theories of race complicated the argument, because so many people believed that they had travelled as a race, in the way Celts, Germanic tribes or Norsemen had migrated and conquered new lands. That the vast Pacific Ocean had been gradually populated over a period of 2000 years or more, and that this movement had created new societies in different areas of the Pacific, was something ethnologists would take a long time to accept.

At the beginning of April, a different type of island came into view, high, steep and isolated. Bougainville named it Le Boudoir, an allusion to a small sitting room. The name bore a flavour of the name *Boudeuse*, which means 'the surly one', or alternatively a seat on which two people could sit back to back. There may also have been some unconscious association in his mind with the French word for candleholder, *bougeoir*, from the way it stood out straight and lonely in the ocean. Its Polynesian name is Mehetia.

Then a much larger island appeared, a long stretch of reef-strewn beaches backed by high forested mountains. He had reached the island of Tahiti. He sailed along the coast for a couple of days, looking for an opening in the reef. On 6 April, he found a way in to a lovely spot – palm and coconut trees down to the very edge of the water, stretches of sparkling sand, and a peaceful lagoon – but it was to prove a 'detestable anchorage', which cost him six anchors. However, as Louis approached, the picture that struck his eyes was delightfully appealing:

In spite of all our precautions, one young woman came aboard on the poop, and stood by one of the hatches above the capstan. This hatch was opened up to give some air to those who were working. The young girl negligently allowed her loincloth to fall to the ground, and appeared to all eyes such as Venus showed herself to the Phrygian shepherd. She had the Goddess's celestial form. Sailors and soldiers hurried to get to the hatchway, and never was capstan heaved with such speed.[2]

On that day the legend of Tahiti as a South Sea paradise was born and it would remain unimpaired for many weeks; in a way it has never died. In fact this episode, or something like it, did take place, but at the end of the stay, as the men were heaving at the capstan to raise the anchor and leave. This does not really matter. It was a nice piece of writing, calculated to appeal to his readers, with its classical allusion to the myth of the judgement of Pâris (the 'Phrygian shepherd') who had to choose the most beautiful of three goddesses, Hera, Athena and Aphrodite. He chose the last named, whose name in Roman mythology was Venus.

The French were given a great welcome. Fruit and refreshments of every kind were provided without delay. Women came forward who were both beautiful and available. There were bare breasts everywhere, and few of the women showed any reluctance to display a lot more. Bougainville mentions that he was offered one island woman – possibly more than once. So was the Prince of Nassau-Siegen, to his embarrassment, because a crowd assembled to watch the spectacle of this European enjoying their special form of hospitality. He was by no means unwilling to enjoy her favours, but not with an audience. Some of the sailors were less inhibited and went in for a little exhibitionism, to the plaudits of the spectators. None of the officers did – or at least none admitted in his journal that he made love surrounded by applauding Tahitians!

The islanders were clearly interested in the newcomers. Bougainville's personal cook, eager to sample the delights of the island, had been the first to go ashore. Meeting a local girl who seemed willing to follow him, he took her under some trees, only to be set upon by a crowd of Tahitians, who promptly undressed him, thoroughly examined his white skin with cries of appreciation and then gestured for him to continue his frolics. The poor man fled back to his ship, vowing never to set foot on land again.

Although the French had no indication that other Europeans had visited the island, it soon became clear that the islanders had had some visitors. They knew about guns and their lethal power. They had discovered this when Wallis had called at Tahiti less than a year earlier. His stay had not been a peaceful one, and he was forced to fire at the islanders. With these unpleasant memories still fresh in their minds, the Tahitians had decided to be friendly towards this second lot of white-skinned visitors, and to give them what they knew they really wanted: fruits, fresh water, and women. These were easily provided and kept the newcomers happy. They did not expect them to stay long, and indeed were able to negotiate with Louis about the length of his intended stay, and reduce it by several days.

There were a few incidents, however, almost all of them the result of theft. Snatching a knife or a cap was carried out with great skill. These were more than trophies for the islanders: they were objects of great value. Louis tried to be understanding and conciliatory. 'No doubt curiosity towards new objects awoke in them violent desires – and anyhow there are rascals everywhere,' he commented. Not all his men were as understanding, though, and there were several clashes, with the locals fleeing into the hills to avoid the expected reprisals.

Overall, though, Tahiti remained in most of the Frenchmen's minds as an enchanted island. Here, thought some like the naturalist Commerson, was conclusive proof that 'Natural Man' existed, living uncorrupted in an isolated island paradise. His enthusiastic reports to friends at home, along with comments by Nassau-Siegen and a number of the younger officers, all helped to create the legend of an Eden, where backbreaking labour was unnecessary, where the sun shone over golden sands, and where men and women were free from the complex and irksome restrictions that morality and property-owning imposed on daily life and on sexual relations. The legend did not survive in this form for very long, as new facts emerged, but enough of it was left, even after the end of the Romantic era, for the very name of Tahiti to retain its aura of magic and idleness.

One of the Tahitians expressed a strong desire to sail with the French. He was delighted when Bougainville, after some early misgivings, agreed to take him to France, although the islander cannot have had any inkling of the enormous distance he would have to travel. Not everyone on board thought it was a good idea. The *Boudeuse*'s clerk, Saint-Germain, had predicted rather gloomily:

> This poor wretch will long repent the foolish thing he has done, because I consider his return to his homeland as impossible. He will be fortunate if the sorrow of spending a long time at sea does not deprive him of the temporary pleasure that will be his when he sees Paris. His main motive is the desire he has of marrying for some time some white women.[3]

His name was Ahu-toru. Bougainville at first called him Louis de Cythère, after Nouvelle Cythère, the name he bestowed on the island, but Ahu-toru preferred to adopt the name of Poutavéry, his approximation of the name of the man who was now his protector. Later, when he came under the protection of Marion Dufresne, who organised the expedition that was to return him to Tahiti, he changed it to Mayoa.

Parisian society would welcome the smiling Tahitian, whose supposed way of life dovetailed so neatly with the popular Rousseauist philosophy. In any case, he was a pleasant young man, exotic in appearance and behaviour. In time he got bored with Paris, but he also chalked up a number of successes among some of Paris's more easygoing ladies. Bougainville, knowing the kind of society Ahu-toru had left, provided him with enough pocket money to ensure that those women who expected some payment for their favours were not disappointed.

He was intelligent and shrewd, with a gift for mimicry, although he never found it easy to acquire a satisfactory knowledge of the French language. Bougainville considered him somewhat lazy and timid, but pleasant and good-humoured. On the other hand, his presence on board was less useful than hoped for. His knowledge of the Pacific was limited to a few outlying islands. The place names he gave the French turned out, in most cases, to be districts of Tahiti itself. Bougainville did not have the time or resources for a leisurely sail around the nearby islands, where Ahu-toru assured him attractive women would be delighted to see him. This caused him to miss the large Leeward Islands north-west of Tahiti, leaving this rich crop to be harvested by James Cook in the following year. He did, however, pass close to the atolls of Tetiaroa and he may have seen the high peaks of Moorea, but essentially he was sailing westwards into open sea.

He had left Tahiti on 16 April. A few days earlier, he had taken possession of the entire archipelago in the name of Louis XV. The document he drew up, with a copy buried ashore in a sealed bottle, refers to 'an archipelago, which we have named Bourbon Archipelago', and to Nouvelle Cythère. Unaware that Wallis had discovered the island before him and called it King George's Island, Bougainville selected a name that was in keeping with his earlier classical allusions. Cythera in the Aegean Sea was reputed to be the birthplace of Aphrodite, a myth made even more famous by Botticelli's painting of a naked Venus drifting ashore in a large shell. Tahitian girls standing naked on canoes around the *Boudeuse* provided a parallel with the Italian's painting.

No further land was seen until 3 May at dawn, when a high island appeared to the north-west. It was soon evident that it was not one but three islands merged together in the early mist. Canoes came out towards the ships, but Ahu-toru was unable to establish contact: he could not understand the language of the islanders manning them. They lacked the charm of the New Cytherans – 'a woman who had come in one of the canoes was hideous'.

The French were more impressed by the quantity of canoes they saw and the skill with which the islanders handled them. At first, Bougainville gave the islands the Greek-influenced name, Small Cyclades, but he soon changed this to the Navigators' Islands, a name that remained in use for many years. These were the islands of Samoa, an important and well-populated group, inhabited by Polynesians, but strongly influenced by nearby Melanesian people. The first three islands they saw – Tua and the smaller Olosega and Ofu – form the Manua group. On the morning of the 5th, the French sighted a long and high island to the north-west. This was Tutuila, and as shown by Bougainville's charts they also had a distant view of the southern coast of Upolu in the evening.

The weather then became overcast and the French had to reduce sail and navigate with a great deal of caution, causing Bougainville to exclaim, 'How much patience, O God, this navigation requires!' The lack of charts, the possibility that a reef might suddenly appear at night, the rapidly dwindling supplies – all these gave him a feeling of growing insecurity. The ships had been at sea almost continuously for six months since their departure from Montevideo, and it was unwise to tarry in these little-known seas. He decided against trying to land. There was no real need to: the supplies he had taken on at Tahiti were still adequate.

At dawn on the 11th they saw a fairly high land to the west-south-west, a lonely island he called first La Solitaire, then L'Enfant Perdu. This 'lost child' soon metamorphosed into two distinct islands; they were the Hoorn Islands, Futuna and Alofi, discovered by Jacob Le Maire in May 1616. The passage of the French is commemorated in the name of the 1310-foot Alofi peak, which is now known as Mount Bougainville.

As the French pressed on towards the west the men's health began to cause Louis some anxiety. Scurvy, that plague of long-distance navigators, was once again making its appearance. 'Several officers have a somewhat inflamed mouth and traces of scurvy in their gums,' he wrote on 14 May. The disease was to be expected, with the constant diet of dried fish, dried meat and hard biscuit. The fruit and vegetables they had obtained at Tahiti were running out, so that the sailors became affected by the lack of vitamin C. They grew weak; the bruises they inevitably suffered in their daily work failed to heal; their legs and ankles became swollen; their gums bled, and their teeth loosened; their breath, already laboured, became foetid.

Another problem also appeared, referred to by the surgeon as 'the venereal distemper'. Saint-Germain reported its appearance in his journal a couple of days later: 'We have begun to notice that some sailors, two in numbers, have caught an illness, it is believed at the island of Cythera; it has manifested itself by chancres [venereal ulcers].'[4] On the following day, he reported that six soldiers were suffering from the same trouble, and on the 22nd mentioned that several cases had also occurred in the *Étoile*, but added: 'in praise of the continence or good fortune of the officers, none has been affected in this way'. Vivès gave the eventual total as approximately twenty in the *Boudeuse* and twelve in the *Étoile*.

This uncomfortable 'distemper' has usually been taken to mean the men had

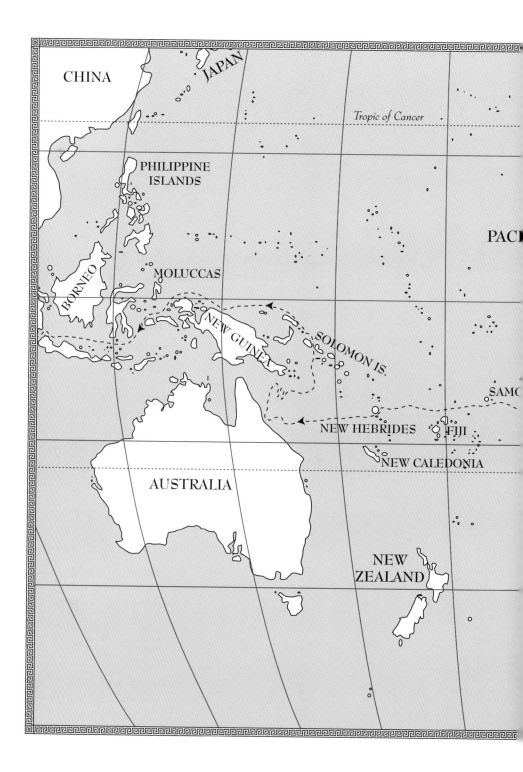

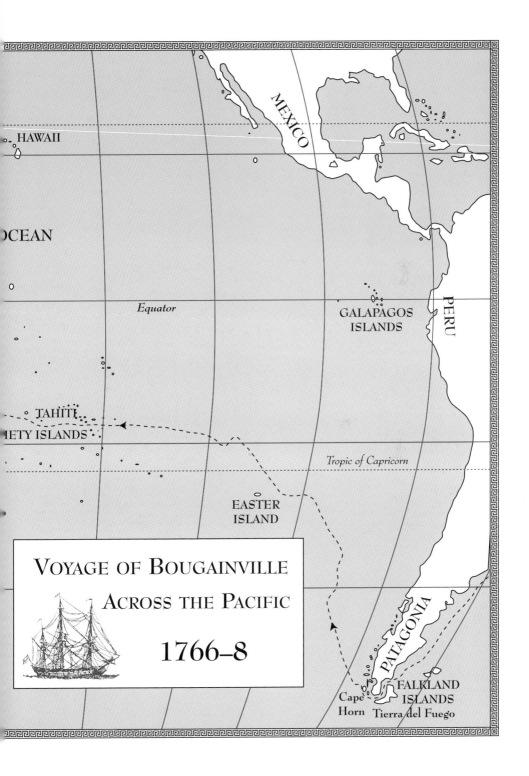

HAWAII

MEXICO

OCEAN

Equator

GALAPAGOS
ISLANDS

PERU

TAHITI

IETY ISLANDS

Tropic of Capricorn

EASTER
ISLAND

VOYAGE OF BOUGAINVILLE

ACROSS THE PACIFIC

1766–8

PATAGONIA

FALKLAND
ISLANDS
Cape
Horn Tierra del Fuego

syphilis, but Bougainville noted that 'Several venereal diseases … have recently appeared on board both ships. They are of all the types known in Europe.' The Tahitian passenger, he noted, was 'ridden with them' and it seemed that 'his compatriots are not greatly concerned about this sickness'. Accepting that it was indeed syphilis and knowing nothing about the arrival of Wallis's *Dolphin* the previous year, Bougainville began to wonder how the disease could have reached these isolated islands, and he even speculated that this might be a case of spontaneous generation. Ahu-toru was correct that it was a disease endemic in the islands, except that he was probably referring to yaws, a tropical disease common in the Pacific, which is caused by a related virus. The symptoms are very similar, and yaws acts, to some extent, as an immunising agent against syphilis. Even today, where yaws remains a problem, syphilis is uncommon, and vice versa: the elimination of yaws is often balanced by a rise in syphilis.

Nevertheless, syphilis did appear in Tahiti and among the sailors who called there. An argument soon developed over which navigator was responsible for its introduction. The easiest answer would be the first shipload of sailors and marines to enjoy the favours of the island women. This would give that dubious honour to the men of the *Dolphin*. Indeed, the Tahitians were to call it *Apa na peritane*, 'the British illness'.

When his ship sailed from Plymouth, Samuel Wallis had up to twenty men affected by 'a disorder too common amongst unthinking seamen', as George Robertson, the master of the *Dolphin*, described it.[5] All were reported as cured before the ship reached Tahiti. The surgeon 'affirmed upon his Honour that no man on board was affected by any sort of disorder, that they could communicate to the Natives'. How sensitive the matter became is evidenced by the addition in red ink and by a different hand of the words 'No Venereal'. When John Hawkesworth wrote his account of the voyage he gave Wallis a public opportunity to put the blame on the French: 'The reproach … must be due either to him [Bougainville] or to me, to England or to France; I think myself happy to be able to exculpate myself and my country beyond the possibility of doubt.'

Not surprisingly, Bougainville reacted angrily against the accusation, which was bitterly embarrassing. In the second edition of his *Voyage*, he replied, 'It is with little justification that they accuse us of having brought to the unfortunate Tahitians the illness that we could suspect more justly was communicated to them by M. Wallas's [*sic*] crew.' The squabble, which spoke of the age-old tension between the British and the French, dragged on for years. The accusations and counter-claims eventually faded as more serious accusations were levelled against European navigators for introducing other illnesses, many of them fatal to the islanders, and bringing about, in the nineteenth century, a serious fall in the island populations.

The Hoorn Islands faded on the horizon, and once again all that lay ahead was open sea. Eleven days went by, then two islands appeared, stretching roughly north-west, with a pass between. The northernmost, Bougainville named Aurora, and the southernmost Pentecost, it being the Feast of the Pentecost, or Whitsunday. The ships had now reached the New Hebrides, present-day Vanuatu. Aurora is Maewo Island, but Pentecost retained its name, though it is also known by its native name, Raga. Bougainville rounded the northern cape of Aurora, sighting far to the north a single peak, which he named Pic de l'Étoile. It was the small island of Mera Lava in the Banks group. Now more islands hove into sight to the south-west and the west. The archipelago was not shown on the charts, so it received the name of the Great Cyclades.

The feeling grew, however, that these islands had been visited before, and that this was the land that Pedro Fernandez de Quiros had discovered in 1606 and called La Austrailia del Espiritu Santo. The search for this 'Land of the Holy Spirit' certainly formed part of Bougainville's instructions. If this was it, the French needed to find the great bay in which Quiros had anchored and which he called San Felipe y Santiago. It was safe and spacious and would provide an excellent anchorage for a few days of rest.

More important still, this could mean that Bougainville had now reached the edge of the fabled southern continent. Playing it safe, Quiros had claimed on behalf of Spain 'all these parts of the South as far as the Pole, together with all its dependencies and appurtenances'. He never lost his enthusiasm for this land, and, as Charles de Brosses mentioned in his *Histoire des navigations*, he had told the King of Spain that 'the extent of the lands recently discovered is equal to the whole of Europe and Asia Minor as far as the Caspian Sea'.

The concept of a great southern continent went back a long way. In earlier times, most people, geographers and churchmen alike, believed that the world was flat. Looking at a wide plain or at a stretch of sea certainly did not give early Europeans the impression that they were standing on a large ball. People spoke – and still do – of 'the four corners of the world'. Some conceded that the earth might be a disc, like the moon, round but flat. This belief in a flat world gradually waned during the Middle Ages, and this brought up another question: was the other side of the globe inhabited? The term 'antipodes' (from the Greek 'against' and 'feet') was used, and suggested that, if there were people down under, then viewed from Europe they would be upside down. It sounded nonsensical in the days when the theory of gravity was unknown. It provided opportunities for satirists, including one famous author, Bishop Joseph Hall, who suggested that in a world that was 'different yet the same', with everything upside down, there could be swans swimming about but, being the very opposite of European ones, they might be black. He was being humorous, but in fact southern hemisphere swans are black!

The discussion then moved further. What was the likely size of this southern continent and were its people wealthy? Whereas the early Middle Ages had pooh-poohed the very idea of a southern continent as dangerous and probably heretical nonsense, geographers now believed that it had to exist, in order to counter-balance the continents of the northern hemisphere. Rocks and soil are heavier than seawater and, if there were no continent down under, the globe would tip over. *Ergo*, there must be one, and it should be equal in size to Europe, at the very least.

Navigators, however, had been gradually whittling away at it. Magellan's voyage had cut a swathe across the old maps, thereby showing that much of the Pacific was open sea. The various voyages of Mendaña, Quiros himself, Schouten and Le Maire, Roggeveen, Dampier and Tasman drove it back into the south-west corner of the charts. The great Australian continent itself, still imperfectly known, was being eroded from the west and north by other voyagers. If a Terra Australis did exist, it could only lie somewhere in that ill-defined and still unknown area where Mendaña and Quiros had discovered their Solomons and their Espiritu Santo.

Some of Bougainville's younger officers were excited by the Great Cyclades. Not only was this a new discovery that could be credited to their expedition, but it might well be the southern continent. Bougainville was rather more down-to-earth. Davis Land, he had already shown to everyone's satisfaction, was a myth. The theory of the southern continent had always been based on very flimsy evidence. The presence of a few islands could not be put forward as proof. And Bougainville could not even find Quiros's famous bay. This was because he was approaching Espiritu Santo from the east, whereas Quiros had sailed down from the north. He did not realise it at the time, but the Spanish had put into San Felipe y Santiago, which lay on the north coast, whereas Bougainville rounded the island along its south coast.

Louis then made his way along various offshore islands and he sailed out through what has become known as Bougainville Strait. This does not mean that sailing into and through the Great Cyclades represents any kind of failure: there was more to his mission that finding Quiros's landfall. Nibbling away at the possible limits of the southern continent was an achievement that geographers would come to appreciate. He would continue his contribution to the elimination of the continent myth in the weeks to come.

Before leaving it, he needed to chart as much as possible of this great archipelago and to describe its features, products and people. This meant landing on an island or two, without taking too much time or endangering the lives of his men. Consequently, on the morning of 23 May 1768, Bougainville went ashore with two boats, accompanied by an armed boat from the *Étoile*. They obtained some firewood, as well as a quantity of bananas and coconuts, in exchange for a few gifts. The Prince of Nassau-Siegen went with him. The presence of this awe-inspiring young nobleman was helpful, for when the islanders began to display some hostility, he advanced towards them and quelled them by his bearing and his obvious courage.

The usual act of possession was buried at the foot of a tree, allowing France to lay a claim to the island group, since the Spanish had displayed no interest in it over the years. It was little more than a gesture – Louis could hardly suspect that one day, under the name of New Hebrides later bestowed on them by James Cook, they would be jointly administered by France and her traditional rival, Britain. When the islands gained independence in the twentieth century they became known as Vanuatu, meaning 'Our Land'.

Suddenly, in the late afternoon, just as the party was about to leave, the islanders attacked with stones and arrows. A few musket shots were enough to disperse them. Communication had not been easy, as Ahu-toru did not speak their language, and their appearance was unsavoury. 'Many of them were covered with running scabs; others had horrible sores covering part of the body.' These symptoms denoted leprosy, yaws and tropical ulcers. The French named the place the Island of Lepers, yet the natives of Aoba, to give it its local name, are today as clean and as healthy as those of the neighbouring islands. Bougainville had obviously landed among an afflicted section of the population, and possibly one that had recently been engaged in warfare with neighbouring tribes.

From Aoba, the ships sailed west, passing between the islands of Malekula and Malo, and entering the vast blank area between Vanuatu and Australia. The officers peered at the map drawn by Robert de Vaugondy for De Brosses's book a mere dozen years earlier. It showed a great bulge on the north-eastern coast of Australia, a gigantic swelling of the continent that went all the way to the Land of the Holy Spirit. This was, according to a number of geographers, the famous Terra Australis – but now the French were sailing right across it. Louis had to admit in his journal that the ships were surrounded by open sea, with not a single sign of land anywhere. 'So where then is his great land?' he wondered, then shrugged and added '*Davus sum, non Oedipus*' – 'I am here to serve my country, not answer riddles'.

At least one other riddle was being finally solved, the Baret affair. Louis's attention had officially been drawn to the matter after an episode in Tahiti when Jeanne was set upon by a group of island men and had to take refuge on the *Étoile*. He probably had had some inkling of the Jeanne/Jean mystery much earlier, but other more pressing things had intervened. The presence of a woman on board a naval vessel was such a breach of the regulations, however, that he could no longer ignore it. He discussed the matter with La Giraudais on the *Etoile*, but little could be done now, beyond making arrangements to contain the scandal, and he returned to his ship in a fairly philosophical mood. 'I admire her determination,' he wrote. 'I have taken steps to ensure that she suffers no unpleasantness. The Court will, I think, forgive her for this infraction to the ordinances. Her example will hardly be contagious.'

Since the two ships were crossing what many had believed was land, officers and sailors permanently on duty in the crow's nest were continually scanning the horizon. This vigilance was rewarded on the evening of 4 June, when they sighted a low island. It was nothing very exciting, merely a stretch of sandbanks and rocks, but it was something of a warning. Louis named it Diane Reef. More substantial and equally dangerous was a set of nasty-looking breakers that appeared on the 6th, covering a wide area. This is now called Bougainville Reef. More were sighted a little later. This was indeed 'a third warning that I should not persist in seeking land along this parallel'. It was a wise comment, for he had reached the edge of the Great Barrier Reef, a dangerous line of low islands and sharp coral reefs that extends for over 1200 miles off the east coast of Queensland. It has proved fatal to many boats and ships over the years, and it brought James Cook's *Endeavour* to the brink of disaster a couple of years later.

As Louis took the only decision open to him, and set a course for north-north-east, he turned away from the coast of Australia, which some of his sailors claimed to have seen. It was, they told him excitedly, 'a low land SW of the breakers'. It certainly was not the mysterious Terra Australis but, as Caro wrote in his journal, 'a part of New Holland … full of shoals and reefs'. Everyone agreed that it would have been extremely unwise to go any closer to this dangerous coast, but he was turning away from a chance to clear up the geographical uncertainty that Vaugondy's map illustrated so well. Louis felt that he needed to defend his decision in his journal.

> I had planned to approach land along the parallel of 15 to 16°, not that I had any doubts that the southern land of the Holy Ghost was anything other than the Great Cyclades, and that Quiros falsified either his discoveries or his narrative … The encounter with this succession of breakers does not allow me to continue to seek here Quiros's southern continent … Other reasons … urge me to sail towards known countries. I have only enough bread for three months at most, wood and water for hardly a month, we have been 7 months at sea … Furthermore I have no anchors left that I could sacrifice to save the ships in such dangerous waters.

He sailed away, believing that the nearby land would offer little opportunity for a colony that would be of any use to France. This stretch of the Queensland coast is indeed difficult for ships to approach; it has a semi-tropical climate, with an arid hinterland, and it would not have appealed to French farming settlers. It might have been possible to make for Carpentaria – indeed, Bougainville's instructions included a mention of it – but this would have meant sailing through Torres Strait, about which very little was known, except that it was dangerous. The charts he had were vague in the extreme, and if there was no navigable channel, he could find himself imprisoned in a wide gulf. It was a risk conditions on board did not allow him to take.

So the great east-to-west crossing of the Pacific Ocean came to an end. The expedition veered north, towards New Guinea and more mysterious seas in which great islands were still waiting to be discovered by Europeans.

24. From New Guinea to Mauritius

June–November 1768

SAILING ROUGHLY NORTH, the expedition came upon the south coast of New Guinea. Had Bougainville taken the risk of entering Torres Strait and veered west a little earlier he could have reached Portuguese Timor, where the supplies he needed so much were plentiful. But if he had risked undertaking this fairly dangerous navigation, it would have curtailed his voyage of exploration and put paid to his most cherished hopes of making more new discoveries. So he sailed ahead until the mountains of New Guinea loomed ahead. He found himself caught in a bay, named the Cul-de-Sac de l'Orangerie, which did not appear safe enough to risk a landing. He struggled on an easterly course, held back for several days by contrary winds and by the fast currents that flow towards Torres Strait. The great mountainous land finally came to an end, but it was replaced by a seemingly endless succession of reefs and small islands that called for exhausting manoeuvres and constant watchfulness.

There was a consolation: these were new discoveries. He named the island chain the Louisiades, after Louis XV. They would be a present the elderly king would surely appreciate, but sailing along them was tiresome and dangerous. When, finally, he reached the end of the chain, he hailed it as Cap de la Délivrance. It was a well-chosen name. Time was pressing. Food was becoming perilously scarce and sickness was making worrying progress among the weakened crew. He was forced once again to reduce the men's rations. The one dog left on board had to be killed for food. The same fate befell their last goat, which the butcher slaughtered with tears in his eyes. She had provided milk on a regular basis and everyone on board had become fond of her. There was a similar pet goat on James Cook's expedition, and he became so fond of her that he took her home to his wife to enjoy a well-earned retirement in their back garden at Mile End, in London. Saint-Germain recorded wryly that he had shared a rat with the Prince of Nassau. They found it pleasant enough, given their circumstances, and he even expressed the hope that the others would not acquire a taste for such a delicacy. He was not sure there would be enough rodents on board to go round.

All the journals reflect the growing weariness. 'O, Bellin, how much you are costing us!' sighed Bougainville. Jacques Nicolas Bellin was one of the few cartographers who had drawn charts of this part of the Pacific, but he had had little information at his disposal and much of his work was little more than inspired guesswork. Caro wrote that he would be a fool if he ever allowed himself to be persuaded into another such expedition. Saint-Germain, soured by his circumstances, grumbled, 'Of what use to the nation is this voyage?' He rued the day he had left his home and family. After sharing his rat with Nassau-Siegen, he even recorded his suspicions that Bougainville and his close friends had extra and better food than others on board.

It is somewhat ironical that, just as Saint-Germain was penning his complaints, the expedition was on the verge of new and important discoveries. The charting of the Louisiades was a significant contribution to the knowledge of the western Pacific, but soon more land appeared as the French sailed north. 'What is this land?' wondered Bougainville. It could not be New Britain or the neighbourhood of Dampier Strait. There was nothing on anyone's charts that could help to identify these new features.

They had reached the southern islands of the Solomons, Gannonga, Baga and Vella Lavella. These were soon followed by others, a group now known as the Treasury Islands. Then a high land appeared to the north, which Bougainville named Choiseul Island, after the duke, his friend and protector. He tried to land, but darkness and tide were against it, and the dark-skinned Melanesians they saw lurking about in canoes were clearly less friendly than the Polynesians of Tahiti. When two longboats did try to look for an anchorage, they were met by some ten large canoes containing 150 men who promptly attacked them with stones and arrows. The French sailors dispersed them with a couple of rounds of gunfire, but this was clearly not a good place for rest and refreshments. Louis named it Warriors' Cove.

All he could do was to continue to the north-west, through a wide strait and along another large island. The passage, 12 miles wide, is now called Bougainville Strait and, rather oddly, forms the present boundary between the modern states of Papua New Guinea and the Solomon Islands. The island across this strait became Bougainville Island. Louis hauled along its impressive northern coast, then past the smaller island of Buka, so named because the islanders called out 'boca, boca' a number of times which the passing French interpreted as invitation to go ashore. They sailed on, however, and the whole island group fell behind, leaving the French to puzzle over their inadequate charts and stare ahead for what might come next.

Although they did not realise it, they had rediscovered the Solomon Islands, two centuries almost to the day since the Spaniard Alvaro de Mendaña had come upon a great island he named Santa Ysabel. It was followed by a succession of smaller ones, and the group became known as the Islas de Salomon. Mendaña died in 1595 while trying to make his way back to them. Quiros, ten years later, also failed to reach them. There were no other attempts by the Spanish to return to that area of the Pacific, and Solomon's Islands began to float about the Pacific in a bowl of uncertainty. The problem was their longitude. Determining a latitude back in the sixteenth century was relatively easy, but calculating a longitude was another matter. Errors of longitude could easily add up to several degrees or many hundred of miles. Mendaña, who was anxious to obtain official support for a return voyage, grossly understated the distance between Peru and the Solomons, so that the task of reaching them would not seem too difficult and therefore too expensive. And, like any good spin doctor, he waxed lyrical over the wealth his new discoveries could bring to his Spanish masters. Solomon's mines, everyone knew, had produced great wealth, so why should these islands not do the same? The King of Spain would surely want to enlarge his possessions by adding these wealth-producing islands to his overseas realm. Mendaña had no evidence to back his extravagant claims, but some of the Solomons have indeed produced gold, mostly alluvial.

Hernan Gallego, the expedition's pilot, underestimated the distance by around 2000 miles. This may seem extravagant, but this was the sixteenth century, a time when few people realised the true extent of the Pacific Ocean. The islands might be a long way to the west of South America, but to Europeans even a long way was manageable – the comparison they had in mind was with the Mediterranean, the Indian Ocean, or the Atlantic. The Solomon Islands might be distant from South America, but not unreasonably so. When Mendaña was appointed Governor of the Western Isles, the title supported the view that these were the western islands of Spanish South America. This did not necessarily run counter to the theory that they were near New Guinea. The Pacific had simply been shrunk by popular opinion.

Not surprisingly, when later expeditions struggled across a vast expanse of ocean and finally reached the Santa Cruz and New Hebrides groups, they tended to give up and veer north. Seventeenth-century mapmakers usually placed the Solomons close to New Guinea, and suspected they might be attached to the famous Terra Australis that everyone was talking about. Others felt that the Solomons actually were the New Hebrides where Mendaña and Quiros had ended up when they tried to get back to the Solomons. A Dutch map of 1622, Hessel Gerritsz's Great Chart of the South Sea, boldly labels the Santa Cruz and New Hebrides archipelagoes Islas de Salomon. This led some to believe that there might be only one group of islands, to which early navigators were giving different and confusing names. Alternatively, if what Mendaña had discovered was really the New Hebrides, the Solomons might not exist at all. Peter Heylen's *Cosmography in Four Books* of 1657, 100 years after Mendaña's voyage, lumps them with imaginary islands such as 'Utopia, New Atlantis, Faierie Land, the Painter's Wives Island and the Land of Chivalry'.[1] Echoing this sentiment, some mapmakers began to leave them out altogether or moved them to some other, less crowded part of the Pacific. Since no one was sure where they were, they might as well be used to fill up some blank space on their charts ...

The cartographer D.R. Dudley changed his mind about them between 1647, when he placed them close to New Guinea in his *Arcano del Mare*, and his second edition of 1661 when they were shown near the Marquesas Islands, 4000 miles further east. On the eve of their rediscovery, doubts about their existence were gaining ground. Both Bougainville and the Englishman Carteret, who also sighted them, questioned their existence or were confused about their possible location. Bougainville had with him Robert de Vaugondy's map of 1756, which shows the 'land seen by Gallegos' to the south of Easter Island, and the Solomons much further east than they really are. Confusion was total. John Callander, who translated and adapted De Brosses's book, suggested that the Solomons were probably a fiction. Bougainville was consequently not in a frame of mind that made it easy for him to identify the islands of Choiseul and Bougainville as part of the Solomons. It would take a careful analysis by European geographers and the detailed work of Buache and, above all, Claret de Fleurieu, to piece together the contributions made by Bougainville, Carteret, Surville and Shortland, and finally solve the problem that had bedevilled Pacific cartographers for more than two centuries.

The *Boudeuse* and the *Étoile* sailed on. There was nothing along the coast that seemed suitable as an anchorage. A few coconuts and bananas were obtained from some islanders, but little more. It was time to press on.

On 6 July, new islands came into view. What could they be? The French remembered that the English buccaneer William Dampier had sailed in this area about sixty years earlier and mentioned a great island he called New Britain. This, according to the charts, seemed to be it. Bougainville sent one of his officers, Du Bouchage, to look for some place where they could anchor. He succeeded: there was a vast bay with a promising harbour that offered shelter for the weary expedition. Louis named it Port Praslin, again honouring the Choiseul family. It was not in New Britain, however, but in neighbouring New Ireland. There was a passage between the two that he never saw, but Carteret had very recently found it, sailed through it and named it St George's Channel.

Port Praslin provided a safe enough anchorage, with one of the most spectacular waterfalls the French had ever seen. It fell majestically from forest-clad hills where they thought they could heard the sound of wild pigs, but they were too steep for the exhausted sailors to climb. Anyhow, there were no coconut or banana trees to be seen anywhere, and no one could be sure that the forest above them would include some. There was shellfish aplenty, easy to collect at low tide, but little else

– apart from a water snake that bit a young sailor and nearly caused his death. Then, walking along the narrow beach, they found part of a metal plaque. They could just make out what was inscribed on it. They were English words. A little further on, they came across clear signs of a camp. They had reached the place where Carteret had put in at the end of August 1767 and which he had called Gower's Harbour.

By and large, Port Praslin was a disappointing place. The daily diet was improved with the addition of cockles and a little fish. The sick could walk along the shore in safety, as there were no natives to worry about; the others could wash their clothes or simply laze about. Commerson went botanising, the Prince of Nassau-Siegen went hunting, Véron observed an eclipse of the sun, the officers supervised the cleaning of the ships and the restowing of the stores. But the rain poured down almost incessantly. 'Shall I always have to write bad weather, strong gale, storm, constant rain?' sighed Bougainville. 'Our crews are worn out, this land is providing them with nothing but an insalubrious air and extra labour.'

The weather delayed their departure, hiding from them the pass Carteret had discovered, which would have provided a much quicker route to New Guinea and the Dutch East Indies. Instead, Bougainville rounded the southern tip of New Ireland and sailed north along the eastern coast.

He passed a succession of islands from which canoes occasionally came out to examine the strange vessels. Attacks and skirmishes were not uncommon: the French were not only arousing the islanders' fears, they were also entering an area of ceaseless inter-tribal warfare. Bougainville named the islands after his officers, respecting their order of seniority. Duclos-Guyot already had his small island in St George Bay; it was now the turn of Bournand, D'Oraison, Du Bouchage and Suzannet. Most of the names have been replaced by the original native ones, Feni, Tanga, Lihir, Tabar.

By the beginning of August, the ships had come to the northernmost island of the New Ireland chain and were making almost due west towards the East Indies. They sailed north of the main Admiralty group until they were close to the equator. It was Commerson's turn to see his name given to an island – and although it is more frequently known as Sae, the French name is still found in use today.

One island, sighted on 8 August and part of the group known as Kaniet, appeared to be well populated, to judge from the number of men fishing around it. None approached the ships or even seemed to pay any attention to them, so Bougainville named it the Anchorites or Hermits Island. On the following morning, a line of low islands came into view. They were well wooded, but protected by fierce-looking reefs. Coming upon them at night would have been 'a disastrous encounter', Bougainville noted. He named them the Echiquier, the Chessboard. It was the Ninigo group, north-west of Manus Island.

On the 11th, this seemingly endless sprinkling of islands was replaced by a view of the high coast of what the French now knew to be northern New Guinea. It was wise not to come too close, but to sail a little further north. That meant almost following the line of the equator, day after day, in stifling heat. With the lack of fresh food and fresh water, the oppressive heat and a general feeling of exhaustion, scurvy was spreading rapidly in both ships; by late August the surgeons counted forty-five cases. The men were in rags, dragging themselves around the deck, struggling to get up the rigging to furl or unfurl the sails. The stench below decks was unbearable, the heat exacerbating the smell of urine and faeces from the sick lying down on makeshift beds of old sailcloth and rotting sacks. Rats scurried about everywhere – which had its bright side, as the sailors could catch them and hand them to the cooks to throw into the watery soup they tried to make each day. 'There have been many arguments over where Hell is situated. Truly we have found it,' said Bougainville.

Eventually, the long journey around New Guinea came to an end, and he reached the island of Ceram, the first of the Moluccas. There was no evidence of any Dutch outpost along the coast, but Louis hoped the islanders would come out to the ships, so he hoisted the Dutch colours. With any luck, they would recognise it as the emblem of their masters, or at least of Europeans they knew and should help. What happened instead was that the locals, who were afraid of the Dutch, took to their heels and fled to the hills. Within moments, the coast was deserted. There was nothing for it but to sail wearily on to the next island, Buru, where he knew there was an important trading post of the Dutch East India Company.

The Dutch, however, had always been worried that other Europeans might undermine their valuable spice monopoly, so Buru was out of bounds to all except Dutch ships. The local governor had strict instructions not to help any foreign vessel, and to arrest any foreigners who ventured near. It took every ounce of tact and courtesy for Bougainville to overcome the governor's scruples. He soon succeeded – he had charmed his way around European courts long enough to be able to deal with a minor Dutch official. He and his officers were invited to dinner, and the way they gulped down everything placed in front of them convinced the governor that their needs were genuine. During the six days Bougainville spent at Buru, he was allowed to buy supplies of rice, oxen, sheep and other supplies – highly priced, but badly needed. The sailors were overjoyed, the sick began to improve and the ships received their first thorough cleaning in weeks.

The *Boudeuse* and the *Étoile* sailed from Buru on 7 September 1768, though without the help of a Dutch pilot. The governor of Buru was not willing to risk doing too much to help the foreigners. A labyrinth of islands lay ahead and the French charts were imprecise. One way the Dutch authorities kept out intruders and defended their monopoly was by publishing as little information as possible about East Indian waters and encouraging the spread of rumours about the dangers of inter-island navigation. Fortunately, the perils were exaggerated, although Bougainville could not know this as he began to thread his way through the seas and straits. He did have the good fortune of having on board a French sailor with experience in the Molucca Sea, 'who has been sailing in these waters for the last six or seven years and has made three or four crossings from Batavia to Amboyna, Buton and Buru'. A local man they met on the way also proved helpful. The French proceeded towards Java with growing confidence, buying supplies from the natives as they went.

On 28 September, they saluted the fort of Batavia (present-day Jakarta) with a twenty-one-gun salute, which was returned in full. On the following day, they went ashore, finding that, as a result of their east-to-west crossing, the date was actually the 30th. The Dutch received them 'in the best manner possible'. The twenty-eight sick on board the two ships were cared for at the local hospital. Supplies were purchased and loaded on board for the return home, but after a week more ill-health began to affect the crew, even though the scurvy cases were recovering. This time, they were falling victim to dysentery, a frequent scourge in Batavia and the cause of many deaths during the eighteenth century. Even Louis was affected, although not seriously, but recurring bouts of dysentery would plague him for much of his life and eventually cause his death.

The city was built on the estuary of the Ci Liwung River, which meandered into sluggish waterways, most of them muddy receptacles for the residents' refuse, stinking in summer and year-long homes for clouds of mosquitoes. The wealthier homes, away from the crowded streets, were surrounded by pleasant and sometimes grandiose gardens, but the sailors were not allowed near them, and even the officers could only go out to receptions and dinners by being rowed ashore and riding or being driven through the filth of the harbourside alleyways. To escape the pestilential climate of the city, Bougainville decided to anchor outside the harbour and then, warned about the impending monsoonal change, he decided to cut short his stay. The monsoon might wash some of the rubbish away and turn the oozy rivulets into canals, but constant pouring rain would not make life any more pleasant. He did not alter the dating of his shipboard journal until he had reached the Isle de France; consequently, according to his reckoning, he left Batavia on 17 October 1768. The route from Batavia to the Indian Ocean was well known. It was the one area of the East Indies the Dutch could not conceal from Europeans. Krakatoa, a slumbering volcanic island that would one day explode into a massive eruption, marked the end of Sunda Strait, between Java and Sumatra. Then it was, literally, plain sailing to the Isle de France, the most important French outpost in the Indian Ocean.

25. From Mauritius to France

December 1768–March 1769

FOR MANY CENTURIES, Mauritius had lain isolated and unknown in the western Indian Ocean. A few hopeful Arab traders may have landed on its deserted shores, but they soon sailed away in disappointment. Left undisturbed, the turkey-like dodo waddled through the semi-tropical forest and fussed around its ground-level nest, where it laid one single, large egg. The first European appeared in 1511, a Portuguese, Domingo Fernandez, but he soon left and the island was left alone again until 1598, when the Dutch arrived and named it after the Stadtholder of the Netherlands, Maurice of Nassau. They stayed – and the fate of the sluggish, friendly dodo was sealed: it vanished sometime in the 1680s, leaving merely a proverbial saying that enshrined oblivion.

By then, a small Dutch colony had been settled, but it never prospered, and it was abandoned in 1700. Mauritius reverted to its isolation and loneliness until 1721 when French settlers arrived. The island had been claimed by Guillaume Dufresne in 1715. He had seen its potential, largely as a staging post for ships on their way to the East, and he had renamed it Isle de France. All that remained of the earlier Dutch activities were old sugar plantations now overrun by the wild bush, depleted forests and a few descendants of runaway African slaves eking out a living by the seashore.

Under its early governors, especially the energetic Mahé de la Bourdonnais, the plantations were restored, establishing a solid basis for a colonial settlement. Another source of income for the colonists was growing food and supplying ships on their way to and from India and China. By 1768, when Bougainville arrived, the population had grown to some 30,000, including 6000 settlers of European descent; the balance consisted of African slaves and people of mixed descent. The French India Company had administered the island until just before Bougainville's arrival. Now, however, run by the Ministry for the Colonies, the Isle de France had its military governor and its civilian administrator, or *intendant*. Not surprisingly, the two were at loggerheads.

As a former army officer and now a captain in the naval service, Louis needed to pay his respects to the governor, Daniel Dumas, a colonel who had served with distinction in French Canada. The two men knew each other, and held each other in the highest regard. Dumas had even, like Bougainville's family, a legal background, having graduated in law and practised for a short and somewhat unsuccessful period. The two men got on well, but Louis was careful not to get embroiled in the ongoing disputes between the governor and the *intendant*.

He had even closer links with the latter, Pierre Poivre: the two had almost come to the Isle de France together, when the Duc de Choiseul envisaged appointing Bougainville instead of Dumas. Poivre was a keen botanist, who created an attractive garden in his French property. A former senior employee of the French India Company, he was a man with considerable experience in the eastern trade, and he made a significant contribution to the island's development. His greatest hope was to set up spice plantations on the Isle de France and elsewhere, that would finally break the irksome Dutch monopoly. Louis, in line with his confidential instructions, had tried to obtain spice plants as he sailed through the Indonesian islands – he requested Commerson to collect some as botanical specimens or to buy some as discreetly as he could – but he had had little success and he had not brought much with him to satisfy Poivre's plans. Still, the information he had gathered about the difficulty, or indeed the absence of difficulty, of navigating through the archipelago was valuable.

Louis steered his way very cautiously between the two rival camps. Poivre was the first to greet him, having gone down to meet him as soon as he heard that the *Boudeuse* had reached the inner harbour. Dumas, however, arrived soon after, and offered his residence as lodgings for Bougainville and his senior officers. It would be an idyllic place after their cramped and noisome quarters on the frigate.

The *Étoile* arrived the following day and provided Bougainville with the first test of his relations with Poivre. La Giraudais and his officers, ever keen to make money on the side, had loaded the ship with sugar, arrack – an alcoholic spirit made from rice – and other items from the East Indies, but unfortunately for him and for Poivre he had no spices either. He knew that he would have little difficulty in selling his trading goods locally at a good price, but there were duties to pay on them, amounting to some 16 per cent of their value. La Giraudais began to argue that naval ships were exempt from these imposts, which was a fairly cheeky claim, since naval vessels were not supposed to engage in trade. Poivre insisted, appealing to Louis to confirm his action. The commander at once sided with the *intendant* and upbraided La Giraudais, not merely for endeavouring to avoid paying taxes on commercial goods, but for trading while in the service of the royal navy.

Dumas, for his part, was endeavouring to get Louis to side with him in his dispute with Poivre, trying to explain to his guest how difficult it was to deal with the *intendant*, but Bougainville steadfastly refused to let himself be drawn into the argument. Poivre, Dumas warned him, would soon be recalled and Louis was backing the wrong side. But Louis remained neutral – and, as it turned out, both the governor and the *intendant* would be recalled at the end of the month by a ministry that had become increasingly irritated by their constant bickering.

The strain between the two men rose to the surface not long after Louis's arrival, when Dumas complained that, instead of joining him on an inspection of the island's defences, and drawing up an authoritative report for the ministry officials back in France, Louis had gone off to visit plantations and an iron works with Poivre. Even worse, he also moved from Dumas' residence, the Réduit, and accepted the *intendant's* invitation to stay with him at his country estate, Monplaisir. To keep the peace, Louis agreed to go with Dumas to inspect the fortifications – 'almost non-existent', he reported to the minister. However, when the time came for Dumas to leave the island, he declined his request to travel in the *Boudeuse*.

The visit to the iron works led to Louis investing some of his own money in the venture. It was situated on a neighbouring estate, where Poivre had taken him with Nassau-Siegen, and he was impressed by what he saw. 'One would find few equal to this one in Europe, and the product is of an excellent quality.'[1] The prince echoed his sentiments: 'One wishes everyone in the colonies showed such enterprise ... Mr Hermans [the landowner] is one of these rare citizens who deserve the gratitude of the state and who should be helped.'[2] Bougainville's enthusiasm was not lost on Hermans, who asked him to help with financing a third furnace. Poivre endorsed the proposal, and Louis invested 30,000 *livres*; this was to be a three-year loan at 5 per cent. Not only did this move upset Dumas, however, but it turned out to be a bad investment. When the time came to send Ahu-toru back to Tahiti, by way of the Isle de France, Louis decided that the capital and the accumulated interest would pay for the Tahitian's stay in the island and his later repatriation – but by then Hermans had gone bankrupt, and Louis was forced to appeal to the king to meet Ahu-toru's expenses.

Bougainville's generosity extended to other areas as well. Whereas the *Étoile* had landed goods that La Giraudais and his officers intended to sell for their personal profit, Louis transferred to Poivre a large quantity of supplies and equipment free of charge: 'I gave, at Mr Poivre's request, the iron and the nails stored in the *Étoile*, my cucurbit, numerous medicines and items which were of no use to us, but of which the colony is in great need.'[3] He also left a number of men on the island. First to disembark were the sailors and soldiers he had picked up in the Indonesian islands: the agreement was that they would serve in the local military forces, 'the legion', in exchange for a full pardon for those who had deserted from other ships.

Then came Philibert Commerson and Jeanne Baret. Poivre was delighted to obtain the services of a botanist he greatly respected. Commerson could help with the collection and classification of plants, locally and in neighbouring islands, especially Madagascar and Bourbon, where the flora needed to be professionally surveyed and classified. The naturalist adopted the idea with his usual enthusiasm, although his ardour cooled somewhat and ended in despair after Poivre was recalled to France and later administrators proved unwilling to finance his work and even help with his living expenses.

The move also solved a problem that had been troubling Bougainville for some time – the reaction of the authorities back home to the presence of a woman on the *Étoile*. Judging by the interest his arrival had aroused in Mauritius, he expected to be greeted effusively once he landed in France, and his officers, too, would be welcomed, invited out and asked to tell their story. Commerson and Baret could not step ashore unobtrusively in Saint-Malo or Brest, and quietly make their way home: Commerson would bask in all the publicity. Leaving him behind on the island, to find his way back a year or two later, was much better. As it turned out, Commerson died on the Isle de France a little over four years later. Baret married locally, left for France soon after and disappeared into relative anonymity.

Others were also left on the island, most of them at Poivre's request. They included the astronomer Véron, the chaplain Lavaysse, the engineer Romainville, and the clerk Saint-Germain, whose health had been deteriorating in recent months. The volunteer Fesche also stayed behind, as did Oury and Oger, the pilots. One of the young officers died on the island, young Du Bouchage who had never recovered from the dysentery he had caught in Batavia. 'He died in my arms,' recorded Bougainville.[4] Another youth, Lemoyne de Montchevry, a volunteer on board the *Étoile*, had also died, in his case of tuberculosis.

Pleasant and restful though most of the stay may have been, Bougainville was increasingly impatient to leave for France, and his officers and men felt the same. It had been a long and wearying expedition, and they all yearned to return to their families and friends. The *Boudeuse* was ready first and there was no need to wait for the storeship. Besides, relations with La Giraudais had been more than a little strained by the recent argument. On 10 December, those on the *Boudeuse* farewelled all their acquaintances and embraced for the last time those they were leaving behind. The next morning, the port captain, Joseph Mervin, came on board for the final goodbyes and Louis gave the signal to raise anchor, but, as so often happened, they had to wait another day until a favourable wind came along. On the 12th, at midday, the *Boudeuse* sailed out of Port-Louis. As a final gesture of goodwill, Bougainville gave Mervin his longboat and a yawl.

The crossing to Cape Town was largely uneventful. The journals record the usual problems with contrary winds, calm days, occasional storms. On Monday 9 January 1769, the *Boudeuse* dropped anchor in Table Bay, and the next day Bougainville travelled with his officers in two coaches to pay a formal call on the Dutch governor, Ryk Tulbagh, at Constantia.

The Dutch had used Table Bay as a stopping place on their way to India since 1616, when the Atlantic Ocean island of St Helena had fallen to the English. A settlement was established in 1652 by Jan van Riebeek. The Dutch were later joined by French Protestant immigrants, the Huguenots, looking for a better life in a new colony. The Dutch East India Company, however, wanted to establish a port of call, rather than build up a colonial settlement. This policy caused a number of disaffected new arrivals to move away in search of farming land – they became known as the trekkers. The company was trying to prevent further immigration, as this was beginning to cause problems with the local Hottentots, and was adding nothing to the company's profits.

By the time of Bougainville's arrival, the Boer farmers had expanded their holdings some 370 miles north of Capetown, where they had encountered the Xosas, part of the Bantu race that had slowly been advancing south, driving aside the earlier inhabitants. Coping with the resulting frequent clashes, when the Dutch East India Company was entering a period of decline, was a constant headache for Tulbagh.

Bougainville and his officers were impressed by the governor, and by the countryside and especially the vineyards. 'A good wine,' Louis noted, 'and we drank a great deal of it, both at table and in the cellar, so that we could appreciate the different vintages.' He was told about some recent discoveries in the field of natural history. An exploring party had found a 'quadruped 17 feet in height, with a young still suckling 7 feet high ... It is said that, in the time of Caesar, a similar type of animal was brought to Rome and shown in the amphitheatre.'[5] It was a giraffe. Also recorded was a 'very handsome' creature, 'with features belonging to the horse, the deer and the bull'. It was a gnu. Louis was given drawings of both animals, to take to the great naturalist Buffon, and he commented: 'It is not without reason that Africa had been called Mother of Monsters.' Louis wrote at greater length about the state of the country's defences. The fort at Capetown did not impress him, and both he and Nassau felt that an alien power could easily conquer it. They were right: the colony fell to England in 1795.

The *Boudeuse* sailed away on 17 January. Louis had learnt that Philip Carteret had also recently called at the Cape, and he was eager, if possible, to catch up with him.

He headed north-west for St Helena which he sailed past on 29 January, making for Ascension Island where he hoped to obtain sea turtles. On 4 February the *Boudeuse* anchored off Ascension's north-west coast at Clarence Bay by Cross Hill. It was a deserted spot, but turtles, a rich source of proteins and vitamins, were easy to find. When the French sailed away two days later, they had fifty-six of them on board. They had actually caught seventy, more than they could take, so they had released fourteen.

Although discovered by the Portuguese in 1501, Ascension had never been settled, but a tradition had grown up for passing ships to record their visit by leaving a note in a bottle in a cave. Messages could also be left in the hope that the next visitors would take them to their destination. Louis found a note by Carteret, which told him that the *Swallow* had departed the island on 1 February, only five days earlier. And on 25 February, the French sighted the *Swallow* a short distance ahead. Bougainville offered Carteret assistance, which was politely declined. The Englishman knew very little about the French expedition:

> My people learned from the boat's Crew that she had been round the Globe with an other ship which they had left at the Island of France (or Maurice), and that they had gone through the Streights of Magellan and had been two months at the Island Juan Fernandes [sic] in the South-Sea. Although this ship was foul from her voyage and we clean, yet he had overtaken and got no less than 4 days sailing of us from the Island of Ascension ...[6]

The officer Bougainville had sent over to offer help was probably one of the volunteers, Duclos-Guyot, who did not wear naval uniform, a fact that surprised and shocked Carteret. Either through mutual incomprehension, or because Bougainville had told the young fellow not to reveal too much about their voyage, Carteret grew suspicious and then angry. He became even more irate when one of his officers reported what he had discovered from the French boat crew. The information included mention of a supposed two-month stay at Juan Fernandez. One young sailor had embroidered on this by saying that he had spent two years on the island – like some Robinson Crusoe.

Carteret had already parted, fairly coolly, with Duclos-Guyot: 'I asked him, how he could presume to think, that I should go and tell him my Voyage, & added, my time is too precious to lose any more.'[7] But he did give him a memento of their meeting, 'one of the Southsea Indian Arrows'. As the *Boudeuse* sailed ahead, leaving the *Swallow* not flying but wallowing behind him, Bougainville wondered how she could have sailed such a distance and how miserable life must have been in the ship.

In early March the French approached the Azores. They sailed through the middle of the island group, passing just to the west of Terceira on 4 March. They went on their way and, on the 14th, sighted the island of Ushant, off the west coast of Brittany. However, stormy weather prevented them from sailing into Brest and forced them north. Then the foremast broke, at which point Bougainville resolved to go to Saint-Malo, and the *Boudeuse* anchored under the city's ramparts on 16 March 1769.

Two years and four months had elapsed since the departure from Nantes. The voyage was an outstanding achievement that placed France in the forefront of naval exploration. Apart from an accident in South America that had claimed three lives, only seven men had been lost. That in itself was an impressive record in eighteenth-century navigation. Louis brought his narrative to an end with a quote from his favourite Virgilian epic, the *Aeneid*: '*Puppibus et laeti Nautae imposuere coronas.*' 'And the sailors, rejoicing, decorated the stern of their ship with crowns of flowers.'

Part 5
War and Revolution

26. Back in France

March 1769–December 1771

EAGER TO REPORT on his mission and to meet his family and friends, Bougainville left without delay for Paris, accompanied by the Prince of Nassau-Siegen and the Tahitian, Ahu-toru.

Outwardly, the capital was unchanged. The streets were still crowded with pedestrians hurrying along the narrow streets, shouting hawkers pushing handcarts, drunks and beggars huddled in doorways or on the pavement. The familiar stench of the back streets, and the cool, odorous air swirling up from the Seine, welcomed them even as it caught at their throats.

But, in many respects, the mood of the people had changed. Louis XV was now almost sixty, secretly wearying of ruling a troubled country as an absolute monarch: he had assumed the role at the age of five. The treasury was still empty, the inequitable and complex tax system had not been reformed, the local assemblies, the *parlements*, were rebellious. The Marquise de Pompadour was no more than a memory. The king's new mistress, the Comtesse du Barry, a seamstress's daughter, was unpopular and far less skilled at political intrigue than her famous predecessor. Only twenty-five, she was much younger than the king, and the thirty-five-year age difference gave their liaison a flavour that some found ludicrous, others increasingly shocking.

Choiseul was gradually losing his influence. He had carried out major reforms, especially in the army and navy, but he had become set in his ways and, like many politicians, was overstaying his welcome. Mounting pressure from his enemies, most of them manoeuvring behind Madame du Barry, was threatening his rule and irritating the king. Louis XV had not yet uttered his famous 'After me, the deluge', but he wanted a change. Above all, he wanted peace for France, peace at court, peace for himself. The thought probably never occurred to him, but what he really would have liked was to retire.

Although Bougainville did not immediately realise it, this complex and evolving political situation weakened his own position. He had been a protégé of both the Pompadour and the Choiseul cousins, and he was about to find himself in the wrong camp.

There were few signs of this at first, however. He made a brief call at Versailles on 19 March, reporting to naval officials, all of whom seemed pleased to see him. He then moved on to Paris, dropped the prince at his residence and took Ahu-toru to his own home in the Rue Basse-du-Rempart. Members of his family rapidly gathered around him, including his cousin Nerville, the one-time governor of the Malouines. They listened eagerly to his tales of the South Seas as his Tahitian guest smiled and nodded, talking still imperfectly the French he had been taught on the voyage. There was just a note of gloom in the household: Louis's brother-in-law, Louis-Honorat de Baraudin, had died, and his sister still wore her widow's weeds. Returning to Versailles, Louis called on the Duc de Choiseul and the Duc de Praslin before having his first audience with King Louis XV. The king congratulated him on his success, and showed appreciation of the seven acts of possession he had drawn up, each laying claim to a group of islands in faraway seas.

Bougainville was once more caught up in the complex court etiquette, with its seemingly immutable rituals, and in the lazy eddies of administrative procedures. Invitations were coming from every side, usually with a request to bring along his colourful Tahitian friend. His list of visits reads like a who's who of Paris society: dukes bearing famous titles such as Orleans and Chartres, the Prince de Conti, the Marshall de Soubise and the Comte d'Estaing, a valuable contact as he was now head of France's naval forces. Scientists wanted to discuss his discoveries, men like Buffon, D'Alembert, La Condamine, who was fascinated by Ahu-toru's native language, De Brosses, the historian, Vaugondy, the famous cartographer.

Ahu-toru had been presented to the king, then taken under the wing of the Duchesse de Choiseul who showed him off in Paris society. He became a regular at Versailles and at the opera and was often seen walking around Paris. He told people that he was Poutavery, having exchanged names with Bougainville in accordance with tribal traditions – those who did not realise this marvelled at the similarity and talked about the two men being predestined to meet. A popular poet, Jacques Delille, included Ahu-toru in his series of poems, *Les Jardins*, picturing him walking in the royal gardens and seeing a tree that he recognised from his native island, wrapping his arms around its trunk and weeping in a romantic expression of homesickness. Ahu-toru, however, had not lost his passion for the ladies and is reported as expressing his desires with a Tahitian frankness that amused many, but is believed to have brought him some successes.

The savants of the day also expressed interest in the visitor. Charles de La Condamine, a mathematician who had also been a great traveller, brought his friend Jacob Pereire to interview him. Pereire had developed a system for communicating with the deaf and dumb, and he was eager to test Ahu-toru's grasp of French phonetics. The Tahitian was as patient as could be expected of someone being asked to repeat a seemingly endless sequence of sounds. Pereire hoped to discover the origins of the Polynesian people by comparing their language with others spoken in the Indian Ocean and the western Pacific, but it was too soon for such endeavours.

La Condamine was told that Ahu-toru had guessed that Commerson's valet was a woman. How could he have done this when so many of the crew had not? His conclusion was that the Polynesians had a more developed sense of smell than Europeans. He came to this view through a rather strange experiment: he showed the Tahitian a painting of Venus in which the goddess wore no more than a veil. Ahu-toru touched it, then sniffed his finger, exclaiming '*moua*', which the French interpreted as meaning good. He had not used the word for woman, '*wahine*', so La Condamine concluded that he had such a fine sense of smell that he could not only tell the difference between a man and a woman, but also between a healthy and a diseased woman. Both scientists left, greatly satisfied, each planning to begin work on an article embodying the fruit of their research.

There were more such visits and more interviews, but not everyone admired Bougainville. There were barbed comments in some quarters. 'He claims to have discovered, among other marvels, an island in the Southern Lands, where the customs are admirable … One may suspect that this new Robinson has acquired that taste for the marvellous that is the hallmark of travellers.'[1] Such quips emerged from the salon of Madame Doublet de Persan, a lady of restricted means who nevertheless managed to gather around her a number of savants, minor poets and wits. She ran a *Bureau de nouvelles*, whose members were expected to bring along news and gossip about the world of politics and French high society. 'Valets acting as secretaries kept the records, and the *encyclopédiste* La Curne de Saint-Palais drew up a card-index of one hundred and fifty thousand anecdotes.'[2] A few days later, from the same salon, emerged a sarcastic comment about Bougainville's hopes of being appointed governor of the wonder-filled island 'which he claims to have discovered … Apparently, he is making every effort to get himself named as governor of this island and thereby make up for the loss of his command in the Malouines Islands.'[3]

The rumour was not entirely without foundation. Still unaware of Wallis's discovery of Tahiti, Louis had broached with Choiseul the possibility of France taking over Pacific islands before the British established their own settlements there, but this was little more than an expression of his early enthusiasm. There were other achievements he could claim: several unchallengeable new discoveries, improvements in geographical knowledge, careful astronomical readings and numerous ethnographical observations. He could even report to Poissonnier that his cucurbit had worked well and, in the words of Voltaire, that 'sea water could be desalted'.[4]

He had less to show in the area of natural history, but he could claim, with justification, that his voyage had not been planned as a scientific one. Even the unsuccessful search for spices had been suggested on commercial, not scientific grounds. The authorities had provided his expedition with a royal botanist in the person of Commerson, who had indeed collected a vast number of botanical and other specimens. But the great bulk of his material, notes, plants, shells and other items, was still with him in Mauritius, largely unsorted and uncatalogued, and at the moment there was not a great deal Louis could show the various scientists who questioned him about his travels.

After the exciting first week or two of his return, he began to discern a certain coolness among the Spanish officials at Versailles. It took him a while to discover the cause: they felt somehow cheated by his previous reports on the potential of the Malouines. He had been enthusiastic about their future, but what the Spanish had found on the islands did not bear out his claims. True, they had insisted that he hand the Malouines over to them, and he had reluctantly bowed to their request, but they were increasingly disappointed by what had become a place of exile. The prospects for agriculture were poor, the islands were treeless and windswept, the buildings were basic and uncomfortable. Some suspected that Bougainville had overpraised the Malvinas so that he could recoup his investments and possibly make a little profit out of the Spanish treasury. Madrid also felt that his voyage was an intrusion into Spanish seas, a reconnaissance intended merely to serve French interests and a danger to their imperial possessions. Some officials had known he had been authorised to come home by way of the Pacific, but few realised how much the French government had done to transform a supposedly straightforward return journey into a major expedition.

Nevertheless, so much was positive in the way Paris and Versailles welcomed Louis home that he could ignore the few disgruntled individuals. And he had work to do: he had to prepare the narrative of his voyage for the king and subsequently for publication. He started work on this in mid-April 1769. He was given full access to his shipboard journal and to other items he had handed over to the naval office, as the regulations required. His first version was ready for a formal presentation to Louis XV on 28 October: 'Today, Mr de Bougainville, Brigadier in the King's armies, had the honour of presenting to the King the manuscript of his Voyage around the world.'[5]

In November 1769 the government granted Bougainville a life pension based on a capital value of 50,000 *livres*, plus 10,300 *livres* in cash, in recognition of the voyage and to offset some of the losses he had clearly incurred over the Malouines affair. It should have been more, but the country's finances were, as usual, in a state of crisis. When, a month later, Bougainville proposed an expedition to the Pacific to return Ahu-toru and explore the region further, the government refused: it could only afford to send Ahu-toru as a passenger on a scheduled trip to the Isle de France. It was hoped that once there he would find some commercial expedition to take him home. The Duc de Choiseul handed over the required travel documents in January 1770, and his wife provided a substantial sum of money to buy tools and other useful items that Ahu-toru could take back to his people in Tahiti.

Bougainville farewelled him in February. The Tahitian arrived safely at the Isle de France, but he had to wait more than a year before an opportunity arose to sail for the Pacific. Marc-Joseph Marion Dufresne, keen to set off on a voyage that combined exploration and trade, took him on board his *Mascarin*, which left Port Louis on 18 October 1771. But the Tahitian was already ill, and he died three weeks later. Marion Dufresne continued on his way, but was killed, with a number of others, in New Zealand.

In January 1770, Bougainville was formally appointed to the royal navy, with the rank of *capitaine de vaisseau*, backdated to 13 June 1763. He had mixed feelings about this formal entry into a corps dominated by members of the aristocracy – in spite of having been in command of a major voyage of exploration, he was still only the son of a lawyer, not a true 'officer of the red' and he had not gone through the period of training normal for officers. He worried that, especially in time of peace, class distinctions would surface and make his life difficult. And in this he was sometimes proved right.

He was attached to the Brest division, with an annual salary of 3000 *livres*, but it was understood that, for the time being, he would remain in Paris, working on a narrative of his voyage for early publication. It was not an easy task. He did not want to load it with navigational details that would mean little to the ordinary reader. He knew his audience and he wanted to appeal to as many cultured people as he could, thereby establishing a wider reputation in the field of Pacific exploration, and strengthening France's position among the exploring nations. In this he was quite successful. His *Voyage autour du monde* never lost its popularity or its readership. But he paid for it by enjoying a lesser reputation among geographers, navigators and scientists, all of whom regretted the lack of the precise information they were able to obtain from James Cook's narrative of his second voyage, the publication of which has been described as 'one of the great events in the history of Pacific exploration'.[6] Cook, in fact, was one who mourned the absence of 'Nautical remarks' about the Pacific part of the voyage – Bougainville had provided much more about the earlier part – and commented that 'had he continued to make [them], his narrative would, not only have been the most entertaining, but the most usefull of any yet published'.[7]

Even so, some of Louis's readers found parts of the book too technical for their taste. He had tried to steer a middle course between a popularised version and one addressed to a specialised audience, and in so doing he displeased people at both extremes of the spectrum. The philosopher and *encyclopédiste* Denis Diderot provides a good example of middle-range criticism: 'I warn [readers] that one will not benefit greatly from it if one is not familiar with the language of sailors for whom, it seems, the author has intended it, judging from the little care he has taken to make it easily readable for others.'[8]

The work took Louis most of 1770, a year which was eventful in many respects. Politically, it was a difficult period, with growing unrest in the provinces and worsening relations between Spain and Britain, this time over the Falkland Islands, which threatened to drag France into a new conflict.

A Spanish frigate had discovered the British settlement of Port Egmont and an argument rapidly developed over the ownership of the islands, each side requiring the other to withdraw. The stand-off lasted through the early part of 1770 and soon involved ministers in Madrid, London and Versailles. Port Egmont was only a small outpost, but its symbolic value was considerable:

> Some English sailors had occupied one of the Malouines. Madrid insisted on their departure. Choiseul saw in this the pretext he was looking for to implicate France into a conflict that would rapidly bring in Europe. He let Spain know that the Most Christian King would defend her claims.[9]

But what Louis XV really wanted was peace. A European war would be too costly and he had enough problems at home with troublesome magistrates and rebellious local parliaments. On 24 December Choiseul was sacked. So, as it finally turned out, Bougainville's Malouines was the last straw that ended the career of the man who had been his main protector.

Another problem was the excitement surrounding a recent report by Philibert Commerson on the island of 'Nouvelle-Cythère'. This caused public attention to centre on life in Tahiti, to the possible detriment of a narrative of the entire voyage.

Commerson's letter, sent from the Isle de France and published in November 1769 in the *Mercure de France*, promptly caused a controversy among the *philosophes*, especially the followers of Rousseau. In the previous century, Louis de Lahontan's *Voyages* had given rise to the hope that a 'Noble Savage', a *Bon Huron*, might be found in America. This hope had vanished as exploration extended – and Bougainville for one, after his experiences in Canada, had few illusions left about the existence of such an untouched type. However, the belief continued that the unknown Pacific might turn out to be his home, and was, to some extent, revived by Rousseau's writings. Commerson's enthusiastic letter, arguing that Tahiti provided the evidence the Rousseauists had been hoping for, led to considerable discussion. In 1770 Bricaire de la Dixmérie wrote *Le Sauvage de Taïti aux Français, avec un Envoi au philosophe, ami des sauvages*, as well as a 'Lettre sur l'Isle de Taïti' published in the *Journal encyclopédique*, backing Commerson's views. Would Bougainville's narrative, once published, favour Commerson's ideas?

First, however, Bougainville had to wait for the royal censors to give their approval. This took several months. Finally, in May 1771, his *Voyage autour du monde par la frégate du roi* La Boudeuse *et la flute* L'Étoile made its appearance. It sold so well that a second, revised edition was soon called for. The print runs can only be guessed at. The first edition probably did not exceed, possibly did not even reach, 1000 copies; the second edition, in two volumes, published in 1772, probably exceeded 1250. In that same year, 1772, an English translation by J.R. Forster appeared in London.

The *Voyage* was undeniably a success, even though it cannot be called a runaway bestseller. It was favourably reviewed, but some scientific journals ignored it. The narrative did not really reflect Commerson's enthusiastic views. The argument switched to whether the Tahitians would have been better off had Bougainville never landed at Nouvelle-Cythère at all. If man in primitive society had retained his original goodness, bringing him into contact with modern civilisation could only do harm. To some extent, and with a different terminology and context, the argument has never entirely disappeared.

Some comments on the book also contained an undercurrent of political backbiting. Critics felt freer to find fault, now that the Duc de Choiseul had left the stage, and his known protégés, like Bougainville, could be more easily attacked. But Louis's reputation was now established and it continued to grow: the book would almost never be out of print, with regular new impressions, popular abridged versions, translations, continuing into our own century.

However, there was nothing more for him to do in Paris. Naval duties called. With little enthusiasm, he set off for Brest. It was a long and often uncomfortable journey. This may be why, more settled financially, he purchased a property at Anneville-sur-mer, just north of Coutances, not far from the boundary between Brittany and Normandy. La Becquetière was a substantial, but by no means pretentious, mansion, in pleasant surroundings and in keeping with his status, and it provided an opportunity for short breaks on the way to and from Brittany.

Brest in peacetime, and especially once the possibility of a major war with Britain had receded, was a dull town, compared with Paris and Versailles. Bougainville soon began to hanker for some challenge, eagerly listening for news from the Indian Ocean or the Pacific. He learned with sadness that Véron, the astronomer he so admired, had died from a fever contracted in Timor. James Cook returned to England in June 1771 after a major voyage of exploration in the *Endeavour*, which had included a call at Tahiti, but reports were still only trickling back to France. Jean de Surville had also led an expedition to the Pacific, in the hope of reaching Tahiti, but it had ended in death and failure and the ship had been impounded by the Spanish in Peru. The interest in Tahiti eventually led the Spanish authorities in South America to send out their own expedition, planning to establish their claim to an island that was arousing so much interest, and now had so many names: King George Island (Samuel Wallis), Nouvelle-Cythère (Bougainville), Otaheite (Cook) and Amat (the Spaniard Domingo Boenechea in 1772). The Spanish plans came to nothing. In time, Tahiti would become a French possession.

There were still rumours about a southern continent. Surville, rather late in the piece, had hoped to discover Davis Land. By now, only a handful of optimists believed it could be found anywhere, although some thought a southern continent might exist in the South Indian Ocean. In May 1771, Yves de Kerguelen sailed for Port-Louis to begin an exploration of South Indian Ocean waters, and Marion Dufresne included in his plans to take Ahu-toru home a sweep into the southern latitudes.

Brest had little to offer Bougainville. The expected antagonism from the 'red' officers towards this middle-class upstart began to make itself felt. They spoke openly about this intruder, *capitaine de vaisseau* though he might be, who had little interest in naval administration. More mutterings arose after Bougainville's election to the *Académie de Marine* on 2 December, just three weeks before his protector, Choiseul, was dismissed. Clashes were inevitable, and one officer, the Marquis de Montalais, who was heard to say, 'One can get a quick promotion in the Navy when one is under the protection of the King's tart', was challenged to a duel.[10] Louis's honour was duly restored when he wounded Montalais in the arm. Louis had not lost the skills he had acquired as a youth in the drawing room of De Chailly. Other challenges were issued over the years, including one to the popular nobleman Du Chilleau de La Roche, who made disparaging remarks about the advancement of men who were really 'officers of the blue'.

It is true, nevertheless, that much of his time in Brest was spent, not on naval duties, vague though they were, but on planning another voyage of exploration. What he now had in mind would be totally different from his previous undertaking, but it reflected the thoughts of a number of scientists: could there be another route to the Far East and the Pacific Ocean than by the Strait of Magellan or the Cape of Good Hope?

On his visits to Paris, he discussed new routes with men like the astronomer Jean-Dominique Cassini and members of the *Académie des Sciences*. One strong influence was Pierre Moreau de Maupertuis, a scientist with an army background who had once travelled to Lapland on a scientific mission. In his famous and controversial *Lettre sur le progrès des sciences* (1752), he had suggested that, once the exploration of the South Seas had led to the discovery of Terra Australis, it should be followed by similar searches in the northern hemisphere. There could be, as many people hoped, 'some passage that would shorten considerably the route to the Indies ... It has been sought in the North-East and the North-West without any success. However, these attempts, fruitless for those who have made them, would not be for those who may wish to continue the search.'[11]

After the tropics and paradises of the South Seas, was Louis now about to tackle the freezing world of the polar regions?

27. Plans and Setbacks

Late 1771–4

LOUIS WAS REVIVING ideas he had discussed with his old mathematics teacher, Clairault, and with his brother Jean-Pierre. It brought back thoughts of Pytheas, the Greek navigator from Marseilles who, in the fourth century BC, had sailed to Britain and beyond to 'Ultima Thule' – which some believed may have been Iceland. Jean-Pierre de Bougainville's *Éclaircissements sur la vie et les voyages de Pythéas* had been published in 1753 and had aroused considerable interest. Now that Louis had earned renown for his voyage to the South Seas, and others like James Cook, Marion Dufresne and Kerguelen were adding to European knowledge of that area, he could seek increased fame by exploring the far north.

Snow and ice would present new difficulties but, after his time in Canada, he was not unfamiliar with such obstacles. The undertaking would require time – this was one element he had always lacked during his circumnavigation – so he allowed two years for the expedition. During the first year, he would carry out a number of preliminary reconnaissances, establish base camps and be ready in the spring to travel further north and west in search of a passage nearer the pole that would lead him to the northern Pacific.

One difficulty was the changed political situation. Choiseul might have looked favourably on his proposals, but he was gone. The new Minister of Marine, Bourgeois de Boynes, was not ill-disposed towards Bougainville, but Louis knew better than to approach him directly. As a courtier accustomed to the convolutions of Versailles politics, he took care to build up support for his plans before presenting them formally to the officials. He had the support of the Prince de Conti, whose receptions were famous and who gathered around him scientists and *philosophes* as well as members of the aristocracy. A painting by Michel Olivier, 'Tea at the Prince de Conti's', shows a large representative assembly of his guests with, seated at the clavichord, a young boy, Wolfgang Amadeus Mozart.

In early January 1772, Bougainville met the influential Duc de Croÿ, an adroit courtier who had remained a friend of the Choiseuls without antagonising their enemies. Croÿ was interested in naval exploration, and had even considered organising an Arctic expedition in the hope of discovering the rumoured Strait of Anian, which was supposed to lead, by way of northern America, to the Pacific Ocean, the equivalent of what others called the North-West Passage. However, he also cherished another plan – the discovery of the exact antipodes of the capital cities of Europe and the erection, if they were on land, of large commemorative obelisks. This was what he had in mind when Louis approached him, but he nevertheless welcomed the explorer's plans and opened a number of doors for him.

By 14 February, Louis felt confident enough to approach De Boynes. The minister's reaction was cautious. He had some doubts about the value of an Arctic expedition and there was practically no money to spare, but he did agree to consider the proposal. As a first stage, he referred the matter to the *Académie des Sciences*.

A committee of three was set up, chaired by Etienne Mignot de Montigny, a specialist in geometry and mechanics who also happened to be Voltaire's nephew. The other members were Cassini and Bougainville himself. They wasted no time, preparing a report which Montigny presented to a meeting of the academy on 4 March. It summarised the research that had been carried out over the previous forty years, included indirect hints about the need for France to match the work of the Spanish, the English and the Dutch, and concluded that:

> Of all the undertakings of this nature that could best contribute to the advancement of the sciences, the most appropriate is a voyage into the ice-seas at the period of the year when they are unencumbered. Four months would be sufficient to go to the North Pole and return … The Academy will offer all the necessary instructions and, if desirable for some of its members to join in, it will supply astronomers and physicists ready to set off on any enterprise for the progress of the sciences, for the honour of our nation and for the glory of Your Majesty.[1]

Duly endorsed, the proposal was forwarded to De Boynes, who wrote back within a fortnight, accepting the scheme in principle but pointing out that more detailed plans would be required, and that they would take at least a year to draw up.

Bougainville had won the first hand, but the game was not over. De Boynes could now put the proposal aside for another year – which had been his intention from the start – and simply leave the academicians to their discussions. If they came back with a favourable report, he would again consider it.

Louis knew he had to strengthen his own position before then, and this would be difficult if he had to spend most of his time in Brest. His uncle, Jean-Potentien d'Arboulin, came to his assistance in quite a practical way: he resigned his position as *Secrétaire de la Chambre et du Cabinet du Roi* and nominated Louis as his successor. The position involved almost no duties, but it gave its holder a high status and easy access to Versailles. D'Arboulin did, however, keep the right to resume his functions if anything should happen to Louis. The king accepted this transfer on 18 April, though Bougainville did not have to carry out any related duties until much later.

Getting to work with his usual energy, Louis had a detailed proposal ready by late August. The plan was to sail from France in April 1773, with a ship that would be strengthened with additional planking and iron to resist the ice it would encounter. As a supply vessel, he suggested the *Étoile*, which, in spite of all her drawbacks, had ample room for the additional food supplies, and above all for the warm clothing that would be needed. The two crews would total 200 men, preferably all volunteers and, if possible, cod fishers with experience in the cold and foggy climate of Newfoundland and the northern Atlantic. Two astronomers and the latest scientific equipment would be essential to ensure a safe navigation and precise observations. Bougainville had talked with people like the famous watchmaker Louis Breguet, who had offered one of his new self-winding watches for the voyage.

De Boynes was rather disconcerted by the proposal: Louis's enthusiasm and experience had defeated him. He was already under pressure to finance a voyage of exploration to the southern ocean led by Yves de Kerguelen, but he did not decline Bougainville's proposal – he simply gained more time by referring it for clarification to a ministry official, Potier. Not realising that he was supposed to take his time, Potier discussed various details with Louis and submitted his report on 5 September.

De Boynes could no longer prevaricate. He had intended to turn down the proposal all along – the kingdom's finances had not improved – and he now made the decision. A mere two days after he received the report he told Bougainville that the undertaking was too costly and the government could not finance it. Devastated, Louis appealed, but De Boynes remained cool. Louis finally lost his temper. When De Boynes repeated that he could not grant him the 'favour' he was seeking, he snapped back, 'Do you think I'm asking for an abbey?'[2] But all he could do was go back to his naval duties in Brest. He felt no better when news came that Kerguelen had returned from the Indian Ocean, claiming to have discovered an attractive southern land, and that the government was preparing to send him back there to found a colony.

If 1772 was a year of dashed hopes, 1773 brought even more frustrations. Returning to Paris in January, Bougainville obtained confirmation that the British were now planning a voyage to the Arctic. He promptly brought out his earlier proposal, stressing how important it was to forestall the British. This had little effect on De Boynes, who considered it more important for France to send Kerguelen back to the southern seas to establish a settlement. The Duc de Croÿ had switched his support to Kerguelen. The expedition would cost an estimated 150,000 *livres* more than Bougainville's would have, but this did not affect the Minister of Marine's attitude. If Kerguelen's reports were correct, an establishment on his 'new world', as Poivre called it, would be far more important strategically and economically than anything Louis might discover in the icy north. And Kerguelen, understandably enough, had waxed lyrical about his 'Southern France':

> I have had the good fortune to discover the Antarctic Continent, and even to find out that it is well placed for the settlement of establishments suitable to command Asia and America … before six years have passed, I am sure that it will repay with interest the services that will have been rendered to it and that, far from needing the assistance of our islands, it will begin to give them in its turn a great deal of assistance, enrich their trade, and finally become their metropolis.[3]

No one could guess, after these glowing reports, that all Kerguelen had discovered was a bleak, windswept, uninhabited island.

Louis had prepared another proposal for the minister, as a sort of backstop should his original scheme fail: keeping an eye on British activities off northern Canada and in the Baltic. A simple survey ship would be enough, and it was important to know for certain what the British were up to. Bougainville could sail with it, having had considerable experience in Canadian waters and on land. De Boynes was too preoccupied with his plans for Kerguelen's colony to waste any time on a new idea. The request was turned down within a week, on 9 March. Three weeks later, Kerguelen sailed from Brest.

Like Croÿ and others, De Boynes recognised that Bougainville was bored. As he wrote to the Duc d'Aiguillon, the Minister of Foreign Affairs, 'His zeal suffers from the inaction he has found himself in since his return from his circumnavigation', but there was nothing either man could do for him. In April, Louis, stuck in Brest, learned to his dismay that a British expedition had indeed sailed towards the North Pole, under the command of Joseph Banks's friend Constantine John Phipps. This voyage, like Kerguelen's, would turn out to be fruitless, but that was a small consolation for Louis at the time.

To make things worse, problems once again arose over the Falkland Islands. Back in Paris for the August-October quarter, Bougainville found himself embroiled in arguments over some back pay that was due to various workers employed either by the king or by the former Saint-Malo Company. The affair irritatingly dragged on until April 1774, when De Boynes finally agreed that Louis could not be held responsible for any claims and that attempting to get Spain to pay a share was a waste of time. The debts were paid out of the French colonial budget.

If, as 1774 dawned, Bougainville felt that his life was stagnating, the same can be said of France as a whole. The king was sixty-four. He had been on the throne for fifty-nine years, and France's ruler since 1723 when he reached the age of thirteen and the regency of Philippe d'Orléans came to an end. Now he ruled over

an elderly country made up of old people ... Everything was immutable: religion, land, social status, position, trade. Obedience dominated life, from the cradle to the grave; obedience to the priest, who presided over every facet of daily life, then to the local lord or his agent, to the colonel who was the owner of the regiment, to the magistrate holding his function by right of inheritance, to the master of the work place and, within the family, to the father who, even though he might be a centenarian, oversaw the actions of his children. And obedience to the king, of course, since he was the summit as well as the very symbol of this human pyramid.[4]

Bougainville must have felt imprisoned in such a system. He depended on the goodwill of the Minister of Marine who was the king's servant. From his 'exile' in Brest, he asked whether he might be allowed to read the journals of the Marion Dufresne expedition, to prepare them for publication. The voyage had a link with his own, since it had been undertaken mainly in order to return Ahu-toru to Tahiti.

De Boynes agreed but, alas, there was little among the expedition's papers that was worth publishing. 'This journal,' Louis wrote in a covering note when he returned the documents, 'is not publishable as it stands.'[5] It was not even Marion Dufresne's own journal, which had never been found, but that of his second-in-command, Julien Crozet. The voyage had not been a failure, by any means. Some islands had been discovered in the South Indian Ocean, the maps of this distant region had been checked and corrected, and there had been some interesting encounters with the Aborigines of Tasmania, but after the tragic death of Marion Dufresne in New Zealand the expedition had effectively collapsed.

A couple of weeks later, Louis was asked to intervene in an argument concerning the Abbé Alexis Rochon, an astronomer who had sailed with Kerguelen, but soon fallen out with him. 'He is a scoundrel,' Kerguelen had told the geographer D'Après de Mannevillette, a feeling the abbé reciprocated. Rochon had been appointed the *Académie de Marine*'s librarian back in 1765, but the library was in Brest, and Rochon was practically always either in Paris or travelling abroad. The minister was asked to formally appoint the man who had effectively been running the library in the abbé's stead for the previous nine years, but Rochon protested and promised to visit Brest as soon as his personal circumstances allowed. The argument dragged on for another three months, with Rochon remaining firmly ensconced in Paris and continuing to draw his salary, amounting to 1200 *livres* a year. De Boynes, siding with Bougainville's logical summary of the situation, finally agreed that the money and the title should go to the person who was doing the work.

There were other matters of greater importance than the Abbé Rochon's spat with Kerguelen. Rumours were beginning to percolate back about the explorer's second voyage and his behaviour: he was said to have smuggled a young girl onboard who shared his cabin. In addition it seemed that his famous southern continent had vanished into a sea mist – and with it France's hope of establishing a colony there.

By the time such matters came to a head, though, Bougainville had gone to Versailles to take up his post as *secrétaire*, and a more immediate and more serious topic of discussion was the king's illness. Louis XV fell ill on 29 April. It soon became evident that he had contracted smallpox; he died on 10 May. Since the illness was highly contagious and frequently fatal, a quarantine was imposed on all those who had been in his presence. This was not easy to enforce, but it was a way of regrouping the various political cabals. The Comtesse du Barry was exiled to a country house, ostensibly for the good of her health, but also for the good of Louis XV's soul, since repentance for sins of the flesh was a requirement for the final rites. The young heir to the throne and his wife Marie-Antoinette were relegated to a distant wing of the château and then to Choisy, a few miles away. Ministers, like D'Aiguillon and De Boynes, who had been near the king, were conveniently kept away, again for health reasons. Bougainville, although a minor player, found his movements restricted for a period of ten days.

Louis XVI, on whom the responsibilities of absolute rule had been so suddenly thrust, called on the elderly Comte de Maurepas, now living in exile, and asked him to take over. 'I am only twenty,' he wrote. 'And moreover I cannot see any of the Ministers, since they were all closeted with the King during his illness.'[6] And so D'Aiguillon and De Boynes were sacked even before their period of quarantine had come to an end, and before long there was a new Minister of Marine, Gabriel de Sartines. Bougainville could feel satisfied with the change, for he had known Sartines in the days when the latter was lieutenant-general of police and in close touch with Paris lawyers.

There were other reasons for Louis to be quietly satisfied with the way things were developing. He obtained a copy of Phipps's account of his voyage to the north, from which it was clear that the Englishman had made no discovery of any significance. By August, it was also becoming evident that Kerguelen's voyage had been an almost total failure – it would lead to a court martial and to Kerguelen's imprisonment. De Boynes and the Duc de Croÿ, who had invested so much in the expedition, were finally discredited.

These various events resulted in Bougainville's full return to favour among ministry officials. They also led to his being asked in November to assess a proposal made by Louis Le Vassor de La Touche for a voyage around the world. It was a well-conceived project by an officer with a good naval and army record. He planned to enter the Pacific Ocean by way of Cape Horn, sail in higher latitudes towards New Zealand, put in at the Bay of Plenty on the east coast and go on to Australia, which he would explore, and then travel to Mauritius.

Bougainville chaired a committee of six specialists, which included Charles de Rosnevet, who had commanded the *Oiseau* on Kerguelen's recent voyage, Joseph Chabert, a naval captain and member of the *Académie de Marine*, Claret de Fleurieu, a gifted administrator and geographer who would one day be Minister of Marine, and Louis Joannis, who had started his career with the French India Company, transferred to the navy and sailed extensively in eastern waters. They concluded that other expeditions, including James Cook's second voyage, then in progress, had left little hope of further major discoveries in the Pacific, and that any detailed survey of the Australian continent would be more easily carried out from Mauritius. There was really no need to sail across the Pacific to get there.

La Touche's plan, like Louis's, was too costly and Sartines was forced to turn it down. In the letter of thanks he addressed to Bougainville in December, the minister wrote, 'I have decided to delay asking the King for instructions until circumstances allow us to consider new discoveries *which you would consider to be of some advantage.*'[7] These words are worth putting in italics. A government minister had stated that his favourable opinion would be a prerequisite for any project. Bougainville was indeed back in favour.

28. BACK TO SEA AND BACK TO WAR

1775–9

LOUIS HAD LITTLE more to do in Paris, and when the spring of 1775 arrived he had no option but to return to Brest. He was able to stay in touch with ministry officials, and keep abreast of political developments, both at Versailles and abroad, but he was nevertheless in some sort of backwater.

Brest may have been a major naval base, but it was still a provincial town, with its small drawing rooms where matrons and their daughters flicked their fashionable fans, in an atmosphere of gossip and backbiting. Admittedly, Bougainville was now in his mid-forties, no longer the dashing young man who had caused dowager ladies and their wards to swoon at his approach, but he was still an excellent catch for any family who had a daughter to marry off – and there were some charming girls among the local families, most of them associated with the navy. The mothers made sure that he was included in their invitation lists and beamed on him when he appeared. He realised that it was time for him to settle down, but he also knew, as did his various hosts, that his career path remained unclear. Service ashore, even with regular duties in Versailles, would not ensure his advancement.

It was with some relief, therefore, that he found himself posted to the *Terpsichore*, a relatively new warship named somewhat romantically after one of the Muses. He was only her second-in-command, but he accepted the limitations his social background imposed on him. The campaign, naval manoeuvres under the Comte de Guichen, he found most attractive. It included a call at La Coruña where the Spanish welcomed their allies with a great banquet punctuated with the firing of guns. They enjoyed the evening, drinking the health of everyone and anyone: '*commandantes, intendantes*, governors' wives and all the ladies on the globe'.[1]

Louis renewed his acquaintance with the young man about town, Charles, Duc de Chartres, one of those who had met Ahu-toru in Paris. Charles had hopes of obtaining the title of grand admiral from his wife's family, the Bourbon-Penthièvres. Such grades were usually the preserve of some great family and could be passed around with the king's consent. In a way, Bougainville had experienced this with the position of *Secrétaire du cabinet*. Charles was a young man with high ambitions.

Bougainville and Chartres travelled overland to Santiago de Compostela, a renowned place of pilgrimage, where they were made especially welcome as the French king had his own chapel there and paid each day a sum equivalent to the price of an ox for the sustenance of French pilgrims. Back in France, they visited other well-known religious sites: the Chartreuse d'Auray, the Abbey of Saint Gildas de Rhuys, where the famous medieval theologian Abélard had been abbot, and another place of pilgrimage, Saint Anne, run by Carmelite nuns.

For the 1776 manoeuvres, the Duc de Chartres, now a commodore, appointed Louis as second-in-command of the *Solitaire*, a ship of sixty-four guns. The campaign was more extensive this time, including Cadiz and West Africa. It was a pleasant, largely uneventful voyage, apart from the *Solitaire* ramming the *Terpsichore*, although causing only slight damage. 'A-Dieu vat,' exclaimed Chartres, an ambiguous exclamation which to a landlubber means 'Put your trust in God', but to most sailors was usually a less fatalistic 'About ship'.[2] Louis certainly expressed some reservations about some of the tactical moves of the squadrons and about the duke's ability as a sailor. On his return, Chartres decided that his duties would henceforth require him to be in Versailles more often.

The navy was by now becoming more efficient. Choiseul's reforms, although unpopular with some traditionalists, had been linked to a substantial shipbuilding programme. In spite of trouble at home, with a young king uncertainly taking up the reins of power, France was thinking of adopting a more positive international strategy – war with England was once again becoming a distinct possibility.

Unrest in the American colonies had been spreading rapidly. At first, it had seemed little more than a case of unruly vassals complaining about their masters, an attitude few members of the French ruling aristocracy considered acceptable. As a protest against taxes imposed by London, the citizens of Boston had hurled chests full of tea into the harbour. To the extent that this was discussed in the salons of Versailles, it was regarded as a joke rather than a real threat to British domination in North America. But the situation quickly deteriorated.

On 19 April 1775, a skirmish at Lexington between American colonists and British troops escalated into a full-scale battle fought at nearby Concord. The British were driven back. The unthinkable had happened: George III was facing all-out war with his colonists. On 4 July 1776, the colonial states declared their independence. The die had been cast, but Louis XVI and his Foreign Minister Charles Gravier de Vergennes remained cautious. Who, after all, were these troublesome American settlers, and what chance did they stand against the military and naval might of Great Britain? Getting openly involved in the struggle could be costly if the British won.

So France resorted to shadowy moves, providing financial help to the insurgents, through the intermediary of minor characters such as the American scientist Benjamin Franklin and the French playwright Pierre de Beaumarchais. Others were more open in their support of the insurgents, but still acting unofficially. The Marquis de Lafayette, not yet twenty, restless and ambitious, sailed for America in March 1777, having wangled the rank of major-general in the revolutionary forces.

To men like Bougainville, the possibility of the states breaking away from London was like a dream coming true. He had been cheered, if a little rueful, when he learned in 1774 that the British had recently vacated the Falklands. The local commander, Samuel Clayton, had left an inscription reminding all nations that 'the Falkland Islands, with this Fort, the Stonehouse, Wharfs and Harbours, Bays and Creeks thereunto belonging are the Sole Right and Property of His Most Sacred Majesty, George the Third'. But the buildings and the so-called wharves had soon fallen victim to the howling winds and the driving southerly rains. Within a year, the occasional fishing vessel putting in at the former Malouines could find only ruins. By 1776, Port Egmont had ceased to exist. And now, with the colonists in open rebellion, who could tell what might happen next? Would Canada also break away, and could Quebec once more become linked with France? It seemed as though all the bitter defeats Bougainville had lived through might soon be avenged.

Meanwhile, he still had his own career to think about. For as long as France remained neutral, the navy would have to restrict itself to harmless manoeuvrings and courtesy visits. In December 1776, he at last got his own command: captain of the *Bien-Aimé*, a sizeable warship. He went to Lorient to take charge and sail her to Brest.

Seventeen seventy-seven was a year of phoney war. The European powers were nominally at peace, satisfied to leave the actual fighting to the British and their troublesome subjects. They simply marked the various advances and retreats on their maps, and quietly discussed the likely outcome in the drawing rooms of Versailles, Madrid and Vienna, rather like onlookers at gaming tables who think it unwise to hazard a bet. The American army was driven back across the Delaware River; but then it defeated Lord Cornwallis at Trenton, forcing his troops to retreat to New York. General John Burgoyne advanced from Canada, captured Fort Ticonderoga, and reached the Hudson River; he was then routed at the Battle of Saratoga. Admiral Richard Howe, the commander of the British fleet, landed at Chesapeake Bay and marched down to Philadelphia, but decided to dig in for the winter at Valley Forge. As the seesawing continued, Louis XVI and his ministers were coming to the conclusion that the colonists had a real chance of winning. They took a gamble and intervened: on 17 December France recognised the independence of the United States. This was an affront to George III. The outcome could only be war.

Until hostilities actually broke out, the French Navy was limited to the standard summer manoeuvres. Back in port, there were important visitors to welcome. In May, the Comte d'Artois, the king's brother who would one day rule France as Charles X, came on a visit of inspection, accompanied by a flurry of noble courtiers: the princes of Henin and of Nassau, the Duc de Liancourt, the Vicomte de Noailles, and sundry other noblemen bearing famous titles, Bourbon-Busset, D'Escars, Crusol, Coigny.

Bougainville's *Bien-Aimé* was selected for a formal reception. There was a solemn mass on board, then forty guests gathered for lunch in the vast wardroom. The Breton sailors danced to the sound of the bagpipes, the local *binious*; there were speeches, compliments and solemn toasts. Even the charming D'Artois tried a few steps, cheered 'wildly by all present, everyone being moved to tears'. He wrote to Du Chaffault expressing his satisfaction at the condition and the 'grandeur' of Brest, and made sure that Bougainville was invited to attend other functions on land.[3]

A month later, another visitor arrived, the Comte de Falkenstein, who was none other than the German emperor, Joseph II, brother of Queen Marie-Antoinette, supposedly travelling incognito. After a tiring series of receptions at Versailles and around Paris, attending horse races at Longchamps – the main passion at the time of the Duc de Chartres, who made sure all important visitors joined him – and visiting the Gobelins tapestry factory at well as the Salpétrière prison, the emperor had toured the provinces. He had also tactfully resisted an attempt to betroth him to Louis XVI's sister. His tour included various ports, such as Toulon, La Rochelle and Brest.

He was not particularly impressed by what he saw, but he was courteous enough to keep his comments to himself and a few close friends. He wrote to Leopold of Tuscany, 'the French Navy does not inspire confidence in me',[4] but Bougainville, whom he had particularly asked to meet, could report to Sartines, the Minister of Marine, 'He told me that … what he saw was even better than he had expected to see.'[5] It was, admittedly, a compliment tinged with ambiguity.

In October, Louis left Brest to return to Versailles. By the time he had to go back to Brest in early 1778, a treaty of alliance had been signed between France and the newly independent American states. On 15 March, he received orders to proceed to Toulon, where he was to take command of a powerful ship of seventy-four guns, appropriately named *Le Guerrier*, the Warrior. This meant leaving Brittany for Provence, a prospect that did not appeal to him. He was a man of the north – the Paris region, Normandy, the Breton peninsula. The people of the Midi were quite unlike his Breton sailors; they had a different accent, unusual turns of phrase, almost a local idiom and their own customs. 'There is half a century of difference between Toulon and Brest,' he wrote.

We are far better equipped in the latter port. And we are less fit for fighting with the type of men we have. We are sailing with neither watch muster nor quarter-bill, with a crew three-quarters of whom know nothing about manoeuvres, guns or the sea. And nearly all are seasick ... I don't know a single officer or petty officer on my ship. I don't even know provençal and I often need to have an interpreter in order to carry out my various tasks.[6]

It had taken Louis a fortnight to settle his affairs in Brest and make his way across France, changing horses at every stop and putting up in uncomfortable country inns. After another couple of weeks, the *Guerrier* was under sail, part of a fleet of fifteen ships commanded by the Comte d'Estaing. They were not told that their destination was Boston until they were all clear of the Strait of Gibraltar – they were to assist the American insurgents in every way possible.

They had hoped to catch the British unawares, but when they reached the Delaware River they discovered that Admiral Howe had taken his ships off to New York. 'The bird has flown,' commented Louis. D'Estaing decided, on the advice of George Washington, to make for Newport. There, General John Sullivan was besieging a force of 6000 British troops. The French would come to his aid, landing 200 men from each ship. Then came news that British naval reinforcements were on their way and likely to trap D'Estaing's ships. Bougainville's *Guerrier* sailed out, sighted the enemy fleet and readied for action – until a thick sea fog came down. When it cleared, the French squadron, by then in some disorder, was ordered to make for Nantasket, near Boston.

The French were confused by all these manoeuvres and counter-manoeuvres, and their mood was not improved by what many of them considered to be confusing and at times contradictory signals from D'Estaing. The Americans were accusing them of having abandoned Sullivan in Nantasket. Arguments broke out ashore, which rapidly turned into street fights. When Lieutenant de Saint-Sauveur, from the *Tonnant*, tried to put an end to the brawls he had his skull smashed in for his pains. Calm was restored and the shocked city fathers offered to provide the equivalent of a state funeral and interment in the local church – but it was a Protestant temple, an improper resting place for a Catholic officer. Instead the state of Massachusetts erected a monument, praising the Frenchman's devotion and his service to the people of America. His death had only tightened the bonds that linked the people of Boston and the French. The inscription ended with a pious hope: 'May any comparable efforts to separate France from America have a similar outcome'.

Bougainville earned the colonists' gratitude by completing a line of defences and a substantial redoubt. If any British troops landed, the French would sweep down on them and cut them to pieces. The thankful locals invited him to various functions, including a dinner at the home of the governor, John Hancock, who sent him to visit his alma mater, nearby Harvard University.

There were other ceremonial occasions on American soil. Lafayette had found Montcalm's sword, bought it from its American owner and had it delivered to Bougainville. With tears in his eyes, Louis kissed the precious relic. There were more reminders of his time in Canada: an Iroquois came to greet him – he was the grandson of chief Onoraguete, from Sault Saint-Louis, near Montreal, who had offered him one of his daughters in marriage when he was adopted into the tribe. Whether he had accepted this gift is not clear: there was gossip that Bougainville had fathered a child in Canada and that the visitor was actually his son.

Six months had now gone by since the departure from Toulon. D'Estaing issued new sealed orders which, when his captains opened them in November, required the squadron to sail for Martinique. British ships were besieging nearby Saint Lucia, a French colony. They captured it on 14 December, a mere five days after D'Estaing reached Martinique. Urgent counter-action was called for, but at first D'Estaing merely showed the flag, hoping this would disconcert the enemy. 'It was no more than a noisy parade and a few fireworks,' complained Louis, and not enough to dislodge the invaders. A landing force was organised. This proved a costly venture: the French suffered over 700 casualties, the British 127. D'Estaing decided to return to Martinique, to ensure at least that this much more important island did not fall to the enemy.

Bougainville was scathing in his comments. 'What comfort our indecision, our endless delays and our wasted manoeuvres are giving to the enemy!'[7] There was worse to come: the local paper welcomed the return of the squadron and expressed sympathy for the losses and the damage it had sustained. This publicised their return and information about French movements was rapidly passed on to the British. After a period of somewhat gloomy recuperation came the cheering news that the Comte François de Grasse was on his way with ten warships. The *Gazette de la Martinique* published a report to that effect, which reassured the locals, but also again warned the British. De Grasse duly arrived on 20 February 1779. A few weeks later, his sailors sighted Admiral Byron's ships in the distance and everyone prepared for battle, but Byron was not looking for a fight and went on his way to Barbados.

Bougainville was chafing at all this inaction when there was a request for help from the island of Saint Vincent, which the British were taking over. The French answered the call and in early June the island was recaptured. The next target was Grenada. D'Estaing arrived on 2 July and a fierce battle ensued. The French took 700 prisoners, and captured 128 guns and 3 standards. They had little time for celebration, for Admiral Byron had finally arrived off the coast. Believing that he had superiority in numbers, he promptly attacked, only to find out that he was outnumbered and that most of the defences were now manned by French troops.

He was driven off with heavy losses, although D'Estaing lost 176 killed, with another 775 wounded. But the attacking ships had suffered heavy damage and Byron was forced to retreat to Antigua. Bougainville's *Guerrier* lost only nine killed and ten wounded.

Had it been a victory? The immediate answer would have to be yes, and the French of Santo Domingo and other islands celebrated it as such. But D'Estaing was a good general who often fell victim to uncertainty. He had hesitated before when circumstances favoured him; he now missed the opportunity to chase four British warships that had been largely dismasted and could have been captured or destroyed.

Overall, the land war was favouring the insurgents in the north, but Britain had decided to strengthen her hold on the south. If the worst came to the worst, the rebellious states could be split between an independent north and a pro-British loyalist south. This would prevent aid from reaching the insurgents through Louisiana and Florida, which were still largely under French-Spanish control and where most settlers were of French or Spanish origin.

Following this strategy, Britain decided to advance on Savannah, an important sea and river port and the capital of Georgia. By December 1778, it had fallen to a large British force. From there, they could advance towards South Carolina, which lay to the north. The colonists sent a desperate appeal to D'Estaing through Colonel de Brétigny, who couched the request in irresistible terms: 'Everything here is in a frightful state of confusion. Truly, Monsieur le Comte, the province has no other saviour to call upon than yourself.'[8]

D'Estaing organised a force of 2500 men and sailed with 22 warships and 10 frigates. On 9 October 1779, the French troops landed on the banks of the Savannah River, while the ship *Truite* started to shell the town. Three columns advanced through marshy land, which it was hoped the British would have left only lightly defended, since they would not have been expecting an attack from that direction. But Savannah itself had been well fortified. A line of guns was manned and waiting, and a hail of case-shot slashed through the French line.

D'Estaing was wounded in the leg and arm. Caught unawares, the French turned away, in some disorder. They lost close on 650 killed and wounded in the space of an hour. 'Oh God,' prayed Bougainville, 'please grant us a miracle!'[9] No miracle came. On 25 October, the French soldiers were left to fight by the side of the insurgents, while the French fleet sailed away, one squadron making for the Chesapeake, another for the West Indies, and the third, Bougainville's Provence Squadron, returning to France.

D'Estaing instructed Louis to make for Rochefort in company with the *Vaillant*. It was time indeed for rest and a thorough refit. The crew were suffering from scurvy and other illnesses; the sick, crowded below in the 'tween-deck, were existing in an atmosphere so foul the other sailors retched when they approached and preferred to seek a place of rest in odd corners on deck, whatever the weather. The *Guerrier* reached Rochefort on 9 December with a mere seventy men still able to stand; another forty-five had died.

Louis learned that he had been promoted to commodore, but that he was to rank below the Marquis de Vaudreuil. This was the eldest son of the Vaudreuil who had been governor of French Canada when Louis was serving there. He was, naturally, an 'officer of the red'. Bougainville resented this ranking and decided to refuse the promotion. On 10 January 1780, he wrote to the Minister of Marine:

> If I were called D'Estaing, Beauffremont, Rochechouard, then I would gladly grant precedence to the Marquis de Vaudreuil, whom I consider one of the best commanding officers the King could have in the Navy. But, born a plebeian, I owe it to the class of useful men, whom a strong sense of vocation drives into the service and whose services should lead to higher ranks, not to endorse by my acceptance the humiliations to which they are all too often exposed. Without expressing any dissatisfaction, or any petulance, I will even give up the rank of *capitaine de vaisseau*. I am adopting once again the grade and the rank that the war enabled me to obtain in the land forces.[10]

Nevertheless, the reaction is hard to explain. Louis-Philippe de Rigaud de Vaudreuil was five years older than Bougainville and had entered the navy at the age of sixteen. His courage during a naval engagement in 1759 had earned him the Cross of Saint Louis; he had served as administrator in one of the French West Indian islands for a total of three years; and his service during the recent campaign had been exemplary. But rumour had it that he was a protégé of Marie-Antoinette, and the lover of one of her favourite ladies-in-waiting.

Bougainville may have considered that there were others of equal or greater talent who lacked Vaudreuil's influence at court and should have been promoted. But it is more likely that Louis's outburst was the product of weariness and ill-health. He was suffering from scrotal pains, which seemed to suggest that he could be affected by a cancer. He was not strong enough when he returned to undergo an operation – anaesthetic was still unknown and, as he well knew, eighteenth-century surgery was relatively primitive and certainly unpleasant.

The minister, and Louis XVI, ignored the revolutionary sentiments that underlay Louis's letter. Without comment, he simply accepted Bougainville's resignation from the navy. And in March, he appointed him *maréchal de camp*, roughly brigadier-general. Bougainville was once more an army officer.

29. A Marriage and a Return to the Sea

September 1780–August 1782

THERE CAN BE little doubt that, when he returned to France, Bougainville was feeling despondent, if not downright depressed. He was worried about his health, and he felt that little had been achieved by D'Estaing's naval operations. The salon talk was all of men like Lafayette, who at the age of twenty-two was being received by the king, honoured by the American Congress and promised 6000 men for his next campaign, or Rochambeau, who was to lead the French forces. Whereas the much older Louis had been wasting his time manoeuvring off the American coast. It is not surprising that he believed that he had made a wrong decision when he adopted a naval career. Would he not have done better if he had remained in the army, or even concentrated on the post of *Secrétaire du Cabinet du Roi* and stayed ashore?

Louis was not operated on until October. The verdict that he was suffering from a benign hydrocelous tumour, a collection of serous fluid that could be simply lanced and cut back, was a relief. The operation was most uncomfortable, but successful. Just as he was about to go under the surgeon's knife, he heard that James Cook's ships were dropping anchor in the Nore after a voyage that had crowned the Englishman as the greatest Pacific explorer of his time. Most of 1780 was, for Bougainville, a period of recuperation and semi-retirement. He had not, though, lost official support. Sartines, the Minister of Marine, remained well disposed towards him – and the king had a greater regard for him than he probably suspected.

Louis XVI was ill-suited to be king in the difficult times that lay ahead. His interests were in more mundane matters: he was a keen huntsman, he liked tinkering with locks and clocks, he was interested in the sciences and in geography. Voyages of exploration were of lasting interest, and this led him to respect Bougainville's achievements and, later, his judgement. Although the king did not openly single him out, his ministers knew of his regard for the explorer and helped to smooth his return to the navy.

As 1780 wound to its close, Bougainville recovered his spirits. At fifty, he was still a bachelor. His sister had been urging him for some time to settle down. Gradually, he became attracted by a young woman living at the manor of Botdéru, in Brest. Flore-Josèphe de Longchamps de Montendre's father had been a naval officer, killed in action in 1760 when she was only a baby. Her mother had remarried, to the Chevalier de Silans, who served for a time as executive officer on the *Réfléchi*. This brought him in touch with the Bougainville family, as the ship's captain, Didier de Baraudin, was connected to Louis by marriage.

Although Flore-Josèphe was his junior by almost thirty years, she was an eminently suitable choice, strong-willed, self-possessed, dependable and resourceful. She would display all these qualities and more during the difficult revolution years. She was also well connected. The Montendres were an old family with wide associations: one of her uncles was Blanc du Bos; another was Nicolas du Botdéru, both of them highly ranked 'red' officers.

There was another reason why the Montendres were well known and respected. In 1741, the *Saint-Géran* was approaching the Isle de France when it was struck by a violent storm and sank close to the shore. On board were a young lady, Mademoiselle Caillou, and an *enseigne de vaisseau*, Louis de Montendre. He urged her to remove her voluminous skirt and bodice and some of her top undergarments that would, he assured her, drag her underwater when the ship went down. Maidenly modesty caused her to refuse. She remained the last person on board as the waves swept over the deck. He seized her unconscious body and began to struggle towards the shore when part of the floating wreckage struck and killed him. Both bodies were washed ashore and eventually buried side by side in the Pamplemousse churchyard. The episode was immortalised by the novelist Bernardin de Saint-Pierre in *Paul et Virginie*, one of the most celebrated books of the period: 'One can still see, near the Île d'Ambre, the Saint-Geran Pass with, at the end of a small valley, the Bay of the Tomb, where Virginie was found half-buried beneath the sand, as if the sea had wanted to give her body back to her family and pay its final respects to her modesty.'[1]

Bougainville had no difficulty in obtaining official permission to marry Flore-Josèphe, a requirement for all members of the naval corps under the Ancien Régime. This authorisation was received on 2 October, and the wedding took place on 27 November 1780 at Kerdreho, near the small town of Plouay, just north of Lorient.

He had only a few weeks in which to enjoy his new status of married man. In March 1781, he formally returned to the naval service, taking over command of the *Auguste*, a ship of eighty guns, part of a division due to sail for the West Indies under François de Grasse with several transport vessels. The plan was to sail for the West Indies, which both France and Spain regarded as their most important and convenient base for any American campaign. Then, De Grasse could decide which ships to dispatch north to land the foot soldiers and especially to secure the mouth of the Chesapeake.

The departure provided an impressive spectacle:

> At dawn on 22 March, Admiral De Grasse's fleet sailed from the Brest roadstead, seen off by the Marquis de Castries who had come, marking his taking over the ministry [of Marine] to see what Sartines had been able to put together before handing over power to him. De Grasse is in charge of 38 warships (five of which will leave him at the Azores, flying Suffren's standard, to try their luck in India), but above all of almost a hundred transports carrying troops and supplies for the islands. This great procession is led by the 'Blue Squadron' of Bougainville.[2]

The route to the West Indies was not going to be easy. Forewarned, the British sent Admiral (later Viscount) Samuel Hood with nineteen ships to bar the way. The two fleets met on 30 April and a first naval battle ensued. Hood, realising he was outnumbered and having suffered enough casualties to dissuade him from further fighting, made for the open sea. De Grasse made only a half-hearted attempt to chase him. His instructions were to escort the troop transports, not to try to sweep the British from the seas – and anyhow Hood's copper-bottomed ships were faster. 'The commander did not attempt to chase deer with tortoises,' commented Bougainville.[3]

In Martinique, De Grasse discussed plans with the governor, the Marquis de Bouillé. They agreed that an attempt should be made to capture British-held Saint Lucia. The ships, Bougainville's *Auguste* included, made a quick foray, but the island's defences were too strong. The island of Tobago was more promising. The French arrived there on 29 May, Bougainville commanding the windward column. Tobago was captured with no great difficulty. However, Admiral George Rodney was in the vicinity with a reported twenty-three ships of the line and a number of frigates. De Grasse sailed out to confront him, but the two fleets missed each other in the labyrinth of islands, and on 18 June the French were back in Martinique.

Little of all this was likely to affect the outcome of the war. The real struggle was on the continent where Lafayette and Rochambeau were planning with George Washington to launch an attack on the British forces led by Cornwallis. The latter had defeated General Horatio Gates at Camden in August 1780 and Nathaniel Greene at Guilford Court in March 1781. These successes followed the capture of Charleston by General Sir Henry Clinton in May 1780. This was worrying for the colonists and their French allies. Washington felt that a concerted attack on Cornwallis, who was now in Virginia, was the only way to reverse the situation. He sent off the frigate *Concorde* with an urgent request for ships and men to be dispatched to the Chesapeake. He also asked for money.

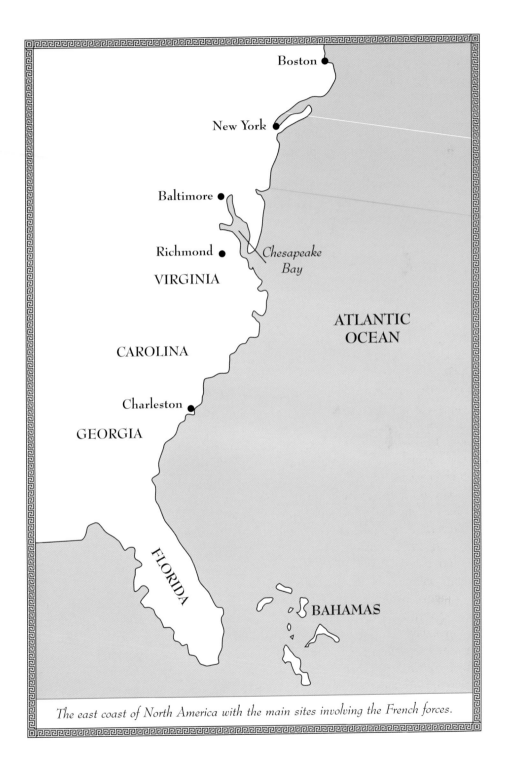

The east coast of North America with the main sites involving the French forces.

De Grasse acted promptly, mortgaging his extensive properties in the Antilles and pressuring the Governor of Cuba for funds and other assistance. He was thus able to raise a total of 1,200,000 *livres*. He then set sail, manoeuvring through the Bahama Channel to avoid British warships, and reached Cape Henry at the head of the Chesapeake at the end of August. The British vessels watching over the Chesapeake fled up the bay, instead of making for the open sea, thus becoming bottled up by De Grasse's ships. Lafayette's troops, meanwhile, were arriving overland to join up with the newcomers. Everything was now going according to plan.

On 5 September, however, Rear-Admiral Thomas Graves's fleet, consisting of twenty-two warships and ten frigates, was sighted, coming to Cornwallis's rescue. De Grasse gave the order to clear the decks for immediate action.

Bougainville's division led the vanguard, leading eight ships, each of seventy-four or eighty guns.

Three o'clock: the English centre and rearguard open fire. Thunder, foam and fire. Those few testing moments for which an entire naval officer's life has been built and for which so many arms have toiled, so much sweat has been poured out in the shipyards to get together all that timber, that iron, those sails. The first English salvo kills Mr de Bourdet, the captain of the *Réfléchi*; eight English vessels manage to concentrate their fire on the *Pluto*, the *Bougogne*, the *Marseillais*, the *Diadème* – which catches fire … when the two lines of battleships sail past each other, spitting out fire, the battle warms up.

But then the *Shrewsbury* lost two masts – and the captain lost his leg. Two yards were snapped off the *Intrepid* and her lower masts were damaged. The *Montagu*, her masts loosened, had to take in her sails. The *Ajax* sprang a leak and was listing. The *Terrible* was badly damaged, 'by the blows that Bougainville [was] concentrating on her. For someone who does not like war, he hides his feelings well.'[4] The battle lasted less than three hours. Graves led the remnants of his fleet towards New York. De Grasse was exultant. When he met Washington and Rochambeau, he stressed that Bougainville's skill and courage had played a major part in the victory. 'That's what I call fighting,' he told Louis.

There were casualties on both sides. The British lost 90 dead and 246 wounded, and the *Terrible*, an imposing ship of 82 guns, was completely destroyed. There were 200 casualties on the French side, 67 of them on the *Auguste*. There were lighter episodes, often repeated in taverns by veterans of the battle: the *Auguste*'s pet parrot, a voluble bird, vanished, terrified by all the turmoil of this battle and of a later engagement against Admiral Hood; he was eventually found cowering under some ropes and canvas, but so traumatised by the constant gunfire that all he ever said from that time on was 'Boom, boom'.

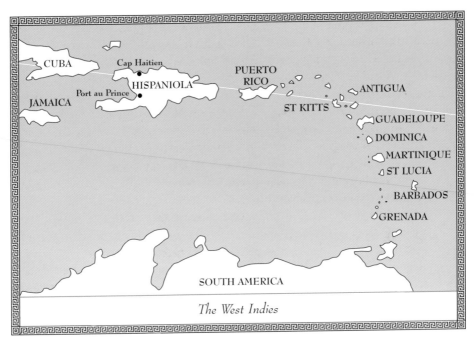

The West Indies

De Grasse's task had been to prevent the British from entering the Chesapeake and relieving Cornwallis, who now found himself totally blockaded in Yorktown. Day by day, the French and American troops, numbering 16,000, increased their pressure. On 19 October, Cornwallis was forced to surrender. Although the war would drag on for some months, Yorktown marked the end of serious hostilities. From then on, the politicians took over, to haggle over the terms of the inevitable peace treaty.

De Grasse could now return to the West Indies, where his own interests lay and where Britain and France still faced each other. Although most commentators regarded the independence of the American colonists as assured, there were still spoils for the main powers to fight over. Holding or capturing islands in the West Indies would place France in an advantageous position at the bargaining table.

Bad weather prevented a landing on Barbados. St Kitts, further north and close to a small island recently taken by the Governor of Martinique, François de Bouillé, looked more promising. On 11 January 1782, De Grasse landed 6000 troops at the main town, Basseterre, causing the small British garrison to retreat to fortified defensive positions.

At this point, Admiral Hood appeared with a fleet of twenty-two ships. De Grasse ordered his vessels to form a line and attack, then changed his mind and told his captains to attack independently. Meanwhile Hood slipped in behind the French, close to Basseterre. Bougainville lamented the confusion and the failed opportunity. 'A shameful day for us,' he wrote. 'It could have been a wonderful one if we had sailed forward, close-hauled and then tacking to cut off the enemy rearguard.'[5] De Grasse tried twice to dislodge Hood, but the outcome was a stalemate, and a costly one at that, with over 300 casualties on each side. De Grasse became irritated by these failures, and complained angrily to his captains. Bougainville exploded: 'By heavens! How much more justified the captains would be if they told him they were dissatisfied with him.'

On land, however, the British were too outnumbered to hold on much longer, and St Kitts surrendered on 13 February. Hood could now be attacked from another angle, but once again he outmanoeuvred De Grasse. He sneaked away with his ships during the night, affixing lanterns to buoys to fool the French. In the morning, De Grasse was astonished to find the anchorage empty.

There was a small consolation on 22 February when the little island of Montserrat surrendered to the French. Hood, it was discovered, had made for Antigua. De Grasse decided to go to Martinique, where the French could celebrate their recent gains. Their victory celebrations could be combined with official rejoicings over the birth of Louis XVI's son. There was a *Te Deum*, a great ball at the governor's and fireworks and bunting for the populace. Bougainville and his fellow officers made merry while they could, but they knew that Hood was merely waiting for Admiral Rodney to join him with reinforcements. Then, together, they could attack the French fleet.

Meanwhile, the French planned to capture the wealthy island of Jamaica. The Spanish would assist in what would be a major enterprise, supplying 15 vessels and enough men to make up a total force exceeding 20,000. The first stage was to take them to Haïti, but Hood and Rodney were waiting for them near Saint Lucia. On 9 April, the two fleets came upon each other in the vicinity of a small group of the Windward Islands known as the Saints.

The first exchanges were inconclusive; Bougainville's *Auguste* was one of the first to fire. The two fleets pulled apart during the afternoon, and at this point De Grasse showed indecision. Navigating the channel of the Saints was not easy but he could have attacked while Hood's ships were struggling with unfavourable winds and at times getting becalmed.

Had he done this, he could have eliminated a quarter of the British fleet, effectively crippling it and regaining overwhelming superiority. The latter course of action was probably too daring for the cautious de Grasse, shackled as he was by the doctrine of mission before all … Had de Grasse fallen on the British van with all his forces, Hood would have suffered huge losses. The remaining British would probably have kept their distance, since Rodney was not a man to take undue risks in the tricky winds.[6]

These delays allowed Hood and Rodney to join forces and get organised for a major battle. This came about on the 12th. De Grasse was now outnumbered, 30 ships to 37 – or 2246 guns against the English's 3016. To make things worse, the winds favoured the attackers. The first shots were exchanged at 7.45 in the morning. De Grasse ordered his fleet to veer about and wear together, a general manoeuvre the situation did not allow. He therefore countermanded this order, but when communication during the smoke of battle depended on flying standards and other visual methods, confusion was all too likely. The casualties mounted rapidly.

Bougainville had been able to make out De Grasse's instructions, but he was unable to take action. The *Auguste* was badly damaged: 'my masts, my shrouds and my rigging, all my braces, bowlines, brails, lifts, stays, halyards were cut. Thirteen cannon shots had put holes in the mainmast, the mizzentop mast and its yards were cut to pieces.'[7] Eighty of his men had been killed or wounded. He was also becalmed so he could neither manoeuvre nor defend himself. Fortunately, Hood turned away to concentrate his own ninety guns on De Grasse's *Ville-de-Paris*. As the sun began to set, De Grasse surrendered.

Vaudreuil led the remnants of the French fleet to Santo Domingo. The Jamaican plan had vanished, and the war was winding down to its close. In poor health and disheartened, Bougainville made his way back to France. He had a wife now and could look forward to rest and home life: his naval career had effectively come to an end.

30. A Court Martial and a Slow Return to Favour

September 1782–late 1788

A DEFEAT USUALLY means recriminations. The Battle of the Saints was no exception. De Grasse was first off the mark. Even while still a prisoner on Rodney's *Formidable*, he fired off a report in which he scattered blame on several of his captains and on Bougainville in particular. He had been left to fend for himself, he claimed, whereas it was the duty of every captain to come to the aid of a flagship under threat. Vaudreuil at first lent some support to the accusation, causing Bougainville to fire off an indignant reply.

> I have never overlooked orders to sail or to anchor; never failed to take up my position or to hold it; I have never run aground and never been boarded; finally I will make bold to assert that no ship of the same rank has been less costly to the King in respect of damage suffered than those I have commanded. And I have fought three times under the order of the Count de Grasse![1]

Louis had never liked De Grasse, who has been described as 'a grumpy hulking giant of a man'. Turning sixty, he lacked the decisive approach of a true commander, often issuing orders that he soon countermanded. Louis, for his part, tended to be impatient and critical.

Both men had their highly placed supporters. When De Grasse was taken to England, he was warmly received – but then he did praise the superiority of the British Navy and the quality of its guns, as well as the ability of men like Hood and Rodney. When he was granted an audience by George III, however, he found that the king praised Bougainville. Cook, he said, was a great sailor, but Bougainville was an inspired one. This caused De Grasse to moderate his criticisms for a while, especially when he discovered that others, including British naval men and scientists, shared their king's opinion.

Nevertheless, De Grasse spent his time writing a more comprehensive report on the Saints, exculpating himself and blaming his captains. This he sent to Louis XVI and his Minister of Marine, Charles de Castries, as well as to George Washington and General Rochambeau. The French king was disturbed by the continuing argument. He was inclined to favour Bougainville, almost siding with him. His first thought was to let the matter be settled in-house, then to die a natural death, but De Grasse's broadcasting of his attack now made this difficult.

The dispute dragged on into 1783. Vaudreuil returned to France in June that year, and De Grasse was freed a little later. At this point, Bougainville, as did most of the other officers directly or indirectly criticised by De Grasse, formally asked the Maréchal de Castries for permission to defend himself publicly – writing, on 4 November 1783, 'God knows that I have no wish to indict the general.'[2] It was a pious thought. A court martial would cause accusations to fly in every direction. It was regrettable, but the king had to placate public opinion.

The court martial met in Lorient in May 1784. Each commanding officer was questioned in turn. Vaudreuil, who had had time to think the situation over and to talk to Bougainville, had already withdrawn his criticism. The proceedings went on for days, but in the end Vaudreuil and most of the captains were exonerated from any blame. It was Bougainville's squadron, the 'blue', that fared the worst. Poulpiquet, who had been in charge of the seventy-four-gun *Hercule*, and Renaud d'Aleins, the captain of the *Neptune*, were formally admonished. Gouzillon, of the smaller *Ardent*, was suspended from any command for three months, for having lowered his colours too early. Cavel, the captain of the *Scipion*, had fought well, but he had failed to hand over command when he was wounded and clearly no longer able to carry on, leaving his officers in total confusion.

When Bougainville's turn came, he could defend himself only by outlining his actions in the early part of the battle – which no one contested – and pointing out the general confusion, the damage suffered by his and his supporting vessels, and an overall shortage of ammunition. He was eloquent and indignant, but had insufficient support. The judgement was not as severe as some of the twelve members of the court martial wanted. The chairman proposed a ten-year exclusion from further service, a commodore and a captain suggested a three-year suspension, two others three weeks, but only one favoured an acquittal. The final decision was the best Louis could hope for:

> The court declares that the actions of Louis-Antoine de Bougainville, commanding the third squadron of the King's forces, or Blue Squadron, in the vessel *Auguste*, were irreproachable until midday of the said day, 12 April 1782. But as this commander failed, during the afternoon, to issue clear signals and manoeuvre his squadron to join together and make as promptly as was possible to the heart of the battle, it condemns him to be formally admonished in the presence of the assembled tribunal.[3]

Louis appealed to the king, but without success: Louis XVI even banned him from returning to Versailles.

De Grasse fared far worse. Not only had he shown a serious lack of judgement at the Battle of the Saints but, as Castries wrote back, 'all your accusations of disobedience to your signals and of failure to assist the admiral ships, have been disproved by the verdict of the court-martial. The result is that you have compromised, by your ill-founded accusations, the reputation of several officers, in the hope of justifying in the eyes of the public your role in an unfortunate affair.' De Grasse was not merely banned from court: he was exiled to his country property, where he died four years later.

This was little consolation for Bougainville, who now decided to spend time with his family. He had a son, Hyacinthe-Yves-Philippe Potentien, born in Brest on 27 December 1781. The name 'Potentien' was a tribute to his uncle Jean-Potentien d'Arboulin, who had always helped him and who had made him a beneficiary in his will, enabling him to buy, in 1785, a small château at La Brosse in the Brie district south-east of Paris. Hyacinthe would one day lead his own expedition to the Pacific, although not on the scale of his father's, since by then there were few discoveries left to make in the great ocean. A second son, Armand, was born on 2 October 1785, like his elder brother at Kerdreho, near Brest. A third son, Alphonse, would be born in 1788, and yet another, Adolphe, in 1796.

The move to La Brosse enabled Louis to stay in touch with relatives and scientists in Paris. He kept his distance from the government, but wanted to be available at short notice if the atmosphere at Versailles changed. In fact, the disaster of the Saints did not have a lasting effect on his reputation, which was strengthened in the eyes of the public when he was appointed a member of the Order of the Cincinnati in 1784.

This association had been formed the previous year by officers of the American Continental Army, and was presided over by George Washington. Provision was made for French officers who had helped during the War of Independence to become members by invitation. Lafayette and Bougainville were among its first foreign members. Ironically, American republicans at first opposed the organisation, fearing that it would create a privileged class, equivalent to an aristocracy on the British model, or turn into something like the English honours system.

In France, the Battle of the Saints coincided with a revival in patriotic ardour. The enemy was still Great Britain – which may have won a victory over the French fleet, but had been humiliated by the loss of its American colonies. Ensuring that France's navy was rapidly rebuilt would further humble the British. An appeal for funds was received with enthusiasm. The people knew there were vast bills to pay, but national honour was at stake. Millions of *livres* were subscribed by organisations in Marseilles, Burgundy and Brittany, and even by the tax collectors. The total was not enough to pay for the cost of the wars, or for the maintenance of the expensive court at Versailles, but it helped.

Appealing for funds from the public at times of euphoria was, however, no substitute for a proper tax system. Over the centuries, new forms of taxation had been tried out, amended and added to, all undermined by a host of exemptions. Public offices were sold to raise funds, many of them mere sinecures, often carrying a title or some form of ennoblement and consequently easier to sell at a higher price. Indirect taxes included the hated salt tax as well as local duties on the transport of goods, which restricted trade within the kingdom itself. And direct taxes, such as the *taille*, a form of poll tax, were the least popular of all. There was no efficient central administration to collect all these, and it was normal to farm out tax collecting to private individuals who made fortunes from the margin between what they forced out of the unwilling taxpayers and the amount they contracted to pay the government.

The response to the Battle of the Saints appeal delighted Bougainville. The people were eager to help rebuild the navy, so at least the losers were not being reviled by public opinion, in spite of all the manoeuvres of the various cliques in the navy and the internal bickering. But he watched the deteriorating political situation with dismay. No fewer than eight ministers had held the post of *Contrôleur-Général des Finances* between 1774 and 1783. Things had only been marginally better in the navy, with four secretaries since the fall of the Choiseul family, who had been in control for ten years, as well as holding the foreign affairs portfolio for a total of twelve years.

After the death of Louis XV, the pressure for reforms mounted, and the young king was unsure how to deal with it. The *Parlements*, less debating chambers than groupings of senior magistrates and wealthy upper middle-class locals, had been challenging royal authority since the middle of the century, more often than not protesting against increased taxation. They had the right to present the king with a formal protest, known as a *remonstrance*, sometimes going so far as to decline to register a royal edict. In 1753, the Paris *Parlement* issued its famous *Grandes Remonstrances*, using such terms as 'the basic principles of the constitution of the State' and 'unlawful procedure'. Further protests were presented by Paris in 1755, 1756 and 1763. Although they were always carefully couched in terms of loyalty and respect for the crown, they were sets of complaints and eventually led to a violent reaction, known as the Flagellation Speech of 1766, in which Louis XV threatened dire consequences for those who created 'the scandalous spectacle of an opposition challenging my sovereign power'.[4]

Louis XVI inherited all this growing dissatisfaction. He may have lacked the decisiveness of his predecessors, but he was no fool. He struggled to maintain the status quo as best he could, but the kingdom itself was changing. The Enlightenment helped to question the very relationship between the citizens and their rulers. The aristocracy, the church, the rich, all defended their privileges, but the *philosophes* were challenging the structure of society itself. The members of the establishment might have been able to hold on for a little longer, but new patterns of trade and what was to become the Industrial Revolution were further helping to undermine their position. Although he was no revolutionary, Bougainville showed his impatience at the old ways. He had obtained advancement through family connections and the help of the Marquise de Pompadour, but had soon found the old aristocracy blocking his way, time and again. And many of his friends – indeed, his own late brother, even though a conservative – could be regarded as *philosophes*, new thinkers moving away from tradition and *idées reçues*.

The eighteenth century had seen too many changes for immobilism, as it would be called, to be acceptable. Steam power was starting to revolutionise the cotton industry; the power loom was about to transform the fabrication of linen and other material, and, although few people realised it at the time, it would destroy cottage industries. In 1787, Antoine Lavoisier would publish his *Méthode de nomenclature chimique* and was already sweeping away most of the old notions on which chemistry, alchemy and medicine were based. Man even began to fly: the Montgolfier brothers had invented the hot air balloon, sending up animals in September 1783, and opening the way for the first manned ascension of 21 Novembre by Pilâtre de Rozier. He was killed in a crash while attempting to cross the Channel in June 1785, but his achievements were none the less dramatic. The world was changing, and at a rate that created both wild enthusiasm and secret fear. Society could not remain static. The old ways were collapsing.

The challenge to absolutism and the inherited privileges were symbolised by Beaumarchais in his dazzling play, *The Marriage of Figaro*, in which Figaro the barber turns on Count Almaviva and issues his famous challenge:

Because you are a *grand seigneur* you believe yourself to be a genius ... Nobility, wealth, rank, offices! All that makes you great and mighty. And what have you done to deserve so much? Just the trouble of getting born and no more: and for the rest you're just an ordinary man.

Not surprisingly, once the audiences had stopped laughing and started to reflect on the implications of these lines, a reaction set in. The play had first opened in Paris in April 1784. Within a few months, the Archbishop of Paris took the offensive, denouncing it from the pulpit; Louis XVI agreed that the play should be banned and that Beaumarchais should be marched off to prison.

The problems caused by the class structure and old traditions can be further illustrated by the case of Alexandre de Calonne, the *Contrôleur-Général des Finances*. Appointed in 1783, he held the position until 1787. This gave him the opportunity of trying to reform France's chaotic financial structure. He had first used loans, then appealed for another *don gratuit*, the kind of voluntary self-tax that had succeeded after the Battle of the Saints, but that could not really be used in ordinary times. When he realised that these and other expedients did not work, he put forward a plan of reforms that required calling together an Assembly of Notables to give their approval.

This was a bold move and, in the new mood, he might have received popular support for daring to challenge the privileges and tax exemptions of the great and the wealthy. He failed for two reasons. One was that by then the people were losing their belief in mere tampering with problems; the other was Calonne's own reputation for personal extravagance:

> He dressed his many servants in full livery and provided fur-lined seats not just for the interior of his coaches but to keep his coachmen warm in winter ... he could choose to reside in one of two châteaux or in the house on the rue Saint-Dominique, where his spectacular collection of paintings – Watteau, Rembrandt, Titian, Giorgione, Boucher, Fragonard and Teniers – was housed ... His kitchen was equally famous, or notorious ...
>
> When he went from his own unofficial palace to the official one at Versailles, Calonne was sure to reproduce its splendours on a suitably regal scale. Under his regime, the last balls of Versailles were thrown with an elegant abandon ... that would create the vision of the old monarchy forever moving at the pace of a minuet, while marble fountains threw perfumed water into scalloped bowls.[5]

The conservative Assembly of Notables dismissed Calonne, but this did little to improve matters. The early popularity of Louis XVI had long since plummeted, partly because of the changing public views, which he could not understand or accept, and partly because of the extravagances of Marie-Antoinette and of her favourites – who included Bougainville's old *bête noire* Vaudreuil.

Louis took little part in the growing political debates, but, although he kept his distance for a couple of years after the Saints affair, he daily edged closer to the new naval administration. He became a close friend and collaborator of Charles-Pierre Claret de Fleurieu, one of the navy's great administrators. He had been appointed Director of Ports and Arsenals back in 1776, and was gradually working his way up the ladder, until in 1790 he became Minister of Marine. A scientist and mathematician of note, he was especially interested in the calculations of longitudes and in naval exploration.

In 1784, Fleurieu met the merchant captain William Bolts, who suggested a voyage to the north-west coast of America, which would combine trade and exploration. Although Fleurieu drew up fairly elaborate plans for such an expedition, Louis XVI turned it down flat. It would have been infra dig for the king's ships to be involved in a commercial enterprise. Louis XVI was in favour of a voyage, but it would have to be a major undertaking, something that could stand comparison with the voyages of James Cook, and not a mere side issue in a trading venture.

A much more important undertaking was already being planned – an exploration of the Pacific by Jean-François Galaup de la Pérouse, which would include the northern coastlines, completing the work done by Cook. The king's role in giving an early green light to this expedition was crucial, because it smoothed away practically all the objections that politicians and administrators might raise. Fleurieu concentrated on this expedition, working with Castries, the Minister of Marine, and a number of scientists. In this context, Bougainville's experience in the Pacific could not be overlooked, and he was called upon, although as yet unofficially, to discuss the areas that still needed to be surveyed, the problems that might arise and the best way to make the most of what the king hoped would be a truly major voyage of exploration.

La Pérouse sailed from Brest on 1 August 1785. His voyage would last almost three years, and figure among the great seagoing expeditions of the eighteenth century. Tragically, right at the end, disaster struck his two ships, which were lost with all aboard during a cyclone in the Santa Cruz group.

The years 1786 and 1787 were relatively quiet ones for Bougainville. Back in 1784, he had been promoted to the grade of Ordinary Member of the *Académie de Marine*. Soon he would apply, successfully, for membership of the prestigious *Académie des Sciences*. Links with his new relatives also helped. In 1787, his young relative Victor de Botdéru had been welcomed at Versailles. He was introduced there and in Paris to a number of Bougainville's friends, and became engaged to a young lady of noble birth, Sophie du Camboust de Coislin. Receptions increasingly included the famed navigator, whose *Voyage autour du monde* was still selling.

When the Duc de Castries gave up the marine portfolio in August 1787, to be replaced by César Henri La Luzerne, a man fairly inexperienced in naval problems, Fleurieu effectively became deputy minister. And once again he called on Bougainville for advice. This time, it was less about navigation than foreign affairs. Complex problems were arising in the East, involving Holland and Britain. The government had to be careful in the way it dealt with the tricky situation. France's position in the East, always tangential, could be strengthened or disastrously weakened, depending on the policies she adopted.

Louis replied with a detailed memorandum in early 1788. He pointed out that, as France had recently fallen out with the Netherlands, supporting the republican estates against William IV, the Dutch ministers were likely to ally themselves with Britain and support their newly formed administration in India, now run by Lord Cornwallis. A mooted visit to France by the ruler of Mysore, the anti-British Tipu Sahib, was not to be encouraged, as France was in no position to provide him with any help, and supporting him could easily lead to a generalised conflict, involving the European powers.

On the other hand, helping the king of Cochinchina would be less fraught with danger. France could benefit from establishing closer links with Indochina, and perhaps set up some kind of base there. Even so, any help to Cochinchina would have to be surreptitious, using the French Indian port of Pondicherry and Port-Louis in the Isle de France, and providing military and other kinds of assistance under the guise of trade.

Two other sections dealt with recent developments in Europe, such as the ongoing war between Russia and Turkey, and relations between Bavaria and Austria.

By the middle of 1788, therefore, Bougainville had regained his status in government circles. His application to join the *Académie des Sciences* had received Louis XVI's full endorsement. He was again made welcome at Versailles. Unhappily, by then, the great revolution was about to topple the throne and utterly transform French society.

31. Paris, Normandy, Paris

1789–96

THE ASSEMBLY OF Notables, which gathered in early 1787, achieved little of value and, if anything, worsened the situation. Louis XVI had expected that, as men of status linked to the establishment, the Notables would agree with the proposals that he and his ministers intended to place before them. He had little to go by. As a group, they had not been called together for a great many years, and he did not realise that their views differed from those of their predecessors. As they filed in, all 144 of them, in due ceremonial order, the princes of the blood in front, the leading archbishops next, then dukes, marquises, counts and senior leaders of local assemblies, he expected that they would follow tradition and bow to his royal wishes.

They began to discuss plans for reform that were pretty drastic. They included a single land tax; the abolition of the *corvée*, by which peasants were required to stop work on their land and carry out public works; and a unified internal duty to replace the host of local taxes. There were arguments and objections, but mostly on points of detail. What soon emerged, however, was a general demand for the dismissal of Calonne. This was quickly granted, but even this no longer satisfied the *Assemblée*. The arguing went on, with no sign of consensus. After almost six months of futile argument, Louis XVI dismissed them.

The only step that now seemed practicable was the calling together of the full Estates General, including not merely members of the nobility, but also representatives of the clergy and of the bourgeoisie – the third estate. The Estates General had not met since 1614; Louis XIV and Louis XV had reigned as absolute rulers with no need for any parliamentary or quasi-parliamentary body to advise them or disagree with their decisions. Calonne's proposals had included provision for local assemblies to assess the collection and impact of taxes. This brought about a call for a full consultation of all citizens before any changes were made to the financial system and everything it implied. Louis XVI accepted this request as a last resort. By bringing the three estates together, he would be able to appeal to the nation to support their king and his kingdom.

The Estates General would bring together representatives who were mostly elected – or selected – rather than handpicked as many of the Notables had been. But with three different estates arguments arose over the proportion of votes each should have. Numerically, the third estate was larger than the other two put together. An assembly in the Dauphiné province requested the third estate should have a number of voters at least equal to that of the other two. But at Bourges, a general assembly asked for fuller proportional representation, pointing out that 'The Third Estate, comprising forty-nine fiftieths of the nation, and carrying, unjustly, nearly all its expenses, should now and always be represented in the Estates General by a number of deputies greater than those of the clergy and the nobility combined ... [and] the nomination of electors or deputies should be effected by free votes and secret ballot'.[1]

Louis XVI did not, indeed could not, go against the mood of the people. Even so, when the Estates General met on 5 May 1789, it was evident that he had not come to hear what the assembly members wanted, but to graciously grant them an audience. First, their credentials had to be verified, and this was to be done separately. Splitting what many were beginning to regard as France's national parliament into three led to endless arguments.

The king then decided to hold a Royal Session in which his will would be made known. To prevent unrest, which had been spreading throughout France in recent months, troops were ordered to guard the members of the third estate. Afraid that this might be a trick or a military coup, they gathered in a nearby tennis court, where they took a solemn oath to stay together until they had provided France with an acceptable constitution. The date was 20 June 1789. Three weeks later, the Paris mob captured the Bastille, the symbol of royal absolutism. The revolution had begun in earnest.

Bougainville remained on the sidelines as the troubles unfolded. Instinctively, he was on the side of the reformers. He came from a middle-class family of lawyers, and he knew from his experiences in the navy how difficult it was to break through the cliques of the privileged nobles. He had first-hand knowledge of parliamentary democracy and of a constitutional monarchy from his time in England – although he realised how powerful the upper class was even there. More recently, he had fought for the republican cause in the United States. And among his closest friends were many of the *philosophes* who had laid the foundations for the new order that now seemed to be coming about. On the other hand, his own progress had depended on the patronage of the great and the powerful; some members of his family, including his own wife, belonged to the lower nobility, and Louis XVI had behaved with some benevolence towards him. He did not take sides, but he did agree to provide two guns for the defence of Fourche, the village close to La Brosse, which was threatened by roaming bands of republicans in the post-Bastille period known as *La Grande Peur* – the Great Panic. He was more involved with discussions over the apparent disappearance of La Pérouse.

According to every calculation, the explorer's two ships should have been back in Brest by now. At the very least, some reports should have arrived from Mauritius. Louis discussed the problem with Fleurieu and with Jean-Joseph de Laborde, a wealthy *fermier-général* who had lost two sons in a boating accident while the La Pérouse expedition was on the north-west coast of America. By the end of 1789, both Fleurieu and Laborde decided that an expedition had to be organised to search for the vanished ships.

There was also the matter of responding to certain claims made by the English navigator John Shortland who was supposed to have discovered some islands in the south-west Pacific. But these had already been visited by Bougainville in 1768 and Jean de Surville in 1769. They were the Solomons. The dispute arose following the publication in London in 1789 of *The Voyage of Governor Phillip to Botany Bay*, which included an account of Shortland's voyage to New Georgia that showed he was largely unaware of earlier French voyages. A counter-claim was prepared, which Laborde turned into an appeal for a rescue expedition to look for La Pérouse's ships.

On 21 March 1790, he submitted to the *Académie des Sciences* a memoir covering both subjects. It was well received, although there were greater experts than he on the cartography of the Pacific: the geographer Philippe Buache was one, Fleurieu another. The reaction was polite, but restrained. Nevertheless, Laborde had his report privately printed under the title *Mémoire sur la prétendue découverte faite en 1789 par des Anglois d'un continent qui n'est autre que la Terre des Arsacides découverte en 1768 par M. de Bougainville, chef d'escadre des armées navales, et en 1769 par M. de Surville, capitaine de vaisseau de la Compagnie des Indes, suivi d'un projet de souscription pour un armement destiné à la recherche de M. de la Peyrouze, qu'on croit avoir fait naufrage sur quelque côte de la mer du Sud*. Arsacides was the name bestowed on the Solomon group by Surville. Laborde had proposed that the search expedition should be led by Bougainville; he cannot have made such a suggestion without first consulting Louis.

Bougainville, however, had other, quite different matters in hand. According to the correspondence of his relative, the Chevalier de Silans, he was being sounded out to lead a delegation to the Russian court in connection with events in France, 'displaying the same kind of wisdom that requires one to remain nearby in order to save what one can from a fire'.[2] A little later, he was invited to attend the *Fête de la Fédération*, which marked the first anniversary of the fall of the Bastille. He felt it was tactful to accept, but he took care not to take a prominent role in the celebrations.

The growing unrest that was spreading throughout the kingdom had affected the navy. On 23 October, Luzerne resigned, finding it impossible to carry on 'owing to the lack of discipline of the sailors worsened by constant rebellious actions'.[3] The navy portfolio was immediately passed on to Claret de Fleurieu, who appointed Bougainville, 'a general who will be agreeable to the men', as commander of the naval forces based in Brest.[4]

Louis left at once, but it was only a matter of days before he was faced with a mutiny.

He had the rebels arrested and given a dishonourable discharge. This show of strength was balanced by inviting the leaders of the republican movement, the *Société des Amis de la Constitution*, to attend the unveiling of the new flag, a combination of the old royal standard and the new red, white and blue colours, which was followed by a series of banquets and displays of patriotic oratory.

This did not prevent further mutinies occurring on four ships preparing to sail for the West Indies. Bougainville managed to contain these by further shows of firmness, but the situation was worsening on all fronts. Experienced officers, many of them aristocrats, were leaving the service. By the middle of 1790, more than half the officers based in Brest had resigned or simply vanished. Some had returned to civilian life and their families; others had emigrated and would soon join anti-republican forces abroad. Republican committees of the *Société des Amis de la Constitution* were being set up everywhere, and several insisted on being fully consulted on naval matters. This made action even more difficult when trouble arose on board a ship.

In February 1791, Bougainville left for Paris for consultations, but even he had to apply for a travel permit. His position had become untenable. Fleurieu could offer no help, and in fact resigned in May. He preferred to devote himself to planning an expedition to rescue La Pérouse, and to his own refutation of Shortland's claims and related matters. His *Découvertes des François en 1768 et 1769 dans le sud-est de la Nouvelle-Guinée* had been published in Paris in late 1790; it was now being translated into English and would appear in London in 1791.

Meantime, a naval officer, Aristide Aubert Dupetit-Thouars, had written to the Ministry of Marine, asking for permission to take up Laborde's proposition and sail in search of La Pérouse. Like him, he set up a subscription list, which was headed by Louis XVI, and obtained the support of the new parliament, the *Assemblée nationale*. The required total was not fully reached, but he was able to obtain an advance equivalent to two years' salary, and sailed in August 1792. His chivalrous attempt to find the lost ships, however, ended in disaster.

Although it had supported Dupetit-Thouars's plan, the *Assemblée* had separately made provision for an official large-scale expedition. It had voted a decree to that effect in February 1791, and Fleurieu gave it official approval in mid-March. This would lead to the voyage of Bruny d'Entrecasteaux, who sailed with two ships, the *Recherche* and the *Espérance*, on 28 September 1791.

By then, the political situation in France had deteriorated considerably. In June, Louis XVI and his family fled Paris, hoping to join the growing number of loyalist supporters and other émigrés overseas. They were arrested at Varennes, some 40 miles from the area where his friends were waiting. The king was brought back to Paris; he was treated for some time as a constitutional monarch, but most of his power had gone, and his fate was practically sealed.

Fleurieu had been replaced by Antoine de Thévenard, a naval officer, but a 'blue', who had been recently appointed naval commander at Lorient. He too found the position of Minister of Marine intolerable and resigned on 1 October, after five months in office. The very next day, Louis XVI, desperately casting around for someone who might be acceptable to all sides, decided to ask Bougainville, who was a renowned navigator and a friend of the *philosophes*, and not a politician. His fame had steadily increased, his views were known to be moderate and he had wide naval experience. Louis wisely declined. The portfolio went to a fairly nondescript local administrator, Bertrand de Moleville.

Bougainville's rejection did not upset the monarch, who realised that Louis had already found it impossible to run the navy at Brest and did not believe that he could do any better with the entire naval forces. Showing that he felt no ill-will towards him, Louis XVI promoted him to the rank of vice-admiral to date from 1 January 1792. But Louis decided to turn down the promotion. In a letter to the minister, he wrote:

> My duty to the fatherland forces me to refuse a high office that would be a mere title without actual duties. Military discipline, without which a naval force cannot exist, has been destroyed. A flag officer cannot carry out his duties without assistants, and I look about in vain for someone who combines a theoretical knowledge of military manoeuvres with the experience of battle. After showing a great deal of patience, they have been driven from their posts by the repeated excesses of insubordination sanctioned by lack of punishment. I beg you, Sir, to express my feelings to the King. I would be unhappy indeed if I could not devote my last days to the service of my country and end my career in the manner I began it.[5]

He was still in Paris, although his family was preparing to move to Anneville. He had stayed by Fleurieu's side, helping him to plan the D'Entrecasteaux expedition. There was little more they could do now, beyond waiting for its outcome. They still met with their friends from the *Académie des Sciences*, but they mostly discussed the political situation. Now, however, it would be safer for his wife and children to live in Normandy than too close to Paris.

War broke out on 20 April. Initially, the main enemy was Austria and the *émigrés* who were planning to overthrow the republic from abroad. The *Assemblée* passed a number of decrees in May and June, which Louis XVI at first refused to sign. For the infuriated republicans this confirmed that he sided with those who had fled France and were now working with the enemy. His action led to riots, including the invasion of the Tuileries, in Paris, where the king and his family were lodged. Among those who gathered to protect the royal family was Bougainville.

The war was going badly. Prussia and Sardinia had joined the Austrians, and their armies had already crossed the frontier and captured several towns. Then, the Duke of Brunswick, commanding the invading forces, issued a declaration threatening 'the rigours of war' against anyone, civilian or volunteer, who resisted, and stating that any further attack against the Tuileries would expose Paris and its inhabitants to 'an exemplary and unforgettable act of vengeance'.[6]

This move, by a commander confident of victory over what he regarded as a mere rabble, was calculated to protect the royal family and encourage royalist supporters, but it backfired badly. More riots broke out, led by radical elements and the national volunteers who had gathered for the third anniversary of the fall of the Bastille and were about to move to the war front. The crowds once more broke into the Tuileries, forcing the king and his family to seek refuge in the main hall of the *Assemblée*. The Swiss guards who had served as their bodyguard were massacred. The king was prevented from ruling and effectively imprisoned. In early September, royalists and people suspected of being their supporters were rounded up in various parts of France and over 1000 were executed.

Bougainville had again been at the Tuileries when the crowds broke in, but he was able to escape and make his way to Anneville. This enabled him to escape the so-called 'September Massacres', but when the republican forces checked the Prussian advance at Valmy on 20 September, he realised that the tide had turned and that the more extreme revolutionaries would take over. Life was now dangerous for anyone associated with the fallen regime.

He lived as quietly as he could on his small property on the southern Cherbourg peninsula. Almost daily, he received news of acquaintances who had fled to England, and of less fortunate ones who had been caught in the waves of arrests sweeping through France, some of them dying on the newly invented guillotine. Vaudreuil was now living in London and would remain there for close on ten years. The Duc de Chartres, whom he had known in the navy, had become a deputy in the *Assemblée*, a body now more radical than ever. Changing his name to Philippe Égalité, he voted in favour of the extremist *Tribunal Révolutionnaire*, and eventually voted in favour of the execution of his cousin Louis XVI, who was publicly guillotined on 21 January 1793. This did not prevent the duke's own arrest, triggered by the desertion and emigration of his own son, and he was guillotined in November of the same year.

Bougainville did not consider emigrating, even though the British-held Channel Islands were a mere 18 miles from the coast, and on a clear day he could see Jersey across the water. He was a moderate, who favoured a constitutional monarchy and had no wish to join the supporters of the former absolutism. Above all, he had family responsibilities. It would have been difficult to take his wife and young children with him, and leaving them behind was unthinkable.

Anneville proved to be dangerous enough. The net of the Revolutionary Tribunal swept far and wide. Some time in early 1794 – the actual date is unclear – Louis was arrested and taken to the prison at Coutances. The arrest warrant merely gave his name, 'Bougainville, former noble', but no specific charges were listed. None was needed by that time: the plan was to hold him until Paris asked for him. Then there would be a brief trial, with death as the likely verdict.

The local authorities, however, had nothing against him, and they were not overly affected by revolutionary fervour. Flore-Josèphe was able to visit him, admittedly with some difficulty, but his children were allowed in more easily: five-year-old Alphonse carried messages to and fro hidden in his shoes. One of these urged Flore-Josèphe to leave La Becquetière without delay and seek refuge in Brittany, where she had friends and family, and where there were numerous anti-republicans who could help.

She moved to Montmarin, a château on the River Rance, south of Saint-Malo. It belonged to Aaron Pierre Du Bosq, a member of the Magon family, who were shipowners and merchants. They traded with Mauritius and India, and had been involved with the 1771–3 Marion Dufresne expedition to Tasmania and New Zealand. Bougainville knew several members of the family, and they were happy to help in these dangerous times. Montmarin had the advantage of being relatively isolated, and the main access to the property was from a landing stage on the riverbank.

To get away, Flore-Josèphe disguised herself as a man and sailed in a small fishing boat across the bay and around Mont Saint Michel. With her went the three boys. One of the crew suspected that she was a woman and, so the story goes, leered at her, saying, 'You're much too pretty to be a man.'[7] A resounding slap across the face put an end to his importuning.

Leaving the boys with a friend, she later made her way back to Normandy, to plead on behalf of her husband with officials in the main town, Caen. There she heard that Louis had just been freed. The overthrow and execution of Maximilien de Robespierre, the extremist president of the convention or national assembly, on

10 July had put an end to the Terror, a mere two days before Bougainville was due to be sent to Paris to face the Revolutionary Tribunal.

The family was reunited shortly after at Anneville. It was still wise to lie low for a while: the revolutionaries remained powerful and a coup against those who had brought down Robespierre was still a possibility. There was no pro-royalist reaction to his death – it was the consequence of the excesses of the Terror, not an anti-revolutionary action. Flore-Josèphe, however, found it difficult to knuckle under in a republican world. She was a devout woman, who had sheltered a priest, the Abbé de Montfrin, when the clerics were under attack and required to take an oath to the republic and even, to prove their loyalty, to marry. She was now openly organising masses for the locals, who were summoned by the traditional loud pealing of bells. This caused mutterings among some officials, but she simply ignored them all.

Throughout the late summer and autumn of 1794, life slowly returned to something approaching normality. The French armies, having now driven back the Austrian-led forces, had marched north, reached Belgium and were preparing to invade the Austrian Netherlands. Where there had been widespread fear, both of the invaders and of the extremist republicans, there was now confidence and a sense of hope in the future.

Although they were slowly eroding, the republican structures and social practices remained in force. Thus, when Bougainville received a letter from the local administrative committee, it was addressed to 'Citizen Bougainville, land owner and farmer residing in Anneville', and used the informal but brotherly *tu*. It required him to travel without delay to Paris to enrol at the new *École Normale Supérieure*:

> The Administration has just appointed you a pupil of the École Normale. Your civic and moral qualities and your knowledge of the useful sciences have determined its selection. You are, according to the terms of the order, to notify us within three days that you are accepting; this response will be governed by your desire to be useful and to do good; these are sentiments that have always guided you …
>
> Greetings and fraternity, [signed] Lefebvre.[8]
>
> Note: You are to be in Paris no later than the 30th of the present month.

The term 'pupil' has puzzled commentators. On the face of it, it reads like an insult to a man who had just turned sixty-five, or hints at a form of political re-education. The 'school', however, was a recently founded tertiary institution for senior teachers and lecturers. The decree that had set it up a mere two months earlier required it to be opened in Paris, 'where would be invited, from every part of the Republic, citizens already knowledgeable in the useful sciences, in order to learn the art of teaching from the best teachers available in every field of knowledge'.[9] What Bougainville actually did there is not clear. He probably helped to build it up – in time, it would become a prestigious national institution – but he most probably simply renewed his contacts with scientists and geographers, and returned to his usual preoccupations.

One of the topics then being discussed was the formation of the *Bureau des Longitudes*, which was set up during 1795–6 and of which he became an early member. In December, Louis was elected to the newly established *Institut National*, in the 'Moral and Political Sciences' section, which included geography. There, once again, he met up with Fleurieu and Buache, as well as the famous mapmaker and geographer Edmé Mentelle, and the writer and philosopher Charles Gosselin.

By then, the revolution was over. The ruling convention had been dissolved in October and replaced by the *Directoire*, a group of five moderate, if not particularly efficient, leaders who were to take the chair in rotation. The change had led to some street rioting in Paris, but the protesters had quickly been quelled by troops led by a little-known general, Napoleon Bonaparte. He would go on, during 1796, to defeat the Austrians in Italy, adding to his rapidly growing reputation by the victories of Lodi and Arcole.

There was one attempt, by the left-winger François Babeuf, to overthrow the *Directoire* and restore the 1793 constitution, but this was promptly quelled, and the progress towards new reforms continued. Freedom of the press was restored, while the jurist Jean Jacques Cambacérès began work on a new set of civil laws: this would become the *Code Napoléon*, the basis for much of the modern French legal system. It was all part of a vast set of reforms that included the educational and scientific world. The Age of the Enlightenment was coming into fruition. Calm had returned, inside France's frontiers at least, and Bougainville and his friends could breathe easy and devote themselves to their families and their other interests. Although he was now sixty-seven, he certainly had no intention of resting on his laurels. There was much to be done in the post-revolutionary world, and he intended to play his part.

32. Apotheosis

1797–1811

Europe was in a state of almost constant conflict. The French armies under Napoleon were going through a period of successes on land and defeats at sea. In Europe, there was much for the French to celebrate. Most of Italy was under French control. Napoleon became the hero of all France, regarded not simply as a conquering military leader, but as a republican taking the message of political reform and 'liberty, equality, fraternity' to other nations suffering under the absolute rule of hereditary kings and aristocrats. The Directors were compelled to concede him full powers to negotiate with Austria, which signed the treaty of Campo Formio and was withdrawing from the struggle, for a time at least. Through it, France obtained most of what is now Belgium, and the possibility of her boundaries extending to the left bank of the Rhine, a long-cherished dream of French rulers. The venerable but sclerotic Republic of Venice disappeared from history, passing firstly under Austrian control, then joining the Italian confederacy in 1805.

Britain was struggling under a severe financial crisis: the Bank of England was forced to suspend payments temporarily, a move that struck fear into the hearts of merchants and ordinary people. An outcome of this was the appearance of small copper coins, the famous pennies, and in 1799 William Pitt introduced the almost revolutionary income tax. On the credit side, the British Navy defeated a combined Franco-Spanish fleet at Cape St Vincent – but on the debit side there were mutinies on British ships at Spithead and Nore.

Bougainville was one of those – sometimes known as the revolutionary or reformist republicans – who gradually entered politics. He became acquainted with Charles Maurice de Talleyrand-Périgord, who had recently returned from exile to take up the position of foreign secretary. A skilful and crafty diplomat, he had begun his career in the church, becoming Bishop of Autun and attending the Estates General as a representative of the clergy, where he supported the new constitution. Later he got himself appointed to the French legation in London. By then, the extremists were beginning to take over, and he cautiously joined the *émigrés*. He returned to France after the fall of Robespierre.

Louis stood for the *Conseil des Anciens*, a kind of senate recently set up as an upper house to the *Conseil des Cinq Cents*. He failed by just a few votes, but does not seem to have been particularly upset by this minor setback. It was more than compensated by the suggestion that he might take up the marine portfolio, which he again declined, and by Talleyrand's address of 3 July 1797 to the *Institut*, entitled 'Essay on the advantages that may be obtained from new colonies under the present circumstances'. He urged members to listen to men of experience, including 'our Bougainville to whom is due the glory of discovering what the famous navigators of England had the honour of visiting after him'.[1]

This rather convoluted speech, with its dig at the claims of Shortland and others, was loudly applauded, and led to a suggestion that it would be to France's advantage if she could secure Egypt, 'not by domination or by a monopoly, but by protection'. And, he added, 'the reopening of the Suez route would be as fatal to Britain as the discovery of the Cape of Good Hope was to Genoa and Venice back in the sixteenth century'. Talleyrand was officially a private citizen – his appointment as minister was still a fortnight away – so he could express views that a member of the government might hesitate to make public. The session ended informally with him, Bougainville and others discussing his comments and their implications.

Bonaparte returned to France at the beginning of December. On the 5th, he held talks with Talleyrand, with Bougainville present. In February, a proposal for a campaign in the Middle East was laid before the *Directoire* and formally approved a couple of weeks later. The idea of a protectorate over Turkish-influenced Mameluke Egypt was modified into a new and broader strategy.

Meanwhile, another plan was being drawn up, the invasion of Britain, and Bougainville was invited to join the committee set up to prepare it. In view of the continuing superiority of the British Navy, getting French troops across the Channel was not going to be easy and the advice of someone with naval experience was essential. Bougainville was first asked to comment on a proposal put forward by a senior inspector of public works, Cessard. The idea was to create an artificial waterway across the Channel by means of a double line of flat-bottomed barges a little over a mile apart, laid out cross-wise from each other and held together by chains. Each of these platforms would be armed with four guns and three mortars. French ships and transports would sail along this channel, hopefully protected from enemy ships.

Bougainville pointed out, in his '*Observations du citoyen Bougainville sur un projet de descente sur les côtes d'Angleterre*' of 23 April 1798, that it would be easy enough for an enemy vessel to sail into such an insecure barrier and that a few small fireships could be set alight and driven towards the barges. He remembered the problems faced along the St Lawrence River during the defence of Quebec. He similarly rejected an alternative plan to bottle up some of the main British naval bases. A line of barges and small gunships laid across a harbour mouth would certainly present problems for the Royal Navy, but it would be too exposed to fireships, gunfire from shore batteries and night-time raids.

None of all this really mattered. Napoleon and Talleyrand had already turned away from any thought of invading Britain. The idea was useful in that it diverted attention from their other plans, and worried the British – who themselves attempted a Channel crossing, landing at Ostend in Belgium at the end of May, and were soundly defeated. In the meantime, Napoleon had been leading his forces to Malta, which he captured in mid-June, and to Egypt, where he landed at the beginning of July.

Bougainville returned to a semi-private life. On 25 June, he read a paper to his fellow members at the *Institut*, an '*Essai historique sur les navigations anciennes et modernes dans les hautes latitudes septentrionales*'. It was something of a homage to his deceased brother. Nostalgia marked much of this year, for the now quite elderly Madame de Hérault, his *chère Maman*, had recently died. His next talk, in the following year, also to some extent looked back to his early years. Entitled '*Notice historique sur les Sauvages de l'Amérique septentrionale*', it included his recollections of the Iroquois people. It was based on numerous notes and diaries he had kept during the Canadian campaigns.

On 5 September, as a member of a special committee of the *Académie des Sciences*, Louis contributed to a report on plans drawn up by the American Robert Fulton to build a submarine. This, the committee concluded, was a terrible means of destruction, because it would travel invisibly and silently under water and it would be practically impossible to avoid it. Such a craft would be particularly appropriate for the French, who had a weaker naval force than their opponents, and the idea was therefore worth taking seriously. The Directory was not too sure whether to proceed and, after long and inconclusive discussions, it set the report aside. Two years went by, until July 1800 when, following Napoleon's personal encouragement, Fulton was allowed to put his *Nautilus* on display at Rouen, on the Seine. The experiment was impressively successful, but again the French Navy did not take it up. Fulton went back to the United States, where he turned to the task of developing plans for a steamboat.

In February 1799, Louis was formally appointed to the *Bureau des Longitudes*, replacing his friend, the famous mathematician Jean-Charles Borda, who had recently died and whose eulogy Louis had been asked to give.

The Egyptian campaign had progressed satisfactorily, gaining Napoleon great notoriety. However, Admiral Horatio Nelson had cut off his lines of communication by destroying French ships at the Battle of the Nile (off Abu Qir, hence its name in French history, the Battle of Aboukir). The Turkish government took advantage of this to declare war on France, causing Napoleon to march on Palestine and Syria. In July 1799, he defeated a joint Turkish-British force that tried to land in Egypt, but decided to make his way back to France while he still could and his fame was still intact. This enabled him to overthrow the Directory, which had only ever given him lukewarm support, and to set up a Consulate of three members. He became First Consul, with a constitution providing for a Senate of 50 members appointed for life, a 'tribunate' of 100 members and a legislative assembly of 300.

Louis de Bougainville was selected as one of the senators. The duties were undemanding, but the emoluments were by no means negligible. He was now in a comfortable financial position, which enabled him to buy the Château of Suisnes, just outside Paris. It had been built in the seventeenth century by De Sainctot, a senior court official, and was more conveniently situated than La Brosse, which the Bougainvilles sold. He enlarged Suisnes, building a dining hall 'with a neo-classical frontage including Tuscan-style columns and pediment'.[2] He also added several summerhouses, and an orangerie in which his gardener, the famous Christophe Cocher, planted tropical trees and shrubs, including palms, bananas, pineapples and sugar canes. Flore-Josèphe, who had always been keen on gardening, had a rose garden laid out. From this a local rose growing industry eventually developed and Cocher called an early variety of rose 'Bougainville'.

For Louis, however, there was other work to do. An expedition to the southern seas had been under discussion for quite some time. An experienced sailor, Nicolas Baudin, had put forward a proposal for such a voyage in early 1798. The *Institut* set up a committee to examine the proposition. It included Fleurieu, the scientist Bernard de Lacèpède, and Bougainville.

Political upheavals and the Egyptian campaign delayed things somewhat, but a favourable recommendation was put forward in March 1800, submitted to Napoleon on 1 April and approved by him a week later. A detailed programme was finalised within a month and accepted by Napoleon with equal promptness. Ships were found and equipped, a crew was assembled and detailed instructions were drawn up in the following months. Baudin sailed from Le Havre with the *Géographe* and the *Naturaliste* in October.

The expedition was intended to survey the coast of Australia and all the outlying islands. As the committee had pointed out, the greatest expanse of uncharted territory still lay along the Australian coast, and the planned voyage of exploration would be:

most interesting for the sciences as well as for politics. It is important for France to become well acquainted with the two straits that divide New Holland – from Van Diemen's Land [Tasmania] in the south, and from New Guinea in the north. This consideration alone would be a sufficient motive to decide on this expedition.[3]

As this comment indicates, it was still believed that the Australian continent consisted of two large islands. The political implications were obvious – and explain to some extent Napoleon's rapid endorsement of the Baudin proposal: the British had colonised New South Wales in the east, and the French could set up their own colony in the still unexplored west.

Did Bougainville really consider leading the expedition, or at least taking part as mentor and guide, as Martin-Allanic speculates?[4] Had he even suggested earlier that he could command the fleet that might supervise the landing of French troops in England, as La Roncière wonders?[5] It is possible that he mentioned to Napoleon that he would prefer action to merely giving advice. The consul had smiled and reminded him of his age, whereupon Bougainville had brought out a classical allusion: 'Nestor was no less prominent at the siege of Troy than the young Achilles'. Louis was famous for his repartée and the reference to the Trojan war was in character.

Certainly, as he entered his seventies, he looked back on the past with wistfulness and yearning. There had been so many things he would have liked to do, so many lost opportunities, he felt, but now that circumstances had brought him so close to the powerful, his age was against him. He had the consolation of seeing his son Hyacinthe join the Baudin expedition, sailing in the *Géographe*. He lent him a copy of the journal he had kept on his first voyage to the Falklands, to use as a model for his own. Hyacinthe would return safely, after an impressive voyage that made some important discoveries, but was rent by personal dissensions on board both ships. Baudin did not return, dying in September 1803 on the Isle de France.

Thinking back to his early days led Bougainville to revive his old idea of a colony on the Malouines. He submitted a paper on 19 March 1800, entitled 'Mémoire du Général Bougainville sur un projet d'établissement dans l'île Malouine'. It made the point that the loss of Newfoundland and French Canada had practically ruined the French cod fishing industry, that the West Indies could all too easily pass into American hands, and that such setbacks could be compensated by a colony in the South Atlantic. 'The settlement I established in 1763 and kept going for three years, gives France the sacred title of first settler … No time is more favourable than the present to get Spain to give up her imaginary rights in our favour and for England to agree to this transfer.'[6]

Napoleon sent the document to the Minister of Foreign Affairs, but the suggestion was not taken up. There were other, more important matters to include in the peace treaty that was about to be negotiated. Known as the Treaty of Amiens, it was signed in March 1802.

It was a minor disappointment, but Bougainville swept it aside. A personal tragedy had struck the family in the intervening year. On 24 May 1801, young Armand de Bougainville went swimming in the Yères, a small attractive river that runs past the village of Gisy-Suisnes. Somehow, he got out of his depth, possibly became trapped between rocks or tree roots, and drowned. He was sixteen. The Bougainvilles were distraught. Flore-Josèphe took Armand's body to be buried in the Calvaire cemetery by Saint-Pierre de Montmartre. The family felt that they could no longer live at Suisnes, which now held such tragic memories for them, and they began to spend more and more time in Paris.

Bougainville had formally retired from the navy on 20 February 1802 with the rank of rear-admiral. He continued to meet regularly with his scientist friends and, now that the troubled times were over, he renewed acquaintance with some of the former *émigrés*. Among them was E.P.E. Rossel who had sailed with D'Entrecasteaux but had been unable to return to France during the revolution. He had now been able to bring back valuable documents relating to the expedition, including remarkable charts by Charles François Beautemps-Beaupré. With the help of both Fleurieu and Bougainville, Rossel began to prepare the narrative of the expedition, which was published in two volumes in 1808, under the title *Voyage de Dentrecasteaux envoyé à la recherche de La Pérouse*.

Almost daily now, old acquaintances were returning to Paris, from abroad or from the country estates where they had prudently kept out of the public eye, and all were eager to exchange news and look back on earlier times. A letter came one day from the elderly Princesse de Rohan-Rochefort: 'My Dear Senator, I am extremely unhappy at not having yet seen you'. It was flattering, but it pleased Louis to feel that he had not been forgotten – or criticised for having stayed in France and not joined the royalists overseas, even though Napoleon at times jokingly referred to him as '*Monsieur le Royaliste*'.

Napoleon was proclaimed emperor in May 1804. Among the innovations that came with the empire was a new decoration to replace the Order of Saint Louis, founded by Louis XIV back in 1693. The new *Ordre de la Légion d'Honneur* reflected the classical Roman flavour so prized by the republicans and their successors – as did the terms 'tribunes', 'senators' and 'consuls' that had come into existence at the fall of the monarchy. The first conferment of decorations took place with great solemnity at the Invalides on 15 July 1804. Bougainville was awarded the rank of Grand Officer.

He suffered from ill-health for much of that year, largely due to a recurrence of the dysentery that had affected so many of his men in Batavia and from which few of them ever completely recovered. By 1805, however, he was well enough to return to the *Académie des Sciences* and serve on several committees set up to examine the reports presented by François Péron, who had sailed with Baudin. The members Louis worked with were all leading figures in science and geography: Fleurieu, Lacépède, the zoologist Georges Cuvier, the naturalist Jean-Baptiste Lamarck, the astronomer and mathematician Pierre Simon Laplace, and Jacques-Julien La Billardière, who had written an account of the D'Entrecasteaux expedition. François Péron was in the process of writing an account, a somewhat biased one, of the Baudin expedition, *Voyage de découvertes aux terres australes*, which was published in 1807.

In April 1802, Baudin had met the English navigator Matthew Flinders at what is now known as Encounter Bay, in South Australia. Flinders, in command of the *Investigator*, had already surveyed much of the southern coast of Australia. His ship eventually proved to be unseaworthy, however, and he was forced to set off for home in a small schooner, the *Cumberland*. His route included a call at the Isle de France but when he got there in December 1803 he was placed under arrest. The passport he had been given for his voyage of exploration referred to the *Investigator* and, as General Charles Mathieu Decaen, the island's governor, pointed out, made no mention of the *Cumberland*. Now that war had again broken out between France and England, Flinders was an enemy and regarded as a possible spy, a charge he denied with mounting indignation. His attitude led to a rapid and acrimonious breach with Decaen, and his imprisonment lengthened into months, then years.

Not without difficulty, he managed to send letters of protest to England and then to France. Through a friendly local merchant, he forwarded letters to Admiral Linois, who sent them on to Fleurieu, to the astronomer Lalande and eventually to Bougainville. By now, it was late 1805. Discussions took place between the three friends, who sought the opinion of the Minister of Marine, Denis Decrès. It was agreed to seek the opinion of the *Conseil d'État*, which authorised Flinders's release. On 21 March 1806, Bougainville took their recommendation to Napoleon. Louis knew enough about the matter to answer any queries the emperor might raise. After a brief and friendly discussion, Napoleon approved the request. It took time, however, for the news to reach Mauritius and even longer for Flinders to be released: Decaen was in no hurry to sign the order releasing the humourless and often discourteous Englishman – in addition to which, the island was being blockaded by English warships. He was finally let go in June 1810.

Flore-Josèphe died on 7 August 1806, at the age of forty-five, and was buried next to Armand. After his wife's death, Louis sold the château and moved to a house at No. 5 Passage des Petits-Pères, in the old heart of Paris where his family had lived for so many years. It was in a way a return to his roots. His youngest son, Adolphe, was still living with him; Hyacinthe, safely back from his time with Baudin, was in the navy as a junior officer and about to be promoted lieutenant; Alphonse was serving in the dragoons. When Alphonse left for Spain at the outbreak of the Peninsular War, his father wrote to him, reminding him that he too had crossed the Pyrenees and ridden to Madrid:

> I four times rode along the route you will be taking. Tell me if your own route caused you, on your way to Vittoria, to pass through a vault cutting into the rock near the top of the mountains. In my day, the plateau one finds on these mountain tops was often a death-trap for travellers.[7]

In Paris, Louis could stroll along the banks of the Seine, which Napoleon was completing and beautifying, and see the changes that were taking place: new bridges, street widenings, new homes, the careful and thorough numbering of the houses, even numbers on one side, odd numbers on the other. As always, perspective remained paramount to French urban planners, and the Rue de Rivoli had been cut through from the Place de la Concorde to the Place des Pyramides, and work was beginning on a great Arc de Triomphe on the Chaillot hill, so that 'This monument will be visible from far away'.

In 1807, Bougainville was elected vice-president of his section at the *Institut*, and appointed president the following year. He was somewhat reluctant to accept this promotion, arguing that his health would not allow him to take over the heavy work this position often entailed. It was agreed that the new vice-president would be available to share his duties when the need arose.

There was a greater honour to come. As emperor, Napoleon needed a formal court, and he could hardly call on members of the old aristocracy to fill these functions. A new aristocracy was created, with the traditional titles, excluding only that of viscount and marquis. Louis de Bougainville became a count, as did most of his fellow senators. The title was formally granted to him on 26 April 1808. The old feudal privileges, including freedom from most forms of taxation, were not restored, but the titles were deemed to be hereditary – although this largely disappeared when the monarchy was restored in 1814.

A coat of arms was designed: 'two golden swords in saltire against an azure background with a silver anchor palewise with a globe similar in abyss brochant over all'.[8] The Bougainvilles had their own coat of arms which Louis had often used, after his father's death and until the revolution, when all titles and armorial bearings were abolished. He could have revived it, but it contained an eagle, a symbol now reserved exclusively for the emperor, so he had to have a new coat of arms designed. After the restoration, Hyacinthe was able to use his family's old coat of arms with the eagle, but he added the globe, in order to commemorate his father's and later his own achievements in world exploration.

Louis still found it hard to give up his old dream of a Falklands colony. Spain had now fallen fully under French influence. Siding with the opponents of the revolution and consequently with Britain, the Spanish had tried to invade France, but had soon been driven back and been invaded in their turn. By 1795, Madrid was forced back into an alliance with France. In 1806 Charles IV abdicated in favour of his son Ferdinand, a committed conservative who proposed to abolish the Spanish assembly, the Cortes, and even considered restoring the Inquisition to put an end to modernist ideas. This was unacceptable to France and Napoleon forced him to return the crown to his reluctant father, who then agreed to give it up in favour of Napoleon's brother, Joseph Bonaparte. The abdication document of 9 May 1808 referred to both Charles and Ferdinand giving up 'their claims to the throne of Spain and the Indies', so that their colonial possessions effectively passed to Napoleon's control. These naturally included the Argentine and therefore the Malvinas.

Bougainville could not resist: he hastily redrafted his earlier memoir on the Malouines, adding a new plea. It contained a double argument – the islands' continuing lack of settlers and the changed political situation in Spain: 'The Malouines, at present uncultivated, have returned to the mass of lands that should belong to their first occupant, all the more so if the Spanish cede to the Emperor their so-called claim'.[9] The French, however, took no action, and the Falklands remained uninhabited and abandoned until the 1820s.

Louis was given other duties. The Battle of Trafalgar in October 1805 had been an epic victory for England, but a disaster for France. It led to the kind of recriminations that had resulted from the Battle of the Saints in 1782 and to a court martial, which met on 13 September 1809, mainly to consider the actions of Rear-Admiral Pierre Dumanoir, who was anxious to defend himself from the constant accusations of incompetence. The chairman was Bougainville himself, with Fleurieu, François Etienne de Rosily, who had sailed with Kerguelen, and Antoine Thévenard, the former Minister of Marine, as members. Dumanoir was totally exonerated, the court stating that he had obeyed all the signals given, and that only the severe damage sustained by his ship had forced him to leave the battle. It was a judgement that Louis wholeheartedly endorsed; it reminded him so much of the slurs that had been cast on him after the Saints.

He became involved with another jury of sorts that year. Napoleon wanted to commemorate the tenth anniversary of his coming to power in 1800 with, among other celebrations, the handing out of prizes to literary and other major figures. As chairman of the scientific committee of the *Institut*, Bougainville was required to provide a short list. This took time, leading to numerous arguments. When the lists were finally published, complaints began to pour in. Some felt insulted at not being included, or ridiculed the choices. The arguments were particularly virulent in the artistic and literary sections. Almost the only poet whose inclusion was not contested was the still popular Jacques Delille who had once written a poem about the Tahitian Ahu-toru: 'They proclaimed their enthusiasm for the good pupil Delille, whom they would have liked to crown three times, for his three poems, *L'Homme des Champs* (1800), *L'Imagination* (1788) and *Les Trois Règnes* (1809)'. When Delille died in 1813, 'his funeral was a splendid one, comparable only to Victor Hugo's … An amazing crowd attended. At Saint-Etienne du Mont and all along the way to [the cemetery of] Père-Lachaise, the streets were crowded, with people at every window … Every speech praised the poet's genius and promised that his name would live for all eternity. Men and women wept in front of his tomb.'[10] Posterity has been less kind to Delille, who is now almost forgotten, as are most of the poets and playwrights selected by the jury. Louis's committee was not immune to the complaints. It had not been easy to decide which were the best geographers and scientists of the day. Napoleon decided that, this time, discretion was the better part of valour, and the contest was somehow buried:

> Excited at the thought of receiving a crown from the hands of the Emperor, those lucky enough to have been selected scanned eagerly through the daily *Moniteur* in the hope of finding the date when the ceremony would be held, but nothing appeared. They had to resign themselves to the great literary competition having fallen into the abyss where abandoned projects disappear.[11]

The year 1810 brought another cause for sorrow. Bougainville's great friend and collaborator, Claret de Fleurieu, died on 18 August. He was younger than Louis by ten years, and this was a harsh reminder of his own mortality.

He was becoming daily more frail. On 20 August 1811, he suffered another attack of dysentery and this time his constitution was too weak to cope. He died on the 31st. He was eighty-one. He had wished to be buried at Montmartre with his wife and his son Armand, but the French state had other plans. In 1806 the Church of Sainte Geneviève, renamed the Panthéon, had been formally reopened for the burial of 'citizens who have rendered outstanding service to the country, in the armed forces, in the administration or in literature'. The emperor ordered that Bougainville should be buried there. First, though, his heart was removed and in a private ceremony interred next to Flore-Josèphe at the Calvaire cemetery (grave No. 65). His body was taken in a procession to the Panthéon on 7 September. Lacépède delivered the funeral oration: 'For close to half a century, Count Bougainville has been honoured by his contemporaries; today it is the turn of posterity to start paying him homage'.[12] Near him were the ashes of Fleurieu, Choiseul-Praslin, Thévenard and of his one-time critic Jean-Jacques Rousseau.

Louis-Antoine de Bougainville was a true man of the Enlightenment. He had grown up in a conformist family and received a traditional education. He was steeped in the classics, but his brother had opened his mind both to the great voyages of antiquity and the potential of a world still full of mystery.

He was a courtier, witty, charming and at home in the salons that dominated the society of his time, as well as in the corridors of Versailles and the reception rooms of Napoleon. In this he linked the days of Louis XV and Louis XVI with the more middle-class world of the nineteenth century.

He was a gifted mathematician, equally able to turn his mind to theory and to practical problems. Attracted by a career in the army, and briefly by the possibilities offered by the diplomatic world, he turned to the sea, studying problems of longitude and latitude, sea currents and magnetic variation. He learned to navigate and to handle a heavy sailing ship; he could read and interpret sea charts and pinpoint their weaknesses. He could discuss botany, zoology and geology with the scientists he took on his voyage.

Experience taught him that Rousseau's theory of the natural man was a fallacy, and he believed that people isolated on distant islands could gain from contact with modern civilisation. He took Ahu-toru to France with him, not as a trophy, but as a guest. For this, he was often criticised unfairly by some of his fellow *philosophes*, including Diderot in his *Supplément au Voyage de Bougainville*, but he was far more generous towards indigenous peoples than many of his contemporaries, and certainly than the colonialists.

Louis had a long life, and lived it through a number of turning points in world history – the fall of French Canada, the opening of the Pacific, the birth of the United States, the French Revolution and the Revolutionary Wars, the crowning of Napoleon and the transformation of France from a still feudal and absolutist kingdom into a new-style democracy. When he died, the boundaries of France stretched from the Pyrenees to Hamburg, her influence from southern Spain to the northern Baltic, and Britain was isolated and threatened with invasion. He was always ambivalent about Britain, which he saw as France's most dangerous rival and traditional enemy, but also as a country with a freedom of thought and a sense of enterprise that he admired. He had many friends among English scientists and writers, and was even admired by George III.

He was a great figure, but also a gentle family man. His three sons and his sister, Madame de Baraudin, erected a simple memorial to him in the cemetery of Montmartre, which summarised his career: 'A la mémoire de Louis-Antoine, Comte de Bougainville, officer général de terre et de mer, le premier circumnavigateur français. 1729–1811'.

Appendix: Bougainville Commemorated

In addition to the well-known bougainvillea flowering climber, the lesser known *bougainvilleia* Lesson jellyfish and the bandicoot *parameles bougainville*, a number of geographical features, streets and educational institutions have been named in honour of Bougainville, among them:

Bahia Bougainville, Strait of Magellan
Bougainville Bay, Papua New Guinea
Bougainville Island, Solomon Islands
Bougainville Reef, Coral Sea
Bougainville Selat, Indonesia
Bougainville Strait, Vanuatu

Bougainville District, Papua New Guinea
Bougainville Peak, New Guinea
Bougainville Strait, Solomon Islands
Cape Bougainville, Falkland Islands
Mount Bougainville, Alofi, Hoorn Islands
Parc Bougainville, Tahiti

Rue Bougainville in the following towns: Blois, Bordeaux, Brest, Brive, Casablanca, Cherbourg, Diego Suarez (Madagascar), Hyères, La Ciotat, Loriol-sur-Drôme, Montigny-la-Bretonneuse, Montreal, Niort, Noeux-les-Mines, Noumea, Paris, Percé (Gaspé), Pornic, Port-Vila (Vanuatu), Roanne, Roche-la-Molière, Reims, Saint-Servan, Toulouse.

Rue de Bougainville in the following towns: Alençon, Aulnay-sous-Bois, Bois d'Arcy, Châtellerault, Grisy-Suisnes, Le Havre, Limoges, Mantes, Quebec, Rèze, Saint-Benoit, Saint-Brieuc, Saint-Hilaire-du-Harcouët, Saint-Laurent de la Salanque, Saint-Sulpice, Viry-Châtillon.

Avenue Bougainville or **de Bougainville** in the following towns: Beau Bassin (Mauritius), Breuillet; and a **Boulevard Bougainville** in Concarneau.

Impasse Bougainville or **Louis de Bougainville** in the following towns: La Roche-sur-Yon, Ludres, Marck, Perpignan.

The following are also found: Allée Bougainville, Sevran; Allée Louis de Bougainville, Ludugris, Quimper; Bougainville Lane, Eau Coulée, Mauritius; Bougainville Playa, Tenerife; Bougainville Road, Penrith, NSW; Bougainville Street, Beenleigh, Qsld, Lethbridge Park, NSW, Manuka, ACT, all in Australia; Whangarei, New Zealand, and Curepipe, Mauritius; Centre Bougainville, Saint-Malo; Passage Bougainville, Saint-Nazaire; Quai Bougainville, Port-Camargue; Quartier (or Centre) Bougainville, Marseilles; Sente de Bougainville, Trappes.

Educational institutions and buildings:

Lycée Louis-Antoine de Bougainville, Nantes, and Port-Vila, Vanuatu; Lycée Bougainville, Brie-Comte-Robert; Bâtiment Universitaire Bougainville and Salle Bougainville École Navale, Lanvéoc-Poulnic; Bâtiment Bougainville, Institut Français de l'Exploitation de la Mer (IFREMEC), Brest; Résidence Universitaire Bougainville, Le Havre.

NOTES

Chapter 1

1 Paganiol de la Force, *Description historique de Paris* (1753), quoted in Constans, Martine, *Le Guide de Paris* (Lyons, 1989), p. 83.
2 Kerallain, R. de, *La Jeunesse de Bougainville*, p. 29.
3 Buffon, G.L.C. de, *Oeuvres complètes*, I, p. 98.

Chapter 2

1 Gaxotte, P., *Le Siècle de Louis XV*, p. 241.
2 La Roncière, Ch. de, *Bougainville*, p. 12.
3 Royal Society Records, ref. A00773. The election date was 8 January 1756.

Chapter 3

1 On these and related campaigns, see Parkman, F., *France and England in North America*.
2 Gaxotte, P., op. cit., p. 177.
3 Ibid.

Chapter 4

1 Kerallain, op. cit., p. 38.
2 Dahlgren, E.W., *Les Relations Commerciales entre la France et les côtes de l'Océan Pacifique (commencement du XVIIIe siècle)*, p. 401.

Chapter 5

1 Bougainville, letter to his brother, dated 29 March 1756, in La Roncière, Ch. de, op. cit., p. 15.
2 La Roncière, Ch. de, op. cit., pp. 16–19.
3 Ibid.

Chapter 6

1 'Report on New France' sent in part through Madame de Hérault to the Minister for War and later part of *Mémoires divers sur le Canada*, published in Quebec in 1924.
2 Bougainville, 'Journal 1756–1758', in *Rapport de l'Archiviste de la Province de Quebec* (Quebec), 1924.
3 Kerallain, R. de, op. cit, p. 23.
4 Ibid., p. 27.
5 Ibid., pp. 46–7.
6 *Société de Généalogie de Lanaudière*, report, 1996, pp. 21–3.

Chapter 7

1 La Roncière, Ch. de, op. cit., p. 39.

2   Bougainville, 'Journal', entry of 1 August 1757.
3   Kerallain, R. de, op. cit, p. 39.
4   Bougainville, 'Journal', entry dated 7 August 1757.
5   Ibid., entry dated 12–13 August 1757.
6   Parkman, F., op. cit., p. 358.
7   La Roncière, Ch. de, op. cit., p. 22.
8   Ibid., p. 26.
9   See Kimbrough, M, *Louis-Antoine de Bougainville*, pp. 218–9; Touchard, M.C., *Les Voyages de Bougainville*, p. 13.
10 Correspondence between Bougainville and Madame Hérault was fairly regular. See La Roncière, Ch. de, op. cit., pp. 26ff, 241; Kerallain, R. de, op. cit.
11 La Roncière, Ch. de, op. cit., p. 50.
12 See Parkman, F., *France and England in North America*, vol. IX, for a full description of the campaign.
13 La Roncière, Ch. de, op. cit., p. 52. Bougainville wrote a detailed account of the battle in his 'Journal'.
14 La Roncière, Ch. de, op. cit., p. 54.

Chapter 8

1   Parkman, F., op. cit., p. 472.
2   La Roncière, Ch. de, p. 60 for both comments.
3   Gaxotte, P., op. cit., p. 258.
4   La Roncière, Ch. de, op. cit., p. 62.
5   See on this, Thiéry, M., *Bougainville, Soldier and Sailor* (1932).
6   De Brosses, Ch., *Histoire des navigations aux terres australes*, I, p. iv.
7   See on this, Campbell, R.J. (ed.), *The Discovery of the South Shetland Islands* (London, 2000), p. 57.
8   La Roncière, Ch. de, op. cit., p. 66.

Chapter 9

1   Letter of 12 April 1759 to the Maréchal de Belle-Isle, quoted in La Roncière, Ch, op. cit., p. 65.
2   Parkman, F., op. cit., p. 487.
3   Ibid, pp. 513–4.
4   La Roncière, Ch. de, op. cit., p. 71.
5   Ibid., p. 72.
6   Oft-quoted last words paralleled by the dying Wolfe's 'God be praised. I die in peace.' La Roncière, Ch. de, op. cit., p. 79.
7   Knox, J., *An Historical Journal of the Campaigns in North America*. See La Roncière, Ch. de, op. cit., pp. 83–4.
8   Parkman, F., quoting from John Knox's *Historical Journal*, op. cit., pp. 582–3.

9   La Roncière, Ch. de, op. cit., p. 85.

Chapter 10
1   La Roncière, Ch. de, op. cit., p. 86.
2   Ibid.
3   Ibid., p. 88.

Chapter 11
1   *Souvenirs* of Baron Charles-Henri de Gleichen, quoted in Levron, J., *Choiseul: un sceptique au pouvoir*, p. 121.
2   'Éloge de Bougainville' by Jean-Baptiste Delambre, reprinted in the *Moniteur Officiel* of 3 March 1813.
3   Williams, G., *The Great South Sea*, p. 256.
4   Green, J., *Remarks in Support of the New Chart of North and South America* (1753), p. 42.
5   Maupertuis, P.L.M. de, *Oeuvres*, 1956 edition, p. 346.
6   Martin-Allanic, J.E., *Bougainville navigateur et les découvertes de son temps*, I, pp. 22, 63.
7   Ibid., p.18.
8   La Roncière, Ch. de, *Bougainville*, p. 93.
9   Comment in Bougainville's 'Mémoires'. See on this Martin-Allanic, J.E., op. cit., II, pp. 961-2.
10 Mitford, N., *Madame de Pompadour*, pp. 241–2.
11 Levron, J., op. cit., p. 176.

Chapter 12
1   Archives du Ministère des Colonies, Paris, ref. Cn 7:508.
2   Martin-Allanic, J.E., op. cit., I, p. 73.
3   Wiltgren, R.M. *The Founding of the Roman Catholic Church in Oceania*, p. 165.
4   'Mémoires sur les découvertes des Terres australes', in Archives nationales de France, Colonies, ref. C7-511. This document seems to have been written in a fair copy by Bougainville de Nerville. See Martin-Allanic, J.E., op. cit., I, pp. 79–82, 103.
5   Martin-Allanic, J.E., op. cit., pp. 82–3.
6   La Roncière, Ch. de, *Histoire de la marine française*, II, p. 300.
7   Goebel, J., *The Struggle for the Falkland Islands*, p. 34.
8   Walter, R., *A Voyage round the World*, p. 113.
9   Gaxotte, P., *Le Siècle de Louis XV*, p. 308.
10 'Mémoires relatifs aux îles Malouines et aux Terres australes', Archives nationales de France, Colonies, 7:507. See also Martin-Allanic, J.E., op. cit., I, pp. 87–8.
11 Martin-Allanic, J.E., op. cit., I, p. 88.

12 Ibid., I, p. 93.
13 La Roncière, Ch. de, op. cit., p. 92.
14 Report by the Chevalier de Lévis on his role in the defence of Quebec, Martin-Allanic, J.E., op. cit., I, p. 97.
15 Martin-Allanic, J.E., op. cit., I, p. 100.

Chapter 13

1   Martin-Allanic, J.E., op.cit., p. 108.
2   Ibid., p. 109.
3   Bibliothèque nationale de France, NAF 9407:20.
4   La Gravière, J. P. E. Jurien de, *Souvenirs d'un amiral* (Paris, 1860), I, p. 105.
5   Bouvier R. and Maynial, E., *Une Aventure dans les mers australes: l'expédition du Commandant Baudin (1800–1803)* (Paris, 1947), pp. 165–6.
6   Martin-Allanic, J.E., op. cit., I, p. 133.
7   Ibid.
8   Bougainville, 'Journal', Bibliothèque nationale de France, NAF 9407: 30.
9   Martin-Allanic, J.E., op. cit., I, p. 144, quoting Pernetty, A.J., *Journal historique*, ch. X, pp. 270ff.
10 Ibid., p. 149.
11 Bougainville, 'Journal', folio 34.
12 Strange, J.S., *The Falkland Islands*, published in 1947, p. 51.
13 Martin-Allanic, J.E., op. cit., I, p. 155.

Chapter 14

1   Mitford, N., *Madame de Pompadour*, p. 68.
2   'Mémoire' with annotations by Bougainville, in Bibliothèque nationale de France, MS fr. 10.776.
3   Martin-Allanic, J.E., op. cit., I, pp. 171–2.
4   *Gazette de Hollande*, Amsterdam, vol. LVI, 13 July 1764.
5   *Gazette de La Haye*, The Hague, No. 97, 13 August 1764.
6   Journal entry of September 1765, folio 81.
7   Duclos-Guyot's Journal in Archives nationales de France, Marine, ref. 4JJ I:6, pp. 15–6.
8   Journal, folio 41.

Chapter 15

1   Reprinted in Pernetty's *Journal historique*, II, pp. 98ff.
2   Darwin, Ch., *Charles Darwin's* Beagle *Diary*, p. 145.
3   Darwin, Ch., *The Voyage of the* Beagle, p. 182.
4   Martin-Allanic, J.E., op. cit., I, p. 208.
5   Gallagher, R.E., *Byron's Journal*, p. 60.
6   Martin-Allanic, J.E., op. cit., I, p. 208.

7   Gallagher, R.E., op. cit., pp. 65–6.
8   Martin-Allanic, J.E., op. cit., I, p. 210.
9   Ibid.
10 Ibid., I, p. 212.
11 Sirandré's Journal is in the Archives nationales de France, Marine, MS 5680A.
12 Bulkeley and Cummins, *Voyage to the South Seas*, pp. 143, 280.
13 Wallis, H., *Carteret's Voyage*, pp. 471–2.
14 See on Bougainville's meetings with the Patagonians, Martin-Allanic, J.E., op. cit., pp. 212–4.
15 Gallagher, op. cit., p. 52.
16 Martin-Allanic, J.E., op. cit., I, p. 215.
17 Bougainville, 'Journal', folio 48, entry of 2 July 1765.
18 Martin-Allanic, J.E., op. cit., I, p. 217.
19 Ibid., I, p. 242.

Chapter 16

1   Martin-Allanic, J.E., op. cit., I, p. 225, quoting from Archivo Historico Nacional, Madrid, E2858:1.
2   Ibid., I, pp. 244–8. The document is held at the Archives des Colonies, ref. 7:530.
3   Quoted in Martin-Allanic, J.E., op. cit., p. 255. Original held in Archives nationales de France, Affaires Étrangères, Angleterre, ref. 465:1, 206–7.
4   Magallon to Grimaldi, 8 October 1765. Quoted in Martin-Allanic, J.E., op. cit., I, pp. 263–4.
5   Ibid., I, p. 279.
6   Ibid., I, p. 281.
7   Choiseul to Durand, 5 July 1766. Quoted in Martin-Allanic, J.E., op. cit., I, pp. 310–1.
8   Report to Durand by the Comte de Guerchy, French ambassador in London, quoted in Gallagher, R.E., op. cit., p. lxx.
9   Gallagher, R.E., op. cit., l, lxvii.
10 Martin-Allanic, J.E., op. cit., I, p. 348.
11 See on this, Martin-Allanic, J.E., op. cit., I, pp. 348–51.
12 Corney, B.G., *The Quest and Occupation of Tahiti*, II, pp. 441–5.

Chapter 17

1   Martin-Allanic, J.E., op. cit., I, p. 436.
2   On their affair and her time on board, see Dunmore, J., *Monsieur Baret: First Woman around the World 1766–68* (2002).
3   Piron, C., *Paris sous Louis XV*, III, p. 108.
4   Letter to his friend Jean Bernard, see Monnier, J. et al., *Philibert Commerson*, p. 93.

5   Martin-Allanic, J.E., op. cit., I, p. 472. The document is held in the Bibliothèque de l'Arsenal collection, ref. MS 6000:15.
6   Reprinted in Martin-Allanic, J.E., op. cit, I, pp. 475–6.
7   Archives nationales de France, Marine, ref. C7: 171.
8   Martin-Allanic, J.E., op. cit., I, p. 477.
9   Ibid., I, p. 489.

Chapter 18

1   Taillemite, E., *Bougainville et ses compagnons*, I, p. 34.
2   Martin-Allanic, J.E., op. cit., I, p. 494.
3   Ibid., I, p. 495.
4   Taillemite, E., op. cit., I, p. 86.
5   Cap, P.A., *Philibert Commerson*, p. 37. The full dedication is reprinted in Monnier, J. et al., op. cit., p. 108.
6   Taillemite, E., op. cit., II, p. 187.
7   Ibid., II, p. 424.

Chapter 19

1   Taillemite, E., op. cit, II, p. 15.
2   Ibid., II, p. 376.
3   Ibid., I, p.209.
4   Groussac, P., *Les Îles Malouines*, p. 162.
5   Martin-Allanic, J.E., op. cit., I, p. 537.
6   Ibid., I, p. 538.
7   Groussac, P., op. cit., pp. 162–3. Catani's report is well summarised, with copious extracts, by Martin-Allanic, J.E., op. cit., I, pp. 532–3.
8   Martin-Allanic, J.E., op. cit., I, pp. 539–40.
9   Taillemite, E., op. cit., II, p. 32.
10 Bougainville, Journal, in Taillemite, E., op. cit., I, p. 223.

Chapter 20

1   Taillemite, E., op. cit., II, p. 34.
2   Ibid., II, p. 423.
3   Dunmore, J., *The Pacific Journal of Louis-Antoine de Bougainville 1767–1768*, p. 228. Quotes relating to the Pacific and Indian Oceans sections of the circumnavigation taken from the various journals all come from this edition unless otherwise stated.
4   Martin-Allanic, J.E., op. cit., I, p. 552.
5   Montessus de Ballore, F.B., *Martyrologe et biographie de Commerson*, p. 123.
6   Martin-Allanic, J.E., op. cit., I, p. 553.
7   Ibid., I, p. 551.
8   Bougainville, L.A. de, *Voyage autour du monde*, ed. by Bideaux and Faessel, p. 113.

9   Comments quoted by Martin-Allanic, J.E., op. cit., I, pp. 559–60.
10   Taillemite, E., op. cit., II, p. 454.
11   Ibid., I, p. 229.
12   Ibid.
13   Martin-Allanic, J.E., op. cit., I, p. 571.
14   Taillemite, E., op. cit., I, p. 231.

Chapter 21
1   Taillemite, E., op. cit., I, p. 239.
2   Ibid., I, p. 246, part of a lengthy complaint about conditions on board the ships.
3   On the stay in Encenada, see ibid., I, pp. 250–4.
4   Ibid., I, p. 250.
5   Ibid., I, p. 252.
6   Montessus de Ballore, F.B., op. cit., p. 40.
7   Bougainville to Minister of Marine, letter dated Buenos Aires, 21 September 1767, in Taillemite, E., op. cit., I, p. 484.
8   Martin-Allanic, J.E., op. cit., I, p. 591.

Chapter 22
1   Dunmore, J., *The Pacific Journal*, pp. 10–1.
2   Taillemite, E., op. cit., II, p. 464.
3   Ibid., II, p. 390.
4   Ibid., I, p. 287.
5   Ibid., I, p. 290.

Chapter 23
1   On David Land, David's Land, Davis Land, see Dunmore, J., *The Expedition of the* St Jean-Baptiste *to the Pacific 1769–1770* (Hakluyt Society, London, 1981), pp. 23–5, 51–3; Dunmore, J., *French Explorers in the Pacific*, I, pp. 118–22.
2   Journal entry of 19 January 1768.
3   Bideaux and Faessel, op. cit., p. 204.
4   La Roncière, 'Routier inédit', p. 213.
5   Ibid., p. 236.

Chapter 24
1   Quoted in Jack-Hinton, C., *The Search for the Islands of Solomon*, p. 200.

Chapter 25
1   Taillemite, E., op. cit., I, p. 433.
2   Ibid., I, p. 414.
3   Ibid., I, p. 437.
4   Bideaux and Faessel, op. cit., p. 347.
5   Taillemite, E., op. cit., I, p. 470 for all three comments.

6 Carteret to Admiralty Secretary, quoted in Wallis, H. (ed.), *Carteret's Voyage*, II, p. 443.
7 Ibid., II, p. 470.

Chapter 26

1 Extract dated 23 March 1769 from Bachaumont's voluminous *Mémoires secrets*. Quoted in Bideaux and Faessel, op. cit., p. 16.
2 Picard, R. *Les Salons littéraires*, pp. 302–3.
3 Martin-Allanic, J.E., op. cit., II, p. 892.
4 Ibid., II, p. 890.
5 *Gazette de France*, issue of 30 October 1769, p. 711.
6 Beaglehole, J.C., *The Life of Captain James Cook*, p. 471.
7 Beaglehole, J.C. (ed.), *The Journals of Captain James Cook*, II, p. 195.
8 Review written in late 1771 for *Correspondance littéraire*, but not published at the time, reprinted in Bideaux and Faessel, op. cit., p. 451.
9 Levron, J., *Louis XV*, p. 257.
10 La Roncière, Ch. de, *Bougainville*, p. 187.
11 Maupertuis, P.L.M. de, *Oeuvres*, II, pp. 388–9, quoted in Martin-Allanic, op. cit., II, p. 1273.

Chapter 27

1 Martin-Allanic, J.E., op. cit., II, pp. 1296–7.
2 Often quoted (see La Roncière, Ch. de, op. cit., p. 181; Martin-Allanic, J.E., op. cit., II, p. 1352), the anecdote was told by Bougainville to his friend Paul de Rossel.
3 'Mémoire sur l'établissement d'une colonie', quoted in Dunmore, J., *French Explorers*, I, p. 215.
4 Manceron, C., *Les Vingt ans du roi*, p. 19–20.
5 Letter of 17 January 1774, Archives nationales de France, Marine, ref. B4: 314, quoted in Martin-Allanic, J.E., op. cit., II, p. 1398.
6 Manceron, C., op. cit., p. 78.
7 Martin-Allanic, J.E., op. cit., II, p. 1427.

Chapter 28

1 La Roncière, Ch. de, op. cit., p. 188.
2 Ibid., p. 191.
3 Ibid., p. 192.
4 Manceron, C., op. cit., p. 519.
5 Kimbrough, M., *Louis-Antoine de Bougainville*, p. 139.
6 Kerallain, R. de, *Bougainville à l'escadre du Comte d'Estaing*, p. 7.
7 La Roncière, Ch. de, op. cit., pp. 199 and 200.
8 Ibid., p. 204.
9 Ibid., p. 205.
10 Ibid., pp. 205–6.

Chapter 29
1 La Roncière, Ch. de, op. cit., p. 207.
2 Manceron, C., *Le Vent d'Amérique*, p. 346.
3 La Roncière, Ch. de, op. cit., p. 208.
4 Manceron, C., op. cit., p. 479.
5 La Roncière, Ch. de, op. cit., p. 213.
6 Kimbrough, M., *Louis-Antoine de Bougainville*, p. 179.
7 Ibid., p. 181.

Chapter 30
1 La Roncière, Ch. de, op. cit., p. 222.
2 Ibid., p. 223.
3 For the court-martial and verdict, see ibid., pp. 221–5.
4 Flammerton, J., *Remonstrances du Parlement de Paris*, II, p. 558.
5 Schama, S., *Citizens*, p. 235.

Chapter 31
1 Temple, N., *The Road to 1789*, p. 97.
2 La Roncière, Ch. de, op. cit., p. 229.
3 Ibid., p. 230.
4 Ibid.
5 Ibid., pp. 231-2.
6 Schama, S., op. cit., p. 612.
7 La Roncière, Ch. de, op. cit., p. 233.
8 Kimbrough, M., op. cit., p. 206.
9 Founding decree by the Convention, 9 Brumaire III (22 October 1794).

Chapter 32
1 Martin-Allanic, J.E., op. cit., II, p. 1536.
2 Municipality of Suisnes website, 'Bienvenue à Suisnes'.
3 Scott, E., 'Baudin's Voyage of Exploration to Australia', *English Historical Review*, April 1913, p. 343.
4 Martin-Allanic, J.E., op. cit., II, p. 1542.
5 La Roncière, Ch. de, op. cit., p. 237.
6 Archives nationales de France, Affaires Étrangères, 'Mémoires et Documents', Indes occidentales 17/14. 257. Quoted in Martin-Allanic, J.E., op. cit., II, p. 1543.
7 La Roncière, Ch. de, op. cit., pp. 237–8.
8 Martin-Allanic, J.E., op. cit., II, p. 1553.
9 Ibid., II, p. 1555.
10 Both quotes are from Bertaut, J., *La Vie littéraire au XVIIIe siècle*, pp. 436, 451–2.
11 Ibid., p. 437.
12 La Roncière, op. cit., p. 239.

SELECT BIBLIOGRAPHY

Abarca, R., 'Classical Diplomacy and Bourbon Revanche Strategy, 1763–1770', *Review of Politics*, 32, 1970.

Aman, Jacques, *Les Officiers bleus dans la marine française au XVIIIe siècle*, Geneva, 1976.

Amherst, William A.T., and Basil Thomson, (eds), *The Discovery of the Solomon Islands by Alvaro de Mendaña in 1568*, 2 vols, London, 1901.

Aragon, Louis Albert Charles d', *Un Paladin au XVIIIe siècle: le Prince Charles de Nassau-Siegen*, Paris, 1893.

Arnaud, Étienne et al., *Colloque Commerson*, Centre universitaire de la Réunion, St Denis, 1973.

Bachaumont, Louis Petit de, *Mémoires secrets de Bachaumont* (ed. P.L. Jacob), Paris, 1859. Original edn Paris, 1777, entitled *Mémoires secrets pour servir à l'histoire de la république des lettres en France depuis 1762*.

Beaglehole, John C. (ed.), *The* Endeavour *Journal of Joseph Banks 1768–1771*, 2 vols, Sydney, 1962.

— *The Exploration of the Pacific*, 3rd ed., London, 1966.

— *The Journals of Captain James Cook on his Voyages of Discovery*, 3 vols, London, 1955–69.

— *The Life of Captain James Cook*, London, 1974.

Bellin, Jacques Nicolas, *L'Hydrographie française ou recueil des cartes dressées au Dépost des plans de la Marine pour le service des vaisseaux du Roy*, Paris, 1756.

— *Le Neptune français*, Paris, 1753.

— *Petit Atlas maritime*, 5 vols, Paris, 1764.

Bertaut, Jules, *La Vie littéraire au XVIIIe siècle*, Paris, 1954.

Bethune, Charles R. Drinkwater, *The Observations of Sir Richard Hawkins, Knt, in his Voyage into the South Seas in the Year 1593*, London, 1847.

Bideaux, Michel, and Sonia Faessel, (eds), *Louis-Antoine de Bougainville: Voyage autour du monde*, Paris, 2001.

Boissel, Thierry, *Bougainville ou l'homme de l'univers*, Paris, 1991.

Bougainville, Louis Antoine de, *Voyage autour du monde par la frégate du Roi* La Boudeuse *et la flûte* L'Etoile *en 1766–1769*, Paris, 1771; second edition in 2 vols, 1772; English translation by J.R. Forster, London, 1772.

Bouvier, R., and Maynial, E., *Une Aventure dans les mers australes: l'expédition du commandant Baudin (1800–1803)*, Paris, 1947.

Brasseaux, Carl A., *Scattered to the Wind 1755–1809*, Lafayette, 1991.

Broc, Numa, *La Géographie des philosophes: géographes et voyageurs français au XVIIIe siècle*, Paris, 1974.

Brosses, Charles de, *Histoire des navigations aux terres australes*, 2 vols, Paris, 1756.

Bruij, J.R. et al., *Dutch-Asiatic Shipping in the Seventeenth and Eighteenth Centuries*, The Hague, 1987.

Buffon, Georges Louis Leclerc de, *Oeuvres complètes* (ed. J.L. de Lanessan), Paris, 1884.

Bulkeley, John, and Cummins, John, *A Voyage to the South-Seas by His Majesty's Ship* Wager, London, 1743.

Cap, Paul Antoine, *Philibert Commerson, naturaliste voyageur*, Paris, 1861.

Carrington, Hugh (ed.), *The Discovery of Tahiti: A Journal of the Second Voyage of H.M.S. Dolphin … written by George Robertson*, London, 1948.

Carver, Jonathan, *Travels through the Interior Parts of North America in the Years 1766–1768*, Dublin, 1778.

Chesnaux, Jean, and MacLelland, Nic, *La France dans le Pacifique de Bougainville à Mururoa*, Paris, 1992.

Chevrier, Raymond, *Bougainville: voyage en Océanie*, Paris, 1946.

Clarke, G.F., *The Expulsion of the Acadians*, Fredericton, 1955.

Combaluzier, F. 'Le Chanoine Paulmier de Courtonne et ses rêves apostoliques vers les Terres australes (1659–1667)', *Revue d'histoire des missions*, Paris, 1935, 12.

Constans, Marie, *Le Guide de Paris*, Lyons, 1989.

Corney, Brian Glanvill, *The Quest and Occupation of Tahiti by Emissaries of Spain during the Years 1772–1776*, London, 1913.

Dahlgren, E.W. 'Voyages français à destination de la mer du Sud avant Bougainville (1695–1740)', *Nouvelles archives des missions scientifiques*, XIV, 1907.

— *Les Relations commerciales et maritimes entre la France et les côtes de l'océan Pacifique (commencement du XVIIIe siècle)*, Paris, 1909.

Dalrymple, Alexander, *An Account of the Discoveries made in the South Pacifick Ocean previous to 1764*, London, 1767.

Darwin, Charles, *Charles Darwin's Beagle Diary* (ed. R.D. Keynes), Cambridge, 1988.

— *The Voyage of the* Beagle, London, 1845.

Daubigny, E., *Choiseul et la France d'outre-mer après le Traité de Paris*, Paris, 1892.

Delille, Jacques, 'Les Jardins' in *Oeuvres de J. Delille*, Paris, 1834, Chant II, p. 18.

Devèze, Michel, *L'Europe et le monde à la fin du XVIIIe siècle*, Paris, 1970.

Diderot, Denis, *Supplément au voyage de Bougainville* (ed. G. Chinard), Paris, 1935.

Dixmerie, Nicolas Bricaire de la, *Le Sauvage de Taïti aux Français*, Paris, 1770.

Dorsenne, Jean, *La Vie de Bougainville*, Paris, 1930.

Doughty, A.L., *John Knox's Journal*, 3 vols, Toronto, 1916.

Dowling, Jack K., 'Bougainville and Cook' in Veit, Walter (ed.), *Captain James Cook: Image and Impact*, I, Melbourne, 1972, pp. 25–42.

Duchet, Michèle, *Anthropologie et histoire au Siècle des Lumières*, Paris, 1971.

Dunmore, John, *French Explorers in the Pacific*, 2 vols, Oxford, 1966, 1969.

— 'The Explorer and the Philosopher: Diderot's *Supplément au voyage de Bougainville* and *Giraudoux's* Supplément au voyage de Cook' in Veit, Walter (ed.), *Captain James Cook: Image and Impact*, I, Melbourne, 1972.

— 'L'Imaginaire et le réel: le mythe du Bon Sauvage de Bougainville à Marion du Fresne', in Mollat du Jourdin, Michel, and Etienne Taillemitte, (eds), *L'Importance de l'exploration maritime au siècle des lumières*, Paris, 1982.

— *Monsieur Baret: First Woman around the World 1766–68*, Auckland, 2002.

— *Visions & Realities: France in the Pacific 1695–1995*, Waikanae, 1997.

Dussourd, Henriette, *Jeanne Baret (1740–1816), première femme autour du monde*, Moulins, 1987.

Duviols, Jean Paul, *L'Amérique espagnole vue et rêvée: les livres de voyages de Christophe Colomb à Bougainville*, Paris, 2000.

Duyker, Edward, *An Officer of the Blue: Marc-Joseph Marion Dufresne, South Sea Explorer, 1724–1772*, Melbourne, 1994.

Ecrits sur le Canada: mémoires-journal, Paris, 1993.

Fairchild, Hoxie Neale, *The Noble Savage: a Study in Romantic Naturalism*, New York, 1928.

Faivre, Jean Paul, *L'Expansion francaise dans le Pacifique de 1800 à 1840*, Paris, 1953.

Ferdon, Edwin N., *Early Tahiti as the Explorers Saw It 1767–1797*, Tucson, 1981.

Ferrando, Roberto (ed.), *Pedro Fernando de Quiros: Descubrimiento de la regiones australes*, Madrid, 1986.

Fesche, Charles Félix Pierre, *La Nouvelle Cythère (Tahiti): journal de navigation inédit* (ed. Jean Dorsenne), Paris, 1929.

Flammerton, Jules, *Les Remonstrances du Parlement de Paris au XVIIIe siècle*, Paris, 1888.

Fleurieu, Charles Pierre Claret de, *Découverte des François en 1768 et 1769 dans le sud-est de la Nouvelle-Guinée et reconnaissance postérieure des mêmes terres par des navigateurs anglois qui leur ont imposé de nouveaux noms*, Paris, 1790.

Gallagher, Robert E. (ed.), *Byron's Journal of his Circumnavigation 1764–1766*, Cambridge, 1964.

Gallet, Danielle, *Madame de Pompadour: l'éternel féminin*, Paris, 1984.

Garrioch, David, *Neighbourhood and Community in Paris 1740–1790*, Paris, 1986.

Gaxotte, Pierre, *Le Siècle de Louis XV*, Paris, 1974.

— *Paris au XVIIIe Siècle*, Paris, 1982.

Goebel, J., *The Struggle for the Falkland Islands*, New Haven, 1927.

Gonnard, R., *La Légende du Bon Sauvage*, Paris, 1946.

Gough, Barry M., *The Falkland Islands, Malvinas: The Contest for Empire in the South Atlantic*, London, 1992.

Graaf, N. de, *Voyages aux Indes orientales et d'autres lieux de l'Asie.* Amsterdam, 1719.

Grégor, Isabelle, 'Bougainville autour du monde: du voyageur à l'écrivain', in *Revue d'histoire maritime*, No. 2, 2001.

Groussac, Paul, *Les Iles Malouines: nouvel exposé d'un vieux litige*, Buenos Aires, 1910.

Hamilton, Edward P. (transl.), *Adventures in the Wilderness: the American Journals of Louis Antoine de Bougainville 1756–1760*, Norman, Oklahoma Press, 1964.

Hammond, L. Davis (ed.), *News from Cythera, A Report of Bougainville's Voyage 1766–1769*, Minneapolis, 1970.

Hank-El Ghomri, Gudrun, *Tahiti in der Reiseberichterstattung und in der literarischen Utopien Frankreichs gegen Ende des 18 Jahrhunderts*, Munich, 1991.

Hargreaves-Mawdsley, W.N., *Eighteenth-Century Spain 1700–1788: A Political, Diplomatic and Institutional History*, London, 1979.

Harlow, Vincent T., *The Founding of the Second British Empire 1763–1793*, 2 vols, London, 1952–64.

Hawkesworth, John, *An Account of the Voyages undertaken by Order of His present Majesty for making Discoveries in the Southern Hemisphere, and successively performed by Commodore Byron, Captain Wallis, Captain Carteret and Captain Cook*, 3 vols, London, 1773.

Henry, Teuira, *Tahiti aux temps anciens*, Paris, 1968, transl. of *Ancient Tahiti*, Honolulu, 1928.

Hommage à Bougainville, special issue of *Journal de la Société des Océanistes*, vol. XXIV, December 1968.

Jack-Hinton, Colin, *The Search for the Solomon Islands 1567–1838*, Oxford, 1969.

Jacquemont, S., 'Le Mythe du Pacifique dans la littérature', in Rousseau, Madeleine (ed.), *L'Art océanien*, Paris, 1951.

Jacquier, Henri, 'Le mirage et l'exotisme tahitiens dans la littérature', *Bulletin de la Société des études océaniennes*, 7, Nos 72–4, 1944–5.

Jurien de la Gravière, Edmond, *Souvenirs d'un amiral*, 2 vols, Paris, 1860.

Kelly, Celsus, *La Austrialia del Espíritu Santo*, 2 vols, Cambridge, 1966.

Kerallain, René de, *Les Français au Canada: la jeunesse de Bougainville et la Guerre de Sept Ans*, Paris, 1896.

Kimbrough, Mary, *Louis-Antoine de Bougainville 1729–1811: A Study in French Naval History and Politics*, Lewiston, 1990.

Knox, J., *An Historical Journal of the Campaigns in North America 1757–1760*, London, 1769.

La Barbée, Linyer de, Maurice, *Le Chevalier de Ternay*, Paris, 1972.

La Montagne, Roland (ed.), *Bougainville: Écrits sur le Canada: mémoires-journal-lettres*, Sillery, 1993.

La Roncière, Charles de, *Histoire de la marine française*, 6 vols, Paris, 1909–32.

— *Bougainville*, Paris, 1942.

— 'Routier inédit d'un compagnon de Bougainville: L.A. de Saint-Germain, écrivain de la *Boudeuse*', *La Géographie*, XXXV, Mar. 1921, pp. 217-50.

Lacourcière, Jacques, *Histoire populaire du Québec, vol. I, Des Origines à 1791*, 1999.

Lacour-Gayet, Georges, *La Marine militaire sous Louis XV*, Paris, 1910.

La Force, Piganiol de, *Description historique de Paris*, Paris, 1753.

Lefranc, Jean, *Bougainville et ses compagnons*, Paris, 1929.

Levron, Jacques, *Choiseul: un sceptique au pouvoir*, Paris, 1976.

— *Louis XV*, Paris, 1973.

Major, R.H., *Early Voyages to Terra Australis, now called Australia*, London, 1859.

Malleret, Louis, *Pierre Poivre*, Paris, 1974.

Manceron, Claude, *Les Vingt Ans du roi 1774–1778*, Paris, 1972.

— *Le Vent d'Amérique 1778–1782*, Paris, 1974.

Mannevillette, J.B.N. d'Après de, *Le Neptune oriental ou Routier général des côtes des Indes orientales et de la Chine*, Paris, 1745.

Margueron, Daniel, *Tahiti dans toute sa littérature*, Paris, 1989.

Markham, Albert Hastings, *The Voyages and Works of John Davis the Navigator*, London, 1854.

Markham, Clements R. (ed.), *The Voyages of Pedro Fernandez de Quiros, 1565 to 1606*, 2 vols, London, 1904.

Martin-Allanic, Jean Étienne, *Bougainville, navigateur et les découvertes de son temps*, 2 vols, Paris, 1964.

Maupertuis, Pierre Louis Moreau de, *Oeuvres*, Lyon, 1956.

Meek, Ronald L., *Social Science and the Ignoble Savage*, Cambridge, 1976.

Mitford, Nancy, *Madame de Pompadour*, London, 1954.

Mollat du Jourdin, Michel, and Taillemitte, E., *L'Importance de l'exploration maritime au siècle des lumières*, Paris, 1982.

Monnier, Jeannine, et al., *Philibert Commerson, le découvreur du bougainvillier*, Châtillon-sur-Chalaronne, 1993.

Montbard, Marie Josèphe de, *Lettres tahitiennes*, Paris, 1786.

Montessus de Ballore, F.B. de, *Martyrologe et biographie de Commerson*, Chalons-sur-Sâone, 1889.

Moutemont, A., *Voyages autour du monde par Bougainville, Cook, Marion, Lapérouse*, Paris, 1853.

Mulert, F.E. Baron (ed.), *De Reis van Mr Jacob Roggeveen*, The Hague, 1911.

Oliver, Douglas L., *Ancient Tahitian Society*, 3 vols, Honolulu, 1974.

O'Reilly, Patrick, 'Le Chanoine Paulmier de Courtonne et son projet d'évangélisation des terres australes (1663)', *Revue d'histoire des missions*, Paris, 1932, 9, pp. 321–39.

Orian, Alfred, *La Vie et l'oeuvre de Philibert Commerson des Humbers*, Port-Louis, Mauritius, 1973.

Parkinson, Sydney, *A Journal of a Voyage to the South Seas in His Majesty's Ship* The Endeavour, London, 1773.

Parkman, Francis, *France and England in North America*, vol. IX, New York, 1965.

Pascal, Marius, *Essai historique sur la vie et les travaux de Bougainville, suivi de la relation de son voyage autour du monde*, Marseilles, 1831.

Pernetty, Antoine Joseph, *Histoire d'un voyage fait aux isles Malouines en 1763 et 1764, avec les observations sur le détroit de Magellan et sur les Patagons*, 2 vols, Paris, 1770.

— *Journal historique d'un voyage fait aux îles Malouines en 1763 et 1764 pour les connaître et y former un établissement*, 2 vols, Berlin, 1769, Paris, 1770.

Picard, Roger, *Les Salons littéraires et la société française 1610–1789*, New York, 1943.

Piton, Camille, *Paris sous Louis XV: Rapports des inspecteurs de police au Roi*, Paris, 1906.

Pritchard, James, *Louis XV's Navy 1748–1762: A Study of Organization and Administration*, Kingston, 1987.

Ramsey, John F., *Anglo-French Relations 1763–1779: A Study of Choiseul's Foreign Policy*, Berkeley, 1939.

'Rapport de l'archiviste de la province de Québec sur le Journal de M. de Bougainville', Quebec, 1924, pp. 202–339.

Ricklefs, Merle Calvin, *A History of Modern Indonesia since c1300*, London, 1991.

Robson, John, *Captain Cook's World*, Auckland, 2000.

— 'A Short Biography of L.A. de Bougainville': website

Roditi, Edouard, *Magellan of the Pacific*, London, 1972.

Role, André, *Vie aventureuse d'un savant: Philibert Commerson, martyr de la botanique 1727–1773*, Saint-Denis, Reunion, 1973.

Ross, Michael, *Bougainville*, London, 1978.

Rousseau, Jean Jacques, *Discours sur l'origine et les fondements de l'inégalité parmi les hommes*, Amsterdam and Dresden, 1754.

Roy, Pierre Georges, *La Famille de Rigaud de Vaudreuil*, Quebec, 1938.

— 'M. de Bougainville aux îles Malouines', *Bulletin des recherches historiques de Québec*, September, 1831.

Schama, Simon, *Citizens: A Chronicle of the French Revolution*, London, 1989.

Scott, Hamish M., 'The Importance of Bourbon Naval Reconstruction to the Strategy of Choiseul after the Seven Years War', *International History Review*, 1, 1979, pp. 17–35.

Ségur-Dupeyron, M.P., *La France, l'Angleterre et l'Espagne après la Guerre de Sept Ans*, Paris, 1866.

Sharp, C. Andrew (ed.), *The Journal of Jacob Roggeveen*, Oxford, 1970.

— *The Discovery of the Pacific Islands*, Oxford, 1960.

Smith, A.D.H. (ed.), *A Voyage to the South Seas in His Majesty's Ship the* Wager *in the years 1740–1741, by John Bulkeley and John Cummins*, London, 1927.

Smith, Bernard, *European Vision and the South Pacific 1768–1850*, Oxford, 1960.

Smith, H.M., 'The introduction of Venereal Disease into Tahiti: A Re-examination', *Journal of Pacific History*, 10, 1975, pp. 38–45.

Somerville, Henry Boyle Townsend, *Commodore Anson's Voyage into the South Seas and around the World*, London, 1934.

Spate, Oscar H.K., *The Pacific since Magellan:* I *The Spanish Lake*, Canberra, 1979. II *Monopolists and Freebooters*, Canberra, 1983.

Stanley of Alderley, Lord, *The First Voyage Round the World, by Magellan*, Oxford, 1874.

Strange, Ian J., *The Falkland Islands*, Harrisburg PA, 1972.

Taillemite, Etienne, *Bougainville et ses compagnons autour du monde 1766–1769*, 2 vols, Paris, 1977.

— 'Le Lieutenant Caro et sa relation inédite du séjour de Bougainville à Tahiti', *Journal de la société des océanistes*, XVIII, Dec. 1962, pp. 11–19.

Taitbout, *Essai sur l'île de Tahiti*, Avignon, 1779.

Taylor, Alan Carey, *Le Président de Brosses et l'Australie*, Paris, 1937.

Temple, Nora, *The Road to 1789: from Reform to Revolution in France*, Cardiff, 1992.

Thiéry, Maurice, *Bougainville, Soldier and Sailor*, London, 1932.

Touchard, Michel Claude, *Les Voyages de Bougainville*, Paris and Papeete, 1974.

Toussaint, Auguste, *A History of Mauritius*, London, 1977 (Translation by W.E.F Ward of the 1971 French edition).

Troudé, Onésime J., *Les Batailles navales de la France*, Paris, 1867.

Vaux, William Sandys Wright, *The World Encompassed by Sir Francis Drake*, London, 1854.

Vibart, Eric, *1767–1797: Tahiti, naissance d'un paradis au Siècle des Lumières*, Brussels, 1987.

Vinson, E., *Célébrités créoles: Philibert Commerson*, Saint-Denis, Reunion, 1861.

Waggaman, Beatrice, *Le Voyage autour du monde de Bougainville: droit et imaginaire*, Nancy, 1992.

Wallis, Helen (ed.), *Carteret's Voyage round the World*, 2 vols, London, 1965.

Walter, Richard, *A Voyage round the World in the years MDCCXL, I, II, III, IV, by George Anson Esq, compiled by Richard Walter*, London, 1748.

Williams, Glyndwr, *The Great South Sea: English Voyages and Encounters 1570–1750*, London, 1997.

— *The Prize of all the Oceans: The Triumph and Tragedy of Anson's Voyage around the World*, London, 1999.

Wiltgen, Ralph M., *The Founding of the Roman Catholic Church in Oceania 1825 to 1850*, Canberra, 1981.

Wroth, Lawrence C., *The Early Cartography of the Pacific*, New York, 1944.

INDEX